THE WARS OF
THE ROSES

THE WARS OF THE ROSES

*Peace and Conflict in
Fifteenth-Century England*

JOHN GILLINGHAM

WEIDENFELD AND NICOLSON
LONDON

First published in Great Britain by
George Weidenfeld and Nicolson Limited
91 Clapham High Street
London sw4

ISBN 0 297 77630 4

Set, printed and bound in Great Britain by
Fakenham Press Limited, Fakenham, Norfolk

for Brenda

CONTENTS

List of illustrations   ix
List of maps   x
Preface   xi
Chronological table   xiv
Genealogical table   xvi–xvii

1   Introduction: the Making of the Myth   1
2   This Seat of Peace   15
3   The Disciplines of War   32
4   Henry VI: the Careless King, 1422–50   51
5   Richard of York: the High and Mighty Prince, 1450–3   65
6   The Road to St Albans, 1453–5   76
7   Margaret of Anjou: the Warlike Queen, 1455–9   92
8   Five Battles, 1459–61   106
9   The War in the North, 1461–4   136
10   Richard of Warwick: the Discontented Earl, 1465–70   156
11   The Return of the Old King, 1470–1   179
12   Coming in by the Windows, 1471–83   189
13   The Usurpation of Richard III: 1483   217
14   Henry Tudor: the Ending of the Wars, 1483–7   233
    Conclusion   254

Bibliographical Guide   258
Index   266

ILLUSTRATIONS

Between pages 112 and 113

Scene in the Temple Garden by J. Pettie (Walker Art Gallery, Liverpool)

Medallion of stained glass in Westminster Abbey (Crown Copyright, Victoria and Albert Museum)

Coronation of Henry VI (Giraudon)

Army on the march from Essenwein's *Hausbuch*

Hand-to-hand fighting (British Library)

Fortified camp from Essenwein's *Hausbuch*

Suit of armour (Crown Copyright, Wallace Collection)

Cannon (Roger Viollet)

Siege (Reproduced by courtesy of the Trustees of the British Museum)

Henry VI leaves London (Bulloz)

Henry VI in All Souls, Oxford (Thomas photos, Oxford)

West Gate at Canterbury (National Monuments Record)

South Gate at King's Lynn (National Monuments Record)

Coronation of Edward IV (British Library)

Jousting (British Library)

Between pages 176 and 177

Tattershall Castle (B. T. Batsford)

Bodian Castle

Battle Scene (Bodleian Library)

The Master of the Staple and Jean de Waurin (Reproduced by courtesy of the Trustees of the British Museum)

Iron dagger (Guildhall Museum)

Pole Axe (Crown Copyright, Wallace Collection)

Battle scene (Reproduced by courtesy of the Trustees of the British Museum)

Sea battle (Bibliothèque Nationale, Paris)

Battle scene (Bodleian Library)

Sir Walter Mauntell and his wife (Crown Copyright, Victoria and
   Albert Museum)
Edward IV groat (Reproduced by courtesy of the Trustees of the British
   Museum)
Henry VI groat (Reproduced by courtesy of the Trustees of the British
   Museum)
The Game and Playe of the Chesse (Bodleian Library)
The Prince in the Tower by Delaroche (Crown Copyright, Wallace
   Collection)
Sir Laurence Olivier as Richard III (Courtesy of the National Film
   Archive/Stills Library and Rediffusion Television Limited)
Henry VII by Torrigiano (Crown Copyright, Victoria and Albert
   Museum)

MAPS

First Battle of St Albans   87
1460–61   121
Second Battle of St Albans   128
The War in the North   143
The Lincolnshire Rising and its Aftermath, March 1470   168
The Barnet and Tewkesbury Campaigns, 1471   198–199

PREFACE

THERE HAVE BEEN many studies of the Wars of the Roses, but none which has concentrated on the wars themselves. Yet long ago the wars came to occupy a pivotal place in an Englishman's sense of his past, came to be seen as a watershed between medieval and modern. When Henry James summed up the course of English history, he did so in words which served to underline both the importance and the violence of these wars: 'foundations bafflingly early, a great monastic life, wars of the Roses, with battles and blood in the streets, and then the long quietude of the respectable centuries, all cornfields and magistrates and vicars.' Yet the battles and the blood have not been much studied, despite their powerful representation in Shakespeare's history plays. Generally speaking, historians of the wars have been historians of politics who have not been much interested in the distasteful business of fighting. They have looked at the breakdown of political stability in England and have tried to explain why that happened, but they have rarely given much thought to the campaigns themselves or tried to see what could be learnt about English society as a whole from a study of the way in which its wars were conducted. For this there are several reasons. For centuries the period of the Wars of the Roses was universally regarded as a low point in English military history. In his classic *History of the British Army* (1899), for example, Sir John Fortescue wrote, 'I shall not dwell upon this miserable and disastrous time, marking as it does the wreck of our ancient military greatness.' 'England', he added, 'now lagged behind other nations in the path of military reform', and of the commanders of the period only Edward IV could claim a share of the military genius of the Plantagenets, those splendid warrior kings who, in Fortescue's eyes, 'had made it a national principle that the English must always beat the French'. Thought of in these terms a period of military history which saw first the French beat the English and then the English fight each other at home was a period to be passed over as quickly as possible. Military historians, many of them patriotic ex-soldiers, do not enjoy recalling their defeats and feel decidedly uncomfortable in the presence of civil strife.

In the second place, the military history of the Wars of the Roses is by no means an easy subject to approach. The contemporary evidence for what happened is astonishingly fragmentary. As a result what historians have written on the major set-piece battles has all too often been composed of conjecture based upon later evidence. All too often they have relied upon details supplied by Edward Hall. But even to a close observer war is a confused business and a chronicler writing in the 1540s cannot readily be accepted as an authority on events which had occurred between sixty and ninety years earlier. In their anxiety to reconstruct battles, military historians have been clutching at straws. It would make more sense to worry less about the irrecoverable minutiae of battles and battlefields and adopt instead a wider perspective, take as our unit of study not the battle but the campaign, look at strategy rather than tactics and compare campaigns in England with campaigns abroad. The question, then, is not what happened in any particular battle but why was it that there were so many battles in the Wars of the Roses? The answer to this question can tell us a great deal about the English political and social system. It will become clear that in England, to borrow Henry James's terminology, the fifteenth century was one of 'the respectable centuries', and the main argument of this book will be the apparently paradoxical one that the Wars of the Roses demonstrate just how peaceful England in fact was.

Yet however wide a perspective we take, the problem of inadequate evidence is one which has to be faced. If we rigorously exclude later chroniclers, what is left? In the first place there is an ever-increasing volume of administrative and judicial records, symptom of a relatively literate and much-governed society. But even here the military historian is unlucky. In this, the first century of effective artillery, the records of the royal ordnance office have been lost. As for contemporary historical narratives, memoirs, chronicles and the like, the historian of fifteenth-century England is notoriously badly off. In many respects the best all-round history of the wars, at least up until 1471, is the work not of an Englishman but of a Burgundian writing abroad, a man who visited England, but whose main sources of information were the dispatches and rumours which reached the Burgundian court. It is significant that Jean de Waurin justifies the writing of his *Anchiennes Croniques d'Engleterre* by pointing to the absence of any English equivalent. Paradoxically one of the reasons for the dearth of fifteenth-century historical writing may be that so much was written. The country seems to have been inundated by lists, manifestos, bills, propaganda pieces, newsletters – all of them ephemera and avowedly so. Their authors were not writing for posterity, but for a particular and present purpose. Some of these ephemera have been preserved, notably the famous collection of Paston letters, but it is clear that we are dealing with the tip of an iceberg. The men of the fifteenth century, however, can only have been aware of the iceberg's immense bulk and, in consequence, they may have been less concerned to keep what they possessed than those earlier generations to whom writings of all sorts had seemed infinitely more precious.

Nonetheless, though the lack of fifteenth-century writings has been the chief problem facing the modern historian, for this historian at least the task of writing this book would have been quite impossible were it not for the relative wealth of recent scholarship devoted to the fifteenth century. Like most books written during the Middle Ages this one contains a good deal of plagiarism: words and ideas borrowed from other people. Their own works are listed in the bibliography, but I would like to take this opportunity of acknowledging the debt I owe to some of them: to Cora Scofield and K. B. McFarlane among an older generation of scholars and, among those who have worked more recently, to Ralph Griffiths, Michael Hicks, J. R. Lander, David Morgan, A. J. Pollard, Colin Richmond, Charles Ross, R. L. Storey and Richard Vaughan. I would also like to thank Jane Thompson for her help in seeing the book through the press; and finally Mrs Nett Capsey for typing the bulk of the manuscript with her usual kindness and unerring skill – and for encouraging me to get on with it.

CHRONOLOGICAL TABLE OF MAIN EVENTS

The Prelude

1422	Accession of Henry VI to thrones of England and France
1445	Marriage of Henry VI and Margaret of Anjou
1447	Death of Humphrey of Gloucester
1448	Surrender of Anjou and Maine
1450	Loss of Normandy. Jack Cade's rebellion
1452	Failure of York's *coup d'état*
1453	Final loss of Gascony. Henry VI's collapse. 'Battle' of Heworth Moor
1454	York's first protectorate

The First War 1455–64

May 1455	First Battle of St Albans
1455–6	York's second protectorate
1458	Warwick defies the court
September–October 1459	Battle of Blore Heath and confrontation at Ludford Bridge
July 1460	Battle of Northampton
October 1460	York claims the throne
December 1460	Battle of Wakefield
February 1461	Battle of Mortimer's Cross. Second Battle of St Albans
March 1461	Edward IV proclaimed king. Battle of Towton
1461–4	See-saw struggle for control of Northumbrian castles
April–May 1464	Battle of Hedgeley Moor. Battle of Hexham

The Second War 1469–71

1469	Robin of Redesdale's Rising. Battle of Edgecote
July–September 1469	Warwick keeps Edward iv in confinement
March–April 1470	Lincolnshire rising. Warwick and Clarence flee to France
July 1470	Reconciliation of Warwick and Margaret of Anjou. FitzHugh's rising
September 1470	Warwick's invasion. Edward iv flees to Holland
March 1471	Edward iv lands at Ravenspur
April 1471	Battle of Barnet
May 1471	Battle of Tewkesbury

The Third War 1483–7

April 1483	Death of Edward iv
Summer 1483	Accession of Richard iii. Murder of princes in the Tower
October 1483	Buckingham's revolt
August 1485	Battle of Bosworth. Accession of Henry vii
April 1486	Lovell–Stafford revolt
June 1487	Battle of Stoke

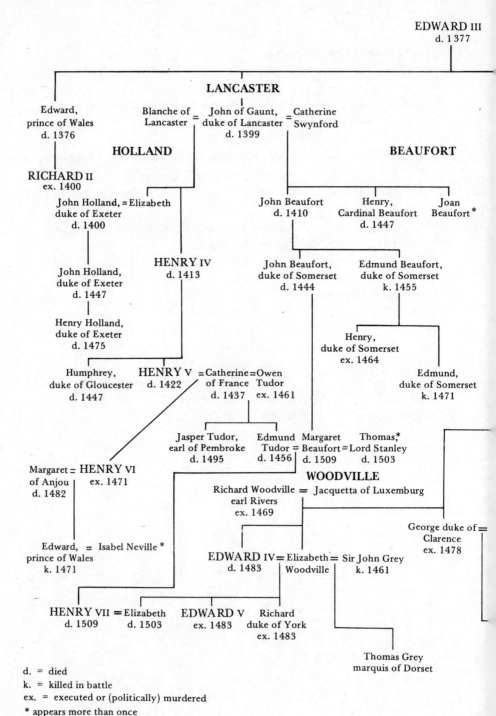

EDWARD III
d. 1377

LANCASTER

Edward,
prince of Wales
d. 1376

Blanche of
Lancaster = John of Gaunt, = Catherine
duke of Lancaster   Swynford
d. 1399

HOLLAND

BEAUFORT

RICHARD II
ex. 1400

John Holland, = Elizabeth
duke of Exeter
d. 1400

John Beaufort
d. 1410

Henry,
Cardinal Beaufort
d. 1447

Joan
Beaufort *

John Holland,
duke of Exeter
d. 1447

HENRY IV
d. 1413

John Beaufort,
duke of Somerset
d. 1444

Edmund Beaufort,
duke of Somerset
k. 1455

Henry Holland,
duke of Exeter
d. 1475

Henry,
duke of Somerset
ex. 1464

Humphrey,
duke of Gloucester
d. 1447

HENRY V
d. 1422

= Catherine = Owen
of France   Tudor
d. 1437   ex. 1461

Edmund,
duke of Somerset
k. 1471

Jasper Tudor,
earl of Pembroke
d. 1495

Edmund
Tudor
d. 1456

Margaret
= Beaufort = Lord Stanley
d. 1509

Thomas,*
d. 1503

Margaret =
of Anjou
d. 1482

HENRY VI
ex. 1471

WOODVILLE

Richard Woodville = Jacquetta of Luxemburg
earl Rivers
ex. 1469

George duke of =
Clarence
ex. 1478

Edward, = Isabel Neville *
prince of Wales
k. 1471

EDWARD IV = Elizabeth = Sir John Grey
d. 1483   Woodville   k. 1461

HENRY VII = Elizabeth
d. 1509   d. 1503

EDWARD V
ex. 1483

Richard
duke of York
ex. 1483

Thomas Grey
marquis of Dorset

d. = died

k. = killed in battle

ex. = executed or (politically) murdered

* appears more than once

NB children are not necessarily in order of birth

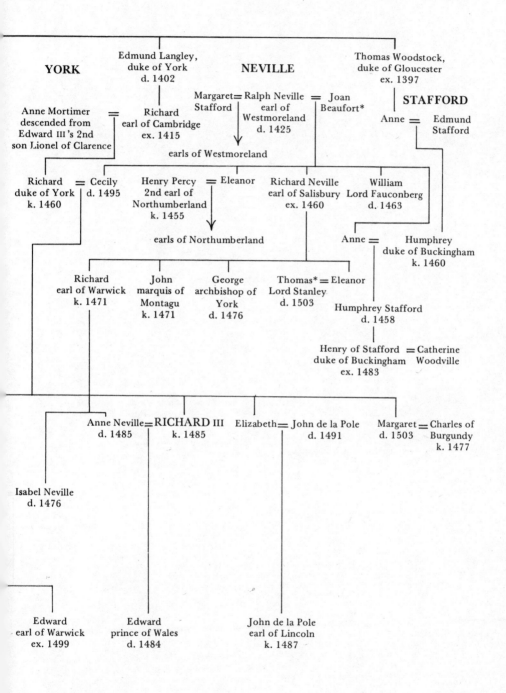

YORK

Edmund Langley,
duke of York
d. 1402

NEVILLE

Thomas Woodstock,
duke of Gloucester
ex. 1397

Margaret = Ralph Neville = Joan
Stafford   earl of   Beaufort*
        Westmoreland
        d. 1425

STAFFORD

Anne = Edmund
     Stafford

Anne Mortimer
descended from
Edward III's 2nd
son Lionel of Clarence

Richard
earl of Cambridge
ex. 1415

earls of Westmoreland

Richard = Cecily
duke of York d. 1495
k. 1460

Henry Percy = Eleanor
2nd earl of
Northumberland
k. 1455

Richard Neville
earl of Salisbury
ex. 1460

William
Lord Fauconberg
d. 1463

earls of Northumberland

Anne = Humphrey
      duke of Buckingham
      k. 1460

Richard
earl of Warwick
k. 1471

John
marquis of
Montagu
k. 1471

George
archbishop of
York
d. 1476

Thomas* = Eleanor
Lord Stanley
d. 1503

Humphrey Stafford
d. 1458

Henry of Stafford = Catherine
duke of Buckingham   Woodville
ex. 1483

Anne Neville = RICHARD III
d. 1485   k. 1485

Elizabeth = John de la Pole
       d. 1491

Margaret = Charles of
d. 1503   Burgundy
       k. 1477

Isabel Neville
d. 1476

Edward
earl of Warwick
ex. 1499

Edward
prince of Wales
d. 1484

John de la Pole
earl of Lincoln
k. 1487

One

INTRODUCTION: THE MAKING OF THE MYTH

THE FIRST WORLD WAR, said Lloyd George, was the worst thing to happen since the Wars of the Roses. Undoubtedly he knew a great deal about the war of 1914–18 but what, we might wonder, did Lloyd George know about the Wars of the Roses? Did he know that the battles were normally fought by armies numbered in thousands rather than tens of thousands? Evidently not. Did he know that battle casualties should be counted in hundreds rather than thousands? Did he know that more British were killed in a single day at the Somme than in the whole of the Wars of the Roses? Evidently not. Yet somehow he knew that the First World War, despite its death roll of millions, was a lesser evil than the Wars of the Roses. Were the Wars of the Roses worse, perhaps, because they were civil wars and the killing of one countryman was infinitely more shocking than the killing of a hundred foreigners? Evidently he did not know that in the Wars of the Roses casualties were limited precisely *because* they were civil wars. On both sides the commanders were anxious to win popular support, not lose it by indulging in bloody massacres. Thus one contemporary observer of the wars, the shrewd French politician Philippe de Commynes noted that 'it is a custom in England that the victors in battle kill nobody, especially none of the ordinary soldiers, because everyone wants to please them.... Even King Edward told me that, in all the battles he had won, as soon as he could sense victory, he rode round ordering the saving of the common soldiers.' For the same reason the commanders generally took good care to see that their marching armies did little damage to the countryside.

Moving away from the battlefield, during the Wars of the Roses private house-building continued – with this difference: that increasingly the nobles were coming to prefer elegant and comfortable homes (even though they might still call them 'castles') to the grimmer and darker fortresses of an earlier age. During the First World War private house-building stopped and by 1918 there was an acute housing short-age. During the First World War direct taxation increased; during the Wars of the Roses it declined.

If all this is true, how then did Lloyd George come to have a view of the Wars of the Roses which was so amazingly wide of the mark? The short answer is that Lloyd George, spell-binding master of the English language that he was, had himself fallen under the spell of a still greater master – William Shakespeare. Not, of course, that Lloyd George was in any way unusual in this. Shakespeare, as has been rightly said, 'was to be the greatest single force in establishing for the Englishman the traditional picture of his past'. Shakespeare, explained the duke of Marlborough, was the only English history book he had ever read. And the duke of Marlborough's admission still holds true today. Insofar as there is a popular understanding of the Wars of the Roses it remains firmly based on Shakespeare's plays and on television adaptations of them. According to one well-known historian of the present day, there is nothing wrong in this. In the concluding sentence of his book *Bosworth Field and the Wars of the Roses*, A. L. Rowse states that 'with so perceptive and sympathetic a mind for a guide, a great master in the understand-ing of human nature to make the past intelligible, a dramatist with penetrating insight into society and politics, anyone deriving his view of the whole story from Shakespeare would not be far out'. In reality, however, there could hardly be a more unreliable guide than Shakespeare.

The trouble with Shakespeare is not that his plays are littered with errors of fact – which they are – nor that he invents totally fictitious scenes like the famous scene in the Temple garden (*1 Henry VI*, II, iv) where the quarrelling nobles pick their white and red roses. The real difficulty comes not with Shakespeare's details, but with his overall interpretation, what Rowse called his 'view of the whole story'. This view is characterized by three distinguishing features. The first is the notion that the period of the Wars of the Roses was saturated with blood, that the battles were so savage, the political murders so brutal that the whole realm became a slaughterhouse. The second is the idea that the origins of this discord were to be found half a century earlier in 1399, in the usurpation of Richard II's throne by the house of Lancaster. The third is the brilliantly theatrical creation of the figure of Richard III. In Shakespeare's hands he becomes the evil genius who not only dominates his own reign but whose malice and cunning overshadow the whole period of the wars.

This conception of Richard III contributes powerfully to our picture of a disastrous age, but it is both the most individual and the most easily dealt with of Shakespeare's distortions of historical reality. Richard makes his entrance in *2 Henry VI*, v, i, where he offers his sword in his father's service. Scene ii takes us to the first Battle of St Albans, fought in May 1455. 'Enter Richard and Somerset to fight. Somerset is killed.' Then Richard speaks the words which at once begin to fix his character in our minds:

> Heart, be wrathful still:
> Priests pray for enemies, but princes kill.

Since in fact Richard was born on 2 October 1452, we can only admire the precocious sword play of the two-and-a-half-year-old, and observe that Shakespeare's Richard has left his mark on the battle which marked the opening of the Wars of the Roses. In *3 Henry VI*, i, ii, set in 1460, we find Richard, now a sophisticated seven-year-old, using ingenious arguments to persuade his father, the duke of York, that it would be no perjury to attack the king to whom he had sworn an oath of allegiance. The boy's speech ends with an image of the white rose turning red:

> I cannot rest
> Until the white rose that I wear be dyed
> Even in the lukewarm blood of Henry's heart.

As history all this is obvious nonsense and not worth dwelling on any longer – except as an illustration of the extent to which Shakespeare was prepared to depart from 'mere' factual accuracy in order to create a dramatic impression on the minds of his audience.

The other two aspects of his interpretation require more extended treatment. In the two great battle scenes in *3 Henry VI*, we find a dramatization of the idea that these struggles were horrifyingly and unnaturally savage. At Wakefield, Clifford, to avenge his father's death, seeks out York's sons and succeeds in killing one of them, the earl of Rutland, still just a boy in the play (though seventeen years old in reality).

> Had I thy brethren here, their lives and thine
> Were not revenge sufficient for me;
> No, if I digg'd up thy forefathers' graves
> And hung their rotten coffins up in chains,
> It could not slake mine ire, nor ease my heart.

> The sight of any of the house of York
> Is as a fury to torment my soul;
> And till I root out their accursed line
> And leave not one alive, I live in hell.

Then York himself is captured but Queen Margaret will not allow Clifford to kill him until after she has finished taunting him, setting him on a molehill and putting a paper crown on his head:

> I prithee, grieve, to make me merry, York.
> What, hath thy fiery heart so parch'd thine entrails
> That not a tear can fall for Rutland's death?
> Why art thou patient, man? thou shouldst be mad;
> And I, to make thee mad, do mock thee thus.
> Stamp, rave and fret, that I may sing and dance.

(In reality York, at Wakefield, is unlikely to have heard the queen's taunts, since she was in Scotland at the time.)

Then at Towton we have the famous scene where a son kills his father and a father his son – the supreme expression of the horrors of civil war. The king, Henry VI, sad but helpless, can do no more than mourn the destruction of his kingdom and the deaths not just of the protagonists, but also of thousands of ordinary people who have been pressed into service. When Clifford, in his turn, is mortally wounded, he blames the feeble king for what has happened:

> And Henry, hadst thou swayed as kings should do,...
> I and ten thousand in this luckless realm
> Had left no mourning widows for our death.

From a historical point of view the importance of these lines is that they reflect the deeply held convictions of the time. This is how all Shakespeare's contemporaries looked back on the Wars of the Roses. One late-sixteenth-century pamphleteer, Thomas Craig, talked of 'the slaughter and blood of 100,000 Englishmen'. At the beginning of the century Sir Thomas More in his *History of King Richard III* wrote of the 'long continued dissension', the many battles 'so cruel and so deadly foughten', which 'hath cost more English blood than hath twice the winning of France'. Inevitably, since this was a hierarchical society, most of the discussion of the casualties of the war focused upon the royal and aristocratic families. The house of Lancaster, of course, had suffered most of all. According to Thomas Craig, as a result of Henry VI's usurpation, by the end of the wars, 'of all his most numerous

Family there was not one left to piss against the wall'. As for the nobility, Thomas More commented that in the 'inward war among ourselves hath been so great effusion of the ancient noble blood of this realm, that scarcely the half remaineth, to the great enfeebling of this noble land'.

What twentieth-century scholars, above all K. B. McFarlane, have done is to demonstrate that this is a mythical view of history. Although many nobles were killed, their families were not extinguished, the 'old nobility' was not exterminated. On average 27 per cent of noble families became extinct in the direct male line in each twenty-five year period during the fourteenth and fifteenth centuries. There had, of course, been civil wars in England as well as prolonged foreign wars before 1450, but even so this apparently high extinction rate was caused not so much by violent death whether in battle or at the headsman's hands, as by disease and infertility – the failure to beget male heirs. The last two quarters of the fifteenth century prove to be no exception to this rule. Measured in these terms the period of the Wars of the Roses is average, not extraordinary. Sixteenth-century writers, of course, did not have the evidence to enable them to carry out this kind of statistical analysis. They dealt with figures in a more creative fashion. William Tyndale, for example, wrote, 'Of their noble blood remaineth not the third, nor I believe the sixth, yea – and if I durst be so bold – I wene I might safely swear that there remaineth not the sixteenth part.'

Today specialists in fifteenth-century history, though they may debate the precise date, are agreed that the origins of the Wars of the Roses are to be found in the 1450s. For Shakespeare and his contemporaries they began in 1399 – as they do also for historians who believe the Tudor myth. 'It all goes back to a revolution,' writes Rowse, 'the Revolution of 1399.' The effect of pushing the origins back to 1399 is to cast a sombre shadow over the whole fifteenth century. According to Rowse the consequences of the 'Revolution of 1399' for the following century included 'deposition of a rightful king, insecurity of tenure of the throne by his successors, dynastic wars, constant domestic turmoil'. This is simply to echo in plainer language the speech which Shakespeare puts into the bishop of Carlisle's mouth on the occasion of Richard II's deposition:

> The blood of English shall manure the ground
> And future ages groan for this foul act;
> Peace shall go sleep with Turks and infidels,
> And, in this seat of peace, tumultuous wars

Shall kin with kin, and kind with kind confound;
Disorder, Horror, Fear and Mutiny
Shall here inhabit, and this land be call'd
The field of Golgotha and dead men's skulls.

This view of the fifteenth century was explicit in the title which the Tudor historian, Edward Hall, gave to his chronicle *The Union of the two noble and illustre families of Lancaster and York, being long in continual dissension for the crown of this noble realm ... beginning at the time of King Henry the Fourth, the first author of this division.* From Hall Shakespeare took not only many of his scenes and images but also the general framework which sees the fifteenth century as one long quarrel over the succession to the throne. It is true, of course, that the succession problem dominated English politics from the 1520s onwards, and particularly the 1590s when Shakespeare was writing, but it does not necessarily follow that the problems which obsessed the Tudors were just as important throughout the previous century. Moreover, in Shakespeare's history plays – no less than eight of which were devoted to the fifteenth century – the succession dispute is fought out with such intense ferocity that we inevitably get the impression that the nobles were anything but reluctant to go to war. 'Then', shouts Warwick at Towton, 'let the earth be drunken with our blood.' In fact, as McFarlane has shown, they were extremely reluctant to take up arms. They went to war because, in the end, they found no other way of coping with some intolerable political situations, with the total incapacity of Henry VI and the tyranny of Richard III. In their efforts to handle these problems the nobles behaved in a manner which their ancestors would have recognized and understood. This, after all, is how their forefathers had behaved during the reigns of John, Henry III, Edward II and Richard II. Yet, whereas both historians and public opinion have often treated the nobles of the thirteenth and fourteenth centuries with marked sympathy, looking upon them as the makers of Magna Carta or as the champions of English liberties, the nobles of the fifteenth century have never enjoyed such favour. The general impression is that they were a savage, turbulent and greedy lot of over-mighty subjects whose only historical function was to commit suicide in the Wars of the Roses, so leaving the way open for the Tudors to take England into a better and more modern world. This conventional view of the fifteenth-century nobility was accurately and fairly summed up by Sellar and Yeatman in *1066 and All That*:

Noticing suddenly that the Middle Ages were coming to an end, the Barons now made a stupendous effort to revive the old Feudal amenities of Sackage, Carnage and Wreckage and so stave off the Tudors for a time. They achieved this by a very clever plan, known as the *Wars of the Roses* (because the barons all picked different coloured roses in order to see which side they were on).

One of the reasons why this mistaken view still retains such a powerful hold is that tales of Sackage, Carnage and Wreckage are memorable, particularly when told by Shakespeare, whereas the absence of Sackage, Carnage and Wreckage is a rather dull prospect, emphatically not memorable. And history, as Sellar and Yeatman pointed out, 'is what you can remember'. The mythical view of English history remains much more obviously exciting than the alternative version laboriously pieced together by pedantic scholars. So, although the pedants are right more often than the poets, the poetic vision of the past is the one which prevails.

In the Tudor period there were other reasons which led men to a sombre view of their recent past. In the sixteenth century men felt that the ship of state was afloat on a rough sea compounded of uncertainties about the succession, religious differences and economic problems and so in increasingly strident tones the cry went up: 'Don't rock the boat!' They emphasized the damaging side-effects of rebellion in the hope of persuading potential rebels that they would be better advised to remain loyal subjects. The miseries of the Wars of the Roses were exaggerated in order to serve as an awful warning to the present generation. John Stow, whose *Annals of England* were published in 1580, believed that it was as hard for a man to read history books and not become wise as it was 'for a well-favoured man to walk up and down in the hot parching sun and not be therewith sunburned'. The readers of Grafton's *Chronicle* (1569) were told that by careful perusal of its pages 'we all may be warned to thank God for the most virtuous wise and peaceable government that we now enjoy in comparison of terrible times heretofore'. Just how sunburned the readers of chronicles became it is hard to say, but those who visited the playhouse where *Henry VI* or *Richard III* was being performed certainly came away deeply tanned. The dark view of the fifteenth century won universal acceptance. Men who opposed each other on everything else agreed on this. Catholics said that the disorders of the fifteenth century were due to the presence of heresy – Lollardy – in England; God brought the Lancastrians down because they had failed to stamp it out. Protestants like Tyndale and John Foxe said that the troubles were caused by the stubborn refusal of the English to listen to the truth as expounded by John Wyclif and the Lollards. But whatever the cause, both sides took it for granted that they had been terrible times.

If we ask why it was that this view of the fifteenth century won universal acceptance, then a partial answer would certainly lie in the artistic skill of some sixteenth-century writers – not just Shakespeare, but also Thomas More, William Tyndale, John Foxe and others. This, however, is only a partial answer and besides the genius of some sixteenth-century writers, we should also bear in mind the social changes of the fifteenth century, changes which it is very hard to interpret as changes for the worse. The first of these is the establishment of English as the language of government and literature. Henry IV was the first king to be able to write English as well as French and Latin. The last will to be drawn up in French is dated 1431. The last parliamentary petitions drafted in French were written in 1447. French had been the vernacular of government and culture ever since the Norman Conquest, but in the fifteenth century it was, except for one area alone, swept aside by the language of Chaucer. The exception was the peculiar jargon known as 'law French', the special language of a group of men determined to uphold the awesome mystery of the workings of justice. (This survived until the early eighteenth century and was a very odd language indeed. A famous entry in one assize roll tells of a prisoner who, on being condemned by the judge, *ject un Brickbat a le dit Justice que narrowly mist.*)

The establishment of English meant that men and women who wished to learn to read no longer had to begin by learning French or Latin; from now on they could read books in their mother tongue. A profoundly important consequence of this was an acceleration of the rise in the level of literacy. More schools were founded. The demand for books and for writings of all kinds increased. The handwriting of the period and the drastic system of abbreviations which they used show that many copyists were in a desperate hurry. It has been estimated that by the 1470s 40 per cent of laymen living in London could read Latin, in which case a higher percentage must have been able to read English. Certainly by 1487 the Goldsmiths' Company was refusing to accept apprentices unless they could read and write. All this brings us to the introduction of printing – the production of printed books using movable type. Even though early editions were small – averaging perhaps only 250 copies – the printing press resulted in an immediate and revolutionary increase in productivity. This technological breakthrough could only be sustained when there was a reading public large enough to support it. Printers were businessmen who would go bankrupt unless they could find a market for the books, news-sheets, proclamations and prophecies – 'prognostications' – which began to pour from their presses. Thus the successful take-off of the printing industry in the second half of the fifteenth century – one of the great moments in European history – is an indication of an existing significant level of literacy. It also, of course, provided the means to improve that level. Wynkyn de Worde, the printer who took over Caxton's business, published about 800 titles between 1491 and 1535. Of these more than 300 were intended for the use of grammar-school boys. He was probably the first publisher to finance his business on the mass sale of school textbooks. A further indication of the close link between printing and education is the fact that the second printer to operate in England was a schoolmaster, the anonymous schoolmaster of St Albans.

The career of the first printer to operate in England, William Caxton, illustrates a different aspect of the early history of the English press – its close relationship with court and government. Caxton's first patron was Edward iv's sister; the first book to be printed in England, *The Dictes and Sayengs of the Philosophres* published in 1477, was translated into English from French by Edward iv's brother-in-law, Earl Rivers; and Caxton's press was set up, not in London, but within the precincts of Westminster. The authorities were quick to perceive the political potentialities, as well as the dangers, of the new machine on their doorstep. From 1485 onwards a royal printer was responsible for publishing the king's proclamations. In 1487 Pope Innocent vii ordered printers to submit their texts to the local bishop for his approval, otherwise, he said, this *ars nova* might cause scandal. But the real impetus for government control of the press did not come until the spread of Lutheranism in the 1520s. By 1526 Henry viii had an index of prohibited books, including works of Luther, Zwingli and Hus. Then with the problems created by his divorce and the break with Rome Henry became more and more determined to curb the freedom of publishers and booksellers. An act of 1534 prohibited the import of books published abroad. A royal proclamation of 1538 required that all books printed in England had to be licensed by the Privy Council. We can trace the effect of this legislation by looking at the publication history of the works of Sir Thomas More. Between 1534 (the year he was committed to the Tower) and 1554 none of More's religious writings was printed or reprinted. Not until Queen Mary's reign did his anti-Protestant line suit the government. But there was not a total ban on all of his works. Anything that suited the government could be published. Thus his *History of Richard III* was reprinted four times in this twenty-year period, twice in 1543, once in 1548 and again in 1550. Government control of the press ensured that there could be no effective challenge to the 'official' Tudor view of Richard III. In these circumstances it was inevitable that there should be a government view of the past, an official, orthodox history of the fifteenth century and the Wars of the Roses. Indeed there were few subjects on which the government did not set out to mould opinion. Uniformity of thought was what was wanted, and a combination of Privy Council and printing press was the instrument by which it was to be achieved. A proclamation of 1543 even insisted that all schoolmasters were to use the same Latin textbook.

The structure of the printing and publishing industry in England meant that it was fairly easy to control. During the whole of the sixteenth century there were very few presses outside London and Westminster. They existed briefly at Oxford, Cambridge, York and Abingdon but in most years all the printers in England lived within easy reach of Westminster Palace and the law courts. Moreover, both printers and booksellers belonged to the Stationers' Company, in other words they belonged to an established guild which was accustomed to regulation and which, for the sake of a good relationship between the crown and the guild as a whole, was interested in ensuring that its members toed the official line. All this was very different from the situation in the more advanced countries in Europe. In Germany there were presses in fifty different towns by 1500; in Italy by the same date in over seventy towns. In Germany or in Italy a printer in trouble with the authorities had at least the option of moving to another town in a different principality. In England he had little choice but to submit. Where men were deeply and passionately involved, in other words in religious matters, there were some attempts to challenge the government monopoly of opinion, but not in less vital areas. What all this means is that as a result of tremendously important social changes in the fifteenth century – the establishment of the English language, increasing literacy and the introduction of printing – all sorts of books, including history books, could now reach a wider audience than ever before. Then, as a side-effect of sixteenth-century religious controversies, the government stepped in to ensure that this wide audience read only the books of which it approved. In this way an official view of English history became universally accepted, and it was on this view that Shakespeare, in the 1590s, set the imprint of his genius. So a view of the past which happened to suit the government of Tudor England became permanently enshrined in the consciousness of men and women of all succeeding ages.

At the centre of this view was an essentially negative picture of fifteenth-century society, even though, ironically, as it happens, some of the developments which made all this possible could easily be described in positive terms. Indeed, there is not much doubt that, for the overwhelming bulk of the population, the fifteenth century, including its politically unstable second half, was a relatively good time in which to live. Compared with the sixteenth century it was an age free of religious controversy – and religious conflicts troubled the hearts and minds of ordinary men and women much more than did the dynastic quarrels at the top of society. The degree of persecution which the fifteenth-century Lollards suffered was mild compared with that meted out to sixteenth-century 'heretics' when the problem, of course, was a more serious one and the authorities' response correspondingly tougher. Compared with the sixteenth century it was an age free of economic difficulties. The real value of wages remained at a high level (higher than at any time before the late nineteenth century) throughout the fifteenth century, only to fall dramatically during the reigns of Henry VIII and Elizabeth, reaching the lowest point in recorded English history in 1597, the year of *A Midsummer Night's Dream*. Moreover, in terms of the development of material culture the sixteenth century saw nothing to compare in importance with the technological breakthroughs of the fifteenth century: the invention of printing and the revolutionary improvements in ship design which made possible the voyages of Christopher Columbus and, from Bristol, of John Cabot.

Yet such is the power of the Tudor myth that none of this counts. The age of Henry VIII and Elizabeth is felt to be a splendid era, a great age in English history, while the preceding period is transformed by a *coup de théâtre* which takes a few disturbances in the aristocratic establishment and turns them into the Wars of the Roses of legend, nasty, brutish and long. In the nineteenth and early twentieth centuries even medieval historians fell victim to the myth. Bishop Stubbs, for example, in the concluding sentences of his influential *Constitutional History of England*, wrote that he was tempted to lay down his pen with a heavy heart.

The most enthusiastic admirer of medieval life must grant that all that was good and great in it was languishing even to death – and the firmest believer in progress must admit that as yet there were few signs of returning health. The sun of the Plantagenets went down in clouds and darkness; the coming of the Tudors gave as yet no promise of light; it was 'as the morning spread upon the mountains', darkest before the dawn.

Even in the second half of the twentieth century it is possible to find Tudor specialists and others calling themselves 'modern' historians who have written in such terms – for example, the statement that 'in the fifteenth century England displayed the characteristics of a stagnant and declining civilisation' in Elton's *England under the Tudors*.

One of the spurious attractions of this approach lies in the fact that it happens to fit neatly into the general framework of another widely held opinion. This is the idea that the Middle Ages 'declined'. According to this theory the fifteenth century or sometimes both the fourteenth and fifteenth centuries, were 'inferior' to the centuries which went before and came after them. This is just silly, yet many people believe it. The root cause of the trouble lies in our habit of dividing history into periods. We have decided that there should be a period called the 'Middle Ages'. It follows therefore that the Middle Ages have ended and it stands to reason that things which end must first decline, otherwise they would not end. Therefore it follows that there must be a period which can reasonably be called 'The Decline of the Middle Ages'. It simply remains to identify it and pin it down with this label stuck firmly upon it. But this whole process exists only in our own minds and nowhere else. It has nothing whatever to do with what was really happening in the thirteenth, fourteenth, fifteenth and sixteenth centuries. It tells us about our own habits of thought but nothing at all about the quality of life in earlier times.

All historians know that dividing history into periods is misleading, but believe that, for practical purposes, it is unavoidable. They may be right. If they are they could at least minimize the distorting effect of 'periodization' by avoiding phrases like 'The Birth of the Middle Ages' or 'The Decline of the Modern Era'. On the whole words like 'Birth', 'Re-birth', 'Renaissance' are loaded with a strong positive content, while words like 'Decline', 'Waning', 'Autumn' carry negative overtones. Moreover, by choosing words which come from the vocabulary of organic life, historians appear to imply that these periods had a life of their own, that in the past such things really did exist, were born and passed away. Because of the convention – it is no more than that – which puts the end of the Middle Ages at about 1500, the period before 1500 tends to get landed with the label of 'decline', and this is a word which is hard to use without an implication of things getting worse. But there is no evidence that they were.

Having said that, it has to be admitted that historians quite often write as though there were evidence to show that the fifteenth century was in some sense worse than previous centuries. The Wars of the Roses are often used as evidence for this, and they are so used because they are believed to corroborate the view that the fifteenth century was, to a peculiar degree, a violent and lawless age. These historians believe that contemporary records bear out the verdict of Tudor commentators and that the fifteenth century was an exceptionally violent, corrupt and lawless age. But in believing this they are making a serious mistake. We know more about disorder and crime in the fifteenth century than in earlier centuries because more records of litigation survive from then than from earlier centuries. There is also a famous collection of private letters – the Paston letters – which sheds a tremendous amount of light on conditions in East Anglia in the mid-fifteenth century. Nothing is easier than to put together a series of quotations from these letters to illustrate the local lawlessness of the day. But no comparable letter collection survives from earlier centuries. This means that all we can say is that disorder is better documented in the late Middle Ages than it was in the early. Whether there actually was more – or less – disorder there is no way of knowing.

Nonetheless, there are more records – therefore there *seems* to be more crime. As it happens, of course, most types of historical evidence concentrate on the problems which society faces. History, as Gibbon observed, 'is little more than the register of the crimes, follies and misfortunes of mankind'. Things that work well, events which go smoothly are not note-worthy or news-worthy. We all know that students are hard-working, sober, conscientious, responsible and underpaid members of the community, but this is not the impression which records of student life tend to give. The evil that men do lives after them. This is true of most types of record, but inevitably it is particularly true of legal and judicial records. Since in the later Middle Ages this class of record is present in greatly increased bulk, not only does this period seem to be worse but it seems to be worse for an ironical reason. There are more legal records because the law courts are becoming increasingly better organized. If this suggests anything, it is that the judicial institutions are becoming more active. In other words the more vigorously the king's courts try to deal with social abuses the more obvious those abuses become and, in consequence, the feebler the monarchy seems to be. We have to be as cautious in analysing fifteenth-century crime statistics as we do when interpreting their modern counterparts.

On the other hand it has to be admitted that in recent years there have been some signs of the growth of a counter-legend, at least among medieval historians, a legend which writes the Wars of the Roses off as a brief and harmless episode. McFarlane's statistics, for example, on the rate of extinction of noble families may well be strictly accurate; nonetheless they tend to conceal the real damage done by the wars. If a family did not become extinct this was because there was a younger son or brother or cousin to replace the man killed or executed. While the rate of extinction remained 'normal', the death rate may have been unusually high. Take, for example, the Courtenay earldom of Devon. No less than four Courtenays in the direct male line perished in the years 1461–71; yet the earldom itself survived. Another piece of arithmetic which tends to minimize the impact of the wars is the statement nowadays commonly repeated that 'the total period of active campaigning between the first battle of St Albans (1455) and the battle of Stoke (1487) amounted to little more than twelve or thirteen weeks – twelve or thirteen weeks in thirty-two years'. This is a re-formulation of W. H. Dunham's calculation that 'actual fighting probably occupied less than twelve weeks between 1450 and 1485'. It all depends, of course, on what is meant by 'actual fighting', but what is certain is that there was a great deal more time spent on campaign than any of these figures suggest – some seventeen weeks in the crucial years 1459 to 1461 alone. At a conservative estimate, the total period of campaigning between 1455 and 1487 was at least a year.

Most of the rest of this book (chapters four to fourteen) will be devoted to a narrative of these campaigns and of their political background. At first glance such a narrative might appear to lend substance to the view that fifteenth-century England was a war-torn society. But this would be a superficial reading of the evidence. What the narrative of these campaigns in fact shows is that England, with the exception of Northumbria and the Scottish border, was a society organized for peace. The wars which interrupted that peace were fought in a manner which brought them to a swift conclusion and so ensured the early restoration of peace. The next two chapters (chapters two and three) are intended to show how this came about.

Two

THIS SEAT OF PEACE

ENGLAND IN THE FIFTEENTH CENTURY was the most peaceful country in Europe. On the continent war was a possibility which always had to be reckoned with. In many areas – the Low Countries, the Rhineland, Central Europe, France, Northern and Central Italy for example – military campaigns were almost annual events. Government and society abroad were moulded by this ever-present menace. States like Burgundy, France and Venice created standing armies. Everywhere towns had to look to their defences and be prepared to spend a considerable portion of the municipal budget on the upkeep of their walls. In England, by contrast, wars were extremely rare. The troubled interlude of the Percy rebellion in Henry IV's reign had been followed by almost fifty years of peace. The Wars of the Roses, when they did come, were intermittent and limited. By Henry VII's reign English society was no more organized for war than it had been in Henry VI's.

Contemporary observers were well aware of these differences between England and the continent. Sir John Fortescue, writing in the 1460s while he was in exile in France, remarked that the English people, free of the heavy burden of war taxation and unharassed by the exactions of a standing army, enjoyed everything that was needful 'for a quiet and happy life'. This was no idle patriotic boast. Every foreign traveller who came to England commented upon the country's wealth and there are no descriptions of a war-ravaged countryside of the type that exists for France. Thus, although it accords ill with the traditional textbook view, no contemporary would have been surprised by Commynes's judgment on England during the Wars of the Roses. 'Now, in my opinion, out of all the countries which I have personally known, England is the one where public affairs are best conducted and regulated with least damage to the people.' The opinions of Philippe de Commynes (1447–1511) are always worth listening to. His *Memoirs*, like many other 'medieval' historical works contain a large element of self-justification and certainly when it came to covering the tracks of his own tortuous career, Commynes had no qualms about the methods he used. But his general observations on the overall European scene are not open to the same suspicion and it is clear that, as a political commentator, he was exceptionally well informed. He had been a counsellor first to the duke of Burgundy and then to the king of France. He had travelled widely on diplomatic missions to Brittany, Castile, Savoy and Italy, as well as to Calais (at that time under English rule). Unquestionably Commynes's motive in praising the English governmental system was, by implication, to criticize the existing regime in France, but the point is that it was England, and not any other country, that he held up as the standard against which France fell short. Moreover, and this needs to be emphasized, it was England during the Wars of the Roses.

Equally, contemporaries had little difficulty in detecting the main reason for the good fortune of the English. As the Castilian writer Gutierre Díaz de Gómez said, 'They are surrounded by the sea and for this reason they have no fear of any other nation.' An English poem written in the 1430s uses the same image as Shakespeare:

> As though England were likened to a city
> And the wall environ were the sea.

If the sea was like a wall enclosing the 'city' of England, the corollary of this was that English towns could afford to neglect their walls. What is most striking in this context is the fact that the contrast with the continent became greater – not less – during the supposedly turbulent fifteenth century. Abroad towns both large and small continued to spend enormous sums on the repair and improvement of their walls. At Rennes in Brittany, for example, the survival of municipal accounts for seventy of the years between 1419 and 1500 shows that, on average, some 40 to 45 per cent of the budget was spent on defence works. Though a slightly higher proportion was spent each year on the walls of Châlons-sur-Marne, a survey in 1491 indicated that it would cost more than 3,000 *livres* to bring them up to date – and this at a time when the town's total annual expenditure was normally in the region of 2,000 *livres*.

Other continental towns, previously unfortified, decided that they could no longer afford to remain so. Caen, for example, had no walls when Edward III captured it in 1346, but in 1417, when Henry V laid siege to it, both the Old and the New Town were completely encircled by new stone walls. As it happened, Henry V took Caen because its citizens had not been able to bring themselves to demolish the two great

abbey churches founded by William the Conqueror which stood outside the walls. Seized by the English, these abbeys acted as artillery
platforms from which guns fired right into the heart of the city. Other
town councils were more ruthless. During the winter of 1475–6, for
example, the mere rumour of an attack by Charles of Burgundy was
enough to persuade the Strasbourg city authorities to destroy no less
than five abbeys and 620 houses, thus creating a two mile wide belt of
open flat land around their walls. Nothing remotely like this ever
happened during the Wars of the Roses or at any time in fifteenth-
century England. Even today the many fine walled towns which still
survive on the continent bear witness to this on-going concern.

In England, on the other hand, the fifteenth century was a period
when 'very little was spent on the walls, even by way of maintenance'.
This is the conclusion which emerges from Hilary Turner's book on
Town Defences in England and Wales AD 900–1500. From the thirteenth
century onwards most towns financed their building operations by
being granted the right to levy a toll on goods coming into the town for
sale. This toll was known as murage. In the fifteenth century several
new sources of financial aid were found, the most popular being the
receipt of a grant from customs duties to meet the cost of a sea-port's
fortification. As a crude barometer of the effect of the Wars of the Roses
on the outlook of municipal authorities we can make a count at ten-year
intervals of the number of towns receiving grants of murage or other
forms of financial aid for the same purpose. In 1460 there were nine;
1470, again nine; in 1480 only six, and by 1490 it was down to four. One
hundred years earlier the same count shows seven in 1360, seventeen in
1370, fifteen in 1380 and fifteen in 1390. Two hundred years earlier it
had been fourteen in 1260, seventeen in 1270, and ten in 1280 and 1290.
The totals for these decades, though somewhat artificial, are very revealing: fifty-one in the thirteenth century, fifty-four in the fourteenth and only twenty-eight in the fifteenth. Measured in these terms it
is clear that during the Wars of the Roses English townsmen were more
relaxed than they had been in earlier centuries, though possibly frac-
tionally more worried than they had been in the previous four decades
(1420–50) when the total is twenty-six. A further indication that
English society in the fifteenth century was, if anything, more peaceful
than ever before can be seen in the design of town gates – the most
important part of the defences. Fortified gates reached their
highest point of development in the late fourteenth century – see, for
example, among those still standing the West gates of Canterbury

and Winchester, the Bargate at Southampton and the Landgate
at Rye. Whereas fourteenth-century gates commonly make provisions
for cannons to be fired from them, fifteenth-century ones do not, and
in general they show a progressive relaxation of their military character. They are becoming thought of as being primarily useful for the
collection of tolls.

   The relatively high number of murage grants in the period 1360–90
(and also in the next two decades) can be explained by the very real
fears of a French invasion which characterized those years. To this
extent the Hundred Years' War, though it was fought almost exclusively in France, had a greater impact on English town defences than
did the Wars of the Roses. This impression is confirmed by the history
of Sandwich which, in Hilary Turner's words, was 'peculiar amongst
the towns of England in that considerable effort was expended on the
fortification of the town in the fifteenth century'. It is clear that what the
Sandwich council feared was not civil strife, but French raids – a fear
which materialized in August 1457 when the town was sacked by a force
of 1,800 men under the command of the famous seneschal of Normandy, Pierre de Brézé – 'the best warrer of all that time', as he was
called by the contemporary English chronicler John Warkworth. There
is some further evidence of continuing work at other south-coast towns
like Portsmouth, Southampton and Dover, but this only serves to
reinforce the point that it was those towns which were nearest the
continent which had most to fear from war. The relatively high count
for murage grants in the thirteenth century can be explained by the fact
that it was then that most towns were replacing their earthwork and
timber fortifications with stone walls. But in the fifteenth century
English towns were no longer trying to keep up to date. In this respect
too there lies a contrast with the continent, where builders and
engineers were evolving new techniques of defence in order to meet the
new challenge of artillery. Here, without a doubt, is an important
moment in the history of warfare: the development and deployment of
effective firearms, and it is to this subject that we must now turn.

By the time of the Wars of the Roses, guns had been used in north-
western Europe for well over a hundred years and there was a wide
variety of types available, many of them with names which sound
strange to modern ears – serpentines, orgues, crapaudeaux, ribaudequins, for example. At one end of the scale there were massive bombards like *Mons Meg* – now in Edinburgh Castle – with a calibre of over

twenty inches and weighing more than 14,000 lb, or the even bigger gun manufactured at Landshut in Bavaria which had a calibre of over three feet. At the other end of the scale there were the small culverins which could either be mounted on tripods or used as handguns pure and simple. During a siege the two types could be used in combination; the bombards to make breaches in the walls, while the culverins picked off those who tried to repair them. Guns were made either of iron or bronze. Iron guns were built by the smith from bars of wrought iron welded into tube-shape and strengthened by thick iron hoops shrunk over the tubes. But most guns were cast and cast in bronze – a field of technology in which there was a well-developed tradition of crafts-manship thanks to the centuries of demand for church bells. When ploughshares were turned into swords, the bell-founders made a nice profit by manufacturing firearms. Not until the second half of the sixteenth century did the techniques of cast iron reach a similar level of development, so throughout the fifteenth century men preferred to use relatively expensive raw materials – copper and tin. Frequently the gun-founders were also the gunners. This was particularly true of the larger siege artillery, where each gun was an individual and its projec-tiles had to be made specially for it. It was only natural that each of these unstandardized pieces should have a name of its own.

To fire his cannon the gunner used a firing iron – an iron bar heated in a pan of coal or charcoal which was kept ready to hand and fanned by bellows. The projectiles varied in size from small pellets or bullets to huge iron or stone balls weighing 500, 600, 700 lb or more. According to a rough rule of thumb it was reckoned to take 1 lb of powder to project a stone weighing 9 lb. Most guns had to be washed out after each dis-charge with a mixture of vinegar and water. The whole process of loading, firing and re-loading was a long one, so that ten shots an hour was reckoned to be a good rate of fire. Thus although guns were commonly employed on the eve of a battle – as at Barnet in 1471 – and most battles actually opened with a cannonade, the slow rate of fire meant that often there was time only for a single salvo before the hand-to-hand fighting began. According to Konrad Kauder's *Feuer-werkbuch*, an artillery manual published in 1429, a cannon using good quality gunpowder had a range of 2,000 to 2,500 paces. Against an enemy force which wished to stay both concentrated and immobile – in order, for example, to dispute a river crossing – the weight and range of cannon shot could be used with devastating effect. In these circum-stances their slow rate of fire was relatively unimportant. In 1465 when

Charles the Impetuous wanted to cross the Seine by pontoon bridge he
used his artillery to disperse the hostile troops on the opposite bank. It
is easy enough to be scathing about early artillery. Garrett Mattingley,
for example, wrote that 'the most experienced gunner might hesitate to
predict whether when next he fired it his gun would send its shot
directly to the target, drop it with a sort of discouraged burp a few
hundred feet ahead, or blow up the breach, probably killing him and his
crew', but the historian who speaks in these terms is adopting an
anachronistic attitude. He is measuring guns by the standards of the
nineteenth or twentieth century and not, as he should, by the standards
set by the earlier weapons which firearms were replacing. Despite a few
famous accidents, like that in which King James IV of Scotland was
killed, the mid-fifteenth-century gun was emphatically not more
dangerous to its user than to his enemy. It had developed, indeed, to a
point at which it was threatening to revolutionize the whole art of
warfare by taking the advantage from the defence, where it had rested
for centuries, and handing it over to the attack.

The crucial advance seems to have taken place in the 1370s. Up to
that point guns had been small, firing projectiles of only two or three
pounds weight, and not particularly effective. Then, at about 1370,
there occurred what has been described as 'the most epoch-making
development in the long history of ordnance'. Suddenly, as it seems,
guns were being manufactured which could fire shot twenty or thirty
times the weight of their predecessors. The momentum of this technological leap forward was maintained and by 1420 we hear of large
cannon able to fire stones weighing seven hundredweight (784 lb). The
high stone walls which had worked well in the age of the ballista and the
crossbow crumbled under the impact of the massive, horizontal blows
delivered by the new heavy artillery. In 1405 just one shot from one of
Henry IV's cannon was enough to make Berwick surrender, so shatter-
ing was its effect on the walls. Three years later when an English
translation of the classic Roman study of war, Vegetius' *De Re Militari*,
was presented to Thomas Lord Berkeley, we find that the translator
had added a sentence not in the Latin original, drawing his reader's
attention to 'great guns that nowadays shoot stones of so great piece
that no wall may withstand them as hath been well showed both in the
north country and in the wars of Wales'.

The first response of military architects was to build thicker walls
and to scarp them, sometimes for as much as two-thirds of their height;
in this way it was hoped that some of the impact of the cannon balls

might be deflected. A further advantage of scarping was that it weakened scaling ladders by increasing the angle at which they could be set against the wall. Since it also meant that assault parties could no longer stand at the foot of a near vertical wall, there was no longer any point in having walls machicolated (the purpose of which was to allow a rain of missiles to be dropped on the attackers' heads), and as a result the defenders began to pay greater attention to flanking fire. The importance of flanking fire had, of course, always been recognized and, in consequence, projecting towers built at intervals along the curtain wall. The initial reaction to gunpowder had been to build gun towers on the model of the old towers, but with thicker walls, and provided with gunports, for the gun, from the point of view of defence, had first been seen as a weapon to be used against assault parties rather than as a long-range deterrent. Up to this point the development can be traced in England. Gunports dating from the second half of the fourteenth century can be found at Southampton and Canterbury, for example. But guns used in this manner had certain disadvantages. They were not as manoeuvrable as bows, and they had a much slower rate of fire. Moreover, in a confined space they produced an uncomfortable amount of smoke. Gradually it came to be realized that guns could be more efficiently used to attack the besieger's encampment and dismantle his artillery. But the big guns which this job required could not be placed inside towers; quite apart from anything else, their arc of fire would have been hopelessly restricted by the small circumference of gunports cut through thick masonry.

Ultimately military architects found the solution to these problems in the creation of the bastion. The bastion is essentially a gun platform thrust forward to obtain as wide a field of fire as possible. Designed to be as solid as possible, it was built on a much more massive scale than a tower, and its height was dropped to the level of the wall in order to facilitate the running of guns from one platform to another. It came to be made of rubble and brick, which absorbed cannon shot, instead of fracturing on impact as stone did. By resisting the new artillery and providing a platform for a heavy gun of its own, the bastion was to give back to the defence that advantage in warfare which had traditionally belonged to it, but which had been undermined by the development of large guns in the late fourteenth century. By the sixteenth century the importance of the bastion had been widely recognized, and almost everywhere town defences remodelled according to the new pattern. As a result the European city, from the Baltic to the North African coast,

took on a new appearance. Indeed wherever Europeans settled over-
seas, from the Caribbean to India, they built towns which conformed to
this basic pattern; at Havana, Mombasa, Goa. Architectural historians
have not written very much about it, preferring the peaceful beauty of
their domes and colonnades; nonethelesss, the bastion was unquestionably the single most significant architectural form evolved during the
Renaissance.

But while everywhere else succumbed to the fascinations of this
international style, England remained stolidly insular. Thus when, in
the nineteenth century, patriotic historians debated the origins of
bastions, there was no English contender for the honour. Italians said
that Italians had invented it, Frenchmen said that Frenchmen had,
Germans gave the credit to Germans. Other candidates included the
Turks and the Bohemians (at the time of the Hussite Wars in the early
fifteenth century), but no one was foolish enough to put forward the
claims of the English. In England the science of military architecture
stood still between the late fourteenth century – when castles like
Bodiam were built as a counter to the threat of French invasion – and
the reign of Henry VIII when a chain of coastal artillery forts in the
foreign manner were built during the years 1538–40. Later on Berwick
and Carlisle, both in the turbulent Border country, were to some extent
brought up to date, but that was all. This crucial difference between
England and the continent can still be observed on the ground. Time
and again on the continent the city centre – the site of the medieval old
town – is separated from modern industrial and residential suburbs by
a ring of wide boulevards or by a pleasant girdle of lawns and gardens, a
kind of miniature green belt. English towns, however, do not conform to
this common European pattern and the reason for this is that the
boulevards or 'green belt' mark the site of the new fortifications based
on the bastion. (The word *boulevard*, linked to the German *Bollwerk* and
English *bulwark*, originally referred to artillery ramparts and then was
later transferred to the promenade laid out on the site of demolished
defence works.) But in England there are no boulevards, because in the
fifteenth, sixteenth and seventeenth centuries there were no bulwarks
and no bastions – or almost none. Thus the differing lay-outs of
English and continental towns continue to reflect their contrasting
histories.

In this respect if there was one period above all others when English
and continental history diverged and took different paths it was the
fifteenth century. For roughly a hundred and fifty years military

architecture in England stagnated at a time when abroad its importance was being fully recognized. It took a long time, of course, to evolve
the fully-fledged bastion, but throughout the century there was a great
deal of experimentation – and in the medium of earth and timber just as
often as in brick and stone. Inevitably the involvement in the Hundred
Years' War meant that English commanders were well aware of what
was going on. They took care that their Gascon towns should be
properly fortified against a besieger's cannon. Thus during the summer
of 1442 earthworks called *boulevards* were thrown up before the gates of
Bordeaux and were well stocked with defensive artillery. Nearer at
home in 1436 the preparations made to defend Calais against the duke
of Burgundy were described by an English chronicler: 'Sir John
Radcliff, the lieutenant of the town, Robert Clitheroe, the mayor,
and Thomas Thirland, lieutenant of the staple of Calais, with the
soldiers, merchants, burgesses and commoners, cast up a fair broad
dike on the south side of the town, and made three strong *bullwerkes*
of earth and clay, one at the corner of the castle without the town,
another at Boulogne Gate and another at the postern by the Prince's
Inn. And at Milk Gate there was a fair bulwerk made of brick.' This
work continued throughout the fifteenth century. Edward IV, in
particular, spent a great deal of money on bringing the Calais fortresses up to date. But in England itself there is almost no sign of
these developments – though here again it is Sandwich which was
one of the exceptions which prove the rule. There is a vivid account of
the French raid of 1457 in the Burgundian chronicle written by Jehan
de Waurin, an old soldier who was well informed on military matters.
According to Waurin the key to the town's fortifications lay in *ung
bollewert rempare nouvellement*.

To the extent, then, that the Channel was a theatre of the Hundred
Years' War, English coastal towns occasionally had to employ continental methods of self-defence, but in England as a whole the architects
found employment only in the arts of peace. Even the castles which
were built in England – Herstmonceux Castle or Tattershall Castle –
were not, despite their names, real castles. The large windows and the
thin walls give the game away. Like the crenellated towers of a
nineteenth-century mansion, their battlements were just for show. For
this there can be only one explanation: England in the fifteenth century
was a uniquely peaceful country; a prosperous and quiet land, un-
troubled by the prospect of war. In these circumstances it was inevitable that a war fought in England might be something very different

from war on the continent. Abroad a victory over an enemy's forces in the field did little to solve the problem of his castles and fortified towns. Thus the Hundred Years' War, despite the fame of a few battles, was chiefly a war of sieges, a war of attrition and blockades. Similarly although the most dramatic moment of the War of the Public Weal, the 1465 rebellion against Louis XI, was the Battle of Montlhéry, it was in fact a battle which decided nothing. Eventually the campaign took shape as a siege of Paris and for eight weeks both sides concentrated on an artillery duel and on digging themselves in. In England there was never anything to approach this war of trenches and gun batteries. By skilful diplomacy Louis XI was able to bring the War of the Public Weal to a swift conclusion but, as Commynes knew well, many continental wars dragged on for years. The Hundred Years' War may be something of a misnomer, but each of the several wars of which it was composed was fought abroad – and each lasted long enough to keep the professional soldiers in business. Moreover in this 'scientific' war of sieges and attrition both sides adopted a 'scorched earth' policy in an attempt to deprive the enemy of supplies.

In a memorandum addressed to the English council in 1435 one of the most experienced of the English commanders, Sir John Fastolf – and anyone less like Shakespeare's plump Jack Falstaff it would be hard to imagine – argued that this policy should be carried through with total ruthlessness. Two strike forces of 750 lances each were to ravage French territory non-stop from 1 June to 1 November 'burning and destroying all the land as they pass, both houses, corn, vines and all trees that bear fruit for men's sustenance and all livestock either to be destroyed or driven off, ... to the intent to drive the enemies thereby to an extreme famine'. What Fastolf advocated was simply making more systematic what was, in any event, the ordinary practice of war. 'First destroy the land,' said Count Philip of Flanders in 1174, 'that is how war is begun.' 'It is better', wrote Vegetius, 'to tame the enemy by hunger than by fighting.' 'War without fire', said Henry V, 'is like sausages without mustard.' What this meant when put into practice by England's efficient hero-king and his subordinates is made very clear in the horrifying list of devastated provinces compiled some years later by a Norman writer Thomas Basin.

> We ourselves have seen the vast plains of Champagne, of Beauce, of Brie, of the Gâtinais, Chartres, Dreux, Maine and Perche, of the Vexin both French and Norman, the Beauvaisis, the Pays de Caux, from the Seine as far as Amiens and Abbeville, the region around Senlis, Soissons and Valois right up

to Laon and beyond in the direct of Hainaut – all this we have seen absolutely deserted, uncultivated, abandoned, empty of inhabitants, covered with scrub and brambles.

War abroad turned on the control of strongpoints and, on the whole, it seemed sensible to avoid battle. According to Commynes, Louis XI 'made his armies so big that there were few princes who could fight them and he supplied them with better artillery than any previous king of France. He also tried to take places by surprise, especially those he knew to be badly provided for, and when he had captured them he placed in them so many troops and guns that it was impossible to recapture them from him. If they had in them a captain who was prepared to deliver the place in return for money he was quick to come to terms.' It reads like a commentary on the dictum which Christine de Pisan attributed to Charles V and which she quoted approvingly: 'That which can be bought ought not to be bought with the lives of men.' From another perspective the same point about the vital importance of strongpoints was made by Leon Battista Alberti, writing in mid-fifteenth-century Italy: 'If you were to examine the expeditions that have been undertaken, you would go near to find that most of the victories were gained more by the art and the skill of the architects than by the conduct or fortune of the generals.' War on the continent became increasingly a struggle between guns on the one hand and artillery fortifications on the other. When Charles the Impetuous of Burgundy marched out to war in 1465 no fewer than 236 carts carrying bombards, cannon, serpentines, ribaudequins, crapaudeaux, mortars and other guns were observed passing through Arras, while a second artillery train went by way of Cambrai. In 1463 the king of France had an artillery budget of 5,000 *livres*; by 1491 it was 25,000 *livres*.

Unfortunately the absence of the relevant records means that we cannot produce equivalent figures for the English government's expenditure on firearms in this period. The fifteenth century remains the 'dark age' of the history of artillery in England. On fourteenth-century firearms we possess a great deal of information thanks to the preservation of the accounts of the king's privy wardrobe in the Tower of London, the crown's main armoury and arsenal. Randolph Hatton, for example, keeper of the privy wardrobe from 1382 to 1396, bought no less than eighty-seven cannon from four gun-founders in his first six years of office. Despite frequent deliveries of cannon to fortresses on the south coast and Scottish border, his executors were able to hand over a stock of fifty guns, as well as 4,000 lb of gunpowder and nearly 600 lb of saltpetre, to his successor, John Lufwyk. Then at an unknown date early in the fifteenth century the privy wardrobe's functions were taken over by the newly created ordnance office. The earliest known master of ordnance was Nicholas Merbury. In that capacity he served Henry v on the Agincourt campaign and ended his career as keeper of the king's jewels and privy purse. Merbury's rise is a clear enough indication of the growing importance of artillery, but unfortunately none of the accounts of the masters of the king's ordnance survive.

In these circumstances the historian of artillery in fifteenth-century England has to make do with scattered fragments of evidence. This is all the more frustrating since the career of one master of ordnance suggests that at the beginning of the Wars of the Roses there were some people who believed that the office might well turn out to be a crucial one. One of these was John Judde, appointed master of ordnance in December 1456. He was a London merchant who attracted Henry vi's attention by offering to provide sixty serpentines and twenty tons of saltpetre and sulphur at his own expense and deliver them to the crown 'under certain reasonable conditions'. Henry and his more forceful wife, Margaret of Anjou, had recently suffered some humiliating reverses and they were now preparing the ground for a political come-back, so Judde's offer was well timed. As the king himself recognized, the crown was 'not as yet sufficiently furnished with guns, gunpowder and other habiliments of war'. Doubtless, like the king's navy, the king's ordnance had suffered from decades of neglect under Henry v's irresponsible son. But now Henry vi was being stirred to take action and one consequence was the appointment of a new broom in the ordnance office. Within a month of taking over, Judde had delivered twenty-six serpentines to the king at Kenilworth and claimed to have manufactured three 'great serpentines to subdue any castle or place that would rebel'. In 1459 the court party's plans came at last to fruition. The king's enemies were scattered. Judde was ordered to seize all their war material. To one Yorkist partisan, the London chronicler Robert Bale, John Judde was a man who 'had maliciously conspired and laboured to ordain and make all things for war to the destruction of the duke of York and all the other lords'. On 22 June 1460, while superintending another delivery of artillery to the king, Judde was ambushed just past St Albans and killed. It was, said Robert Bale, 'a wretched end, as the caitiff deserved'.

Edward iv's masters of ordnance were more fortunate; indeed they

served a king far more aware of the importance of artillery than Henry
VI had ever been. An Italian visitor to London in 1475 observed how the
king inspected all his artillery every day. From 1463 to 1477 Edward's
master of ordnance was John Wode, a man whose experience in the
Calais administration gave him the background appropriate to the job.
His successor, John Sturgeon (1477–82), was well-versed in another
related field, that of naval supplies. Unlike Judde the London
businessman, both Wode and Sturgeon were esquires of the king's
body, members of that small political élite (two or three hundred
strong) which comprised the royal household. That the status of the
office continued to rise is indicated by the fact that both Richard III and
Henry VII appointed knights as masters.

Yet for all the growing importance of artillery, it remains true that
this arm played only a minor role in the campaigns of the Wars of the
Roses. The reason for this was the fact that in England battles could be
decisive. Once the enemy's forces had been cleared from the field, his
castles and towns proved relatively easy to capture. In England the art
of fortification had lagged behind the skill of the gunner and precisely
because of this the gunner found he had but little work to do. In the
Wars of the Roses there were few sieges and only one of any consequence. Thus Commynes commented on some English troops who
were serving in the Burgundian army in 1477 that 'because the English
had not fought outside their kingdom for so long, they did not understand siege warfare very well'. At the court of Charles of Burgundy, by
contrast, where they took this business very seriously indeed, they even
played games based on siege warfare. In the autumn of 1473 while
Duke Charles was residing in the ancient and famous monastery of St
Maximin outside Trier, he and his friends were entertained by a
spectacular struggle waged between the retinue of the 'King of the
Crows' on the one hand and a company of cooks on the other. For an
account of this absorbing game we are indebted to the letter of an
eye-witness: 'The company of cooks made a defence of wood and
manure around a cesspool in the courtyard at St Maximin's. They had
many ways in and round about it and they put up a lively defence from
these ways, using three serpentines which they had ready inside, with
old cushions, etc. The King of the Crows had two serpentines which
fired at and stormed against the castle and they hurled manure and dirt
at one another and struck each other. They had such a time that
everyone had to watch and they all got very wild.'

In England, however, battles, not sieges, were decisive and it was for this reason that, as Commynes observed, the English were 'of all the people in the world the most inclined to give battle'. Commynes was in no doubt what the consequences of this were. 'If any conflict breaks out in England one or other of the rivals is master within ten days or less. Our affairs, however,' he added ruefully, 'are not conducted in this fashion.' It was this contrast which persuaded him that 'out of all the countries which I have personally known, England is the one where public affairs are best conducted and regulated with least violence to the people. There neither the countryside nor the people are destroyed, nor are buildings burnt or demolished. Disaster and misfortune fall only on those who make war, the soldiers and the nobles.' Commynes's view of England in the period of the Wars of the Roses as the best regulated realm in Europe might well come as a surprise to those who know their history chiefly through Shakespeare, but in the light of the contrast between warfare here and warfare abroad, it is a perfectly sensible judgment.

If we take this contrast a step further we can observe that in England, unlike France, Burgundy and some Italian states, there were no standing armies of any significance. From the point of view of society at large this was undoubtedly a blessing. Standing armies had to be paid for – and in more ways than one, as we can see from, for example, the proceedings of the chapter of the Order of the Golden Fleece. One of the traditions of this order (the most prestigious order of chivalry in Europe) was that its member knights were encouraged to criticize each other and their sovereign, the duke of Burgundy. In 1473, along with other criticisms of Duke Charles such as that he endangered his health by working too hard and that he sometimes spoke sharply to his servants, they complained of the burdens occasioned by the presence of a standing army. 'He is not aware of the great evils and damages they do, but thinks they are content with their wages. It is his noble wish that, through the agency of the financial contributions and taxes which they willingly pay, his people will be preserved from oppression by these troops. But the contrary has happened and happens frequently without his knowledge, for some of these troops do a great deal of damage to goods, and some of the said men-at-arms go through the country ransoming villages by threatening to lodge in them.' In his reply Duke Charles admitted the justice of these grievances and blamed the officers for allowing their troops to get out of hand. Exactly the same complaints were heard in other countries. Commynes said of Charles VII of France:

He has heavily charged his own soul and those of his successors and inflicted a cruel wound on his kingdom which will long bleed, by establishing, after the manner of Italian lords, this terrible burden of a standing army.... They live off the country continuously without paying anything, committing other crimes and excesses as we all know. For they are not content just to live but in addition they beat and abuse the poor and force them to go to look elsewhere for bread, wine and victuals, and if any good man has a beautiful wife or daughter he would be very wise to protect her carefully.

The only way to tackle these problems was to ensure that the troops were paid well and regularly. No fifteenth-century ruler was able to do this entirely satisfactorily and mutinies were fairly common. Indeed the mutiny became as much an accepted part of the social framework as the strike is today; essentially mutinies, like strikes, were a means of exerting pressure in negotiations about pay.

Inevitably the reappearance of the first standing armies since classical times meant the reappearance of that heavy taxation which had characterized the Roman Empire. And, just as in the Roman Empire the rich had found ways of avoiding paying taxes, so also now the main burden fell upon the mass of the population. Thus, in Commynes's words, 'it was pitiful to see and learn about the poverty of the people. Our master [Louis xi] took everything and spent everything. He built more imposing fortifications and defences for towns and other places in the kingdom than any of his predecessors. He gave much to churches. In some respects it would have been better if he had done less, because he took from the poor to give to those who had no need of it.' Moreover, since standing armies created the need for permanent war taxation it became possible for princes to levy taxes without first obtaining the consent of their subjects given in parliaments or in meetings of Estates. In France therefore, as Commynes pointed out, Charles vii became the founder of both standing armies and arbitrary taxes.

In England the nearest approach to a standing army was the king's personal bodyguard of two hundred archers formed in 1468. Outside England, in the shape of the Calais garrison, the king did possess a permanent military force of about a thousand men, and the fact that this played an important role in the Wars of the Roses only serves to show just how unmilitarized England itself was. The one exception to this was in the far north on the border with Scotland. Only here in the Marches towards Scotland was the danger of war real enough for it to have an impact on the political and social structure. From the late fourteenth century onwards wardens of the Marches were appointed to provide the border counties with permanent military guardians. The warden of the west March, based at Carlisle, was normally paid £1,000 or more in peacetime and his colleague in the east based at Berwick, twice that amount. Since they were expected to use these salaries – higher than those received by any other royal officer – to employ troops, it is clear that there was a standing army of a kind in the north. It is usually said that these troops were not really royal armies but private armies raised at the crown's expense. This, however, would also be true of large sections of the French standing army; the position of the count of Saint-Pol, in command of 400 men-at-arms on the France–Burgundy border, was very similar to the position of a Neville or a Percy as a warden of the marches. But it is equally clear that if this was a kind of standing army it was a very small one. According to the indentures drawn up by Henry IV, the warden of the west march was supposed to maintain a peacetime force of 50 men-at-arms and 100 archers and double this in time of war. The cost of maintaining his peacetime force was put at about £2,000 a year, but after 1411 the warden rarely received much more than half this amount. The warden of the east march was paid twice as much as the warden of the west, and this suggests that the combined peacetime force of the two wardens would have been in the region of 75 men-at-arms and 150 archers.

In practice, of course, when they needed to, the wardens could raise larger bodies of troops from their own tenants and retainers – and the borderers were hardy warriors. Even when Scotland and England were formally at peace the marches were rarely quiet. For men on both sides raid and counter-raid were a way of life to which they had grown accustomed in the century and more which had passed since Edward I had tried to conquer Scotland. Every landowner built his own little fortress, a stone pele tower where he and his men could take refuge during enemy raids. This was a society where the military values of constant vigilance and skill in arms were the ones which counted. There were times during the Wars of the Roses when the tough fighting qualities of the northerners were much in evidence and sent shivers down the spines of their less warlike southern cousins. An Italian traveller, Aeneas Sylvius Piccolomini, later Pope Pius II, passed through the border country during the winter of 1435–6 and gave a vivid description of his first night spent in an English village just south of the border. He and his companions were put up in a farmhouse and enjoyed a good supper of hens and geese (which their host offered them) as well as red wine and white bread (which they themselves provided, to the amazement and delight of the locals, some of whom had never seen such luxuries, much less tasted them). Suddenly the men and boys rose and left the farmhouse in order to take refuge in a pele tower some way off in case the Scots should come south on a raid. The women, however, stayed sitting round the fire. Aeneas, somewhat surprised, asked why it was that no effort was made to protect the women. In reply he was assured that they had nothing to fear from the Scots 'since they do not count rape as harm'.

Three

THE DISCIPLINES OF WAR

In England, then, the outcome of the Wars of the Roses was to depend upon battles rather than sieges, battles fought not between standing armies but between forces raised just for the occasion. How was this done? The only English army of this period on which we are reasonably well informed is the expeditionary force which Edward IV took across the Channel in 1475. This was a 'contract' army. It was composed of nearly 200 contingents and each contingent leader had contracted to bring so many men. Sir Richard Tunstall, for example, had entered into indentures to provide ten spears and one hundred archers 'to do service of war for one whole year'. These men would then usually be raised by means of sub-contracts. In one surviving indenture an esquire named Richard Hyde promised to bring five archers to the duke of Clarence's contingent and to serve himself as a man-at-arms. Was this how the armies which fought in the Wars of the Roses were raised? Unfortunately the evidence is far too scrappy for us to be able to reconstruct these forces with anything like the same degree of precision. Late medieval noblemen kept records in abundance but only a few fragments of their archives still survive today. There are, however, some clues to be found in the fifteenth-century family archive which has suffered least from the ravages of time, that belonging to the Staffords. We know, for example, that ninety men from Surrey and Kent were paid 6s 8d a head for being with Humphrey, duke of Buckingham, at the First Battle of St Albans (1455). Five years earlier the Staffordshire receiver had incurred expenses of £17 10s in bringing a force of seventy-four mounted yeomen to London in anticipation of Cade's revolt. Clearly these men were paid for their services. Probably their wages were based on the rates paid by the king when he went to war. Equally clearly the numbers involved show that on occasions like this a lord was not content to rely on his retainers alone. The total number of people on Duke Humphrey's payroll in 1457 was only 129 – and 15 of these were waiting women. Out of 114 potential combatants there were 17 gentle-men, 51 yeomen, 34 pages, 4 chaplains, one herald and 7 members of his clerical staff. If as many as 90 came from Surrey and Kent, or 74 from the Staffordshire circuit, then plainly Duke Humphrey's officials were mustering men from other sources. That this was so is confirmed by what we know of the composition of the Percy army at the 'Battle' of Heworth (near York) in 1453. In June 1454 the victorious Nevilles brought indictments against 710 named Percy followers. They included 6 knights, 32 esquires, 26 gentlemen and 24 clerks (among them several belligerent parish priests). The city of York provided a sizeable con-tingent (about 100), but by far the largest single group was the yeomen (330). Since another 44 were described as husbandmen it looks as though the Percies had been able to call out many of their tenant farmers. (As late as the Napoleonic period when the duke of Northum-berland maintained 1500 riflemen, cavalry and artillery to meet the threatened French invasion, the force was known as the 'Percy Tenan-try Volunteers'.) Of the 710 named in the 1454 indictments, only a tiny proportion were Percy retainers, but doubtless these few were import-ant in providing leadership and organization. That this was part of a retainer's job was spelled out in his indentures, i.e., in the contracts made between him and his lord. For example, sixty-nine of the inden-tures drawn up by Lord Hastings (one of Edward IV's closest advisers) still survive. Sixty-one retainers agreed to come to Hastings's call with as many men as they might assemble, and in fifty-one cases it was explicitly stated that these men were to be 'defensibly arrayed'. The normal arrangement was that Hastings should bear the costs and expenses incurred by these men. In other words, the troops whom Hastings's retainers led to war were paid wages, since at this date the function of all soldiers' wages was to meet their expenses. Their profit was expected to accrue from what they could lay their hands on by way of plunder. But this arrangement, though it worked well enough in wars fought in foreign territory, was not a satisfactory one for soldiers involved in civil wars. To the extent that their commanders, anxious not to lose popular support, succeeded in keeping a tight rein on looting, these campaigns were unprofitable ones for the ordinary soldiers.

In addition to soldiers who followed their lords to war for reasons of personal private obligation, there were also troops who could be said to serve in consequence of a public duty – though the line between these two was always a fluid one. At any given moment in the Wars of the

Roses, there was one side which enjoyed the advantage of controlling the country's administrative machinery. It was thus able to summon the subjects to render on its behalf the services due to the crown. From 1458 to 1461 the Lancastrian government issued commissions of array to various counties, authorizing the commissioners to muster the shire levies and bring them to the king's presence. In the absence of unofficial accounts of county court proceedings, what actually happened when the king's commission was read out must remain a matter of guesswork. When a particular magnate was quite obviously the dominant figure in the region, the levies doubtless attached themselves to his following. Thus in 1484 Howard of Norfolk reckoned to have command of a thousand men, both levies and retainers. At other times the balance in the shire was presumably less clear-cut and much may have depended on the kind of manoeuvring familiar to historians of the county communities in the civil wars of the 1640s. A letter written by John Paston gives some idea of the uncertainty which prevailed in Norfolk early in 1461. Apparently the levies had been ordered to stand by, but had instead taken some kind of independent initiative.

Most people out of this country [the term commonly used to denote 'county'] have taken wages, saying they will go up to London. But they have no captain assigned to them by the commissioners and so they straggle about by themselves; in all likelihood only half of them will reach London. Moreover men coming from London report that not more than four hundred of them have passed through Thetford, though doubtless the towns and country that have paid their wages will consider that they have already discharged their obligation. It will not be at all easy to get more men when they are needed.

The survival of records from cities like York, Norwich, Coventry and Salisbury means that the system for raising town levies is more readily accessible than that for the mustering of the shire. For example, on 18 May 1455 Henry VI wrote from Westminster asking the city authorities of Coventry to provide as many troops 'as ye goodly may in their best and most defensible array'. The king's messenger delivered this letter into the mayor's hands on 22 May and was given 6s 8d for his trouble. The mayor then called a council meeting. They decided to send 100 archers and appointed a captain to lead them. But by this time the First Battle of St Alban's had already been fought and won (on 22 May); the city contingent stayed at home. In 1455 it was early days and in the first flush of enthusiasm the council had ordered a new banner, new sashes in green and red for the men and a splendid new garment in green, violet and red for the captain. By 1460 Coventry was already feeling the problems of divided allegiances among its citizens. Despite this it was still prepared to send 100 men in support of Edward IV in March 1461 (the Towton campaign) at a cost of £80. Then later that same year another £40 was raised to pay the wages of the forty men who were sent to join Warwick's campaign in the north. As it turned out they were away for longer than anticipated and a further £11 13s 4d had to be found to recompense the thirty-four men who returned home after a total of six weeks' service. In 1469, however, the Coventry council was embarrassed by receiving requests for troops from both Edward IV and the earl of Warwick, by this time the king's enemy. It was decided to send fifty men for twenty days' service in the king's army, but in these awkward circumstances they found it impossible to levy troops at the rate of 8d a day and were forced to raise the daily wage to 10d. Next year the city was having to pay its soldiers 12d a day as well as plying them with wine and ale. By 1471 the collectors who went round the wards raising the money were finding great difficulty in raising the amount due. The evidence from other towns tends to bear out the impression created by the Coventry records that, as the years went by, subjects were becoming increasingly unwilling to answer the government's summons to war. This was an attitude which townspeople shared with lords and their retainers. Whereas a very high proportion of the English nobility participated in the war of 1459–61, thereafter they became increasingly reluctant to risk life and limb until finally, at Bosworth in 1485, the issue was decided, in effect, in their absence.

What kind of army was it that gradually assembled as lords, retainers, tenants and others came in, willingly or unwillingly, to the muster? The best visual impression of a fifteenth-century army is provided by the drawing of an army on the march in the late-fifteenth-century *Hausbuch*, an essential corrective to the superficially pretty atmosphere of chivalry which pervades so many late medieval illustrations of war. The *Hausbuch*, of course, is concerned with continental armies, not with English ones, but fortunately we do possess a detailed description of the way English troops looked to a continental observer. This was written for the archbishop of Vienne by an Italian cleric, Dominic Mancini, who visited England in 1482–3. What impressed him most were the archers.

Their bows and arrows are thicker and longer than those used by other nations just as their arms are stronger than other peoples', for they seem to have hands and arms of iron. As a result their bows have as long a range as our crossbows. Almost every man has a helmet and each carries an iron shield and a sword which is as long as our sword, but heavy and thick as well. Only the wealthy wear metal armour; ordinary soldiers prefer comfortable tunics (stuffed with tow) which reach down to their thigh. They say that the softer they are the better they withstand blows; besides which in summer they are lighter and in winter more useful than iron.

Mancini stayed in London and seems to have been a spectator at the martial games which were a traditional part of the city scene. 'On holidays the youths fight in the streets with blunted swords or staves clashing on shields. When they are older they go out into the fields with bows and arrows – indeed even the women go hunting with them.' Mancini was also struck by the relatively small numbers of cavalry, and observed that the English used their horses 'not to fight on horseback but to carry them to the field. Then they dismount, and they all fight together under the same conditions; no one can hope to flee more easily than his fellows.'

Although the troops which Mancini saw were assembling for an ostensibly ceremonial occasion (Richard III's coronation), it seems certain that this clear numerical superiority of archers was the norm. We know from surviving pay records that the army with which Edward IV planned to invade France in 1475 was composed of at least 11,451 combatants. Of these, 1,278 were men-at-arms and 10,173 were archers. This was the largest English force to cross to France in the fifteenth century, about 2,000 more than Henry V mustered for the Agincourt campaign. But since 1415 the ratio of men-at-arms to archers had changed. Whereas Henry V usually took with him three archers to one man-at-arms, the ratio in 1475 was nearer seven to one. This may well reflect the long years of peace. Law required every free-born Englishman between the ages of sixteen and sixty to bear arms and to the extent that this was observed it may have helped to keep in being a pool of archers. But the expensive equipment and unusual skills required of men-at-arms may well have meant that their numbers were likely to dwindle during a prolonged period of peace. This was certainly Commynes's opinion. In his view, the 1200 men-at-arms in Charles the Impetuous army at the battle of Montlhéry in 1465 were 'poorly armed and inexperienced'; only about fifty knew how to lay a lance in the *arrêt* and only 400 had breastplates. This he put down to the fact that they had enjoyed some thirty-six years of peace 'except for some small wars against the men of Ghent which did not last long'. By contrast he pointed out that so many archers had come to the muster that Charles's captains had been able to pick and choose, taking only the best and dismissing as many as they enrolled. In the light of these considerations it would seem probable that the armies which fought in the Wars of the Roses were based on a ratio of seven or more to one rather than three to one.

The man-at-arms was a heavily armoured front-line soldier. Ideally, from the egg-shaped bassinet on his head to the short pointed sections on his feet, the man-at-arms was completely sheathed in plate armour, each section overlapping the next and each presenting a glancing surface to his enemy. Padded clothing was worn underneath to help prevent bruising. The weight, though enormous, was well distributed and it was extremely difficult for an opponent to do damage to the man-at-arms inside his carapace. It was possible to smash a sledge-hammer on to the best armour from Milan or Nuremberg and do virtually no injury to the knight who could afford such expensive protection. It was impossible, however, and, from the point of view of cost and mobility, hardly desirable to protect the horse as completely as his rider. As the French discovered on several catastrophic occasions during the Hundred Years' War, this made the mounted man-at-arms very vulnerable to the deadly shower of arrows launched by English bowmen. If his horse fell and the knight came crashing down it was very difficult for him to get back on to his feet. And there was always the danger that, once helpless on the ground, his last sight might be his vizor being forced open and the flash of a dagger in the eye. For this reason the old and well-known tactic of making the men-at-arms dismount before a battle came to be even more frequently adopted during the fifteenth century. On the continent it was regarded as 'the English method' and we can hardly doubt that, as Mancini said, this was the method normally employed in the Wars of the Roses where both sides were well provided with archers. Not even a contingent of English bowmen could bring to a halt the steady and sinister advance of heavily armoured knights on foot.

Not, of course, that the dismounted man-at-arms was totally invulnerable. Arrayed against him was his counterpart on the other side and the climax of most battles was the hand-to-hand mêlée of these steel-clad figures, each trying to bludgeon the other to the ground. Since sword and spear thrusts tended to be deflected by the sophisticated fluted armour now being worn, other kinds of weapons were growing in popularity: the battleaxe, the mace and the flail, a great spiked ball of iron attached to a staff by a long chain. These were designed to crush rather than to pierce armour. It was hoped that the sheer weight of the blow would knock an opponent off his feet. Thus battles could easily develop into fierce slugging-matches, like two heavyweight boxers forgetting their ring-craft and trading blow for blow. But encased as he was in heavy armour and wielding a heavy weapon the chief enemy of the man-at-arms was probably sheer physical exhaustion; for this reason most of the battles, though hard-fought, were fairly brief.

Once the struggle between two fairly evenly matched armies had reached the stage of the general mêlée, the issue might be decided by any one of a number of chance factors. Battlefields were a muddle in the fifteenth century – as in other centuries. Marston Moor, we should remember, was fought out in the absence of the senior commanders on both sides, Prince Rupert and the earl of Leven. Both of them had turned and fled, each believing that the other had won. That fifteenth-century battles were just as chaotic is clear from Commynes's vivid eyewitness account of the Battle of Montlhéry (1465). Poorly informed as we are about the battles of the Wars of the Roses, one thing at least is certain: all the ingredients for confusion were there – with one additional factor, English weather. One battle took place in the snow; one in a thick early morning mist; another in a rain-storm.

One constant source of uncertainty was the absence of uniform. Not until 1645 and the formation of the New Model Army do we find the first general order requiring a uniform colour for the whole army. Before that date men wore their lord's livery, or town soldiers might wear the colours provided by the municipal authorities, such as the green and red of the Coventry contingent in 1455. With multicoloured armies on both sides almost anything could happen. This, for example, is how the chronicler John Warkworth described what he believed to be the decisive moments in the Battle of Barnet (April 1471) between the earl of Warwick, aided by the earl of Oxford, and Edward iv, fighting to recover his throne.

And divers times the earl of Warwick's party had the victory and supposed that they had won the field. But it happened that the earl of Oxford's men had upon them their lord's livery, both before and behind, which was a star with streams, which was much like King Edward's livery, the sun with streams [the blazing sun of York]; and the mist was so thick that a man might not properly judge one thing from another; so the earl of Warwick's men shot and fought against the earl of Oxford's men, supposing them to be King Edward's men; and soon the earl of Oxford and his men cried, 'Treason! Treason!', and fled away from the field with 8,000 men.

Whether this really happened must be regarded as doubtful. It was a 'good story' and Warkworth was writing between six and ten years after the event, plenty of time for an anecdote of this type to be elaborated and given undue significance. But in this context whether or not it happened is of less importance than the fact that contemporaries knew that this kind of thing *could* happen.

In the confusion of battle it was the great banner of the commander-in-chief which provided the most readily visible rallying point. Carried by a trusted standard-bearer, the banner signalled the presence of the prince or noble whose device it bore. In an age when the army commanders were both political leaders and at times front-line soldiers, the fortunes of battle could best be observed by following the movement of their banners. The banner's fall symbolized the prince's defeat and perhaps his death.

If a prince chose to participate in person in the fierce hand-to-hand fighting of the mêlée he was exposing himself to great danger, no matter how well he was protected by the bodyguards of his household. Inevitably he became the main target for enemy attacks. On the eve of the Battle of Agincourt eighteen French men-at-arms joined together in a sworn association, vowing that they would make a combined attack on Henry v and either 'strike the crown from off his head' or die in the attempt. They kept their vow. With princes faced by threats like these as well as by the ordinary 'accidents' of the mêlée, it is hardly surprising that the question of whether they should be allowed to take part in battle was one which was much debated.

The problem was tackled in Christine de Pisan's *Le Livre des faiz darmes*, a book which was translated and printed by William Caxton as *The Book of Fayttes of Armes and of Chyvalrye*. Despite her sex Christine was one of the most respected of all fifteenth-century writers on matters of war, and a copy of her book would undoubtedly have been a most suitable gift for the redoubtable Margaret of Anjou – a point appreciated by John Talbot, earl of Shrewsbury, himself the most renowned English soldier of his generation, for he gave one to her as a wedding present. According to Christine, a sensible prince would be well-advised not to take the terrible gamble of risking his life in battle. Even though, as she admitted, his presence would encourage his men to fight harder, the damage to the kingdom were he to be captured or killed would be out of all proportion – and she was thinking here of the political crises in France which followed the capture of King John at the Battle of Poitiers in 1356. The same lesson was hammered home in 1477 when Duke Charles the Impetuous fell in battle at Nancy and with him fell the Burgundian state founded by his great-grandfather. As an example to all princes Christine held up King Charles v of France. Without stirring from his palace, he recaptured the lands lost by his all too chivalrous predecessors. To this rule, however, Christine was prepared to make one important exception: the case of civil war. Against rebels the king should be prepared to take the field with his army 'since in the nature of things the subject fears to offend the majesty of his sovereign lord, especially when the latter is present in person'. The truth of this observation was borne out by the almost farcical events at Ludford Bridge in 1459 (see below p. 105). For this reason kings – or those who claimed to be kings – normally took part in the campaigns of the Wars of the Roses. In consequence a high proportion of battles ended with a king's capture or death. In this way too battles, precisely because of the grave risks involved, could be decisive. Here then is an additional reason why the army commanders in these English civil wars adopted a battle-seeking campaign strategy very different from the normal practice of war on the continent.

Even in England, however, there was a great deal more to war than the bloody climax of the hand-to-hand mêlée and the success of the English under Edward III and Henry v had shown that, in terms of value for money, the most useful soldier was the archer, in particular the mounted archer. By the mid-fifteenth century this lesson had been well and truly learnt. Whereas *c.* 1400 the men-at-arms in the French royal armies had outnumbered the mounted archers and crossbowmen by two to one, by 1430 and thereafter this proportion was reversed. Thus Commynes wrote that 'in my opinion archers are the most necessary thing in the world for an army – though they should be counted in thousands, for in small numbers they are almost useless'. Though his weapon lacked the weight and penetration of the crossbow, the bowman could shoot ten or twelve arrows a minute against the crossbowman's two. His rapid rate of fire also meant that he still had the edge over the soldier who would one day supplant him: the hand-gunner. For this reason, the hand-gunner figures rarely in the Wars of the Roses and even Duke Charles the Impetuous, that most self-consciously up-to-date of generals, employed more archers than gunners and crossbowmen put together. According to his ordinance of 1472, there were to be 1,200 hand-gunners, 1,200 crossbowmen and 3,600 archers in the Burgundian standing army. The archer's rate of fire, filling the sky with clouds of deadly shafts, gave rise abroad to a literary image: 'thicker than arrows in an English battle'. As we have already noticed, Dominic Mancini was particularly impressed by the archers he saw in England, and this feeling was a general one. They were, said Commynes, 'the world's best'. The systematic Charles the Bold always made sure that his army included a contingent. Moreover, he paid them more than his other mounted archers. In a letter to a friend one of the duke's captains, Philippe de Croy, reported that, 'In our army the English have been more watched and admired and better esteemed than were our robes of cloth of gold and costly adornments at the last feast of the Golden Fleece.' Just how highly Charles valued them was graphically highlighted by an incident at the siege of Neuss (1475):

On Monday after supper the English quarrelled over a woman and wanted to kill each other. As soon as the duke heard of this he went to them with a few people to restore order but they, not recognizing the duke – or so they claimed – shot two or three times directly at him. Their arrows only just missed his head and it was extraordinarily lucky that he was not killed, since he had no armour on at all. A rumour got about, however, that he had been wounded and so everyone rushed over and began to attack the English. This upset the duke but he was unable to prevent some of them being killed. Next morning he issued a proclamation. Anyone who had taken anything from the English was to return it; there was to be no quarrelling with them, for he regarded them as his friends and subjects.

In the hard daily grind of campaigning archers were indispensable. They were relatively cheap and their missile weapons meant that they were superior to men-at-arms in every field of military activity except close combat – and close combat, of course, took up only a minute fraction of the total time spent in the field of war. Moreover, even in the preliminaries to close combat archers had a valuable role to play. If the enemy had taken up a tight defensive formation, archers could be used to disperse them. Philip the Good employed this tactic to defeat the Ghenters in the summer of 1453. It was difficult for men-at-arms to advance through terrain which abounded in hedges and ditches held by the enemy unless archers had gone on ahead to clear a way. This, for example, was how Charles the Impetuous beat the army of Liège at Brustem in October 1467. It was the absence of archers which led to the earl of Pembroke's defeat at Edgecote in July 1469. Archers and men-at-arms had to be used in combination. On their own both of them were vulnerable. This was an elementary fact of military life which had been recognized for centuries. Though their arrows might dent many a cuirass, if archers were caught on their own they would be driven back

and slaughtered – the fate which befell a contingent of English bowmen
at the hands of Burgundian knights at the Battle of Brouwershaven (in
Holland) in 1426. Thus at the moment of battle archers had to be
protected either by men-at-arms or by other infantry – pikemen or,
more commonly in England, billmen. The theory of how this was to be
done is made clear in Duke Charles's military ordinance of 1473 (in the
section on training and drill):

> The captains are to exercise the archers with their horses, to get them used to
> dismounting and drawing their bows. They must learn how to attach their
> horses together by their bridles; to march briskly forwards and to fire without
> breaking rank. The pikemen must be made to advance in close formation in
> front of the archers, kneel at a sign from them, holding their pikes lowered to
> the level of a horse's back so that the archers can fire over the pikemen as if over
> a wall. Thus, if the pikemen see that the enemy are breaking rank, they will be
> near enough to charge them in good order as instructed. The archers must also
> learn to place themselves back to back in double defence, or in a square or
> circle, always with the pikemen outside them to withstand the charge of the
> enemy horse, while their own horses are enclosed in their midst.

Occasionally, in continental sources – though not in English ones –
we find those small but graphic details which make it possible to
visualize archers in action. In a letter written in 1475 by Charles the
Impetuous himself there is a description of his English archers 'making
the sign of the cross on the ground and kissing it, according to their
custom' before advancing to the attack. Commynes remembers seeing
the archers at a quiet moment before the Battle of Montlhéry 'with their
boots off and with a stake driven into the ground in front of them. Many
barrels of wine had been broached so they could drink.'

In order to complete our picture of the armies of the period it is
necessary to have some idea of their size. The first essential is to
disregard the numbers given by chroniclers. Where it has been possible
to check chroniclers' figures by comparing them with exchequer pay
records, the chroniclers have been shown to exaggerate numbers by
anything between ten- and sixtyfold. Although there are no complete
sets of pay records for any of the armies of the Wars of the Roses, there is
no reason to think that fifteenth-century writers were any more accurate than their predecessors. Take, for example, the figure for Edward
IV's army at Towton (1461) as given in *Gregory's Chronicle*: 200,000 men.
For several reasons we might be disposed to trust the author of this
chronicle. By this date a London citizen might reasonably be supposed
to have some knowledge of arithmetic. The author, though not himself

an eyewitness of Towton, had been present at a slightly earlier battle, the Second Battle of St Albans. Moreover the figure of 200,000 is supported by other contemporary writers. A letter written only a week later by Richard Beauchamp, bishop of Salisbury – a man who claimed to be high in Edward's confidence – gives the same figure. As befitted a member of a more numerate society, the Milanese ambassador at Bruges was at first sceptical. 'My lord,' he wrote to Francesco Sforza, 'I am ashamed to speak of so many thousands which resemble the figures of bakers.' Nonetheless, his later reports are full of high numbers and tall stories. He passes on, for example, the figure of 28,000 for the number of casualties at Towton, which would make it the bloodiest battle ever to be fought on British soil.

It is obvious, however, that figures such as these, no matter how widely circulated, are totally incredible, worthy of belief only by those naïve historians who wish to take Tudor myths about the Wars of the Roses at something approaching face value. All the sources indicate that the Lancastrian army at Towton was bigger than the Yorkist, so if we accept 200,000 for the latter, we arrive at a total of nearly half a million men engaged on both sides. Now since at the time the population of England was probably less than three million, and of these about 20 per cent – some 600,000 – were men of fighting age, it follows that most adult Englishmen were present at the battle of Towton! But if we cannot rely on the figures given in literary sources, what can we do? Fortunately pay records do survive for some fifteenth-century English forces, and, even though these are not for armies which fought in the Wars of the Roses, they can at least give us some idea of a possible order of magnitude. The 11,500 soldiers who went to Calais with Edward iv in 1475 have already been mentioned. In 1415 Henry v crossed the Channel with about 9,000 men – and won the battle of Agincourt with considerably fewer. The largest army to leave England during this period was the 20,000 strong force with which Richard of Gloucester invaded Scotland in 1482. Since by definition none of the commanders in the Wars of the Roses had the united resources of England and Wales to call upon, it is unlikely that any of the civil war armies can have exceeded this size.

Another approach to the problem of numbers is offered by the practical considerations of logistics. To put an army into the field and maintain it in good condition required quite an array of tradesmen, servants and specialists of various kinds. The men-at-arms had servants to carry spare weapons, dress them, help them mount, pick them

up if they fell down and look after the horses when they fought on foot.
Behind the lines there were many more. Chaplains and their servants,
minstrels, heralds, fletchers, labourers, carpenters, grooms, bakers,
trumpeters, physicians, women. In his ordinance of 1473 Duke Charles
commanded that the individual appropriation of women camp-
followers should stop; from now on women were to be kept in common,
no more than thirty to a company. Chroniclers who report the size of
armies rarely trouble to make the crucial distinction between combatants and non-combatants, but one who did, commenting on the Burgundian army raised by Duke John the Fearless in 1417, gives an
interesting, if exaggerated, idea of just how numerous the non-
combatants could be: 'This army numbered 3,600 men-at-arms and
more than 2,000 bowmen. And one would have found in it, on any one
day, 200,000 people and at least 150,000 horses, including the transport, which was loaded with every sort of war equipment and took up
more than two leagues when on the move.' Occasionally by bearing in
mind the distinction between combatants and non-combatants we may
be able to resolve apparent discrepancies in the sources. In March
1471, for example, Edward IV set sail from Flushing in the hope of
reconquering his lost kingdom. The official Yorkist account says he had
2,000 Englishmen with him; the Burgundian soldier-chronicler Jean de
Waurin says he had 1,200 combatants. In other words there may well
be no conflict of sources here though historians have tended to write as
though there were.

All these people had to be fed, clothed and sheltered. In front of every
army rode the harbingers, the fore-riders whose job it was to seek out
and arrange lodgings for the troops. Theirs was a job which called for
considerable skill. The soldiers' morale could easily suffer if they spent
too many uncomfortable nights, while an army's cohesion was readily
lost if one contingent quarrelled with another over who was to enjoy the
best billets. According to John Warkworth it was precisely such a
quarrel which led to the fatal division of Pembroke's and Devonshire's
forces on the eve of Edgecote (1469). Moreover a good harbinger was
more than just a tactful administrator. It often happened that the first
inkling of an enemy's proximity came when the harbingers of one side
clashed with those of the other. By the same token this well-known
accident of war could be used to deceive an enemy. The harbingers
would be sent in one direction (to be 'found' by the enemy), while the
army moved in another – a trick which was used by Warwick in 1470
and by the Lancastrians before Tewkesbury in 1471.

Normally the harbingers came under the command of the army's marshal, but the latter's biggest headache was to see that the troops were properly fed: 'An army is a beast that hath a great belly.' To put this problem in perspective we must bear in mind the size of English towns in the fifteenth century. York, Bristol and Norwich may each have had 10,000 inhabitants. Only London, with 30,000 to 50,000 inhabitants, was larger; most of the others were much smaller. In other words an army of 10,000 combatants plus several thousand non-combatants would be like one of the kingdom's major cities on the move. Merely to keep an army of anything like this size in being for a few weeks was a formidable administrative achievement. How was it done? Usually by one of three methods, or by a combination of them. Either the troops carried their supplies with them, or they bought them from merchants who followed the army, or they lived off the country. English government records for 1481 show the immense labour and expense involved in laying in supplies for Edward IV's planned invasion of Scotland. As it turned out the effort was wasted since Edward postponed the invasion; nonetheless it gives an insight into the scale of preparations. Beef (on the hoof) and large quantities of mutton, bacon, fish, grain, peas, beans and salt were sent north. Flour, of course, was the biggest single item. To meet the army's demand for bread, bakers were to be drafted from Newcastle, York, Durham and other northern towns. In London coopers were set to work collecting the materials of their craft and stockpiling finished barrels. Newcastle was designated as the army's base and as much as possible was transported there by sea. On arrival it was to be off-loaded on to the carts which Richard of Gloucester and the earl of Northumberland had been ordered to assemble. Some of these carts were to move to and fro between the army and its base, while another five hundred were to accompany the invasion force itself.

Just how important carts were to an army can again be deduced from the illustrations to the *Hausbuch*. A document from St Gall (in Switzerland) gives further details. It contains an inventory of everything that was loaded on to the two carts, each drawn by five horses, which accompanied the St Gall contingent to the Swiss army of 1476 which defeated Charles the Impetuous at Murten. One was piled high with eight sides of bacon, two sacks of salt, dried beef, barley, oatmeal, butter and other provisions. Since the food had to be cooked and eaten, the other cart contained kettles with hooks and tripods, copper and tin ladles, dishes and other kitchen equipment as well as shovels, axes, scythes and sickles. Elaborate calculations had to be made in advance of any campaign by the army's logistical experts. Thus when Philip the Good's advisers were planning a crusade in 1456 they worked out that 200 carts would be needed to carry the gear belonging to 4,000 archers. If contemporary accounts of the campaigns of the Wars of the Roses hardly ever mention the wagon trains, this is presumably because the writers took their presence for granted, while they very rarely go into sufficient detail to make incidental references at all likely. An exception, from an exceptional source, *The Historie of the Arrivall of King Edward IV* (see below p. 189), is the reference to a brook which did little to quench the army's thirst, 'It was so soon troubled with the carriages that had passed it.' Even the small 'private' armies of the time needed a baggage train. When, in September 1451, the earl of Devon marched against his local rivals, Wiltshire and Bonville, his force was accompanied by five carts loaded, it was said in judicial proceedings brought against the earl, with guns and other weapons.

Naturally so prominent a part of the army as the wagon train was put to a variety of uses besides those of transporting food and guns. At the end of the day's march, the wagons would be formed into a protective circle around the encampment. This device was commonly adopted by a smaller force fighting on the defensive – as was reported of the earl of Salisbury's army at Blore Heath in 1459. On the other hand, an advancing army could plan to use its baggage train as a rallying point in the event of its attack being repulsed – as the Liégeois did at Brustem in 1467. Even the disaster of the capture of the baggage train could at least be used to facilitate flight while the victorious enemy concentrated on the plunder they found there. This, according to the memoirs of Jehan de Haynin, was how the Battle of Brustem ended. 'Some of my archers seized a cart with a barrel of wine which lasted the nineteen of us two days; also another cart with bread, salt meat and cheese which lasted fourteen days.... Several people thought that if our vanguard had continued its advance it would have done very well, but nothing was done.'

It was clear though, no matter how carefully a campaign had been prepared, that no army could carry with it all that it needed. At one extreme the earl of Devon's small force had not been self-sufficient. There was consternation in Glastonbury when his men billeted themselves in the town for a night and took what food they wanted. At the other extreme, we have the calculations made by a Hungarian historian, G. Perjés, of the supply needs of the large armies of the seventeenth century. According to his estimate if an army of 60,000 combatants took with it provisions to last for one month, this would require a baggage train of 11,000 carts, 22,000 drivers and helpers and 50,000 to 70,000 draught animals. Calculating a length of twelve metres for one cart with horses, and a distance of six metres between carts, the overall length of the train, in single file, would be 198 kilometres. Given a marching speed of twenty-five kilometres per day the rear of the column would be eight days behind the head. Even divided by six to approximate to the needs of an army of 10,000 – a more normal size for a large fifteenth-century force – these figures show just how hopelessly cumbersome and vulnerable the wagon train would become if an army tried to be self-sufficient for a month. In practice baggage trains contained a reserve of food sufficient for a few days only and commanders assumed that they would have to find alternative sources of supply. Normally they could count on some merchant victuallers following the army. Christine de Pisan suggests that the marshal should assign to no less than 200 men-at-arms, 100 crossbowmen and 100 archers the job of ensuring that these vital entrepreneurs should not be set upon and robbed.

The third method, living off the country, was at times the most important. It also created many problems. Sending men out to forage and others to guard them could entail a dangerous dispersal of one's forces. Then there was the obvious political problem – which in a civil war could be a crucial one – of the relationship between the army and the country people whose provisions they were consuming. Taking food, even when promising to pay for it, could easily turn into looting, and failures of this kind of army discipline were to cost the Lancastrians dear in 1460–1.

At a still more basic level there is the fact that an army could count on finding more food in a densely populated region than in one which was thinly populated. Commenting, for example, on the 1465 campaign in France, Commynes observed that 'the Île de France and Paris are well-placed to maintain two very powerful armies.... All in all I have never seen a city surrounded by more fertile and verdant country than Paris.' This made it possible for the two sides to settle down to a long-drawn-out struggle of trenches, counter-trenches and artillery duels. This problem of supply, then, was a constraint which played an enormous part not just in limiting army size but also in determining the strategy of any war. Fifteenth-century experts were just as aware of this as were later generations of military men. In the spring of 1430 one of

Philip the Good's advisers sent him a detailed memorandum from
which the following passages are taken:

Advice on the strategy to follow when the king of England and his army
disembark in France. The following points must be borne in mind:

1   It is likely that few or no provisions will be available in enemy-occupied
countryside, yet such provisions are essential to undertake sieges and keep
armies in the field.

2   As things stand, it looks as though the loss of Paris, now surrounded by
the enemy, would entail the loss of the whole kingdom.

3   It follows that first priority ought to be given, in the strategy of the king
and my lord of Burgundy, to clearing the enemy from around Paris, and they
must advance to do this through areas where provisions are available, i.e.,
through Normandy and Picardy.

The fact that we do not have this kind of documentation for the Wars
of the Roses does not mean that the English fought their domestic wars
oblivious of the constraints which logistics imposed upon strategy –
even upon the strategy of wars which did not last for long. In March
1470, for example, Edward IV was moving at top speed to counter the
Lincolnshire rising and the revolt of Warwick and Clarence. Yet on
reaching York he stopped and waited there for four days. Behind this
period of immobility lay the problem of supplies. The author of the
Chronicle of the Rebellion in Lincolnshire – probably a member of the king's
secretariat – explains. While at Rotherham Edward had been informed
that Warwick and Clarence were seeking reinforcements in Lancashire.
He wanted to cross the Pennines in pursuit but it was not easy. 'He
could not conveniently proceed with so great a host, for the said duke
and earl, with their fellowship, had consumed the victuals ahead of
him, and the country there was not able to sustain so great a host as the
king's highness had with him without a new refreshing.' For this reason
he made for York 'fully determined there to have refreshed and victualled his said host, and, so victualled, to have entered into Lancashire
that way'. At York he tarried four days, spending the time both on
political arrangements for the north and 'for sufficient provision of
victuals for his host for the accomplishing of his purpose into Lancashire'. And there were other occasions too, for example at Wakefield in
1460 and during the Tewkesbury campaign of 1471, when the absence
of adequate provisions played a crucial part in determining events.
Indeed, most important of all, it may be that the prospect of supply
shortages was among the pressures which moved civil war commanders, anxious not to antagonize local feeling, to adopt a battle-seeking

strategy whenever and wherever possible. This certainly seems to have been in the earl of Lincoln's mind in 1487.

It is important to remember that this aggressive strategy went against everything which generals and military theorists had practised and preached for centuries – and against everything which contemporary continental experts were continuing to practise and preach. By far the most popular military manual throughout the Middle Ages was the *De Re Militari* written by Vegetius in the fourth century AD. It survives both in the Latin original and in translations; it survives in editions with long additional passages bringing it up to date; it even survives in manuscripts which are folded for ease of carrying in the pocket. Vegetius' strategy is crystal clear. Anything is better than pitched battle. Manoeuvres, diplomacy, taming the enemy by hunger – all should be tried in preference to putting the lives of men and the fate of kingdoms to the hazard of battle where that fickle and unpredictable goddess Fortune reigns supreme. Fifteenth-century writers fully accepted Vegetius' advice. Analysing Louis XI's success, Commynes wrote that 'he never risked anything and never hankered after battle'.

Commynes's observation reads like a commentary on the practice of the famous war-lords of the Middle Ages – there was no gulf here between theory and practice. How many pitched battles did Charlemagne or Richard the Lionheart fight? They were successful generals because they used precisely the methods which Commynes attributes to Louis XI. There is no generalization more misleading than the notion that medieval warfare consisted of little more than the headlong clash of two cavalry armies under the command of two empty-headed princes. It may, of course, be true that according to some notions of chivalry the knight who charged received more praise than the knight who waited. In practice, however, most knights preferred to wait. To an outside observer like the twelfth-century Arab writer Usamah, Europeans were 'of all men – may Allah's curse be upon them – the most cautious in warfare'. What this means is that if the struggles of the Wars of the Roses do at times seem to be little more than the headlong clash of two parties both in great haste to have their brains knocked out, then there was a very good reason for this. These were not the actions of men blindly following the precepts of military tradition.

This discussion of warfare in England and abroad in the fifteenth century points to two broad conclusions. Men did not like fighting battles and England was a very peaceful country. Yet an Englishman who was born in 1450 and survived to be forty years old would have lived through a time of dramatic political turmoil. Moreover, if he enjoyed watching battles – in later centuries a well-known spectator sport – he could have had a feast of them. He would have lived through no less than three civil wars, known collectively as the Wars of the Roses. On at least five occasions he would have seen kings pushed off the throne by force (Henry VI twice, in 1461 and 1471; Edward IV in 1470; Edward V in 1483; and Richard III in 1485). In terms of sudden and violent swings of the political pendulum there is no period in English history which can compete with this one. Simply as a story it is full of excitement, quick reversals of fortune, desperate flights and startling comebacks. But it is also a puzzle. If England was indeed such a peaceful country, how on earth did it happen? What is the real significance of those turbulent events? How was it that men came to blows in the first place?

It is at least clear that the wars began in the reign of Henry VI. But should their origins be sought even earlier than that? In 1422, when Henry came to the throne, were the signs of trouble already there? In particular, had Bolingbroke's usurpation of the crown in 1399 cast a shadow long enough to darken the early years of Henry's reign? This is what many Tudor writers and some modern historians would have us believe. On the other hand, there were contemporary and late-fifteenth-century observers who believed that the start of the trouble lay not in 1399 but in the 1450s. For Jean de Waurin it all began with the defeat of the English in the Hundred Years' War and the consequent recriminations between the dukes of York and Somerset. At the heart of Philippe de Commynes's analysis lay the clash of factions at court, also in the 1450s, and for this he blamed the characters of the king and queen – an imbecile king and a queen who took sides instead of mediating between them. To see whether either of these interpretations makes sense we must take our story right back to the beginning of Henry VI's reign.

Four

HENRY VI: THE CARELESS KING, 1422–50

ON 14 SEPTEMBER 1422 a funeral procession left the castle of Bois de Vincennes on the outskirts of Paris, at the start of a sombre, slow journey along the roads of northern France. On top of the coffin there reposed a more than life-sized effigy of the man whose corpse – dismembered, boiled and well spiced – lay within. The effigy was dressed in royal robes, wore a crown and held a sceptre, the symbol of dominion, in its right hand. Henry v, king of England, would-be conqueror of France, had died a fortnight earlier and what remained of his body was being taken home for burial in Westminster Abbey. The cortège was heading for Calais, just as, seven years earlier, in the autumn of 1415, Henry v himself had headed for Calais on that famous and fortunate journey which took him to the field of Agincourt. But now the thirty-five-year-old soldier-king was dead and his heir, Henry vi, was a nine-month-old boy.

A few weeks later on 22 October 1422 another king, Charles vi, the old mad king of France, died in Paris. Over his grave a herald proclaimed a new king, *roi Henri* ii – an eleven-month-old boy: Henry vi of England was also Henry ii of France. By the terms of the Treaty of Troyes (1420) Henry v had married Katherine, Charles vi's daughter, and secured the succession to the throne of France for himself and for his heirs. Henry v had failed to live long enough by less than two months, but now his young son could enter into this magnificent inheritance. Whether he would enjoy it for long was another matter.

Henry v had died with his work in France unfinished. According to the letter of the Treaty of Troyes Charles vi's son, the Dauphin, had been debarred from the succession, but in fact he still held court at Bourges. As Charles vii of France he remained a legitimate focus of loyalty for all who resented English rule and, although he was anything but an inspiring leader, he was probably an attractive alternative to an infant king. In the fifteenth century – as for centuries to come – people looked to the person of the king to provide the mainspring of government. It was hard to see how a war of conquest could be brought to a successful conclusion when it was waged in the name of a ruler who, in the nature of things, could not himself provide the necessary driving force. If Lancastrian prospects in France looked bleak, they were hardly much better in England. A royal minority had always been a time of unrest and upheaval. The last royal minority in England, that of Richard II from 1377 to 1389, had seen both aristocratic war (1387) and, more alarmingly still, peasants' revolt (1381). Even the so-called new monarchy of the Tudors was unable to cope with this old problem; witness the troubles which beset the minority of Edward VI (1547–53). 'Woe to thee, O land, when thy king is a child.' In the Anglo-French dual monarchy of 1422 this great cliché of medieval politics must have seemed doubly appropriate.

Yet clichés are only mostly true. As it happened, 1422 did not mark the turning of the tide of war in France. The English and their Burgundian allies continued to win victories and push southwards. Although Joan of Arc has stamped her image for ever on the year 1429, the real turning-point did not come until 1435, the Council of Arras and the end of the Anglo-Burgundian alliance. But even this marked the beginning of the slow erosion rather than the rapid collapse of the English position. As late as 1444–5 when Henry VI was twenty-four years old, English politicians believed that, in discussing peace with France, they were negotiating from a position of strength; and since by the terms of the truce of Tours, agreed in May 1444, they still held Normandy, Maine, Anjou and much of Guienne, it is clear that they were right to believe this.

At home the story of Henry VI's minority is an even more remarkable one. The Lancastrian council ruled economically and well. The personal rivalries between the king's uncles which, at other times and in other places, spilled over into civil war, were here confined to quarrels in the council chamber. Disputes between one noble family and another – the kind of dispute which, in the 1450s, led to the violence of private warfare and so helped to trigger off the Wars of the Roses – were in the 1420s and 1430s brought before the council and settled there.

As usual Shakespeare gives a totally false impression when he writes, in *1 Henry VI*, III, i:

> This late dissension grown betwixt the peers
> Burns under feigned ashes of forg'd love
> And will at last break out into a flame

As it happened, the quarrels of the 1420s and 1430s did *not* escalate into the Wars of the Roses. If Henry VI's minority has any significance, it is not as the beginning of the end but as evidence showing that in fifteenth-century England there existed a stable political system, containing in the council an institutional framework within which tensions could be contained and resolved.

Yet although Henry VI's reign began surprisingly well, it ended in calamity. In one of his kingdoms, England, he was deposed twice – a rare achievement. But as well as losing the throne of England, he managed to lose all of France except Calais. Though to lose one kingdom may be regarded as a misfortune, to lose both looks like carelessness.

Is this a fair verdict? Was Henry VI indeed an incredibly careless king? Unquestionably if we are to understand the causes of the Wars of the Roses we have to understand the character of the king. Was he simply the 'holy king' described by Shakespeare?

> gentle mild and virtuous
> fitter for heaven than earth.

There survives a pen-portrait of Henry, written by a man well placed to know him, his chaplain John Blackman, and it could be argued that this account lends support to Shakespeare's view.

He was, like a second Job, a man simple and upright, altogether fearing the Lord God, and departing from evil. He was a simple man, without any crook of craft or untruth, as is plain to all. With none did he deal craftily, nor ever would say an untrue word to any, but framed his speech always to speak truth.

He was both upright and just, always keeping to the straight line of justice in his acts. Upon none would he wittingly inflict any injustice. To God the Almighty he rendered most faithfully that which was his, for he took pains to pay in full the tithes and offerings due to God and the church: and this he accompanied with most sedulous devotion so that even when decked with the kingly ornaments and crowned with the royal diadem he made it a duty to bow before the Lord as deep in prayer as any young monk might have done. . . .

And that this prince cherished a son's fear towards the Lord is plain from many an act and devotion of his. In the first place, a certain reverend prelate of England used to relate that for ten years he held the office of confessor to King Henry; but he declared that never throughout that long time had any blemish of mortal sin touched his soul. . . .

This King Henry was chaste and pure from the beginning of his days. He eschewed all licentiousness in word or deed while he was young; until he was of marriageable age, when he espoused the most noble lady, Lady Margaret, daughter of the king of Sicily, by whom he begat one only son, the most noble and virtuous Prince Edward; and with her and toward her he kept his marriage vow wholly and sincerely, even in the absences of the lady, which were sometimes very long: never dealing unchastely with any other woman. Neither when they lived together did he use his wife unseemly, but with all honesty and gravity. . . .

It happened once, that at Christmas time a certain great lord brought before him a dance or show of young ladies with bared bosoms who were to dance in that guise before the king, perhaps to prove him, or to entice his youthful mind. But the king was not blind to it, not unaware of the devilish wile, and spurned the delusion, and very angrily averted his eyes, turned his back upon them, and went out to his chamber, saying: 'Fy, fy, for shame, forsothe ye be to blame.'

At another time, riding by Bath, where are warm baths in which they say the men of that country customably refresh and wash themselves, the king, looking into the baths, saw in them men wholly naked with every garment cast off. At which he was displeased, and went away quickly, abhorring such nudity as a great offence, and not unmindful of that sentence of Francis Petrarch, 'The nakedness of a beast is in man unpleasing, but the decency of raiment makes for modesty.'

Besides, he took great precautions to secure not only his own chastity but that of his servants. For before he was married, being as a youth a pupil of chastity, he would keep careful watch through hidden windows of his chamber, lest any foolish impertinence of women, coming into the house should grow to a head, and cause the fall of any of his household. . . .

The lord king complained to me once in his room at Eltham, when I was alone with him and working with him over his holy books, and hearing his serious admonitions and devout observations, one of the most powerful of the English dukes knocked at the door. The king said: 'See how they disturb me!'

The problem is, can we accept Blackman's vivid picture of a pious and puritanical king at face value? It was written during the reign of Henry VII at a time when that king was hoping to secure his predecessor's canonization. To back up the petitions to Rome a case had to be prepared. A book of miracles, for example, was compiled. Over 130 assorted cures and even the occasional resurrection from the dead were attributed to Henry VI. Many of these miracles of healing were said to have occurred at the royal tomb at Windsor, the centre of a flourishing cult of the dead king. Particularly revealing is the story of how a girl called Agnes Freeman was cured. She suffered from scrofula, the skin disease which was known as the 'king's evil'. According to a widespread belief which survived until the eighteenth century, the victims of this disease could be healed by a king's touch. Agnes's friends urged her to visit the reigning monarch, at that time Richard III, but her parents, following better advice, prayed for Henry VI's assistance and vowed to go on a pilgrimage to his shrine. No sooner had the vow been taken than Agnes's condition improved and within three or four days she had completely recovered. This was a miracle which made it perfectly plain who was the true king and who the usurper.

Like the book of miracles, Blackman's portrait is not history but propaganda. It is hagiography; part of the process of making a saint. Moreover, it is hagiography written at the behest of a king, Henry VII, who had an obvious political interest in proving that Henry VI had been a pure and blameless king. Since Henry VII had seized power at the expense of the Yorkist dynasty it suited him to portray Henry VI as an innocent man unjustly turned off his throne by the Yorkists. This does not necessarily mean, of course, that we can dismiss Blackman's book as a pack of lies. Like most effective propaganda, it told the truth. Henry VI had been an exceptionally pious man and, after his death, there were many who regarded him as a saint, though – as the example of St Thomas Becket shows – a violent end was undoubtedly a help in this respect. But the question is, did it tell the *whole* truth? Was Henry essentially a man of pure religious simplicity? Or was he also a simpleton? Yorkist writers naturally described him as a man of small intelligence. Their partisan statements are to some extent corroborated by evidence which suggests that as early as the 1440s popular opinion held Henry to be a foolish young man. In 1442, for example, a Kentish yeoman was reported to have said that the king was a lunatic like his grandfather. There were several cases brought before the courts in which reference was made to Henry's childlike appearance and behaviour. In 1450 a Sussex man was indicted of having publicly declared 'that the king was a natural fool, and would ofttimes hold a staff in his hands with a bird on the end, playing therewith as a fool, and that another king must be ordained to rule the land, saying that the king was no person able to rule'.

A further question concerns the extent of Henry's involvement in politics. Was he – as Blackman implies – totally absorbed in higher things? Or did he find time and energy to take part in affairs of state? Were the troubles of his reign the result of his action or inaction?

Whichever was the case, the king was ultimately responsible and it is clear that either way disaster lay at the end. Nonetheless they are different roads.

The nature of the evidence is such that it is by no means easy to decide whether it was the king or his ministers who were, in reality, making policy. The evidence of government records always tends to make the king appear responsible, and equally evidence from anti-government sources such as rebel manifestos tends to make his ministers appear to be responsible. Whose hand, for example, lay behind the surge of new elevations to the peerage which characterized the 1440s? Whereas there were only nine additions to the English nobility during the first thirty-six years of the Lancastrian dynasty, in the next twenty-five (between 1437 and 1461) there were twenty-five. Undoubtedly the turning-point here was Henry vi's coming of age, but was it Henry or his chief minister William de la Pole, earl of Suffolk, who effectively decided that there should be this lavish distribution of titles accompanied by a massive squandering of royal lands? In the light of Blackman's picture of a king who disliked worldly business, it is tempting to assume that the initiative was always Suffolk's. Yet Blackman's king, however unworldly, could hardly be called meek or timid. Outspoken and interfering perhaps, at least in those fields which interested him, but certainly not a man who lacked a mind and will of his own. The question we then have to ask is, did he confine himself to matters of religion and morals? Or did he also lay down the law on affairs of state? Affairs of state, after all, were not Blackman's concern, since his object was to portray the saint, not the politician. What we need is a test case, an issue over which Henry and Suffolk can be shown to have disagreed, so that it becomes possible to separate the views of the king from those of his chief adviser. Such a test case is provided by the Anglo-French peace negotiations of 1445 to 1448, negotiations which culminated in the humiliating surrender of Anjou and Maine in March 1448. Moreover, this test case has the advantage of introducing us to Henry's wife, Margaret of Anjou, a dominating figure in the history of the Wars of the Roses.

In the early part of 1445 the English were still in a position of strength in France; they held Gascony, Anjou, Maine and Normandy as well as the territory around Calais. Although the king himself never appeared in France after 1430, this may actually have helped his lieutenants there to govern efficiently. Then, in the autumn of 1445, Henry recalled his commander-in-chief, the duke of York, and for over two years no one was sent to replace him. With York out of the way the king felt free to pursue a French policy of his own. On 22 December 1445 he wrote secretly to Charles VII promising to surrender Maine and Anjou by the end of the following April. This letter apparently confirmed a promise which he had earlier made verbally to the French king's ambassadors. But the promise was easier to make than to perform. It had to be kept secret because it was obvious even to Henry that neither parliament nor his own council could possibly have been persuaded to agree to this surrender and, officially at least, the king's council was kept in ignorance of his promise for the next eighteen months. It would be hard to imagine a more chaotic way of conducting the business of the realm. We will never know just how much Suffolk knew about Henry VI's secret diplomacy, but what is clear is that he disapproved of it. On 25 May 1447, at his own request, he was allowed to make a formal declaration in the king's chamber that he had never been a party to any proposals to surrender Anjou and Maine. By this time the secret had leaked out and most people seem to have believed that Suffolk's must have been the guiding hand in this as in so much else. In fact on this occasion rumour was mistaken. Henry VI was making his own policy – and one which was sharply at variance with the 'official' policy of his ministers.

What was Henry up to? Why had he decided to strike out on an independent but highly problematical line of his own? Probably he had two reasons; one general and one more specific. In the first place, he wanted peace and believed in the virtues of peace-making. All princes, of course, wanted peace – or so they said. But Henry really meant it. Moreover he seems to have believed that Charles VII meant it too, so that English concessions would be interpreted purely as gestures of friendship between kings and not as signs of weakness prompting the French king to make further preparations for war. In this naïve spirit Henry dreamed of a personal meeting with Charles VII and an end to the differences which divided their two countries. In the second place, Henry was a newly married man and wanted to please his wife, Margaret of Anjou.

Margaret had arrived in England in April 1445. A fleet of no less than fifty-six ships had been chartered to transport her household and her baggage across the Channel. But the crossing, though on a magnificent scale, does not seem to have been a smooth one. On landing, Margaret spent several days recuperating in Portsmouth before she was well enough to travel further and meet her husband. (The actual marriage

had already taken place a month earlier at Nancy, with Suffolk standing as a proxy for the king.) A nice story of her arrival in England was
told a dozen years later by Raffaelo de Negra, an Italian writer who
claimed to have heard it from an Englishman:

> When the queen landed in England the king dressed himself as a squire, and
> took her a letter which he said the king of England had written. While the
> queen read the letter the king took stock of her, saying that a woman may be
> closely observed while she is reading, and the queen never found out that it was
> the king because she was so engrossed in the letter that she never looked at the
> king in his squire's dress.

If this Italian gossip was true, it was the only time in his life that Henry
VI held the advantage over his queen. When Margaret arrived she was
fifteen years old and widely regarded as a charming and attractive
young woman. According to Raffaelo de Negra she 'is a most handsome
woman, though', he added – for he was writing to the duchess of Milan
– 'she is somewhat dark and not as beautiful as your highness'.

On 30 May 1445 Margaret was crowned queen in Westminster
Abbey. The day before she had been acclaimed by the populace as she
was carried in procession from the Tower to St Paul's. Dressed in white
damask and powdered gold and with her hair combed down to her
shoulders, the young French princess was given a rapturous welcome –
not surprisingly since the city conduits ran with red and white wine. A
dozen years later it would not have been so easy to arrange a political
pageant in her honour; not only was she widely blamed for the loss of
English possessions in France, but the loss of Gascony had been
followed in 1456 by a steep decline in the level of wine imports from
Bordeaux.

Margaret's father was René of Anjou, titular king of Sicily and
brother of the French queen. Charles VII, therefore, was her uncle, and
on 17 December 1445 she wrote to him saying she would do all she
could to make Henry consent to the surrender of Maine and Anjou. Just
five days later Henry sent the secret letter in which he promised to do
this, but it would probably be a mistake to conclude from this sequence
of events that Margaret was the driving force behind the secret royal
diplomacy. In later years this could indeed have been said of her, but it
is unlikely that a fifteen-year-old girl could wield so much influence
within a few months of her arrival at a strange court where most people
spoke a language which she had yet to learn. Whatever may have
happened later, it is hard to imagine even Henry VI being pushed

around by a domineering wife in 1445–6. The decision to surrender Maine and Anjou, though undertaken partly to please Margaret, must have been one which the king himself chose to make. It was a decision which dramatically revealed just how out of touch he was with all shades of English political opinion, not just with those who, like his uncle Duke Humphrey of Gloucester, wanted to prosecute the French war more vigorously, but also with those who, like the earl of Suffolk, advocated a policy of peace with honour. Henry VI's own peculiar brand of peace-making only served to tarnish the reputation of anyone who was in any way associated with the policy of peace.

Among these people, of course, was Margaret herself. The marriage had been arranged as a preliminary to peace talks and her arrival in England was followed, some weeks later, by the arrival of Charles VII's ambassadors. As the princess who was meant to bring the gift of peace, and as the daughter of a – by royal standards – impecunious father, she brought no dowry with her, so the initial popular enthusiasm for her soon waned. She came to be seen as the queen who had brought nothing and taken much away. None of this would have mattered very much if she had held the restricted but secure position of wife to a competent king. Unfortunately, with a husband like Henry VI, it gradually became clear that her role at court was to be very different from that normally assigned to a queen. Her primary political function was to produce an heir to the throne, but this, it seems, was not easy. It was to be ten years before their first child, a boy, was born, and they were to have no more. In over twenty years of marriage she was pregnant only once – and this in an age when annual pregnancies were fairly normal. Clearly this could have been the result of any one of a number of physiological or psychological conditions; nonetheless there are a few pointers which suggest that, as usual, the problem was in Henry VI's mind. Blackman portrays a man with strong and, on the whole, disapproving views on sex and nudity. Other evidence shows that some people believed that the king's spiritual advisers exercised an undue influence over him. Bishop Ayscough of Salisbury was held responsible for the long wait for an heir, being accused of counselling Henry not to 'come nigh her'. Perhaps most telling of all is the fact that the king's one total mental breakdown occurred in 1453 during his wife's pregnancy.

In the meantime, by virtue of his rash promise to Charles VII, Henry VI had landed himself in a political mess from which it was impossible to extricate himself with honour. Although no one would approve the cession of Maine and Anjou, it was certain that the most vigorous

opponent of this step would be the king's uncle, Humphrey, duke of
Gloucester. He was a man with wide intellectual interests and a great
patron of scholars, the founder of Duke Humphrey's Library at Oxford.
In many ways an erratic and unstable politician, he nonetheless had
one guiding principle to which he consistently held. As Henry v's sole
surviving brother, he saw himself as the executor of the dead king's
policy of conquest. In his eyes all peace-making was anathema. He had
bitterly opposed the truce of 1444 and though he had been outvoted
then, the terms which were now being mooted would make it easy for
him to win widespread support. As the heir presumptive to the throne
whose views were decidedly out of line with the prevailing policy at the
court, he was an uncomfortable figure to have around. There had been
an earlier attempt to embarrass him when, in 1442, his wife Eleanor
had been accused of plotting the king's death by sorcery. Five years
later it looks as though the court had finally decided to silence him for
good. A parliament was summoned to meet at Bury St Edmunds, a
centre of Suffolk's influence. As Gloucester rode into the town on 18
February 1447 he was arrested preparatory to being put on trial in
parliament. Five days later he died. Most probably he suffered a stroke,
but the circumstances of his death were undeniably suspicious. Fore-
seeing the outcome, Suffolk ordered that the body should be exposed to
view. Those who inspected it, could see no sign of a wound or any other
indication of how he had died, but this did little or nothing to check the
rumours. As one chronicler put it, 'Some said he died of sorrow; some
that he was murdered between two feather beds; and others said that a
hot spit was put in his fundament. And so how he died God only knows,
from whom nothing is hidden.' But his enemies gained nothing from his
death. Gloucester turned out to be one of those men who are more
dangerous once dead than when alive. The 'Good Duke' returned time
and again to haunt the subsequent careers of Suffolk, Margaret and
Henry vi. He had been made into a political martyr to whose memory
all those who opposed either the court or peace with France could
appeal.

    With his uncle out of the way, Henry vi's schemes became a little bit
easier to implement. On 28 July 1447 he appointed commissioners to
hand over the fortress-town of Le Mans to the French. So unpopular,
however, were Henry's instructions that his commissioners connived
with the local commanders to delay matters still further. It was now two
years since the king's rash promise and inevitably Charles vii became
more and more exasperated by so much procrastination. Eventually,

despite the formal existence of a state of truce, he brought up an army to lay siege to Le Mans. Only then did the English bow to the necessity of carrying out their king's promise. At midnight on 29 March 1448 the commissioners met their French counterparts in the ditch beneath the walls of Le Mans and completed the formalities of the surrender, formalities which included the exchange of documents extending the truce to April 1450.

The documents were handed over in darkness 'without so much as a candle', and the French neglected to look closely at the content of the text they were given. They had, after all, no reason to suspect that the English would stoop to the falsification of diplomatic papers. Yet this is precisely what they had done. Since the truce was simply being extended, the French had assumed that the terms of truce were to remain the same as before – and the English had encouraged them in this assumption. As before, the allies and liegemen of the king of England were included in the truce, but the list of these allies as drawn up by the English in 1448 was different in one crucial respect from previous lists – the name of the duke of Brittany had been inserted. In fact the duke was an ally of the French king and this alteration in the truce terms was made without his knowledge. The extraordinary behaviour of the English had a point, of sorts. Should there ever be conflict between the king of England and the duke of Brittany, then the king could claim on the basis of the 'revised' terms of the truce, that it was a purely domestic affair, a quarrel between a lord and his vassal, and the king of France had no legal right to intervene in the matter. A year later, in March 1449, an English army led by an Aragonese mercenary captain, upon whom Henry VI had bestowed the Order of the Garter, attacked, without warning, the Breton town of Fougères, took it by escalade and sacked it. The duke of Brittany naturally sought Charles VII's help, but at a series of conferences held during the early summer of 1449 the English argued that Fougères was none of Charles's business. To base a legalistic argument upon a piece of sharp practice was dishonourable, foolish and unavailing. On 31 July 1449 Charles declared that he no longer considered himself bound by the truce. Open war began. The king of France launched a full-scale invasion of Normandy. Incredible as it may seem, Henry VI's government had done nothing to put the Norman defences into a state of readiness, though it is clear that the sack of Fougères had long been planned and it is hard to see how else Charles VII could have responded to an attack on his ally. In October, Rouen fell. By August 1450 the last

English stronghold in Normandy had been captured. It is hard to imagine a more sorry tale of dishonesty, underhand dealing, vacillation and mismanagement than the conduct of French affairs by Henry vi's government in the years 1445–50. For all this Henry vi himself must bear the responsibility, directly in the case of Maine and indirectly in the case of Fougères, which seems to have been a scheme devised by the man who was still his closest adviser, William de la Pole, now promoted duke of Suffolk.

Retribution came swiftly. During the last few years Henry vi's government had been dominated by a small inner ring of councillors – a 'gang of three', Suffolk, the king's confessor William Ayscough of Salisbury, and Adam Moleyns, bishop of Chichester and keeper of the privy seal. Within a period of six months all of them were dead, not put on trial and duly executed, but dragged off and lynched by angry men. Never in the whole sweep of English history has a governing clique been so brutally swept away on a roaring tide of popular indignation. On 9 January 1450 Moleyns was set upon and murdered at Portsmouth by a mob of soldiers and seamen after a violent altercation in which they accused him of withholding their wages. In the heat and frenzy of the moment he apparently made some damaging remarks about his patron, Suffolk, and these were used to fuel the agitation against him. Three days later there was a riot in London, when a crowd chanted this refrain:

> By this town, by this town,
> For this array the king shall lose his crown.

In Kent there were armed demonstrations led by men who took names like Bluebeard, Robin Hood or the King and Queen of the Fairies. For the moment a troubled calm was imposed on the countryside following Bluebeard's execution at Canterbury on 9 February. But an order issued on the same day by King Henry shows just how alarmed he was. Each groom and page of the royal household was to be supplied with a bow and a sheaf of arrows 'for the safety of our person'. Ten days later the carrying of weapons was banned in London and the whole south-east – the unenforceable edict of a panic-stricken government.

By this time the storm of popular indignation had been taken up by the gentry, represented by the commons in parliament. On 28 January, at the insistence of the commons, Suffolk was committed to the Tower of London. A ballad of the time makes plain what most people thought about this:

> Now is the fox driven to hole!
> Hoo to him, hoo, hoo!
> For if he creep out
> He will you all undo.

Two separate indictments were drawn up, the first accusing him of treasonable dealings with the French; the second accusing him of various corrupt and violent practices in the central and local administration of the country. Although on the charge of treason he was clearly not guilty, there was a good deal more substance to the second indictment. His hand and that of some of his more unsavoury political associates had lain heavy on East Anglia. So great was the need for a scapegoat and so deep the resentment against the all-powerful position of Suffolk's group at court, that the duke would almost certainly have been found guilty on all charges had it ever come to a formal trial in parliament. Henry intervened to save his favourite. As a sop to public opinion he banished him for five years.

On leaving the Tower, Suffolk had a narrow escape from another angry mob. He then spent six weeks in his new country house at Wingfield, putting his affairs in order and preparing to leave the realm. On 30 April he set sail from Ipswich. On 2 May his ships were intercepted off Dover by a small fleet which was lying in wait for him. To shouts of 'Welcome, traitor' Suffolk was taken aboard the fleet's flagship, the *Nicholas of the Tower*, under the command of an unknown captain. What happened then was told to John Paston in a letter sent to him from London just three days later, a letter which, according to the man who wrote it, had been so thoroughly washed by tears that it was scarcely possible to read it.

And Suffolk asked the name of the ship, and when he knew it, he remembered a prophecy that said, if he might escape the danger of the Tower, he should be safe; and then his heart failed him for he thought he was deceived, and in the sight of all his men he was dragged out of the great ship into a boat; and there was an axe, and a stroke, and one of the lewdest of the ship bade him lay down his head, and he should be fairly dealt with and die on a sword; and took a rusty sword and smote off his head with half a dozen strokes, and took away his gown of russet and his doublet of mailed velvet and laid his body on the sands of Dover.

The courtiers, shocked by Suffolk's murder, blamed it on the lawlessness of the men of Kent and threatened dire reprisals. The treasurer, Lord Saye, and his son-in-law, William Crowmer, the sheriff of Kent, announced that they would turn the county into a deer forest. Kent's response was a massive uprising, the revolt of Jack Cade. For a few weeks in June and July 1450 the government seemed to be at the mercy of the large rebel army drawn up at Blackheath. Over two thousand men received pardons for their participation in the revolt, so presumably the total number involved was many times greater. Their manifesto, the *Complaint of the Commons of Kent*, caught with fine propagandist skill the mood of the country. An advance guard of the royal army was caught in an ambush and destroyed. Uncertain of the reliability of the rest of his troops, Henry VI retreated to Kenilworth. In Wiltshire, on 29 June, a mob, said to be 600 strong, hauled Bishop Ayscough of Salisbury, the last of the gang of three, out of the chancel of the church where he was saying mass, and put him to death on a nearby hill. On 4 July Cade's army entered London. Saye and Crowmer were captured, tried and executed. But now, intoxicated by their success, some of Cade's followers began to get out of hand. The Londoners turned against them and Cade agreed to disband his troops in return for a free pardon and a promise that some at least of their grievances would in due course be redressed. With his men dispersed, he was killed on 12 July. The government which, a week before, had seemed to be on the verge of total collapse, began to pull itself together. A commission was appointed to investigate the abuses and oppressions which had troubled Kentish society for the last dozen years. Though there were fresh outbursts of local disorder in Sussex, Wiltshire, Essex and Kent, in the succeeding months the country gradually returned to normal, but the summer of 1450 was a crucial moment. Jack Cade's revolt had brought Henry VI's government to its knees and, in its manifesto, had produced a telling diagnosis of the ills which beset the realm. For the first time, moreover, men had decided to take up arms to remedy those ills. Although as yet the aristocracy stood aloof, large numbers of gentry had been involved, and it would not be long before the most powerful nobleman in the country was prepared to follow where the commons had led.

Five

RICHARD OF YORK: THE HIGH AND MIGHTY PRINCE, 1450–3

EARLY IN SEPTEMBER 1450 the duke of York left Ireland and stepped ashore at Beaumaris harbour. From this moment on he became the dominant figure in English politics and he remained so throughout the whole decade. Time after time during these ten years he tried to seize power until, in the end, his sheer persistence won a grudging half-recognition from his fellow peers. Was his return to England in 1450 the first of his bids for power? Was this why he had left Ireland without asking for the king's permission? To answer these questions we have to try to understand something of York's character and of the dilemmas which were facing him.

Born in 1411, he became a royal ward in 1415 and was then brought up by the Nevilles, one of the greatest families of northern England. His father, Richard, earl of Cambridge, executed for treason in 1415 on the eve of the Agincourt campaign, was the son of Edmund Langley, duke of York, Edward III's fourth son. His mother, Anne Mortimer, was a descendant of Lionel, duke of Clarence, Edward III's second son. With the death of Humphrey of Gloucester, Henry VI became the last surviving member of the house of Lancaster. If he were to die childless, Richard of York would be in a strong position to claim the throne, and by 1450 it was beginning to look as though the marriage of Henry VI and Margaret of Anjou was barren. Richard of York was also the wealthiest English landowner of the day. From Edmund Langley he had inherited great estates in Yorkshire, the Midlands and the Home Counties. To this he added the vast Mortimer inheritance in Wales and the Marches. Moreover, in his role as earl of Ulster he was also a leading Anglo-Irish landowner. Altogether these estates yielded about £7,000 a year gross

(£5,800 net). It was only natural that a man of his standing should play
an important part in national affairs, and for many years he had done
so. In 1436–7 he had been the king's lieutenant in France. In 1440 he
had been engaged to serve a five-year term as lieutenant-general and
governor of France and Normandy. But in March 1443 John Beaufort
was appointed lieutenant and captain-general of France and Gascony
for seven years. York was understandably furious, all the more so when
Beaufort, now created duke of Somerset, was given a larger army than
his own. The sting in the tail of this humiliating episode lay in the fact
that Somerset was provided with £25,000 to pay the advance wages of
his troops, while York got nothing and was told to be patient. By the
end of his term in France, York was owed nearly two years' wages and
was unable to pay his captains and garrisons. Even so he was anxious to
remain in France where Henry vi's personal foreign policy meant that
events were now boiling up to a crisis, but not surprisingly the king, and
following him, the court party, now looked upon York with a degree of
suspicion which Humphrey of Gloucester's death served only to inten-
sify. They determined to exclude him from the corridors of power and
so, in July 1447, as Henry prepared to hand over Le Mans to the
French, York was appointed lieutenant of Ireland. The lieutenancy of
France which he had coveted went instead to John Beaufort's younger
brother Edmund, created duke of Somerset in 1448. Once again an
exasperated York felt that he had been outmanoeuvred by the court
party. He quarrelled violently and publicly with Adam Moleyns and
not until July 1449 did he eventually sail for Ireland.

York had every right to feel aggrieved. The crown's dealings with
him had wounded not only his pride but his pocket. By 1446 the
government owed him the enormous sum of £38,666. In order to secure
payment of part of this, York agreed to forego £12,666. Even so, the
money was very slow in coming in, and by 1450 his financial plight was,
if anything, worse still. The government's failure to pay his wages as
lieutenant in Ireland together with the arrears of his hereditary pension
at the Exchequer meant that he was owed a further £10,000. Through
no fault of his own he was being forced to contemplate selling some of
his manors and to endanger good relationships with his friends by
borrowing heavily from them. Two considerations made this particularly frustrating. In the early 1440s he had not only been active in the
king's service abroad; he had also, in large measure, put his purse at the
disposal of the government. By 1446 his loans to the crown totalled
some £26,000. This was a great help to a government which was in

financial difficulties throughout the decade, and, as its largest single creditor, Richard of York was surely entitled to fair treatment. This, however, he did not receive. The crown's normal method of discharging its debts was by handing out tallies of assignment on some regular source of income, such as the customs, but the receipt of such tallies did not, in fact, guarantee prompt payment. The assigned revenue might well be committed already. In this case the unfortunate recipient had nothing more in his fist than a bundle of 'bad' tallies. In the years 1442–52 the duke of York received no less than £21,000 worth of bad tallies. Given the size of the overall government debt – £372,000 in 1449 – one might have expected to find that all its creditors were in an awkward position, but this was not the case. Those who had access to the inner ring at court could normally ensure that the tallies which they were given were good ones; thus repayment was less a matter of the crown's general financial situation and more a question of politics: of whether you were 'in' or 'out'. The number of bad tallies received by York demonstrated in a particularly galling fashion just how 'out' he was.

Richard of York may not have been the world's finest administrator, but this was shabby treatment for a man who had given years of service to the crown and who was, moreover, the king's most powerful subject and his heir presumptive. York was not alone in thinking this. According to Jack Cade's manifesto:

> The king should take about his noble person men of his true blood from his royal realm, that is to say, the high and mighty prince, the duke of York, exiled from our sovereign lord's person by the suggestions of those false traitors the duke of Suffolk and his affinity.

This, however, was not so much a 'Yorkist' proclamation as a statement of the commonplace view that sensible kings did not exclude the greatest nobles from their council. The next sentence runs as follows: 'He should also take about his person those mighty princes, the duke of Exeter, the duke of Buckingham and the duke of Norfolk, together with the true earls and barons of his land. Then shall he be the richest king in Christendom.' A few weeks earlier, similar opinions had been expressed by a Yorkshire shipman who barged his way into Henry's presence and thrashed about with a flail, saying that this was how the duke of York should deal with the traitors. Unexpected incidents of this kind could serve only to deepen a timid king's mistrust. As the government plunged into a state of near collapse in the early months of 1450, all sorts of wild rumours were given undue currency. Suffolk had been scheming to make his son first in line of succession in place of York. York on the other hand, was planning to raise an army in Ireland and seize the throne for himself. Was Cade's revolt a pre-arranged part of York's political programme? Why else had Jack Cade taken the name Mortimer if not to remind people of the York–Mortimer claim to the throne? Some of these stories may have been deliberately started by the court party in an attempt to discredit Cade by portraying him as a Yorkist agent whose aim was not to reform the realm but overthrow the dynasty. Whether or not any of the king's household believed these innuendoes, it is quite possible that the king himself did. Such was the atmosphere of suspicion, uncertainty, rumour and counter-rumour into which York sailed when he left Ireland in September 1450, return- ing via North Wales to England.

Why had Richard decided to return unannounced? Clearly there was no real connexion with Cade's revolt, otherwise he would have come back at least two months earlier than he did. What in fact he seems to have been worried about was the return of Somerset from France. Who was going to take Suffolk's place as the king's chief counsellor? Once the panic occasioned by Cade's rebellion had died away, this was the most important question in English politics. Would it be the senior duke? Or would, once again, his 'rightful' place be usurped by a favourite of the king's own choosing? On 1 August Somerset returned to England, and the news of his reception at court was soon transmitted to York, possibly by Sir William Oldhall his chamberlain and political chief of staff. In York's eyes everything about Somerset was detestable. As lieutenant in France he had obtained the very office which York himself had wanted. Then he had presided over the loss of Normandy; in October 1449 he had in person surrendered the city of Rouen to Charles VII. Unlike York, he had lent relatively small sums to the king and had received mainly good tallies in return. Moreover, as a member of the Beaufort family, he could rival York's claim to be heir presumptive. Like the Lancastrians, the Beauforts were descendants of John of Gaunt, Edward III's third son, but their lineage was of doubtful legiti- macy. An act of parliament had legitimized Gaunt's children by his mistress Katherine Swynford, but Henry IV had later issued letters patent debarring them from the succession to the throne. But how much would such legal devices and limitations be worth in terms of practical politics fifty years later? It was hard to know. All York did know was that the duke of Somerset was the hated rival who, despite having failed in France, now seemed to be on the point of scooping up all the rewards of power in England.

Whatever Richard's intentions, his arrival was a cause for grave concern to the king's servants. They did not know what was in his mind; all they knew were the reports that spoke of him as the leader of a plot to depose their master. Very naturally, therefore, they tried to apprehend him, but he gave them the slip and arrived at Westminster, accompanied by a large retinue, and complaining bitterly that he had been treated as though he were a traitor. Nonetheless, when he met Henry he showed him all the deference due from a subject to a king. He wanted to clear the air. In recent years too many rumours had brought about the downfall of too many men, of whom Gloucester and Suffolk were the greatest, and York wanted to ensure that this would not be his fate. Henry's reassurances on this point then led him to go a stage further. In a bill which he presented to Henry and then had circulated, York put himself forward as the champion of law and order and publicly offered his services to the king, in effect suggesting that he should be made principal counsellor with a mandate to reform the royal household.

The successful propaganda campaign against Suffolk and the widespread support for Cade's revolt had shown just how unpopular some of the old ruling clique had been. In the hope of preventing further disturbances, the government had set up commissions to investigate the accusations of corruption, perversion of justice, unlawful violence and the like, but many of those accused were still members of the royal household and it was not easy to believe that these would, in fact, be made to pay for their crimes. To those who regarded the offer of royal justice with cynicism, York's sudden arrival in London at the end of September offered fresh hope. Here, it seemed, was an upright man, untainted by connexions with the Suffolk affinity, and so powerful in the kingdom that he could insist that the law should take its course. At once the propaganda war against Suffolk's old cronies, men like Heydon and Tuddenham in East Anglia, was taken up with new energy. A letter written in London on 6 October 1450 reveals with great clarity just how such campaigns were waged and how public opinion was systematically manipulated by the fifteenth-century equivalent of the mass media.

To my master, John Paston, in right great haste
Sir, if it please you, I was in my lord of York's house and I heard much; I heard much in Fleet Street too. My lord was with the king and he put things in such a way that all the king's household was, and is, afraid right sore. And my

lord has put a bill to the king, desiring much which is after the commons' own heart, with all the emphasis on justice and on arresting those who have been indicted.... Sir Berle Yonge and Josse are working hard on behalf of Heydon and Tuddenham; they have offered more than £2,000 to Sir William Oldhall to have his good lordship. Therefore your only course of action is to get the Swaffham men to meet my lord next Friday at Pikenham and hand him a bill against Sir Thomas Tuddenham, Heydon and Prentice, and cry 'Out' on them, and call them extortioners and beg my lord to take stern measures against them. You should persuade the mayor and all the aldermen and commoners to ride to meet my lord, and have bills drawn up for my lord's attention, and have all the town cry 'Out' on Heydon, Tuddenham, Wyndham, Prentice and all their false maintainers, and tell my lord in piteous terms how much damage they have done to the city. For, sir, unless my lord hear some foul tales of them and a hideous noise and cry, by my faith they will all be restored to favour. And, sir, many groups of commoners should be organized in those parts of the town which my lord will visit, to cry out to my lord for justice.... Sir, I send you a copy of the bill which my lord of York handed to the king; and, sir, see that enough copies of this bill are distributed about the city, for the love of God.

York did his best to live up to the expectations which, by the publication of his own bill, he had encouraged men to place in him. During mid-October he travelled around East Anglia and the east Midlands meeting those men who, as they hoped, were to be his local associates in the new regime. Efforts were made to ensure the return of the 'right' kind of MPs for the forthcoming parliament. But if Henry VI stood firm, no amount of this kind of manoeuvring could get York the place he wanted. And Henry did stand firm. In reply to York's bill, he issued a statement of his own, rejecting the idea that he should be advised by one man alone and declaring his preference for a council in which each member had an equal voice. This was little help to York since, at this stage, only the duke of Norfolk and the earl of Devon among his fellow peers, were willing to go along with his open criticism of the court. While parliament was in session (November 1450 to May 1451), York could hope to wield some extra influence. His anti-household stance had won him considerable support with the commons who traditionally looked upon the court as a conspicuous waster of the taxpayers' money. They elected Oldhall as their speaker and passed several measures of financial reform and retrenchment. But York knew that once parliament was dissolved then he was back where he started – unless, in the meantime, something was done to strengthen his position. It was presumably in the forlorn hope of achieving this that he allowed

Thomas Young, a friend of Oldhall's and MP for Bristol, to present a bill asking Henry to recognize York as his heir. The court was outraged, parliament dissolved, and Young sent to the Tower.

In the last eight months York had employed constitutional methods and they proved to be ineffectual. Somerset, indeed, was still in the ascendant at court – in 1451 he was appointed captain of Calais; this meant that he had charge of the largest military establishment at the king's disposal – but York had certainly not given up. He had consistently maintained his pose as champion of law and order – even to the extent of protecting his rival Somerset from the anger of a mob of ex-soldiers – and in the autumn of 1451 he was given a new opportunity to shine in this role. This came about when the most famous feud in the south-west flared up yet again.

Traditionally this part of the world was Courtenay country. The Courtenays had been earls of Devon since the early fourteenth century, but in the last few years Thomas, the twelfth earl, had found his position at the head of south-western society challenged by the emergence of an energetic, capable and ambitious rival, William Bonville. A member of a gentry family, Bonville had climbed into prominence by making himself useful not only in local affairs, on commissions of the peace and the like, but also in the business of the realm. As a young man he had served in France under Henry v and John, duke of Bedford, and in the 1440s he spent three years as seneschal of Gascony. This was an office of great responsibility which he presumably filled well enough to be raised to the peerage as Lord Bonville of Chewton in 1449. To the twelfth earl this *parvenu* was all the more irksome because he had dared to insinuate himself into the domestic affairs of the Courtenays. He had married Thomas Courtenay's aunt and, in one of those quarrels between senior and junior branches of a family which were so characteristic of this period (as also of most others), he had sided with the Courtenays of Powderham.

As early as 1440 there had been trouble between Bonville and the earl of Devon and this was considerably exacerbated next year when Henry vi appointed Courtenay steward of the duchy of Cornwall – apparently oblivious of the fact that the office was already held by William Bonville. For the next decade their quarrel continued to simmer. Inevitably it took on the complexion of the greater conflict between York and the court party. Since Bonville's career had brought him into close association with Suffolk and the Beauforts, it was natural that Thomas Courtenay should attach himself to the duke of York. In September 1451 violence flared up again, when the earl and his friend and neighbour Lord Cobham raised an army and led it in search of their enemies. The king's council made a few ineffectual gestures in the direction of keeping the peace, but the earl was not to be so easily deflected from his purpose. The climax of a demonstration of Courtenay's armed might came when he caught Lord Bonville in Taunton Castle. For three days his retainers surrounded the castle while carpenters worked hard at making siege engines. While the government was still thinking about acting, Richard of York marched to Taunton. He persuaded Courtenay to disband his forces and Bonville to hand over the castle. He even compelled the enemies to come to terms with each other. York was acting on his own initiative, showing the world that he could do the government's job more effectively than the government itself. Such action could only strengthen York's claim to be the chief of the king's counsellors. It is also possible that he realized that his ally the earl of Devon had gone too far and had to be brought to his senses before he was arrested and punished. Fortunately for York, Henry vi's government moved so slowly that its moves were easily forestalled.

Soon after this York began to plan a more dramatic action. Since constitutional means had failed, he would try to impose himself on the king by force: armed rebellion together with demonstrations in support of his cause in as many towns as possible. We do not know when he and Oldhall got down to the secret work of organizing this *coup*. If the later accusations of his enemies are to be believed, he was already thinking of it when he went to Taunton, and by November the details were being fitted into place. Certainly by the end of the month Sir William Oldhall was feeling distinctly nervous. Believing himself to be in danger of imminent arrest he took refuge in the sanctuary of St Martin-le-Grand and remained there, except for brief intervals, until 1455. Not, however, until February 1452 was York ready to come out into the open. Once again he made a systematic attempt to influence public opinion by outlining his complaints in letters which were given a wide circulation. One such text still survives in the copy which was sent to the citizens of Shrewsbury. It emphasized the continuing disgrace of further defeats in France. With the fall of Bordeaux on 30 June 1451, Gascony too had been lost – after being three hundred years in the possession of the English crown. Now the French were advancing to the siege of Calais. For all this York held Somerset personally responsible. The salutary advice which he had given the king after his return from Ireland had likewise been neglected 'through the envy, malice and untruth of the

said duke of Somerset ... who works continually for my undoing....
Wherefore, worshipful friends, to the intent that every man shall know
my purpose, I signify unto you that with the help and support of
Almighty God and of our Lady, and of all the company of heaven, I,
after long sufferance and delays, it not being my will or intent to
displease my sovereign lord, but seeing that the said duke ever pre-
vaileth and ruleth about the king's person and that by this means the
land is likely to be destroyed, am fully determined to proceed in all
haste against him with the help of my kinsmen and friends.'

But York's bid for popular support failed. Only in a dozen small
towns where the local overlord was either York or his ally Devon were
there 'spontaneous' risings in his favour. Though he could command
widespread sympathy for his views when ventilated through the
medium of parliament, rebellion against an anointed king was a very
different matter indeed – and, however much York protested that he
was taking up arms not against Henry but against Somerset, this was a
distinction which made more sense in theory than in practice. Despite
his popularity in London in the autumn of 1450, the city now refused to
admit him. Even in Kent, where York now marched in the hope that
the thousands who had followed Jack Cade would muster to his
banner, he found his expectations confounded. He had no tenants here.
Unruly Kent remained obstinately quiet. So, in the end, as perhaps it
had done all along, York's fate depended on the number of lords who
were prepared to follow him and on the size of their retinues, but in his
encampment on the south bank of the Thames at Dartford there were
only two lords to be found: the earl of Devon and Lord Cobham. As the
king's army drew up at Blackheath on 1 March, it was clear that far
more peers, including even York's own kinsmen, the Neville earls of
Salisbury and Warwick, had chosen to remain loyal. No one, however,
was very anxious to fight. York may have been outnumbered, but he
was well entrenched 'with much great stuff and ordnance'. Moreover,
the earls of Salisbury and Warwick, whatever they may have thought of
York's action, cannot have wanted to draw their swords against him. So
the king's council decided to open negotiations. Their delegation
included both Nevilles as well as another of York's relatives, the bishop
of Ely. York stood by his stated intention. Only if Somerset were
arrested and put on trial for his conduct of the war in France, would he
disband his troops. The delegation agreed and apparently King Henry
also gave his verbal assent. The rebel army dispersed.

York was an honourable man and he believed that the king had given his word, but when he entered Henry's tent, he found Somerset standing in his accustomed place at the king's side, and when they returned to London, it was York who was compelled to ride before the king as though he were a prisoner. Compared with his associates Devon and Cobham, who were detained for some time in Berkhamsted and Wallingford Castles, York was fortunate. On 10 March he was released – possibly helped by a rumour that 10,000 Yorkist Welshmen were marching on London. Though he had undeniably committed treason, he was not put on trial. To do this would have been to dishonour Salisbury, Warwick and the other envoys who had pledged their word at Dartford. Moreover, as the behaviour of these envoys suggests, he had prepared so damning an indictment of Somerset's handling of the war that any trial of York was likely to be turned into a trial of Somerset, in other words to be as damaging to the government as was the trial of Adolf Hitler after his attempted *coup* in November 1923.

Nonetheless, before being released, York was made to grovel. Before a great assembly in St Paul's he had to swear an oath of loyalty in terms which explicitly spelt out that any future misconduct would bring down on his head the full penalties of treason. Later in the year some of York's tenants and retainers were brought to trial for their part in the rising. In order to emphasize the full extent of York's failure, the court was presided over by Somerset and it sat at Ludlow in what was supposedly the very centre of York's power. Whether or not York himself was present at Ludlow to witness this humiliation, we do not know. In the eighteen months between September 1450 and March 1452 he had done everything he could and he had been defeated. It was hardly surprising, then, that for the next eighteen months he preferred to stay out of politics. In his absence things began to go well for Henry and Somerset. In October 1452 an English expeditionary force under the command of old John Talbot, earl of Shrewsbury, recaptured Bordeaux. And by next spring it was clear that Queen Margaret was pregnant at last.

But early in August 1453 two events shattered this modest revival of the fortunes of the court. In the first place, news reached England of a catastrophic military defeat in Gascony. On 17 July the English army had been overwhelmed at Castillon and Talbot killed, brought down by a ball fired from one of the French guns. In the second place, Henry VI suffered a complete breakdown. Some of the king's subjects put this down to necromancy, but most knew that his mental health had always been fragile. In view of his maternal grandfather's madness this may have been an hereditary condition. But whereas Charles VI is said to have believed that he was made of glass and that if anyone touched him he would shatter, Henry's breakdown took the form of complete immobility. For nearly eighteen months he was unable to speak or use any of his limbs. It has been pointed out that this condition bears a resemblance to a period of stupor in a case of catatonic schizophrenia, though at this distance of time confident diagnosis is not really possible. Just what it was that brought on Henry's collapse we do not know. It occurred during his wife's one and only pregnancy and this may have increased the general sense of strain under which he was suffering. Possibly it was the news of the defeat at Castillon that proved to be the final straw.

Henry's collapse occurred while he was visiting the royal hunting lodge at Clarendon near Salisbury. For two months he was kept here while the government of the country carried on as though nothing had happened. This reticence reveals the extent of Somerset's embarrassment; he and his friends were now in an extremely awkward position. Only the king had sufficient authority to keep York out of the place to which his rank entitled him, and once he was back in the council there would be precious little room for Somerset, but the pretence could not be carried on indefinitely. Finally a great council was summoned to meet late in October to discuss the problem of Henry's incapacity. The duke of York had not been invited to attend this meeting. Presumably Somerset still hoped that the attempted *coup* of 1452 had so damaged York's reputation that his fellow peers would sit quietly by and allow him to be left out in the cold, but in the meantime, York's position too had changed – and for the better. There was now an important group of nobles interested in obtaining his help in the furtherance of their own quarrels. Violent events in the north – events in which, initially, York had no direct involvement – were conspiring to bring his political isolation to an end.

Six

THE ROAD TO ST ALBANS, 1453–5

ON 24 AUGUST 1453 on Heworth Moor on the north-east outskirts of York, a thousand or so men lay in wait for a bridal party. The ambush had been planned by Lord Egremont, the second son of Henry Percy, earl of Northumberland. The bridal party consisted of Sir Thomas Neville, the groom; Maud Stanhope, his bride of a week; the earl and countess of Salisbury (the groom's parents) and Sir John Neville (the groom's younger brother). They had celebrated the wedding at Tattershall Castle in Lincolnshire and were now travelling north to conduct the bride to a new home in one of the Neville castles in Yorkshire. Fortunately for them, the Nevilles had a large retinue and they managed to fight off the Percy assault and continue on their way. On both sides, however, many men were beaten, wounded and slain. The Nevilles claimed that the Percies had intended to kill them all, and from this moment the old feud between the two families reached new heights of violence and bitterness. To one contemporary chronicler, indeed, it seemed that the 'battle' at Heworth marked the beginning of the time of troubles, not just in the north, but in the whole of England.

What, then, lay behind the ambush? Why had the Percies turned out their Yorkshire tenants in their hundreds – and even gone to the trouble of bringing some along from their lordship of Cockermouth in Cumberland – in order to attack a bridal party? Discourteous it may have been, but it cannot be denied that there was a certain rough logic about Lord Egremont's decision to lay on a special reception for the newly-weds. Maude Stanhope was the niece and co-heiress of Ralph, Lord Cromwell. Cromwell was one of the oldest and most experienced of Henry VI's ministers and, as was only to be expected, he had done very well out of his long service to the crown. His splendid new house at Tattershall had been built – in brick, in the new fashion – out of the profits of his official career. Among his other gains were two manors: Wressle in Yorkshire and Burwell in Lincolnshire. Once upon a time these manors had belonged to the Percies, but they had lost them, together with their earldom and the rest of their estates in the great crisis of the family: the rebellion of the first earl of Northumberland and his son Hotspur against Henry IV; Hotspur's death in the Battle of Shrewsbury in 1403 and their defeat at the king's hands; the consequent forfeiture of their honours. The memory of these disastrous events rankled still, half a century later. With patience and tenacity, Hotspur's son had recovered the earldom and had reassembled most of their estates, but not yet all of them. It was bad enough that someone else should hold Wressle and Burwell, but that these estates should ever come into the possession of the Nevilles was worse – much worse. To the Percies, the marriage of Cromwell's heiress to Sir Thomas Neville was an intolerable affront.

The Nevilles and the Percies had been at each other's throats for longer than anyone could remember. The estates of the two most powerful families in the north lay so intermingled in Cumberland and Yorkshire that any acquisition made by one family could be seen as an opportunity missed by the other. The traditional crown policy of using the one as a counterweight to the influence of the other served to reinforce, rather than to check, their rivalry. But the Nevilles had suffered no such catastrophe as that which overtook the Percies in Henry IV's reign. In the last half century they had enjoyed a record of almost unbroken success. Ralph Neville, the first earl of Westmorland had married, as his second wife, Joan Beaufort, a daughter of John of Gaunt. They had twelve children and taking full advantage of their close association with the house of Lancaster, they pushed their interests without scruple and to great effect. One became the bishop of Durham (the richest see in the north), but for those who did not go into the church, good marriages had to be found – and the sooner the better. As a result, no less than thirteen of the parties to eleven marriages were under sixteen years of age on the day they became a husband or a wife. The eldest son, Richard Neville, was married to a rich heiress, Alice Montagu, through whom he acquired the title and estates of the earldom of Salisbury. Three of his brothers married other heiresses, though one of them, the nine-year-old Joan Fauconberg, had been a declared lunatic since her birth. The daughters also married into the greatest families in England. Between 1450 and 1455, five Neville brothers and five brothers-in-law were sitting in the house of lords. In addition, the earl of Salisbury's eldest son, another Richard Neville, when six years old, had married Anne Beauchamp when she was nine. In time she inherited the earldom of Warwick, thus providing her husband with an income of about £4,000 a year, and making him the wealthiest of the English earls. All in all, it was probably the most amazing series of child marriages in English history. The chief victim of it all was another Neville, Ralph, second earl of Westmorland, the first earl's grandson by his first wife. In name he was the senior member of the family, but since the bulk of the property had gone to the descendants of his grandfather's second wife, he had good reason to feel disgruntled. In reality the head of the family was the earl of Salisbury, and he it was who held the important lordships in Yorkshire where Neville and Percy lands lay dangerously intermingled. Altogether, his estates were probably worth more than £3,000 a year. Moreover, the crown had recognized his commanding position by making him warden of the west March towards Scotland, an office he held from 1420 to 1435 and again from 1443 onwards.

The wardens of the Marches were responsible for defending the border in wartime, and for preventing the Anglo-Scottish war from continuing unofficially during periods of official peace or truce. Given the deep resentments which had developed in the century and a half of almost incessant strife since Edward I's invasion of Scotland, the second was probably the harder task. To maintain some degree of military control over the turbulent border society where every landowner had his own fortress required a warden who was well supplied with men and money as well as being a tough and experienced politician. The wardens received salaries higher than any other royal officers, out of which they were expected to retain the troops needed to carry out their duties. The effect of this was that the wardens of the Marches were able to raise private armies at the crown's expense. In consequence, the office became a most desirable prize for ambitious nobles with confidence in their own ability to master the challenge and opportunity which it presented. Local realities and the traditional royal policy of balancing Percy against Neville meant that, needless to say, the warden of the east March at this date was a Percy: Henry, Lord Poynings, Northumberland's eldest son.

The angry feelings which had been stirred up again on Heworth Moor continued unabated in the next few months. Bands of partisans of both families rode round the county, attacking their enemies' tenants and property. The king's council wrote letters remonstrating with the protagonists, but otherwise did nothing. With the king incapacitated, the council was insufficiently sure of its own authority to act with the necessary firmness. Somerset, in particular, was reluctant to take a severe line with magnates whose support he might need to bolster his own highly vulnerable position. To the earl of Salisbury this degree of conciliar restraint, not to say feebleness, was very frustrating. For years now he had been a regular and prominent member of the king's council and he doubtless expected the council to help him to bring Egremont and the rest of his crew to justice. On 20 October 1453 both families mustered their full strength. The Percies – Northumberland, his sons Poynings and Egremont, with their cousin Lord Clifford – assembled at Topcliffe in the North Riding; the Nevilles – Salisbury, Warwick, Sir Thomas and Sir John Neville, together with their allies, Lord FitzHugh and Scrope of Bolton – at Sandhutton, just four miles away. On this occasion the confrontation was bloodless, but four days later at Westminster the king's council decided to invite the duke of York to join its deliberations. Present at that council meeting were the earls of Salisbury and Warwick. Evidently the Nevilles had ridden south in haste. It looks as if they had decided that only with York's help could they defeat the Percies.

Unquestionably Richard of York was their most natural ally. He was married to Salisbury's youngest sister Cecily and, though he visited them rarely, he possessed substantial estates in south Yorkshire. By this date, moreover, one of the Nevilles was himself at odds with York's great enemy. On 15 June 1453 Somerset had been granted custody of estates in Glamorgan which, up to that moment, had been held by Warwick. If he had known anything of the Neville earl's character, Somerset must have realized that this was a step which took him on to dangerous ground. But in mid-June, of course, he was still basking in the favour of a king who was more or less sane. In addition, Somerset's own financial position was in some ways an awkward one. Although as a Beaufort he belonged to one of the very greatest families in the land, his own landed inheritance was a relatively small one, bringing him in little more than £300 a year. Lacking independent wealth, he was therefore peculiarly dependent on his position at court and on the grants, pensions and profits of office which he could derive from the king's favour. In these circumstances it is not to be wondered at if he acquired a reputation for being extremely avaricious. In accumulating crown pensions and offices to the tune of £3,000 a year, he inevitably trod on a few toes, and it was only a matter of time before he offended the wrong man. In the event, it turned out to be the earl of Warwick, later to be known as the kingmaker. Twenty-five years old in 1453, this ambitious man was to prove a deadly enemy. A momentous bargain was struck: in return for York's active help against the Percies, the Nevilles would support his attempt to oust Somerset and reform the government. Other lords also swung round to York's side. His claim to be the senior member of the council was much stronger now that the king himself was no longer capable of presiding over its meetings. Shortly before Christmas, Somerset was confined to the Tower, and York's old charges relating to his conduct of the war were revived.

Even in the Tower, Somerset was a force to be reckoned with. According to a London newsletter written in January 1454 he employed friars and seamen to act as his spies and enter the house of each lord in the land. And what sinister design lay behind the story that his billeting officer had rented all the lodgings round and about the Tower, in Thames Street, Mart Lane, St Katherine's and Tower Hill? But scaremongering of this kind probably tells us more about the tense atmosphere of the time than it does about Somerset's real plans. With him in prison, the leadership of the court party had passed to the queen. Margaret's position, of course, had recently been transformed by the fact that on 13 October 1453 she had given birth to an heir to the throne. She now had a son, Prince Edward, for whose rights she would fight with all the fierce energy at her command. Were he to die, however, York would once again stand closest to the throne. Not surprisingly, the queen looked at York with redoubled suspicion and was determined to prevent his being appointed regent of the kingdom in the parliament which was due to meet in February 1454. According to the same newsletter: 'Item, the Queen hath made a bill of five articles, desiring these articles to be granted; whereof the first is that she desireth to have the whole rule of this land.' With the queen and the duke of York lining up against each other, it was apparent that this was going to be an uncomfortable session of parliament. While the avowed supporters of both sides entered London in force, most people were reluctant to commit themselves. As a result, so many lords stayed away that York, who had been empowered to open parliament as the king's lieutenant, went to the lengths of actually fining peers for non-attendance – the first and only time in English history that this had happened.

The first few weeks of parliament were characterized by the

manoeuvres and counter-manoeuvres of the queen and the duke of York. On 14 March, York's old ally, the earl of Devon, was formally cleared of the charge of treason brought against him for his part in the field at Dartford. On the next day, the queen's baby son was created prince of Wales. The death of the chancellor, Cardinal Kemp, on 22 March finally precipitated a decision, since it was beyond the customary competence of the council to make a new appointment to so central an office. Moreover, the second item of the queen's bill was: 'that she may make the Chancellor, the Treasurer, the Privy Seal, with sheriffs and all other officers of this land'. Even so, the lords were terribly reluctant and looked desperately for a sign from the king that would absolve them from taking the responsibility upon themselves. They commissioned twelve of their number to ride to Windsor on 25 March and try to discuss the matter with Henry. An account of this pathetic and fruitless mission was then entered into the official record of the parliament's proceedings.

And anon after the king's dinner was done ... the bishop of Chichester showed to the King's Highness the first three articles, as was advised by the lords ere they went; that is to say, the humble recommendation of the lords to the King's Highness, their great desire for his good health, and their great diligence in this parliament. And then forasmuch as it liked not the King's Highness to give any answer to the said articles, the bishop of Chichester declared and opened to the King's Highness the other matters contained in his instructions; to the which matters they could get no answer nor sign, not for any prayer or desire, lamentable cheer or exhortation, nor for anything that any of them could do or say, to their great sorrow and discomfort. And then the bishop of Winchester said to the King's Highness that the lords had not dined, but that they should go dine them, and wait upon his Highness again after dinner. And so after dinner they came to the King's Highness in the same place where they were before; and there they moved and stirred him, by all the ways and means that they could think, to have answer of the matters aforesaid, but they could have none; and from that place they willed the King's Highness to go into another chamber, and so he was led between two men into the chamber where he lieth; and there the lords moved and stirred the King's Highness the third time, by all the means and ways that they could think, to have answer of the said matters, and also desired to have knowledge of him, if it should like his Highness that they should wait upon him any longer, and to have answer at his leisure, but they could have no answer, neither word nor sign.

Unable to get any help from an insane king, the lords eventually appointed York as protector – a position they defined as being chief councillor with a special responsibility for the defence of the realm, both against foreign enemies and rebels. Five days later, the earl of Salisbury became the new chancellor. York then set about reasserting the government's authority. An act of parliament was passed, imposing forfeiture on all who ignored a summons to appear before the council. Another act denounced wardens of the Marches who illegally extended their powers southwards into Yorkshire. Although these could undoubtedly be construed as anti-Percy moves, they also indicated a determination to come to grips with the problem of the provinces and the disintegration of royal authority.

The Percies, of course, had no doubt how these measures should be interpreted, particularly since they were followed by a series of orders commanding them to appear before the council – orders which they naturally had no intention of obeying. By this time they had found an ally of their own, not as powerful as York certainly, but a duke nonetheless: Henry Holland, duke of Exeter, hereditary admiral of England and constable of the Tower. Like the Percies, Holland had a quarrel over property with Cromwell. In addition, he had, until fairly recently, been a ward of the duke of York and he may have harboured a grudge against his former guardian. Such grievances, however, hardly constituted an effective rallying cry for rebellion. Holland's central demand was that he, not York, should be protector. This claim was based on the fact that, as a grandson of Henry IV's sister Elizabeth, he was one of Henry VI's closest living relatives. He is alleged to have offered tax relief to all those who would swear allegiance to him. Although his abilities in no way matched his ambitions, Exeter could usefully serve as a figurehead for the Percy revolt. Early in 1454, he and Egremont had met and sworn an oath of mutual assistance. On 14 May they met again and rode into York. Dissension among the citizens, possibly exacerbated by York's economic problems, opened up prospects for rebels who wanted to capture the second city in the kingdom. For five days they held York, but when Duke Richard, accompanied by Cromwell, arrived, they promptly fled. The protector had wasted little time in following up his words with action. This was precisely the kind of thing which Henry VI had signally failed to do, and doubtless York was anxious that men should observe the contrast between them.

In his anxiety to act quickly, however, it seems that York had not brought enough troops with him. For a while he was more or less held a prisoner in York while Egremont and Exeter overran much of the shire. But by the beginning of June the protector had a force large enough to take control of the situation; for the rest of that month he remained in the north, setting in motion the judicial processes which were meant to bring hundreds of Percy supporters to book. Following the collapse of his shortlived attempt to oust York from the protectorship, Exeter made his way incognito to London and then took sanctuary in Westminster Abbey. York, still playing the part of the stern guardian of law and order, returned to London and removed him, much to the consternation of the abbot and his monks. Exeter spent the next nine months in gaol in Pontefract Castle. York went north again in August but Egremont and his followers remained at large throughout the summer and autumn. Finally it was left to the protagonists of the Battle of Heworth Moor to meet again and decide the issue of their private war for a while at least. On 31 October or 1 November 1454 Egremont clashed with Sir Thomas and Sir John Neville at Stamford Bridge, the site of the last great victory of Anglo-Saxon England. The flight of Peter Lound, bailiff of the nearby Percy manor of Pocklington, taking with him two hundred of Egremont's retinue, lost them the day. Egremont and his brother Richard Percy were captured. The Nevilles at once brought a civil action against Egremont for damages, and he was condemned to pay £11,200. Since he had an income of barely £100 a year, he had no hope of paying this huge sum. It was simply a means of keeping him and his brother in debtor's prison. So they were taken to Newgate and remained there for the next two years. When eventually they left the prison, it was in a characteristically adventurous fashion. A warder was bribed and weapons smuggled in. Then, during the night of 13 November 1456, they attacked and wounded the keeper and released the other prisoners. While the latter climbed on to the prison roof and fought off attempts to recapture them, the Percy brothers made good their escape on horses which had been held in readiness for them. In November 1454, however, not only were they still in prison, but so too were York's main enemies, the dukes of Somerset and Exeter. York could look back over the events of the last twelve months with a good deal of satisfaction.

Then, on 9 January 1455, Edmund Clere wrote a letter to John Paston:

Right well-beloved cousin, I recommend me to you, letting you know such tidings as we have.

Blessed be God, the king is well amended, and hath been since Christmas Day... On Monday afternoon the Queen came to him, and brought my Lord Prince with her. And then he asked what the prince's name was, and the Queen told him Edward, and then he held up his hands and thanked God. And he said he never knew him till that time, nor knew what was said to him, nor knew where he had been whilst he hath been sick till now.

And he saith he is in charity with all the world, and so he would all the lords were.

And now he saith matins of Our Lady, and evensong, and heareth his Mass devoutly.

But, as has been well said, 'If Henry's insanity had been a tragedy, his recovery was a national disaster.' York's protectorate was over and the king, no matter how incompetent, could not be refused the right to please himself in the choice of his advisers. The lords picked their own councillors, controlled their own households, so how could the king be any less free than his subjects? Although York had clearly been partisan in the Neville–Percy dispute, he had, on the whole, made an effort to rule the country with the help of a fairly broad-based council and administration. With Henry's return to what passed for his right mind, the administration again fell into the hands of a narrow clique. On 4 February 1455 Somerset was released from prison. A month later Salisbury resigned the chancellorship. His position on the council had become untenable as the result of an alliance between the courtiers, headed by Somerset, and the Percy family. The earl of Northumberland, one of his sons – the bishop of Carlisle – and his old friend Lord Clifford, were all present at the meeting which witnessed Salisbury's resignation. Following decades in which he had held himself very much aloof from Westminster, it seems that the success of the York–Neville alignment in 1454 had persuaded Northumberland that he must adopt a similar policy. And so the sides for the first battle in the civil war were drawn up: York and the Nevilles against the court and the Percies.

A little later York, Salisbury and Warwick left London without taking their formal leave of the king. They acted precipitately, apparently afraid that Somerset was plotting their destruction. Possibly they had already decided to raise an army, seeing no other way in which they could recover their political advantage. In mid-April they were summoned to attend a great council at Leicester on 21 May. Its stated purpose was 'to provide for the king's safety' and this York and the Nevilles took to be aimed against them, since the phrase, as they pointed out, 'of common presumption implieth a mistrust to some persons'. The assembly was to include representatives of the shires, but they were to be representatives nominated by the court, not elected members. It looks as though Somerset dared not run the risk of open elections to parliament resulting in the return of a pro-York house of commons. Nor, knowing his own unpopularity with the Londoners, did he dare risk a meeting at Westminster. Unquestionably the Leicester council was to be a 'put-up job'. Possibly the intention was to put York on trial, but the meeting never took place and we cannot be sure of this. What is clear is that Leicester was not the first move in a campaign to dispose of York and the Nevilles by military means. Somerset was always a politician rather than a soldier. He made no attempt to mobilize an army until after he had heard that a large Yorkist force was advancing rapidly southwards – and by then it was too late. Somerset and the court had been taken by surprise – so much for the spies which Somerset was rumoured to have in every noble's household.

It looks as though Somerset's first inkling of what was afoot came on 18 May while the court was still at Westminster. Measures were at once put in hand to raise an army. Then, on Wednesday 21 May, not wishing to remain in such dangerous proximity to London, Somerset and the royal household set off for St Albans where they expected to await the arrival of borough contingents and the retinues of absent magnates. Not all of those who accompanied the king on this occasion could be relied on to support the king's favourite. James Butler, earl of Wiltshire, whom Somerset had recently appointed treasurer, was a member of the inner circle. Northumberland and Clifford might well relish the chance to strike a blow at the Nevilles; on the other hand, York's old ally, the earl of Devon was there and William Neville, Lord Fauconberg, would surely prefer to be on the side of his brother Salisbury. A third group, amongst whom the outstanding figure was Humphrey Stafford, duke of Buckingham, though ultimately loyal to the king, would be extremely reluctant to take up arms on behalf of Somerset. In many ways Henry VI's advance towards St Albans resembled a court progress rather than an army on the march: only the fact that the queen was not accompanying them revealed the seriousness of the situation. By ten o'clock in the morning they had just reached Kilburn, when they were overtaken by John Saye, keeper of the privy palace at Westminster, bearing a letter sent by the Yorkists. In it they protested their loyalty to the king, their willingness to renounce all private quarrels in return for the appointment of a council of their own choosing and disclaimed responsibility for anything 'inconvenient' that might occur. This was reading matter which can have contained little which was not already known to King Henry and Somerset; they continued on their way undeterred and spent the night of 21/22 May at Watford, sixteen miles from Westminster. At two o'clock in the morning of Thursday another messenger arrived with another letter from York, Salisbury and Warwick. Again it had nothing fresh to say, but these night-time comings and goings are a sign that every hour was precious. Time was running out.

In the early hours of Thursday morning the royalists left Watford, intending to reach St Albans in time for dinner. They had not, however, travelled very far when yet another messenger arrived. This one bore the startling news that the Yorkist lords were close at hand. Since their last letter had been sent from Ware, twenty-two miles away to the north, and written only the day before, Somerset had clearly not expected them to follow so quickly behind, but they must have left Ware that same day and spent the night somewhere near St Albans. By sheer speed of movement they had succeeded in catching their enemy before his mobilization had been completed. Several of the magnates summoned by Somerset arrived at St Albans on 23 May, one day too late. All this suggests determined and competent generalship in the Yorkist camp.

Hastily Henry VI took counsel with his lords. The messenger had made it clear that they were outnumbered – perhaps by two to three thousand – and too close to be able to retreat in safety. In this difficult position Henry had to choose between conflicting advice. Somerset and his friends argued that they should stay where they were and prepare for battle in the open country. Another group, whose spokesman was Buckingham, favoured carrying on as planned. Buckingham believed that, much as the Yorkists loathed Somerset, they would, in the last resort, prefer to negotiate with a man of known moderate views like himself, rather than step over the brink and attack the person of the king. In order to create an atmosphere favourable to negotiation it would be better if the royalists were to dine in peace at St Albans. Henry had to make up his mind quickly and, for once, he decided against Somerset. At Dartford, after all, York had drawn back; perhaps Buckingham was right and York and his friends would do so again. The king dismissed Somerset from the office of constable and in his place appointed Buckingham.

The royalists reached St Albans at about nine o'clock in the morning. They found the Yorkists encamped in Key Field, east of the gardens behind the houses in Holywell and St Peter's Street. Henry took up his quarters in the town centre, in the market-place, from where he could most easily direct operations. Heralds then went to and fro between the sides. This civilized behaviour was normal procedure before a battle, practised in the hope of avoiding bloodshed – and indeed sometimes

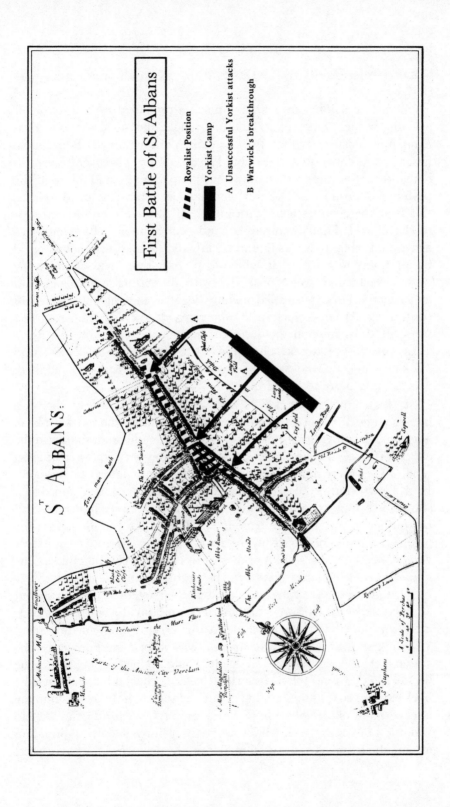

First Battle of St Albans

Royalist Position
Yorkist Camp

A Unsuccessful Yorkist attacks
B Warwick's breakthrough

practised successfully, as at Dartford in 1452 and, later, in 1459 at Ludlow.

On this occasion, however, the negotiators failed to find a way of averting battle. Somerset, in fact, had judged the mood in the Yorkist camp more accurately than Buckingham. York remained obdurate. So far as he was concerned, there could be no compromise over his central demand that Somerset be handed over to prison; he had followed the path of compromise at Dartford and had been humiliated. Moreover, this time the Nevilles were with him, and they were no influence for moderation. If Henry refused to hand over Somerset, Buckingham's attempted mediation was bound to fail, and further discussions could be used only to win time in which to prepare the defence. Inevitably these preparations were observed with increasing impatience and anger by the Yorkists and skirmishing began even while talks were still continuing. At ten o'clock in the morning, as York's herald returned from his third mission to the town, he met the duke and his army advancing to the attack. They had waited long enough. 'Now', said York, 'we must do what we can.' He had crossed the Rubicon and there was nothing more to be said.

St Albans, though unwalled, was certainly not defenceless; the town houses could themselves act as a wall surrounding the market-place. The roads leading into it were blocked by barricades and, thanks to the efforts of successive abbots of St Albans, these barriers were in good repair. They were manned by forces under Lord Clifford's command. In the town centre the royal standard was displayed as a sign that a state of war now existed. In spite of this, Henry and his household did not bother to put all their armour on. They were confident that the barricades would be too strong for York. They were right. Despite their advantage in numbers, the Yorkists were soon in great difficulties. The narrowness of the lanes up which they surged, meant that only a few men could engage at a time and that, bunched together, they presented an easy target for Clifford's archers. For an hour the royalist defence held firm and the attack faltered. At this critical moment the earl of Warwick showed why it was that he was to become known as 'the kingmaker'. Seeing that the barricades could not be taken by storm, he decided to go round them. Ignoring the lanes, he led his men into the back gardens so that they could fan out and then fight their way into the backs of some of the houses in Holywell Street. Once inside they were to tear the houses down, in this way creating further entry points and forcing the royalists to draw off men from the defence of the barricades.

The ploy worked. Sir Robert Ogle, in command of six hundred men from the Scottish Marches, took the houses between two inns, the Sign of the Cross Keys and the Chequers, and broke into the market-place. A sudden blare of trumpets and the ringing war-cry of 'A Warwick! A Warwick!' announced the success of this flanking manoeuvre. The royalists in the centre sounded the alarm and flew to arms, but once again they were too late. The decisive breach had been made.

At first the king's household put up a brave show of resistance, but they were in no condition to withstand the hail of arrows now descending upon them. Many Lancastrians, including Henry himself, received face, neck, arm and hand wounds – sure signs that they were caught up in the fighting before they had finished arming themselves. After half an hour or so, they broke and scattered. Some managed to get clean out of the town. Discarding their tell-tale armour as they went, they escaped into the relative safety of the countryside. Some, like the earl of Wiltshire and the duke of Buckingham, withdrew into the abbey where they could hope for the sanctuary of a famous shrine. Others, King Henry and Somerset among them, were driven to retreat into the nearest available building. The king of England, wounded in the neck, sheltered in a tanner's cottage, while his standard lay abandoned in the street.

As soon as it was clear that the field of battle was his, York ordered the king's removal to more dignified quarters in the abbey. He then turned his attention to the Castle Inn, at the corner of Holywell and St Peter's Streets, where Somerset had taken refuge. For him there was to be no escape. York's soldiers surrounded the inn and broke down the doors. Knowing only too well the bitterness of York's feelings towards him, Somerset, after a hasty consultation with his followers, resolved to die fighting. Striking out to right and left, Somerset charged into the midst of his enemies. He was said to have killed four men with his own hand before he was out-felled by an axe and then hacked to death. According to one contemporary chronicler, he 'had heard a fantastic prophecy that he was going to die under a castle and for this reason had persuaded the king never to summon him to Windsor Castle'. If this story pleased an unknown chronicler's sense of the irony of an unrelenting providence, there can be no doubt that Somerset's death mightily pleased the duke of York. Equally, the Nevilles had cause to celebrate the deaths of Northumberland and Clifford. In all, only three Lancastrian nobles were killed in the defence of St Albans, and the fact that it was precisely these three is certainly suspicious. The battle had been fought over the issue of the right governance of the realm, but it was also an act of private vengeance; 'and when the seyde lordes were slayne the batayle was ceased'. There were not many casualties – the best estimates suggest that less than a hundred, mostly Lancastrians, were killed – and for this reason the first battle of St Albans has been described as 'a scuffle in the streets', but the deaths of Somerset, Northumberland and Clifford suggest that York and the Nevilles had intended, not merely to defeat their enemies, but to kill them.

The problem for the Yorkists was that they still claimed to be loyal to Henry VI. In these circumstances how could they remove Somerset and his allies from their positions of power on the king's council except by taking their lives? In the moment of victory they might be able to force Henry to dismiss Somerset, but in the long run they could not prevent the king from reasserting his authority over his own court and inviting back a friend whom he liked and trusted. That this would happen was as certain as anything in politics could be – particularly while Margaret was at Henry's side. York and the Nevilles had therefore pushed themselves into a position where they could either depose the king or kill the king's friends. Such was the majesty of kingship, so great its sacred quality as the focus of national life, that killing seemed the more acceptable course of action. But the legacy of this policy was the blood feud.

With Somerset gone, the duke of York was prepared to spare those nobles who, he felt, would not stand in the way of his taking his rightful place in the government of the realm. He sent a herald into the abbey and told the king to hand over Buckingham and Wiltshire if he wanted to save their lives. Henry, who had little choice in the matter, agreed. Buckingham was handed over, but Wiltshire was nowhere to be found. Somehow he had slipped through the net. Unlike Buckingham who had suffered three arrow wounds, Wiltshire seems to have come through the battle unscathed. According to popular opinion, he had fought with his heels, being a pretty knight whose main aim in life was to preserve his good looks. At a pinch, however, he was apparently less concerned about fine clothes, for it was rumoured that he had made his way through the Yorkist lines dressed in a monk's habit. By this time the Yorkist soldiers were presumably fully absorbed in enjoying the rewards of victory: despoiling dead and captured Lancastrians and plundering the townsfolk. A poorly dressed monk might pass unnoticed where a wealthy churchman like William Percy, bishop of Carlisle, was set upon and stripped of jewels and horses.

While the looting continued, York entered the abbey. Coming into the king's presence, he dropped on his knees before him, begging forgiveness for any offence he might have committed and lamenting the fact that Henry's life had been imperilled. He assured the king that he had never intended to harm him, only the traitors around him. There being nothing else he could do, Henry pardoned the duke and received him into his royal grace. The duke was on his knees, but it was the king who was the captive. Next day, Friday 23 May, Henry was escorted to London. York rode on his right hand, Salisbury on his left, while Warwick went on ahead, bearing the sword.

Seven

MARGARET OF ANJOU: THE WARLIKE QUEEN, 1455-9

Two days later, on Whitsunday 1455, Henry VI wore his crown in state at St Paul's. Appearances were preserved, but for the moment it was York who held the reins of power and patronage. Already the offices which Somerset and his friends had accumulated had been redistributed. York became constable, Warwick was made captain of Calais (both posts formerly held by Somerset), and Viscount Bourchier appointed treasurer in place of Wiltshire. On Monday, 26 May, writs were sent out summoning parliament. To secure his position York needed to win the collaboration of a wide circle of peers and commons alike; at St Albans, after all, he had been accompanied by only a small minority of peers, some Nevilles and Bourchiers. But compared with Somerset who had relied almost exclusively on the court, York was fairly confident that he could win the support of the political nation at large. Parliament assembled on 9 July. Its chief business was to secure the passage of a bill blaming Somerset and two of his minions, Thomas Thorp and William Joseph, for the inconvenience at St Albans. Somerset, Thorp and Joseph were said to have concealed the letters which York had sent to the king on 20 and 21 May – letters which were now being given wide circulation in order to prove that the Yorkists were, in fact, loyal subjects who had done their best to avoid bloodshed. By fixing responsibility on a few named individuals, everyone else could feel exonerated and free from the fear of recrimination. In this way some of the tension could be taken out of the atmosphere and a climate favourable to a policy of reconciliation be created. The bill which became law on 18 July went on to grant immunity to the 'Yorkist army' and their sympathizers throughout the country for everything that happened at St Albans. This parliamentary pardon was an attempt to devise a more effective amnesty than the general pardon which had been offered by the crown for all those who had taken part in the Dartford fiasco in 1452. When one of York's followers had pleaded this pardon he was told that it would not help him even if it were sealed with a whole cartful of wax. It was hoped that the added authority of parliament would make it less easy to pour scorn on the pardon of 1455. But as supposed champions of reform York and the Nevilles had to do more than look to their own future safety. Fresh proposals to regularize and limit the expenditure of the royal household were enacted. The promise of government economies was well calculated to win the hearts of taxpayers, as was also the last act of this parliamentary session: a proclamation declaring that Humphrey, duke of Gloucester, had lived and died a true subject. This was a clever move, since it associated the Yorkists with a man who, whatever his real worth, had come to stand in the public imagination for the vigorous and successful prosecution of the war in France in contrast with the air of failure and defeatism which clung to the court party. As the myth of the 'good duke Humphrey' gathered momentum, so it provided the Yorkist movement with a patron whose name they could invoke in moments of doubt or crisis.

The trouble they took to obtain a parliamentary pardon shows that York and the Nevilles knew perfectly well how precarious their hold on power was. The tense atmosphere which prevailed in London during that summer and autumn is well illustrated by a prophecy reported in a letter written to John Paston:

It is talked that one Doctor Green, a priest, hath calculated that by St Andrew's Day next coming shall be the greatest battle that was since the battle of Shrewsbury, and it shall fall between the Bishop's Inn of Salisbury [in the Strand] and Westminster Bars, and there shall die 7 lords, whereof 3 should be bishops. All this and much more is talked and reported. I trust to God it shall not fall so ... so much rumour is here. What it meaneth I know not.

In an effort to consolidate his position, York planned to secure a second term of office as protector when parliament reassembled in November. A private war in the south-west and the need for a strong hand in suppressing riots provided a convenient justification for this step, since Henry VI, never strong, was at this time not even well enough to attend parliament. York, therefore, was already acting as the king's lieutenant in parliament when William Burley – a member of York's council – led a commons' deputation to the lords asking for the appointment of a 'Protector and Defensor of this land'. The lords were reluctant, but the news from the south-west grew daily more alarming and was ably orchestrated by Burley in order to achieve the desired end. Within a week the lords bowed to this pressure and, on 19 November 1455, Henry gave his assent to York's nomination. Burley may have exaggerated the extent of the threat in the west country – 'unless these riots and disorders are firmly dealt with, the land will be lost, and if that land is lost, it might be the cause of the subversion of the whole realm' – nonetheless the trouble was real enough. The Courtenays and the Bonvilles were at it again.

In the summer of 1455, faced by the disintegration of the court party following the battle of St Albans, Lord Bonville judged it wiser to come to an understanding with the Yorkists. This change of allegiance was sealed by the marriage of his grandson and heir to a daughter of the earl of Salisbury. Bonville's manoeuvre infuriated the Courtenays and they reacted savagely. Their first victim was Nicholas Radford, Bonville's legal adviser. On 23 October a gang led by the earl of Devon's son, Sir Thomas Courtenay, the Egremont of the south-west, attacked Radford's house at Upcott, on the southern edge of Exmoor. A petition presented to parliament by Radford's heir, despite its legal jargon, gives a frighteningly graphic account of the events of that night:

They made there a great shout and the gates of the said place set a-fire. And the said Nicholas Radford woke, and hearing a great noise and stirring about his said place, arose and opened his window of his chamber. And he seeing the said gates on fire, asked what they were that were there and whether there were any gentlemen among them. And the said Nicholas Philippe answered and said, 'Here is Sir Thomas Courtenay.'

And then the said Sir Thomas Courtenay hearing the said Nicholas Radford speak, called to him, saying in the wise, 'Come down Radford and speak with me.' And then the said Nicholas Radford knowing the voice of the said Sir Thomas Courtenay knight answered saying to him these words: 'Sir, and ye will promise me on your faith and truth, and as ye are true knight and gentleman, that I shall have no bodily harm, ne hurt of my goods, I will come down to you.' And then the said Sir Thomas Courtenay knight answered the said Nicholas Radford again, and said to him in this wise, 'Radford come ye to me, and I promise you as I am true knight and gentleman ye shall be save both of your body and of your goods.' Whereupon the said Nicholas Radford trusting faithfully upon that promise, came out of his chamber with torch light, and did set open the gates and let him in – and then pressed in with him the said misgoverned people And the said Nicholas Radford seeing so much people within his said place, was sore a-feared, and said to Sir Thomas Courtenay knight, 'Sir, what do all this people here?' and he answered again and said, 'Radford, ye shall have none harm,' and thereupon the said Sir Thomas Courtenay had the said Nicholas Radford bring him to his chamber whereas he lay in, and he did so, and there the said Sir Thomas C. both ate and drank, and from thence came out into the hall, and the said Nicholas R. with him, and there stood together at a cupboard, and drank of his wine. And there the said Sir Thomas Courtenay subtly held the said Nicholas R. with tales, while the said Sir T. Courtenay's men brake up the chamber doors and coffers of the said Nicholas R., and then and there the said mis-doers abovenamed and others, the said Nicholas Radford of £300 and more in money numbered being in his trussing coffers, and other goods and jewels, bedding, gowns, furs, books, and ornaments of his chapel, to the value of £1,000 marks and more, feloniously robbed, and the goods they trussed together and with the said Nicholas Radford's own horse, carried them away.

And among other rifling then and there, they found the said Nicholas Radford's wife in her bed, sore sick as she hath been this two year and more, and rolled her out of her bed, and took away the sheets that she lay in, and trussed them with the remnant of the said goods.

And after that, the said Sir Thomas Courtenay left his talking with the said Nicholas R. at the cupboard, and said to the said N.R. – 'Have do Radford, for thou must go with me to my lord my father', and he said he would go with him all ready, and make him ready to ride, and bade his servant make him ready an horse, and his servant answered him, 'Sir your horse has been taken all away and charged with your goods', and the said Nicholas R. hearing that, said to the said Sir Thomas C., 'Sir, I am aged, and may not well go upon my feet, and therefore I pray you that I may ride'; and the said Sir Thomas Courtenay answered again in this wise, 'Have no fear, Radford thou shalt ride enough anon, and therefore come on with me.' And he went forth with him a stone's cast and more from his said place and there the said Sir Thomas Courtenay knight communed privily with Nicholas Philip, Thomas P., and John Amore and forthwith spurred his horse and rode his way and said 'Fare well Radford'. And the said Nicholas P., Thomas P. and John Amore and other forthwith turned upon the said Nicholas Radford, and then and there the said Nicholas P. with a glaive smote the said Nicholas Radford a hideous deadly stroke overthwart the face, and felled him to the ground, and then the said Nicholas Philip gave him another stroke upon his head behind that the brain fell out of head. And the said Thomas Philipe that time and then with a knife feloniously cut the throat of the said Nicholas Radford, and the said John Amore that time and there with a long dagger smote the said Nicholas Radford behind on his back to the heart. And so the said Nicholas P., T.P. and John Amore thus gave the said Nicholas Radford several deadly wounds, and him then and there feloniously and horribly slew and murdered.... And forthwith after the said horrible murder and felony thus done, the said Sir Thomas Courtenay with all the said misdoers rode to Tiverton in the said shire of Devonshire where the said earl the Friday next after the said Thursday feloniously recetted, comforted, and harboured the said Sir Thomas Courtenay, N.P., T.P., and J.M.

and other misdoers abovenamed, with the said remnant of misdoers with the said goods, knowing them to have done the said murder, robbery and felony in the form aforesaid.

And the Monday next after the said Thursday, Henry Courtenay late of Tiverton in the shire of Devon squire, brother to the said Sir Thomas C. knight, and godson to the said Nicholas Radford, with divers of the said misdoers, came to the said place where the body of the said Nicholas Radford lay in his chapel, and there and then the said Henry C. and those misdoers took upon them the office of coroner without authority and made one of them sit down, and called afore him an inquest of the persons that murdered the said Nicholas Radford, by such estrange names as no man might know them by, ne never men heard tell such dwelling in that country. The which misdoers by such names as they were called scornfully appearing, and made such a presentment as pleased them, and such as is reported that they should indict the said Nicholas Radford of his own death, in great despite and derision of your laws. And anon after that, the said Henry and divers of the said misdoers with other misdoers to a great number, constrained certain persons there that were servants to the said Nicholas Radford to bear his body to the church . . . And there the said misdoers took the body of the said Nicholas Radford out of his chest that he was laid in, and rolled him out of his sheet in the which he was wound; and there and then cast the body all naked into the pit, and with such stuff of stones as the said Nicholas Radford had late purveyed for his tomb to be made there, cast upon his body and head, and it horribly brake and quashed, having no more compassion ne pity than though it had be a Jew or a Saracen.

Radford's murder was the signal for the Courtenays to muster all their forces at Tiverton. On 3 November an army, said to be a thousand strong, entered Exeter and took charge of the city. While some of them ransacked Bonville's town house, others went on to lay siege to Powderham Castle, the strongly-fortified residence of Sir Philip Courtenay. For seven weeks the earl of Devon held Exeter and besieged Powderham. The area between the rivers Exe and Axe became the theatre of a local war of raid and counter-raid. On both sides houses were pillaged, cattle driven off, and plenty of plunder taken. While York at Westminster used these events to push through his appointment as protector, it was left to Lord Bonville to try to retrieve the situation. But the task was beyond his resources. Twice he led a force to the relief of Powderham, and twice he was driven back.

Not until after the second of Bonville's defeats, at Clyst on 15 December, did Richard of York take action, but when he eventually did move, the effect was instantaneous. As soon as he heard of the protector's approach, Devon abandoned his war. He set out to meet York. At Shaftesbury in Dorset he submitted tamely to being arrested and was sent to the Tower. It is all very reminiscent of a modern prime minister's method of allowing a dispute to come to a head and boil for a while before he intervenes, demonstrating not only that he can bring peace but also that others cannot. But York, of course, had other matters besides the Devon–Bonville quarrel to worry about during the autumn and winter months of 1455. Above all, perhaps, he wanted to settle the problem of Calais.

It is hard to overestimate the military importance of Calais. According to Philip de Commynes it was 'Christendom's finest captaincy'. For more than a hundred years since its capture by Edward III in 1347 the town had been in English hands. While other lands in France were won and lost according to the ebb and flow of the tide of war, Calais remained English, 'a little bit of England beyond the sea'. For a brief while indeed, from 1542 until its eventual fall in 1558, Calais was to send an MP to Westminster just as though it was an English borough. Throughout the fifteenth century Calais served as a reminder of Edward III's claim to the French crown, and for as long as the idea of conquering remained alive, it functioned as a convenient gateway into and out of France. As late as 1544 Henry VIII, that unpleasant but thoroughly conventional king, was still using Calais as a base for an invasion of France. In 1415 Henry V had been on his way to Calais when he met the French on St Crispin's Day; and after his untimely death his body was taken home via Calais. By 1455 when everything else in France, both in the south and in the north, had been lost, Calais remained the only English possession across the Channel, and in Calais was concentrated a great part of England's wealth and military strength. At times the town of Calais and the other castles in the March, Guînes, Rysbank and Hammes, contained as many as a thousand soldiers – by far the largest military establishment at the crown's disposal, and its only standing army. Control of this strong-point would be a priceless asset to any regime, and York was naturally determined to possess it. Unfortunately, as he knew only too well, this was easier said than done.

Calais cost money, a great deal of money. In the three years from June 1451 to June 1454 the wages of the garrison averaged over £17,000 per annum. Then there were the maintenance and improvement of the fortifications, which were very necessary now that Calais was the only place which Charles VII still had to recapture. In 1453 £9,300 was set aside for this purpose. By fifteenth-century standards these were immense sums. In some years Calais could have cost the king as much as a quarter of his English revenues. Fortunately the town was able to make some contribution to its own upkeep. Ever since 1363 England's export trade in wool had been channelled through Calais. Edward III had granted a monopoly of this trade to a company of the greater merchants engaged in it, on condition that all their wool was taken there and sold in Calais market. This made it easier for the king to control the trade and collect customs dues. It also had the effect of concentrating the cash received for the wool in the hands of a privileged company – the Company of the Staple – and their anxiety to preserve their privileged status made it hard for them to refuse when the king asked for a loan. Since the wool trade provided, and the Calais garrison absorbed, a substantial part of the royal revenue, it was an easy and natural step to link the two. It became normal practice to set aside part of the wool custom in order to help pay the garrison whose job it was to guard the warehouses where the sacks of wool awaited the arrival of the foreign purchasers. In theory it was an excellent system, but there were two problems. The underlying one was a gradual change in the structure of England's foreign trade. Each year fewer and fewer sacks of raw wool were being sent abroad; in their place greater quantities of woollen cloth were exported. But whereas the declining trade was channelled through Calais, the developing one was not. Cloth merchants were free to seek their markets wherever they could. In consequence the wool custom brought in less money each year, and each year the gap between Calais income and Calais expenses grew wider. It was up to the English Exchequer to bridge the gap, and this brings us to the second and more immediate problem. As always there were too many calls on the resources of the Exchequer. This meant that the garrison, like other government creditors, generally had to wait for their money. But if the soldiers found their pay too much in arrears, they had a resource not available to most other creditors: they could mutiny and, by seizing the wool which they were supposed to guard, they could win for themselves a valuable bargaining counter. In the last half-century the Calais garrison had mutinied roughly once every ten years.

When York became protector in March 1454 he also, on paper at least, took over the captaincy of Calais from Somerset. In fact, however, neither he nor his officers were ever able to enter the port. In May the garrison mutinied and refused to open the gates until they had received either some payment of their arrears or licence to sell the wool which they had seized. York, who was generally preoccupied with business in the north of England – the Neville–Percy feud and Exeter's rebellion – refused to authorize any payment until his admission was assured. The negotiations were still deadlocked when Henry VI recovered his senses and Somerset recovered the captaincy. Immediately after St Albans, York bestowed Calais on the earl of Warwick, the man who had done more than anyone else to win the battle for him – 'the most courageous and manliest knight living', as he was described by a London chronicler. But Warwick, in 1455, faced exactly the same problems as York in 1454, with the difference that the garrison's arrears were by now greatly increased. Not until January 1456 was the basis for an agreement finally worked out. For the Company of the Staple the prolonged closure of Calais to trade was disastrous, so to end the dispute they eventually agreed to lend the government the £25,000 needed to meet all the arrears. By April 1456 the bulk of the money had been paid over, the gates opened and the mutineeers pardoned. During the summer the earl of Warwick marched into Calais to take up his command.

York's second protectorate lasted barely three months. On 25 February 1456 the king came into parliament and relieved him of his commission. But Henry was still 'in charity with all the world' and, earlier in the month, a London letter-writer reported that the king wanted York as 'his chief and principal councillor'. Once Henry was fit again there was no justification for a protectorate, but York and the Nevilles remained the most influential group in the council. The threat to their position came not from the peace-loving king, but from Margaret of Anjou. She was, said the same letter-writer, 'a great and intensely active woman, for she spares no pains to pursue her business towards an end and conclusion favourable to her power'. Twice she had seen York grasp the reality of power, and twice she had seen her friends scattered, the expenditure of the royal household cut back and the patronage of the court eroded. At all costs she was determined to prevent a third protectorate. Naturally, she found ready allies in the private enemies of York and the Nevilles. Much less keen to see the *status quo* overturned and the country once again thrown into a state of confusion were the Londoners, especially the Company of the Staple, and the administration. This meant that Westminster was not the place where the queen felt most comfortable. So early in the summer she left the neighbourhood of London and, taking Prince Edward with her, travelled round the midland castles of the royal duchy of Lancaster as well as the castles of her son's earldom of Chester. She was beginning to carve out a new power base for herself. By early June one of John Paston's London correspondents was commenting: 'My lord York is still at Sandal [in the West Riding]. He watches the queen [at Chester] and she watches him.' She was, after all, a French princess and this was how French kings governed – keeping well away from the turbulence of Paris.

For several months Henry remained behind, living in his palaces near London, but towards the end of August he went to join his wife at Kenilworth. Once the queen had persuaded him to leave Westminster she could use him as a means of taking the control of appointments into her own hands. In September her own private chancellor Laurence Booth became keeper of the privy seal. In October a new chancellor and a new treasurer were appointed. Next month the treasurer, the second earl of Shrewsbury, was said to have joined with the feckless Exeter, now released from prison, and the new duke of Somerset, seeking revenge for his father's death, in an attempt to ambush Warwick on his way to London. A few days later Egremont escaped from Newgate. His elder brother, the new earl of Northumberland, came to court in February 1457 and was given a new contract as warden of Berwick and the east March. Later that year Salisbury's brother, the bishop of Durham, died and was replaced by Laurence Booth.

That the political tide was flowing against York and the Nevilles was evident to all, but as yet the speed of the drift was very slow. There were several reasons for this. No one was anxious to repeat the experience of St Albans. On 28 August 1457 a French raiding force landed on the Kent coast and sacked Sandwich, awakening real fears of invasion. At this juncture York and Warwick, as the acknowledged men of action, were indispensable. To his chagrin Exeter was removed from his office of admiral and the keeping of the seas was entrusted to Warwick. In addition, for four years after St Albans the king's own genuine desire for peace and reconciliation was supported by the duke of Buckingham. Although Buckingham had been irritated when his two half-brothers lost their posts as chancellor and treasurer in October 1456, he did not react by going over to the Yorkists. On the other hand, he was widely believed to exercise a restraining influence on the court and since, together with York and Warwick, he was one of the three richest noblemen in the country, his was a voice which had to be listened to. Between November 1457 and March 1458, capitalizing on these feelings, a determined attempt was made to halt the slide into civil war.

Eventually York, Salisbury and Warwick promised to endow a chantry at St Albans, where masses would be celebrated for the souls of the slain, and agreed to pay compensation to the Percy and Clifford families. At the so-called Loveday of 24 March 1458 the rival parties marched arm-in-arm to St Paul's; Somerset and Salisbury, Northumberland and Warwick, even Richard of York and the queen. Perhaps Henry believed that he had achieved something, but few others can have been so sanguine. This grand gesture of reconciliation had been acted out against a backcloth of thousands of armed retainers quartered inside and outside London, with the mayor and city authorities working overtime to keep the peace. Here was an ominous trend which the Loveday did nothing to check. Each time the lords were summoned to a public occasion they were turning up with bigger and bigger retinues – a sure sign of the steady growth of mutual mistrust.

Even so, it was to be another six months before the next incident on the road to war. In this intervening period the spotlight switched to Calais and to the earl of Warwick. As the queen strengthened her hold on the machinery of English government, so the Exchequer, obedient to her will, sent less and less money across the Channel, and Warwick found it correspondingly harder to pay the garrison under his command. His response was characteristically vigorous. If the money would not come to him, he would go out and get it. As captain of Calais he was perfectly placed to make a successful career as a pirate and he built up a small fleet of about ten ships of his own (this at a time when Henry v's fine fleet had been sold off and the royal navy was down to one). At the end of May he attacked a Spanish fleet, capturing six ships. A few days later it was the turn of the famous Hanseatic Bay Fleet, the great annual convoy which carried salt from the Bay of Bourgneuf on the Atlantic coast of France to the Hansa towns of North Germany and the Baltic. Such profitable excitements kept his soldiers happy and made the earl himself something of a hero; for the last thirty years there had been almost no military exploits worth cheering, so even acts of flagrant piracy were chronicled with pride. But though a patriotic public liked nothing better than seeing foreigners being given a drubbing by Englishmen, these attacks on neutral shipping were deeply embarrassing to the government. Moreover, the stories which reached the court about Warwick's diplomatic relations with the duke of Burgundy seemed to indicate that he was conducting a pro-Yorkist policy of his own. These activities led the queen to seek his resignation, though she was probably less concerned about the international repercussions

than she was about the desirability of having the Calais garrison on her
side in the coming quarrel. Summoned to London in October 1458 to
answer charges of attacking the Hansa fleet, he was set on by the royal
guard after a brawl between his servants and those of the king. He
managed to escape by fighting his way to his barge. Margaret blamed
Warwick for the incident and demanded his arrest, but he withdrew to
Calais in open defiance of the government, claiming that there had been
a deliberate plot to murder him.

Warwick's rebellion – for this, in essence, is what it was – naturally
led the court to step up its preparations for war. In May 1459, for
example, three thousand bows were ordered for the royal armoury.
Those who, like Buckingham, had been occupying the middle ground
of politics, were gradually being squeezed out; they could either withdraw or, if they still wanted to have a hand in shaping events, they must
choose sides. Believing, perhaps, that Warwick had now gone too far
and, on a personal level, irritated by a long-standing property dispute
with him, Buckingham chose to throw all his influence on the side of the
court. This was a decisive shift in the precarious balance of the last four
years. The queen decided that her moment had come at last. In June a
great council met at Coventry, but not all the peers were summoned to
attend. York, Salisbury, Warwick, Warwick's brother, George Neville,
bishop of Exeter, the Bourchiers and a few others were pointedly
excluded. At this partisan council indictments were laid against the
Yorkists. In the face of the queen's evident determination to crush
them, the Yorkist leaders made plans to hold a meeting of their own at
Ludlow. There the duke of York would be joined by Salisbury with an
army of northerners and by Warwick with a contingent from the Calais
garrison led by a famous soldier of the day, Andrew Trollope. They
believed that King Henry still wanted peace, but that only a show of
armed might would gain them access to the hostile court. All that
summer both sides were busy raising troops.

In September Warwick sailed from Calais leaving Lord Fauconberg
in command of the remainder of the garrison. Later that month Salisbury set out from Middleham. He was accompanied by his sons Sir
Thomas and Sir John Neville and by his leading retainers, Sir Thomas
Harrington, Sir Thomas Parr and Sir John Conyers. At the same time
several royalist armies took the field, hoping to prevent the Yorkists
concentrating their forces. The king himself lay at Nottingham; the
queen and their son were stationed at Chester; the duke of Somerset
patrolled the West Midlands. At Coleshill (between Birmingham and

Coventry) Warwick narrowly escaped being intercepted by Somerset, and in consequence was able to reach Ludlow unscathed. His father was less fortunate. Warned of Salisbury's approach, two or three royalist armies took steps to block his path. The earl managed to evade Henry VI's force, but Margaret, on reaching Eccleshall, was well placed to block Salisbury's advance from Newcastle-under-Lyme to Ludlow. But then she stayed where she was, apparently waiting to be joined by Lord Stanley, while Salisbury went by a few miles farther north. At this juncture the attitude adopted by the Stanleys, Lord Thomas and his brother Sir William, seems to have been critical. Both royalists and Yorkists had reason to look for Stanley support. Lord Thomas indeed sent several messages assuring the queen that he was on the way, even offering to take command of the royalist van in order to allay the suspicions aroused by his apparent dilatoriness. In the event, however, he kept at a safe distance and was later on accused of having hindered Margaret's attempts to raise troops in the Wirrall and other parts of Cheshire where he had influence. But his brother, less cautious, decided to throw in his lot with the Nevilles. As a result of these manoeuvres and delays the earl of Salisbury, now joined by Sir William Stanley, was halted at Blore Heath on the road between Newcastle and Market Drayton, not by a combined royalist army but by a subsidiary Cheshire force under the command of Lords Audley and Dudley.

About the events of that day, 23 September 1459, we know very little. Audley was killed, Dudley captured and the Lancastrians defeated – but just how these things happened we cannot say. According to the London chronicle known as Gregory's Chronicle, compiled some ten years later, the fighting lasted from 1 p.m. to 5 p.m. Only one writer, however, gives any details of the fighting and we would do well to distrust his account. This is Jean de Waurin, normally a valuable source, but not on this occasion. This is because his account of Blore Heath occurs in a section of the chronicle which was written later than the rest and which can be shown to be highly unreliable. According to a local tradition Queen Margaret observed the fighting from Mucclestone church tower and, when it was over, took flight, reversing the horseshoes on her horse in order to evade pursuit. As a story this one is typical of local tradition – its fundamenal uselessness half-concealed by the veneer of topographical precision.

But although we do not know how it was that Salisbury won the upper hand in the encounter at Blore Heath, what is reasonably clear is that even after his victory he was in an awkward position. Margaret of

Anjou was close at hand and her husband probably not far off. In Gregory's Chronicle this became the occasion for an anecdote. Salisbury, it is said, moved on under cover of darkness, but managed to trick the royalists into believing that he was still encamped in a wood behind Blore Heath by having a friar fire off guns at intervals throughout the night. Even after they had reached Market Drayton in safety, Salisbury's advisers were conscious of their strategic plight. When a letter from Thomas Stanley reached them, congratulating them on their victory, and promising to stand by them as he would have done already if only he had been able to reach Blore Heath in time, Sir Thomas Harrington took the opportunity to rally doubters: 'Sirs, be merry, for still we have more friends.' Lord Stanley, however, soon regretted the excessive show of enthusiasm he displayed under the immediate impact of the news of Blore Heath. He stayed for a few days at Newcastle but then, as it became clear that the skirmish had settled nothing, he went back home and waited on events. In consequence Salisbury made his way to Ludlow without the benefit of Stanley's assistance – and not without serious loss. His two sons and Sir Thomas Harrington were ambushed and taken to Chester Castle where they remained as prisoners for the next nine months.

From Ludlow the Yorkist leaders published a manifesto in the form of a letter to the king, excusing and justifying their actions. The court responded by offering to pardon all who were prepared to lay down their arms, except those who were involved in Audley's death. Neither side trusted the other, however, and on 12 October, as the Lancastrian army approached Ludlow from the south, the Yorkists took up a fortified position at Ludford Bridge, their guns in carts (their field artillery) placed in the front of their line of battle. At St Albans the Yorkists had taken Somerset unawares, but for this day the queen had long made her preparations. Even though York, Salisbury and Warwick had managed to effect the union of their forces, it was still the court which held the initiative. Moreover the Lancastrian army was a royal army in the strict sense of the word – the king in person was there at the head of his troops – and a large number of the peers had rallied to his banner. In the Yorkist camp there were only six peers: York himself and his sons, Edward, earl of March (now seventeen years old), and Edmund, earl of Rutland, the earls of Salisbury and Warwick; besides this narrow family group there was only Lord Clinton, the poorest of the English barons. They had clearly failed to mobilize any widespread support; in terms of the number of peers present they were outnumbered by three to one. On 12 October their position was already so weak that any defection would be fatal to their cause.

The élite corps of the Yorkist army was the Calais contingent brought over by Warwick. It seems probable that he had assured Andrew Trollope that they would not have to fight against the king himself, but now Henry was there – though the Yorkists did their best to pretend that he wasn't. They brought men into their camp to swear that the king was dead. They even had priests singing masses for his soul. But the elaborate charade failed. Trollope and the Calais veterans changed sides; the oath of allegiance to the king, even to King Henry VI, clearly still meant a great deal. This did not stop the Yorkist guns bombarding the royal army, but when evening came, and with it time for reflection, York and his friends realized that they were lost. Announcing that they were returning to Ludlow for the night, they fled, abandoning their troops and all their equipment. York even left behind his duchess and his two youngest sons. He and his second son Edmund eventually found sanctuary in Ireland. His eldest son, Edward of March, took a different road, riding south through the night with the Nevilles. While the Lancastrian troops enjoyed themselves pillaging Ludlow, Edward, Salisbury and Warwick, trusting to the guidance of a Devonshire squire, John Dinham, made their way to the shelter of the Dinhams' home near Newton Abbot. Then they sailed for Calais in a ship bought with John Dinham's money. The young earl of March did not forget these services and later, as Edward IV, he raised Dinham to the peerage. On 2 November they arrived at Calais, safe enough for the moment, but with their cause in ruins. Their flight from Ludford Bridge, prudent though it undoubtedly was, was too precipitate to be honourable. They had concentrated all their strength at Ludlow only to be scattered more widely than before, to see their followers captured or helpless. England was now ruled by Margaret of Anjou.

Eight

FIVE BATTLES, 1459–61

THE NEXT EIGHTEEN MONTHS witnessed more violent swings of the political pendulum than any other period of similar length in English history. First Lancaster was ousted by York, then York by Lancaster and finally Lancaster by York again. Moreover, these were political upheavals brought about by force of arms. This same period saw no less than five battles, culminating in the biggest bloodbath until the seventeenth-century Battle of Marston Moor.

It began, of course, with the ascendancy of Margaret of Anjou. A parliament of her partisans met at Coventry in November 1459 and proceeded to pass a bill of attainder on their opponents. By this procedure twenty-seven Yorkists (six peers and twenty-one others) were condemned as traitors, had their estates confiscated and their heirs disinherited. As rebels levying war against the king they can have expected no other fate. Even so, only those who had fled were attainted. Other known Yorkists escaped with fines or were pardoned. Evidently by adopting this merciful approach the government hoped to emphasize the isolation of the 'hard-core' Yorkists. But for this policy to work it had to be accompanied by firm action against the hard core itself; and this Margaret and her supporters were unable to take.

With remarkable ease the fugitive duke of York set himself up as the ruler of Ireland, claiming to be the king's lieutenant. According to the abbot of St Alban's he was received with open arms, the Irish welcoming him as though he were a second Messiah. On paper a new lieutenant of Ireland, the earl of Wiltshire, was appointed on 4 December, but the queen did little or nothing to enable him to take up this office – unless we accept the claim made by Yorkist propaganda that privy seal letters were sent to the native chiefs encouraging them to drive the English out of Ireland. York was not in Ireland often, and then only for brief periods, but his success there suggests that he had political gifts greater than most historians have been willing to allow. It was not in

Ireland, however, but in Calais that the crisis came. Whereas English governments have usually preferred to shelve the problem of Ireland, Calais was a very different case. Its crucial strategic position, at a crossroads of northern Europe within striking distance of London and conveniently placed for the conduct of negotiations with Burgundy and France, meant that it simply could not be ignored.

Even before the rout at Ludford Bridge, the duke of Somerset had been appointed captain of Calais. He made what haste he could to assemble ships, men and artillery, but when his fleet approached Calais it was greeted with gunfire both from the town itself and from the tower of Rysbank guarding the harbour entrance. The Lancastrians had blundered badly; the preparations for an expedition to Calais should have been made before the result of Ludford Bridge was known. If the queen and her friends wanted a decisive victory they should have tried to capture Warwick's base while he was away. As it was, Somerset came too late. He did not give up. His force included not only Lord Roos and Lord Audley (whose father had been killed at Blore Heath) but also Andrew Trollope and his men. Their local knowledge and contacts meant that Somerset still had a chance. He sailed west, landed at Scales' cliff and advanced towards the fortress of Guînes. By offering to pay the garrison their arrears of wages, he gained an entrance. Others of Somerset's force were less fortunate. Carried in ships which were blown into Calais harbour they were brought before the earl of Warwick and those of them who had been with Andrew Trollope at Ludford Bridge were executed.

From Guînes Somerset launched almost daily attacks against Calais, but always he was beaten off, sometimes with heavy losses. Once again his cause suffered from inadequate preparation and administrative inefficiency as the looked-for reinforcements from England failed to arrive. In Calais, meanwhile, so long as they could keep the garrison happy, the Yorkist earls were comfortably placed. Fortunately for them, despite the Lancastrian government's attempt to impose trade sanctions, both foreign and English ships continued to land their cargoes there, some, indeed, even being granted safe-conducts by the government. Furthermore, Warwick had succeeded in negotiating a truce with Burgundy which allowed raiding parties from the garrison to pass through Burgundian territory on their way to plunder and pillage the French king's subjects. But Warwick's greatest asset was his reputation, and in particular the popularity which his piratical exploits had won for him among some sections of the Kentish people. His supporters there kept him fully informed of the slow progress of the fitting-out of a big expeditionary force at Sandwich which was intended to flush him out of Calais once and for all. By mid-January 1460 the Lancastrian fleet under the command of Lord Rivers was just about ready to sail. But on 15 January, between four and five o'clock in the morning, John Dinham landed at Sandwich with a force of eight hundred soldiers plus an apothecary, a tailor, a butcher, a servant, two yeomen, a merchant and a chapman, all of them citizens of Sandwich – doubtless the men who kept Warwick up to date with the latest news from their home town. The complacent Lancastrians were taken completely by surprise. Lord Rivers, his wife the dowager duchess of Bedford, and his son, Sir Anthony Woodville, were captured while still in bed. All the ships in the harbour which had been made ready for sea – at Lancastrian expense – were seized by the economical Yorkists and sailed off in triumph to Calais.

Henry VI's government feared an immediate invasion and was reduced to panic stations. Clearly they lacked the equivalent of Warwick's intelligence service and had little idea of what was going on in Calais, but their attempts to organize coastal defences and sea patrols were crippled for lack of ready cash. They had lacked the forethought to ask the pliable parliament of November 1459 for a subsidy, and now they lacked the nerve to summon a new one so soon after the dissolution of the old. With its most energetic figure isolated at Guînes, the government shifted from one feeble expedient to another. On 1 February the sheriff of Devon, Sir Baldwin Fulford, was commissioned to raise a new fleet, but this had still not put to sea when, in March, the earl of Warwick sailed to Ireland to confer with the duke of York. He encountered no opposition and paused only to seize a few merchant ships which ran across his path. He stayed in Ireland for two months, doubtless – as Henry's government suspected – laying the final plans for a two-pronged invasion of England. Unquestionably he and York intended to secure their own reinstatement, but was this all? This would have meant a return to the position as it was after 1455 – hardly a comfortable position for them, and one which gave them no guarantee for their future security. Or did they discuss more far-reaching possibilities?

In the meantime Warwick's long absence from Calais should have given Somerset the opportunity to strike a powerful and possibly decisive blow. Unfortunately for the duke, he was hamstrung by lack of men and money. He had not even been able to pay the garrison of Guînes the

£5,000 in wages which had been owing to them when they had admitted him in return for the promise of payment. Lord Audley and Humphrey Stafford of Southwick had been sent with some reinforcements, but bad weather forced them to put into Calais, where they were promptly added to the growing list of prisoners. Eventually, on 23 April 1460, Somerset launched an attack up the Boulogne road, but his inadequate force was defeated at Newnham Bridge. By the time the painfully slow-moving Lancastrian government was again ready to dispatch aid to Somerset, Warwick was back at Calais.

He had set sail from Ireland late in May. This time a fleet was waiting to intercept him. In addition to Fulford's force, a formidable navy had been mustered by the duke of Exeter. Exeter had lost his office of admiral to Warwick in 1457 and was now anxious to prove that he was the better man. He had been given command of Warwick's old flagship, the *Grace Dieu*, and his fleet included one Venetian and three Genoese carracks (big, three-masted ships) which the government had hired for £100 a month each. An attempt had even been made to hire the great Venetian galley fleet, but rather than get involved in the English king's quarrels, the galleys had slipped quietly out of London. Their hopes dashed, Henry's ministers retaliated by arresting all Venetian merchants in the city, releasing them only after they had given security to the amount of 36,000 ducats. The measure doubtless alleviated their immediate cash crisis, but it was short-sighted in the extreme. Yet even without the Venetian galleys the duke of Exeter's fleet was a strong one and the well-informed Burgundian chronicler, Jean de Waurin, has a vivid description of the circumspection with which Warwick made his way up the Channel. He took the precaution of sending a fast-sailing caravel on forward reconnaissance. After the caravel (the frigate of the fifteenth century) had done its job and reported the presence of a fleet, some fishermen were captured and interrogated. From them Warwick and his admiral, the much-respected Gascon Lord Duras, learned the identity and size of the force ahead. At once all Warwick's captains were summoned aboard his ship and asked for their opinions. Their unanimous advice was that they should attack: apparently they had the advantage of the wind, and the earl's reputation as a fighting man doubtless helped to give them confidence. Exeter, it seems, had counted on his superiority in numbers – according to Waurin he had fourteen ships in all – and was dismayed on seeing the enemy, whom he had expected to flee, heading straight towards him and clearly spoiling for a fight. An encounter at sea between two fleets was a rare event in fifteenth-century naval warfare and Exeter's nerve was not equal to the occasion. On his orders his fleet turned and took shelter in Dartmouth. The Channel was now clear and Warwick made good speed. Next day he was given a rousing reception at Calais by the friends and kinsmen who had been looking anxiously for his return and for news of his conference with the duke of York.

Somerset meanwhile had still not given up hope. His look-outs indeed had initially identified Warwick's fleet as the reinforcements for which they had waited so long. The mistake had been a very natural one, since they knew that a force of two hundred men-at-arms and two hundred archers had mustered at Sandwich under the command of Sir Osbert Mountfort, a veteran of the French wars, and was only waiting for a favourable wind to cross the Channel. Once again, however, it was the Calais garrison which struck first. Early in June 1460 John Dinham, assisted this time by Sir John Wenlock and Lord Fauconberg, led a raiding force to Sandwich and after a fierce fight they seized the town. Dinham carried Mountfort off to Calais just as, five months earlier, he had carried off the Woodvilles, but this time Lord Fauconberg remained behind in Sandwich. The Yorkists had won a bridgehead. The first stage of the invasion had begun.

Besides their military preparations Warwick and his associates had conducted a vigorous propaganda campaign. They had manifestos circulated throughout England, claiming that their intention was purely to remedy the sufferings of the realm. They were able to make some effective points in criticism of the Lancastrian regime, harping particularly on the theme of the greed of evil councillors. As a result, by the time they landed, they had won a lot of popular support, particularly in the south-east.

On 26 June the earl of Warwick joined Fauconberg at Sandwich. With him were the earls of Salisbury and March, Lord Audley (who had been persuaded to join his captors), Sir John Wenlock and a force of between 1,500 and 2,000 men. There was also the papal legate to England, Francesco Coppini, bishop of Terni. He had been sent by Pius II to make peace and to win Henry VI's support for a crusade against the Turks which the pope was trying to organize, but for motives of his own, instead of standing between the parties, he became an active partisan of the Yorkists. They moved on from Sandwich at once, and before nightfall they reached Canterbury. There the three captains whom

Above Choosing the red
and white roses:
a picture which
reflects the hold
of Shakespeare's
view of the past on
subsequent artists
and writers.

Right The white rose
was the most famous
badge of the house of
York and so, when
Henry VII adopted
the red rose as his
badge, it became
possible to see his
marriage as the
union of the roses.

Above Henry vɪ's failure to retain
the lands he inherited in France was
to prove fatal to his reputation.
Here we see him being crowned at Paris as
king of France: from Jean de Waurin,
Chroniques d'Angleterre.

Below This depiction of a
wagon train on the move gives
a more realistic picture
of day-to-day campaigning
than is gained from most
battle scenes.

Above The hand-to-hand mêlée between heavily armoured knights formed the usual climax to a hard-fought battle. Many were fought, like this one, outside the walls of a besieged town.

Below The baggage train was formed into a circle when the army encamped for the night.

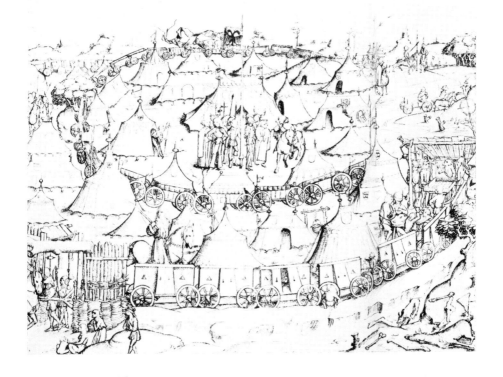

Above A fifteenth-century cannon.

Opposite The best fifteenth-century
armour was manufactured
either in Germany or
in Italy.

Below A full-scale siege:
the besiegers have prepared
for a long struggle, erecting
wooden fortifications of
their own and placing their
cannon behind palisades.

Above Henry VI's and
Margaret's inability to
keep London's loyalty was
to play an important part
in their fall. Frequently
they had to try to govern
England from outside
London, allowing the city
itself to fall into the
hands of the Yorkists.

Right Henry VI in
All Souls College Oxford

These two gateways demonstrate the difference between fifteenth-century city gates and those built earlier. The West gate at Canterbury (*right*) is clearly meant for defence, whereas the South gate at King's Lynn (*below*), with its wide doorways and windows, was primarily for municipal purposes, such as collecting tolls.

Below A coronation of a king at Westminster was a carefully stage-managed event, as is clear from this mid-fifteenth-century artist's impression of Henry IV's coronation in 1399.

Above Jousting, shown here without the tilt (or banner) which was introduced about 1430, and with sharp spears. The king and the ladies of the court are on the central stand.

Henry had appointed to defend the city, John Fogge, John Scott and Robert Horne, decided to join them. That evening the Yorkists knelt in prayer at the tomb of Thomas Becket, an act of shrewd piety. Soon thousands more came flocking to their standard, 'like bees to the hive', wrote the abbot of St Albans. Their most important recruit was York's old ally, Lord Cobham. Two days later the march on London began.

By this time, of course, there was great agitation in the capital. On 27 June the common council of London had agreed that everyone should help the mayor and aldermen to resist the rebels, but they were anxious to keep their independence and they had refused to allow a Lancastrian peer, Lord Scales, to act as the city's captain, claiming that they were quite capable of withstanding the Yorkists on their own 'without any aid of lords'. Next day men-at-arms were stationed on London Bridge, with orders to guard the gate. The common council also sent a deputation to the Yorkists, warning them that they would resist any attempt to enter the city. But Warwick had passed safely through London only a year before, and he was not to be dissuaded. As the Yorkists continued their advance, growing stronger by the hour, the determination of the city authorities wilted. Once again the rebels insisted that they had not come to attack the king but to reform the realm. So far as the Londoners were concerned, this was a face-saving formula which enabled them to avoid the risks of confrontation. Another deputation was sent, this time telling the Yorkists that they were welcome to enter the city. At this juncture Lord Scales might have decided to join the Lancastrian court in the Midlands, but instead he chose to withdraw his troops into the Tower. He was accompanied by several other lords, Hungerford, Lovell, de la Warr, de Vescy and the earl of Kendal. Possibly Scales calculated that with this strong point held against them threatening their direct line of communication with the Kentish ports and Calais, the Yorkists might well hesitate before advancing any farther inland. Besides, he may well have known that Henry would move in the direction of London as soon as he heard of the earl's landing, in which case the Yorkists might be caught between two Lancastrian forces.

On 1 July the earl of Warwick's army reached St George's Field at Southwark. By now it had been joined by so many 'footmen of the commons of Kent, Sussex and Surrey' that various writers, including at least two eyewitnesses, estimated its size at between twenty thousand and forty thousand – figures traditionally used to mean 'a great many'. Next day the Yorkists marched across London Bridge and into the city.

The earls took up residence in the house of the Grey Friars at Newgate, while their army camped near Smithfield. They stayed in London for two days, and during that time concentrated their energies on two tasks. Firstly, they took advantage of a meeting of convocation to put their case to the bishops. Their reiterated declaration that they intended nothing that was contrary to their allegiance to King Henry clearly won a sympathetic hearing, for when they marched out of London no less than seven bishops, including the archbishop of Canterbury, went with them. Secondly, while talking of peace they prepared for war. They asked the city authorities to provide them with a baggage train and to appropriate the king's guns which were stored at Whitechapel 'for the city's defence' – a phrase which meant for use against the Tower. Having let the earls in, the common council found it impossible to refuse their requests and, willy-nilly, found themselves being inexorably drawn deeper into the Yorkist camp. When the Lancastrians in the Tower asked if they might send men to obtain victuals in the city, the council, at Warwick's insistence, said No. Finally, on 4 July, the city made a corporate loan of £1,000 – 'for the sake of peace and of prosperity for the king and kingdom', as the official record somewhat optimistically puts it.

That day the Yorkist vanguard moved out of London. The rest followed a day later. In view of a report that King Henry was on his way to take refuge in the Isle of Ely, one part of the army marched via Ware while the rest took the St Albans road. Their fighting strength had been increased by the adhesion of several more peers, the duke of Norfolk, Viscount Bourchier and the Lords Abergavenny, Saye and Scrope of Bolton: and this meant that they could now afford to leave Salisbury, Cobham and Wenlock behind to contain the defiant garrison in the Tower. King Henry meanwhile had left his wife and son in Coventry but, far from fleeing to Ely, was in fact making his way slowly towards London. Having advanced as far as Northampton he halted and waited, possibly hoping that this would give time for loyal northerners to join him, possibly made hesitant by a division of opinion within his council – some willing to give the rebels a hearing, others convinced that the time for talking was long since past. But though immobile, the Lancastrians were far from being idle. They had sited their camp and artillery park outside the walls of Northampton, half-way between Delapré Abbey and the River Nene, and they now dug themselves in. A trench carrying water from the Nene and enclosing their whole position was the main feature of defence works, which were strong enough to impress visitors and make the royalists confident of the outcome of battle.

Once the Yorkists had definite news of the king's whereabouts they united the two parts of their army and advanced cautiously north of Dunstable. Their progress was slow, partly to give time for negotiation, using some of the bishops as ambassadors, partly because heavy rain was making the roads unusually difficult. The peers in Henry's camp included the earl of Shrewsbury and Lords Beaumont, Egremont, and Grey of Ruthin, but the dominant voice there was that of the duke of Buckingham. By all accounts he was against any form of compromise. The embassies of the bishops came to nothing. By the morning of 10 July the earls of Warwick and March had approached to within striking distance of the Lancastrian camp. A last attempt to negotiate was made by Warwick herald, rejected by Buckingham, and so, at two o'clock, to a blast of trumpets, the Yorkists advanced to the attack. Their soldiers were under orders to spare the king and the commons, but to slay the lords, knights and squires. The Yorkist van was under Fauconberg – 'little Fauconberg, a knight of great reverence', in the words of a Yorkist ballad. Warwick and March were in command of the main battle. On paper the strength of the Lancastrian army lay in its artillery and in its well-entrenched position, but two factors combined to undermine both these advantages: rain and treachery. In the first place, another heavy downpour put the Lancastrian guns out of action; in the second place, and more crucially, one of the Lancastrian lords had become a secret Yorkist. What it was that persuaded Lord Grey of Ruthin to change sides just at this critical moment we shall never know. He was evidently a ruthless man. His behaviour at Northampton is itself sufficient proof of a lack of scruple, but there is also the fact that ten years earlier he had been deeply involved in the murder of William Tresham, the speaker of the house of commons. So far as we can tell he had hitherto avoided taking an active part in the armed clashes of the last twelve months, but that he was, by July 1460, looked upon as a trusted member of the court party seems clear from the fact that he and his men stood in the front line of the Lancastrian defence. In later years he did well: he became treasurer in 1463; in 1465 he was made earl of Kent and his eldest son married into the family of Edward iv's queen. These rewards came too late, however, to make it likely that he had been bribed to change sides. Had this been his motive he would surely have demanded prompt payment once he had carried out his side of the bargain with such cynical efficiency.

What does seem clear is that the earl of Warwick had been informed of what was going on in Lord Grey's devious mind. As the earl's troops advanced they were given instructions to spare all those who bore Grey's badge – the black ragged staff – for these were the men who would allow them entry into the Lancastrian encampment. And so it proved. Indeed, according to one writer, John Whethamstede, the abbot of St Alban's, Grey's men actually helped to pull the attackers up the steep slope of the ramparts. The shock of Grey's treachery gave the Lancastrians no chance to recover. The fighting may have lasted no more than half an hour, by which time the king's army was broken and in flight. Buckingham, Shrewsbury, Egremont and Beaumont had stationed themselves by the king's tent and they died there, struck down, it was said, by the Kentishmen. Many more died as they tried to escape from the battlefield, some of them drowned in the river to which they had once looked for protection. But in the opinion of a Yorkist writer, even more would have been killed had it not been for Lord Grey's timely and humane action. Among the three hundred or so casualties, the most unfortunate, according to common report, was Sir William Lucy. A knight who lived not far from Northampton, he heard gunfire and decided to come to the king's aid. As it happened, by the time he got there, the battle was all over, but his arrival was noted by John Stafford, and, since Stafford was in love with Sir William's wife, he took the opportunity to make her a widow. Not long afterwards he married her.

Still proclaiming their loyalty to the crown, Warwick and his friends took possession of the hapless King Henry. They rested at Northampton for three days and then returned to London with their prisoner, entering the city on 16 July. This turn of events put the Lancastrians holding the Tower in an impossible position. During the last fortnight Lord Scales had organized a spirited resistance. However, although he had sufficient artillery and ammunition to make life in London very uncomfortable for a while, there was not enough food to enable him to stand a long siege. Too many non-combatants, including ladies, had taken refuge in the Tower. They not only consumed provisions; their fears and complaints helped to undermine the morale of the garrison. The earl of Salisbury had placed some bombards on the river bank opposite the Tower, but though their shot did some damage to the walls and doubtless added to the alarm of the Lancastrian ladies, it is clear that the Yorkists were relying chiefly on a tightly drawn blockade to starve the Tower into submission. Undoubtedly Lord Scales could have held out for longer, but what was the point? The outcome of the battle of Northampton had settled the fate of the defenders of the Tower. On 19 July they capitulated. Lords Scales and Hungerford were to go free, but not all of the besieged were offered such generous terms. Warwick, sitting in judgment in the Guildhall, had a number of them, mostly members of the duke of Exeter's household, condemned to a traitor's death at Tyburn. Warwick, however, was not the only man in a vindictive frame of mind. The Londoners had not enjoyed Lord Scales's bombardment of their city and as he made his way by barge to safety (and possibly sanctuary) at Westminster he was set upon by some boatmen and murdered. He was stripped of all he had and his body 'naked as a worm' dumped at the porch of the church of St Mary Overy in Southwark.

With his enemies scattered, Warwick proceeded to take over the reins of government. His brother, George Neville, bishop of Exeter, was appointed chancellor and Viscount Bourchier made treasurer. On 30 July writs were sent out summoning parliament to meet on 7 October. Its primary purpose was evidently to reverse the sentences of attainder passed at Coventry. Had anything else been intended? They had captured Henry VI, but not his wife or his son, and this particular outcome of the battle of Northampton cannot have been foreseen when York and Warwick met and conferred in Ireland. London gossip said that they planned to make one of York's sons king, passing over Prince Edward on the grounds that he was not Henry's son. But whatever York's intentions may have been, he was still in Ireland. From Warwick's point of view it must have been apparent that if there were now far more peers prepared to support the Yorkists than the bare half dozen who had stood by them last summer, this was due in no small measure to a propaganda campaign directed against the 'corrupt and evil counsellors'. Crucial to the success of this campaign had been the fervent protestations of loyalty to the crown. To change policy now would have been to risk losing that new and possibly fragile support. With Queen Margaret still at liberty this was a risk which Warwick, whatever he may have thought once, was in no mood to take. For the moment, moreover, he had more immediate problems, notably the safety of his power base at Calais.

Across the Channel the military stalemate had continued: Warwick's garrison in Calais (together with his wife and mother); Somerset's troops holding Guînes. During Warwick's absence the inhabitants of Calais had understandably been nervous, but in reality the result of the

battle of Northampton had been to make Somerset's position untenable. As soon as the earl reached Calais, the duke indicated his willingness to come to terms. They met at Newnham Bridge, and Somerset
agreed to surrender Guînes in return for his own freedom to go wherever he wanted. According to Warwick's version of events, Somerset
also swore that he would never again take up arms against him.
Somerset then took refuge in France, while the victorious earl returned
to England. Here, however, matters were still far from being settled.
The Yorkists had a tolerably firm grip on the south and east, but in the
north many Lancastrians were at large, able to meet each other and
muster troops. When Warwick went on a pilgrimage to Walsingham
and then on a tour of his estates in the Midlands, rumours of ambush
kept his followers on their toes. On the other hand, it could not have
been easy for the scattered Lancastrians to regroup and plan a march
on London. If they had tried any such thing, the duke of York might
have crossed the Irish Sea and landed in their rear. Throughout these
weeks, indeed, York's intentions were the big unknown factor in the
political and military equation.

But at last he began to show his hand. He landed near Chester at the
end of the first week in September and soon made it clear to his English
and Welsh followers that he had come to claim the throne. During a
leisurely progress through the Welsh Marches and West Midlands he
gathered his supporters about him. Then he turned towards Westminster and the meeting of parliament. When he reached Abingdon,
observed a London chronicler, 'he sent for trumpeters and clarioners to
escort him to London, and there he gave them banners with the royal
arms of England without any diversity and commanded his sword to be
borne upright before him.' On 10 October he reached the city. Delaying
there only long enough for his formal reception by the mayor and
aldermen, he rode on to Westminster, accompanied by five hundred
armed men, trumpets and clarions sounding, the sword still borne
upright before him. The scene in the palace of Westminster was
described by John Whethamstede, the abbot of St Albans, who may
well have been an eyewitness. 'He went straight through the great hall
until he came to the chamber where the king, with the commons, was
accustomed to hold his parliament. There he strode up to the throne
and put his hand on its cushion just as though he were a man about to
take possession of what was rightfully his. He kept it there for a while
then, withdrawing it, he turned to the people and, standing quietly
under the canopy of state, waited expectantly for their applause.'

Instead of the acclamation he looked for, however, York was greeted by a stony silence. Eventually the archbishop of Canterbury approached and asked him if he wanted to see the king. Though York's reply was a proud one, there could be no getting away from the fact that the question had devastated his hopes.

The lords, of course, had by now known of York's intentions for some time and were determined not to give way. York, however, pressed on with his claim. Possibly, if he and Warwick had agreed on something like this while they were in Ireland, his determination was stiffened by resentment at the earl's going back on his side of the bargain. On the other hand, Warwick, who may have met York at Ludlow in September and could have tried to dissuade him from going ahead, may well have been angered by what he would have seen as York's failure to take account of political reality. If York did not like that present reality, then he should have done something about it, instead of waiting in Ireland while others risked their lives. All this, of course, is speculation, but two things at least are clear. First, Warwick and York were now at logger-heads. Second, York's claim to the throne was undeniably, in law, a strong one, and now that he had insisted on pressing it in the high court of parliament, it required an answer in law. The reluctant lords did their best. They had sworn oaths of allegiance to Henry VI; the house of Lancaster had enjoyed possession of the throne for sixty years. To these arguments York's lawyers replied that Henry IV had been a usurper, and his descendants were no lawful kings. Against the fact of their possession, York argued his right to the throne: 'For though right for a time rest and be put to silence, yet it rotteth not nor shall not perish.' Yet even while admitting the justice of York's cause, the parliament of October 1460 was unable to bring itself to depose Henry VI. Given the fact that Henry's reign had been disastrous and that parliament contained no Lancastrians, this was a remarkable indication of the crown's place as the symbol and guarantee of political stability. Eventually a compromise was reached. Henry was to retain the throne, but when he died he was to be succeeded by York and then by York's heirs. In the meantime ten thousand marks a year were to be provided for York and his sons.

While the Yorkists were struggling to achieve this constitutional and dynastic settlement, their enemies were gathering in an attempt to overthrow it. In some ways the Act of Accord of 24 October 1460 simplified their task. While the king himself had appeared to accept the government foisted upon him, it could not have been easy for the queen to find an entirely acceptable reason for renewing the civil war. After the battle of Northampton, indeed, Margaret had found herself in a very tight corner. Accompanied by a small escort only, she had headed for Wales, but was ambushed by some of Lord Stanley's followers, and though she and her son escaped, she lost her jewels and other valuables. In this impoverished plight she managed to find a refuge in Harlech Castle, temporarily out of touch with those of her old associates who were still alive. But in passing the Act of Accord the Yorkists had gone beyond the stage of replacing one set of counsellors by another. They had disinherited a king's son. In doing so, though paradoxically they had acted in the name of a just inheritance, they had offended against that same principle, the corner-stone of the world of a landowning nobility, the 'sacred' principle of inheritance – the principle which seemed so natural to the essentially unchanged society of Shakespeare's day. Take the son's rights away

> and take from Time
> His charters and his customary rights;
> Let not tomorrow then ensue today.   (Richard II, ii. i)

With her young son disinherited, Margaret now had a powerful motive to continue the struggle, and a cause which attracted sympathy and support. How many sons might not be ousted if lawyers were to resurrect every ancient pedigree?

As autumn passed, more and more men joined the swelling stream of Lancastrian resistance. In Wales Jasper Tudor, earl of Pembroke, had stood by Margaret in her darkest hour and was now ready to go over to the offensive. Margaret herself had taken ship to Scotland and was seeking allies at the Scottish court. The duke of Somerset, having returned to England via Dieppe, was now at Corfe Castle, raising the south-west with the assistance of the earl of Devon. Much of the north was under the control of the earl of Northumberland and Lords Clifford and Roos. Orders sent out from the Yorkist government at Westminster were ignored. Far from being able to bring the dissidents to book, the Yorkists could not even protect their own. The York and Neville estates in the north were devastated and some of their tenants forced, on pain of death, to join the ranks of the Lancastrians. From a government point of view all this was bad enough, but the military threat would become much greater if their opponents in the north, in Wales and in the south-west were allowed to join forces. Late in November, apparently taking the Yorkists by surprise, Somerset and Devon headed north.

They marched through Bath, Cirencester, Evesham and Coventry to rendezvous at York with the Percies and their allies. By early December the rumour had reached London that there was to be a massive gathering of all Lancastrians at Hull. It was high time the Yorkists took some counter-action.

The earl of March received his first independent command and was dispatched to Wales. The earl of Warwick stayed behind in London to 'protect' Henry VI and supervise the government. As warden of the Cinque Ports and Keeper of the Sea it was his job to hold the Channel and guard against the danger of French raids on the south coast. His retainer, Geoffrey Gate, appointed governor of the Isle of Wight, succeeded in capturing Somerset's brother, Edmund Beaufort. But given the Lancastrian troop movements of the last few weeks it was likely that the decisive confrontation would take place in the north. Thus the main Yorkist force, possibly six thousand strong, was sent north under the command of the duke of York and the earl of Salisbury, together with their sons Edmund of Rutland and Sir Thomas Neville. On 9 December they left London. Their march did not go unchallenged. The duke of Somerset, whose contingent was still effectively under the command of Andrew Trollope, that 'very subtle man of war', lay in wait at Worksop and inflicted some losses on the Yorkist advance patrols. Nonetheless, by 21 December they had reached the relative security of York's castle at Sandal and the neighbouring town of Wakefield. Here they spent Christmas. Whether they were able to enjoy it in traditional fashion is another matter. Not far away at Pontefract, lay the main Lancastrian army under Somerset and the earl of Northumberland and the quantities of Christmas food and drink which might have allowed them to forget that menace for a while were notably absent. Their enemies' control of the countryside must have made it impossible for York's officials to stockpile supplies in readiness for their master's arrival. At any rate it is clear that from the moment of his midwinter arrival at Sandal, York's campaign lay under the shadow of a victualling problem. Instead of being able to hold his army together as a single fighting unit, he found himself forced to disperse his troops in extensive foraging operations. Even so, had they remained behind the walls of Sandal Castle, the duke and his friends should have been safe enough.

But they did not. At the end of December, despite being outnumbered, they sallied out and suffered a disastrous defeat. York himself was killed on the battlefield, as were Sir Thomas Neville, Sir Thomas

Harrington, Sir Thomas Parr and many others, no less than two thousand in total (according to the estimate of the Neville chronicler). Edmund of Rutland died in the pursuit, killed on the bridge at Wakefield by Lord Clifford. Later that evening the earl of Salisbury was captured. Next day, at Pontefract, he was executed. His head was displayed at York, as were those of his friends. The Lancastrian council had ordered that their dead bodies be decapitated. If, in the decision to treat them as traitors, an element of personal vindictiveness had crept in, this would not be altogether surprising. The leaders of the Lancastrian army, Somerset, Northumberland and Clifford, were sons of the men killed five years earlier at the battle of St Albans. Spite of another kind may have been displayed if, as the Neville chronicler complained, the duke of York's head was decorated with a paper crown: an obvious comment on his claim to the throne

The Battle of Wakefield is a puzzle. What had induced the Yorkists to come out from behind the shelter of their walls? But dead men tell no tales and the battle had turned into a slaughter of the men who had taken this seemingly foolish decision. If the victors left behind an account of the events of those days, it does not survive; despite this Yorkist setback the climate of the next twenty-five years was far from being favourable to Lancastrian historical writing. Thus modern historians have tended to write Wakefield off as being simply the last of York's many miscalculations. Miscalculation it certainly was. Even so, we should try to understand the circumstances which lay behind it. After all, the duke of York was not alone. He is unlikely to have launched an attack if Salisbury had been against it – and Salisbury was a man whom Waurin described as 'sage et ymaginatif'. On Salisbury's council, moreover, were men like Harrington and Parr, veterans of Blore Heath and of subsequent campaigns. What then had persuaded these men to run the risk?

The most detailed account of what happened is that written up later in the 1460s by Jean de Waurin. According to him the Yorkists were tricked by the redoubtable Andrew Trollope. It was his idea to have four hundred of Somerset's men dress up in Warwick's livery (the ragged staff) and get themselves admitted into the town on the pretence of being an advance guard of reinforcements on their way from Lancashire. Next morning, Trollope himself, with more troops similarly disguised, sent in the news that the rest of the 'reinforcements' had now arrived. Thoroughly taken in, York decided to move out and bring the main Lancastrian army to battle. But as soon as York's army, still

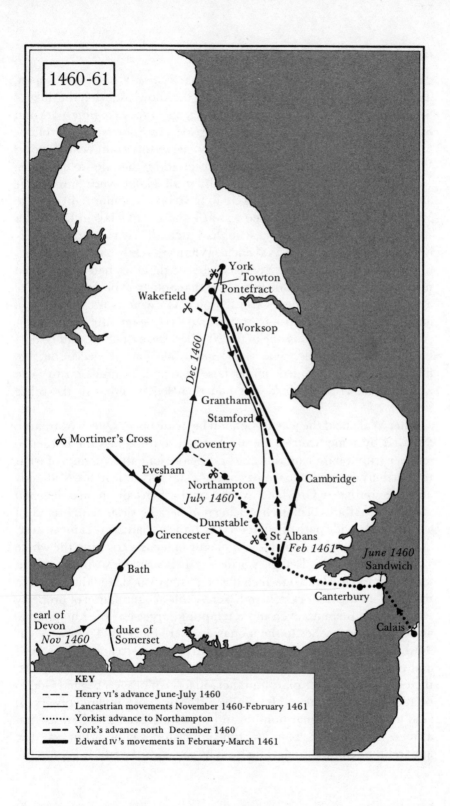

1460-61

York
Towton
Wakefield   Pontefract

Worksop

Dec 1460

Grantham
Stamford

Mortimer's Cross   Coventry

Evesham   Cambridge
          Northampton
          July 1460

                    Dunstable
Cirencester   St Albans
                                 Feb 1461
                                         June 1460
Bath   Sandwich

earl of   duke of   Canterbury
Devon   Somerset   Calais
Nov 1460

KEY
- - - - Henry VI's advance June-July 1460
———— Lancastrian movements November 1460-February 1461
·········· Yorkist advance to Northampton
- - - - York's advance north December 1460
━━━━ Edward IV's movements in February-March 1461

depleted by the absence of foraging parties, was out in the open, Trollope threw off the mask, confident in the knowledge that the duke of Somerset was close at hand. Within a very short space of time York and Salisbury were being attacked on three sides, by Somerset, by Trollope and by the 'advance guard'. Can we believe this complicated story? Would Warwick's father have been deceived by the tales told by men wearing his son's livery? Undoubtedly it all sounds very improbable and Waurin's source is more likely to have been an informant close to Warwick, that is, someone who was at London or Calais in December 1460 rather than someone who had actually witnessed the preliminaries to the Battle of Wakefield. Whatever really happened it does at least seem clear that the Yorkists believed that they had been tricked in some way; several chroniclers assert that Somerset broke the terms of a local truce. Yet another variation on this theme is provided by an anonymous Yorkist chronicler writing very soon after the event. According to him, it was one of the Nevilles, the earl of Westmorland's brother, Lord Neville, who was responsible for the deception. He had sought and obtained 'under false colour' a commission to raise an army on York's behalf, but had then led it across to the other side.

After Wakefield the way to London lay wide open. Queen Margaret, followed by some Scottish troops, hurried south across the border to join her triumphant captains at York. Before long the rumours of what the northerners might do were creating a state of panic in the Midlands and the south. At Croyland Abbey in the Fens the monks listened anxiously to stories of churches being plundered, priests slaughtered, of a thirty-mile-wide path of pillage as the Lancastrian army came nearer, 'a whirlwind from the north, . . . a plague of locusts covering the whole surface of the earth'. Refugees bringing their valuables with them fled for shelter to the island on which the monastery stood, and this added to the fears of the prior of Croyland. Surely this accumulation of property would make them an even more tempting target for 'the abominable army'. All approaches to the monastery were blocked. Trees were cut down and laid across the causeways. Rivers and streams were staked and palisaded. The monks, meanwhile, hid their precious vestments, their jewels and silver plate and then, in fervent prayer, begged God to be allowed to keep them. Mercifully, as the prior of Croyland observed, God took notice of their humble and contrite hearts. The Lancastrian army came to within six miles of the monastery's bounds but was not, apparently, tempted to deviate from its southward path. It kept to the

Great North Road. Croyland and its community of refugees remained unscathed. Moreover, if we wish to know what places were actually pillaged it is very noticeable that the prior of Croyland does not tell us. He names no names, gives no precise information. His whole account is couched in the vague and emotional rhetoric of unsubstantiated atrocity stories.

Another monastic writer, and one who saw the queen's army in the moment of their victory at St Albans, Abbot John Whethamstede, described the 'northern invasion' in similar terms. In a characteristic display of his learning, Abbot John compared the Lancastrians to some notorious war-lords of the past and concluded that they were worse than Attila's Huns. But it is only with their stay at St Albans itself that he descends from the peak of eloquence to give a few factual details – though even these are couched in high-flown language. What then becomes clear is that the queen's army left St Albans in a shambles, dirty, messy and stripped of food and drink. But it is hardly surprising that the town's stores and sanitary arrangements were inadequate to meet the needs of a fairly large army. On the other hand, the abbey precincts were not damaged; nor were the townspeople harmed. Abbot John also tells us that the soldiers themselves felt that they were entitled to behave in the way they did. What all this points to is that the Lancastrian army was behaving much like most armies on the move, quartering itself on the civilian population, commandeering supplies and paying for them inadequately or not at all: a practice by no means easy to distinguish from looting. Inevitably this would lead to tension and all manner of unpleasant incidents in which the soldiers generally held the whip hand. Obviously anyone who wanted a quiet life and uninterrupted enjoyment of his goods would be wise to keep out of the path of an advancing army. Nonetheless, all this is very different from the systematic plundering and devastation which armies adopted as a terror weapon in the war in France. Only in one or two cases – places like Grantham and Stamford which 'deserved punishment' as towns belonging to the duke of York – is it possible that the northerners were deliberately let loose to do all the damage they could. But whatever the realities of the Lancastrian march south may have been, the fact remains that Yorkist propaganda presented that march in a very different light, and did so with great success. In the words of one Yorkist ballad:

> All the lords of the north they wrought by one assent,
> For to destroy the south country they did all their entent.

The conflict which had so recently crystallized into a dynastic struggle for the crown was now portrayed as a war of the north against the south.

In the west, Edward heard reports of the coming northern invasion. With troops raised in the Welsh Marches he prepared to set out for London, but then news from another quarter caused him to change his plans. The earl of Wiltshire had landed in south-west Wales with a force of Bretons, Frenchmen and Irishmen. He had joined up with Jasper Tudor and they were now marching on Hereford. Edward succeeded in intercepting them at Mortimer's Cross, not far from his castle at Wigmore, and bringing them to battle on either 2 or 3 February 1461. We know nothing about the battle, except that it provided Edward with the first of a remarkable series of victories, and that it was said to have been preceded by a remarkable meteorological event: three suns 'in the firmament shining full clear'. According to Edward Hall, this was the origin of one of Edward's badges, the golden sun of York. After the battle several of Edward's prisoners were executed in the market square at Hereford, among them Jasper Tudor's father, Owen. In the words of Gregory's Chronicle:

> His head was set upon the top step of the market cross and a mad woman combed his hair and washed the blood from his face, and she got candles, and placed them about him, and lit them, more than a hundred of them. This Owen Tudor had wedded Queen Katherine, Henry vi's mother, and all the way to the scaffold he had not believed that he would be beheaded till he saw the axe and the block and the collar of his red velvet doublet was ripped off. Then he said, 'That head shall lie on the stock that was wont to lie on Queen Katherine's lap', and he put his heart and mind wholly unto God, and full meekly took his death.

His son, the earl of Pembroke, however, managed to avoid capture, as also did the earl of Wiltshire, one of the great escapers of the age.

It may have been the fact that these two were still at large that kept Edward in the west and left Warwick to take sole charge of the defence of the Yorkist south-east. At the end of January, as soon as he heard that the queen's army had begun to move, Warwick sent out commissions of array to East Anglia and the southern counties. His chief supporters were the duke of Norfolk and the earl of Arundel. The duke of Burgundy sent a contingent of hand-gunners. The city of London made a contribution of two thousand marks. By 12 February Warwick was ready to march out of the capital. Evidently he was in no hurry, for by the morning of Shrove Tuesday (17 February) he had advanced no further than the neighbourhood of St Albans where he was occupying a strongly fortified position.

In reconstructing the events of the next twenty-four hours we should rely chiefly on the accounts written by two men who were there that day, William Gregory, a Londoner in Warwick's army, and John Whethamstede, watching anxiously from the relative safety of his abbey. Their accounts are very different in type and, to some extent, complement each other. Gregory's has many of the characteristic features of a participant's version. He shares to the full a footsoldier's disdain for the easy life of the cavalry. 'As for spearmen they be good to ride before the footmen and eat and drink up their victuals, and many such pretty things they do,' but, he goes on, 'in the footmen is all the trust.' It is clear that certain scenes stand out in his memory and he describes them vividly. He was impressed, for example, by the amount of 'hardware' at the disposal of Warwick's troops, and in particular the Burgundian contingent, who seem to have been equipped with all the latest gadgets. They had firearms which could 'shoot both pellets of lead and arrows of an ell [forty-five inches] in length with six feathers, three in the midst and three at the end, with a mighty piece of iron at the head, and wild fire withal. Also they had nets made of great cords of four fathoms [twenty-four feet] of length and four feet broad, like a rabbit net, with a nail standing upright at every second knot, so that no man could move across it without being hurt.' Among the other devices noticed by Gregory were the caltrap (a sort of starfish made of steel spikes so arranged that in whatever position it lay one spike always projected upwards) and the pavise (a kind of sandwich-board to protect an archer, containing a window through which the man could shoot, and thickly studded with nails so that when the archer had exhausted his arrows he could lay the pavise flat on the ground in front of him to make yet another prickly hazard for charging horses and men). But Gregory makes no attempt to give an ordered sequence of events and for this we have to turn to Whethamstede's account. Written by a man who was comparatively detached in his political outlook and who naturally possessed an excellent knowledge of the topography of St Albans, the abbot's description of the battle is by far the more useful one.

Warwick had mustered a large army, Whethamstede refers to more than twenty-five thousand Yorkist troops, while Gregory went so far as to assert that he was one of a vast host of a hundred thousand. Such figures are unreliable, but it was clearly a sizable force. Whether it was larger than Queen Margaret's army, it is impossible to say. The equally wild estimate of the Neville chronicler put the Lancastrian army at eighty thousand. More reliable is his list of Lancastrian lords: the dukes of Exeter, Somerset, the earls of Northumberland, Devon and Shrewsbury, the Lords Roos, Grey of Codnor, FitzHugh, Greystoke, Wells and Willoughby. Clifford was there also, and all of them, wrote Gregory, wore the ostrich feathers of the prince of Wales as well as their own livery. In Gregory's opinion many of the northerners were just a rabble; the battle, he said, was won by the retinues of the lords. On the Yorkist side there were Warwick and his brother John, recently created Lord Montagu, the duke of Norfolk, the earls of Suffolk and Arundel, the Lords Berners, Bonville, Bourchier, and Fauconberg. So the Lancastrians outnumbered the Yorkists by twelve lords to nine, but this count, of course, tells us nothing about the size of their retinues. The battle, moreover, was not won by weight of numbers. Both the most reliable account and the fact that not a single Yorkist lord was killed in the fighting make it clear that a very large proportion of Warwick's army never came to grips with their enemy.

Why then, at the scene of his triumph six years earlier, did Warwick lose the second battle of St Albans? Warwick, we know, claimed that he was betrayed. After the defeat a man called Lovelace, the commander of the Kentish troops in the Yorkist vanguard, was accused of all manner of offences, accepting bribes from Queen Margaret, passing information about Yorkist troop movements, withdrawing his Kentish men from the line of battle, organizing the return of Henry VI to his queen. But unlike Grey of Ruthin's treachery at Northampton, that of Lovelace is vouched for only by sources close to the defeated general; nor do these partisan sources agree amongst themselves about what Lovelace is supposed to have done. Furthermore, the two best accounts of the battle mention neither treachery nor a man named Lovelace. On balance it looks as though Lovelace became a scapegoat for other men's failures; probably Warwick's own.

The earl of Warwick had evidently decided to adopt a cautious campaign strategy. The pace of his advance from London suggests that he wanted to confront the queen's army while his own forces were still within easy reach of the city and its store of supplies and war material. This defensive strategy may well have been a sensible one. After all, he was the man in possession of two trump cards, the capital and the king. But every strategy, if it is to be successfully carried out, requires good reconnaissance, and it was here that the Yorkists made their first, possibly crucial, mistake. On 16 February one of their outposts was overrun. Its commander, Edward Poynings, and two hundred men (according to the Neville chronicler) were killed. This was at Dunstable, fourteen miles from St Albans. Next day, thinking that the queen's army was still some distance away, Warwick made the mistake of ordering his troops to move out of their fortified camp and take up a new position. As Gregory observed, 'Their scouts had given them no tidings of the queen's army, save one who told them it was nine miles off.' In consequence, Warwick's vanguard, which had advanced to Barnet Heath (on the Luton road just to the north of St Albans) was attacked before it could get into battle order.

What had happened is that the Lancastrians, pressing on swiftly down Watling Street, had tried to drive straight through the centre of St Albans in order to bring Warwick's army to battle as soon as possible, but a contingent of Yorkist archers stationed in the market-place met them with a hail of arrows. As a result, they got no farther than the Great Cross, before being driven back to the west end of the town by St Michael's mill. Undaunted they immediately worked their way northeast along a lane which skirted the town 'Backsides' in order to force an entrance near St Peter's. Once again, however, they encountered some stiff opposition from a contingent of Yorkist infantry. After fairly heavy losses on both sides, the Lancastrians turned away and moved yet farther north to Barnet Heath where they ran into Warwick's vanguard, still in a state of disarray. Here the fiercest fighting of the day took place, involving the largest numbers. According to Whethamstede there were four to five thousand men in the Yorkist vanguard. At first they held their own, but eventually they were forced to give way and then the retreat turned into a rout. The Yorkists scattered and were pursued through the thickets and copses of the surrounding countryside. As always in a pursuit there were heavy losses, which might have been yet heavier had it not been for the coming of darkness. Up to this point the main Yorkist force, estimated by Whethamstede to contain no less than twenty thousand men (as well as the king) and commanded by Warwick himself, had taken no part whatever in the fighting. According to Whethamstede, indeed, it was their failure to come to the aid of the vanguard that had finally broken the morale of that hard-pressed body of men. To make matters worse still, Warwick's troops proved incapable of steeling themselves to face a night in the proximity of the now confident Lancastrians. Depressed by what had happened to the vanguard and unhappily conscious that their theoretical commander-in-chief – the king – was at heart a Lancastrian, they

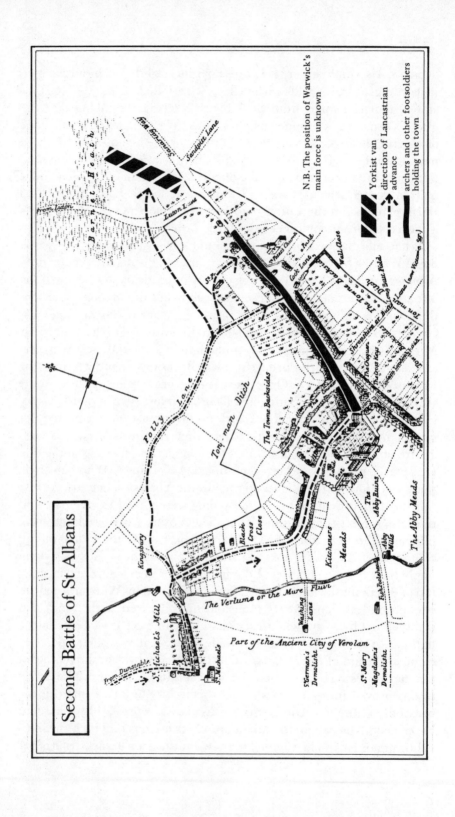

Second Battle of St Albans

N.B. The position of Warwick's
main force is unknown

▨ Yorkist van

⇠ ⇠ direction of Lancastrian
advance

⬛➤ archers and other footsoldiers
holding the town

Barnet Heath

From Luton

Sandpit Lane

Folly Lane

Tonman Ditch

Kingsbury

St Michael's Mill

From Dunstable

St Michael's

The Verlume or the Mure Fluin

Part of the Ancient City of Verolam

St German's Demolisht

St Mary Magdalen Demolisht

Washing Lane

Kitcheners Meads

Black Cross Close

The Towne Backsides

Abby Mills

The Abby Meads

The Abby Ruins

Abby Church

too began to melt away. Before the night was over Warwick's mighty
army had crumbled into nothing and the earl himself was riding
westwards. Possession of the most advanced military technology that
the fifteenth century could offer counted for little when weighed against
poor reconnaissance, uninspired leadership and consequent loss of
morale.

It speaks volumes for the state of confusion in the Yorkist ranks that
night, that they failed to keep possession of an asset as valuable to them
as the person of the king. Left to his own devices, Henry VI joined his
wife and son, and together they took up quarters in the royal chambers
in the abbey of St Albans, while outside, in the town, the victorious
army celebrated. Among those with most cause to rejoice was Andrew
Trollope, knighted by the young prince of Wales in recognition of the
part he had played in the attack on the Yorkist position. According to
Gregory, Trollope received the honour with mock modesty. His foot
had been spiked by a caltrap and, with his mobility impaired, he
claimed to have been unable to perform his usual deeds of valour. 'My
lord, I have not deserved this for I slew no more than fifteen men. I
stood still in one place and they came to me but still they stayed with
me.' A less pleasant occasion was the now traditional beheading of
some of the captured leaders, but in this case it was only two: Lord
Bonville and Sir Thomas Kyriel. Warwick's brother, Lord Montagu,
was spared and, on the whole, the English nobility suffered very little:
an outcome which reflects accurately enough the fact that many of the
Yorkist lords had been sensible, rather than wholehearted in their
commitment to the second battle of St Albans.

With their enemies scattered, the way now lay open for the Lancastrians to march into London, or so it seemed. The city authorities sent a
deputation of ladies, the dowager duchess of Buckingham and the
dowager duchess of Bedford, to Queen Margaret to say that the gates
would be opened if there was no pillaging. On 19 February as a token of
her determination to prevent any such thing, Margaret ordered her
army to return to Dunstable. This, commented the Neville chronicler,
was fatal to her cause. Had she and the king advanced on London
everything would have turned out as they wished. But it was at this
point that the propaganda campaign which the Yorkists had waged
against the 'northern invaders' proved to be of decisive importance.
While the mayor and aldermen were still nervously trying to remain on
good terms with the king and queen, popular feeling in the city turned
out to be resolutely pro-Yorkist. William Gregory reports an incident in

which the mayor gave instructions for some carts to be loaded with bread, victuals and money for the Lancastrians, but when this became known, a group of citizens, led by Sir John Wenlock's cook, seized the carts and distributed the food among the people. 'But as for the Money,' observes Gregory, 'I know not how that was distributed; I trow the purse stole the money.' A news-letter written on 22 February and sent to Michele Arnolfini, a Bruges-based Italian merchant, by his London agent Carlo Gigli, tells how two days earlier, when the dowager duchesses returned with Queen Margaret's assurance that all would be well, the city authorities issued a proclamation 'that everyone should keep fast to his house and should live at peace in order that the king and his forces might enter and behave peacefully. But less than an hour later all the people ran to arms and reports circulated that York with sixty thousand Irish and March with forty thousand Welsh had hastened to the neighbourhood and would guard their place for them; and they said that the mayor must give them the keys of the gates. They called for a brewer as their leader and everything that day was in uproar.' Much to the relief of Arnolfini's correspondent the excitement passed. His letter is a precious indication of the mood in the city as well as of the infinitely precarious political balance. On 20 and 22 February Carlo Gigli fore-saw no better outcome than that 'since the queen and the prince have not descended in fury with their troops, the gates may be opened to them and they may be allowed to enter peacefully. God grant this may happen!'

God granted otherwise. On the day that Margaret ordered her army back to Dunstable, Edward, earl of March, heard the devastating news of St Albans. He moved east at once with all the troops he had mustered. On 22 February he met Warwick in the Cotswolds and together they rode for London. Four days later, to the cheers of the crowd, they entered the capital. Now that Henry was in Margaret's hands, the earls had to take the dynastic struggle a stage further. They had either to give up the contest altogether or depose Henry and set up a new king. And in the person of the nineteen-year-old Edward of March there was a new king ready to hand. He can have needed no prompting from Warwick. Whereas Warwick's reputation was sullied by defeat, Edward was fresh from his victory at Mortimer's Cross and confident that his hour had come. The backbone of the army which escorted him into London was provided not by Warwick's men, but by his own, by retainers and tenants drawn from the Welsh and Marcher estates which he had inherited from his father, Duke Richard, just as he had inherited from him the obligation to seize the moment and claim the throne. And so it was done. During the first four days of March 1461 in a series of carefully stage-managed ceremonies – ceremonies which stopped just short of being a formal coronation – Edward of March was proclaimed king of England. There were not many magnates by his side when he took his momentous step, perhaps only Warwick, Norfolk, the archbishop of Canterbury and the Beauchamp and Neville bishops of Salisbury and Exeter, but that he offered a popular alternative to a regime dominated by Queen Margaret is not in doubt. On 4 March an Italian in London wrote of the 'great multitude who say they want to be with him to conquer or die'. Something of this same mood can be sensed in the lines recorded by William Gregory: 'Let us walk in a new vineyard, and let us make a gay garden in the month of March with this fair white rose and herb, the earl of March.'

How long this favourable mood would last would depend in the first place on how successfully Edward tackled his immediate military problem. The queen, cheated of her prey, had withdrawn north of the Trent, but she was still undefeated, and even now could command the allegiance of a majority amongst the English nobility. An assessment of the situation written by an Italian observer at the court of France suggested that Margaret could afford to remain on the defensive 'as they say she is well content to do'. Simply by standing firm and holding off Yorkist attacks she could undermine the new king's fragile authority until the people 'seeing that they are not, after all, on the road to peace, can easily be induced to change sides – such being the nature of the people'. By implication, if Edward was to survive he had to attack. In a proclamation issued on 6 March he announced that any adherent of Henry VI who submitted within ten days would be pardoned – with the significant exception of anyone who had an income of more than 100 marks a year. This suggests that Edward's strategy was to look for popular support and try to thrust a wedge between the Lancastrian lords and their followers: a continuation on a wider scale of the policy adopted at the battle of Northampton. In addition a reward of £100 was offered to any man who put to death certain named enemies of the house of York, prominent among them the Lancastrians' chief military adviser, Sir Andrew Trollope.

Edward stayed in London for another week, overseeing the central administration of his war effort and persuading the city to add another £4,000 to its financial contribution. Most of the other Yorkist leaders dispersed in order to raise troops in their own areas, chiefly East Anglia and the Midlands. On 11 March Lord Fauconberg left the city at the head of an infantry force made up of Kentishmen and those king-making contingents from the Welsh Marches which had come to London a fortnight earlier. Two days later Edward himself set out, accompanied by the duke of Norfolk and the rest of the army, some Burgundian troops once again included. Their advance northwards through Cambridge was taken at a measured pace, giving time for other contingents to join the main army. By the time he reached Pontefract (on 27 or 28 March) close to the scene of his father's death, Edward was in command of an exceptionally large army. Gregory's Chronicle gives a figure of two hundred thousand men and this can at least be taken to mean that it was bigger than the Yorkist force at St Albans. Although there were only eight or nine noblemen in Edward's army, this figure is misleading inasmuch as it ignores the fact that the king himself now represented all the wealth and political connexions of the house of York. The combined magnet of the York and Neville estates continued to exert an enormous pull and draw in large numbers of gentry. Even so, it is likely that Queen Margaret's army was at least as big. It contained nineteen or twenty lords and a very considerable array of gentry from all over England. Some sixty knights and gentlemen were later attainted for their activities in March 1461 and of these, twenty-five were men of sufficient standing to have been MPs. Not surprisingly, modern historians who tend to be very sceptical of large numbers are nonetheless prepared to admit that on this occasion there may have been as many as fifty thousand present on both sides. At any rate it looks as though half of the entire political establishment was there, squaring up for a decisive encounter. Some men must have been continuously under arms for three months now and they can only have hoped that, one way or another, an end would soon be put to the debilitating uncertainties of the last year and a half.

Unfortunately, despite the crucial importance of this encounter, we have no eyewitness description of the Battle of Towton to match Whethamstede's account of the second battle of St Albans. On the subject of the northern battle, so far distant from his own local interests, the abbot has little to offer except classical allusions and pious reflections. The most detailed account is that written by Edward Hall and this one has been the most influential, but it was composed some eighty years after the event and clearly should not be relied on. Closest to the event is a letter written by Warwick's brother, George, bishop of Exeter, on 7 April 1461, itself based on news which had just reached

London via messengers and letters. But, like most political letters, this one is more concerned with the consequences of the battle (notably the list of important casualties) than with describing its ebb and flow. Thus all George Neville says of the events of 29 March which preceded the rout is that 'there was a great conflict that day, beginning at sunrise and lasting until ten o'clock at night, so great was the determination and boldness of the combatants, none of whom took any heed of the possibility of a miserable death'. To some extent Neville's letter can be supplemented by the relevant chapters from Jean de Waurin's history, for, although they were composed after 1465, they were at least based on information provided by men who were present at the battle. Nonetheless, even with the addition of a few sentences taken from Gregory's Chronicle and from some contemporary notes apparently compiled at Ely, these scraps simply do not allow us to reconstruct the events surrounding Towton with any confidence.

What is clear is that the weather was bitterly cold – there was snow about – and that there were two separate actions on two consecutive days, 28 and 29 March, Saturday and Palm Sunday 1461. On the first day the struggle centred around control of the passage of the River Aire on the road between Pontefract and York. At Wentbridge Edward's reconnaissance patrols made contact with a Lancastrian force which had been given the job of holding the line of the Aire. This clash of arms brought the Yorkist vanguard hurrying to the aid of their patrols, and for the next few hours the crossing was fiercely contested. According to George Neville, the Lancastrians had broken the bridge at Ferrybridge and held a strongly fortified position at its northern end. 'Our men could only cross by a narrow way which they themselves made and over which they forced a way at sword point, many men being slain on both sides.' Although the Lancastrians eventually had to retreat and concede the crossing, it seems evident that both they and the ice-cold waters of the River Aire claimed many victims. One Yorkist peer, Lord FitzWalter, was killed and the earl of Warwick himself received an arrow wound in the leg.

Having crossed the river, Edward's army then had to spend a cold and uncomfortable night in the open. They were running short of provisions for both men and horses, and the main Lancastrian army was still intact somewhere to the north of them. In this unfriendly terrain a long-drawn-out campaign was a grim prospect. Fortunately for Edward the morning brought news that the Lancastrians too were anxious to fight and settle the matter once and for all. They were drawn up in battle array on the road between Ferrybridge and Tadcaster, probably just behind the valley of Dintingdale. All we know for certain about Towton itself is that it was long and hard, in the end one of the bloodiest battles ever fought on British soil. It opened, presumably, with an exchange of archery fire and here one of Whethamstede's pious reflections may be significant. Through God's agency, he wrote, the wind suddenly changed direction and began to blow hard in the faces of the Lancastrians, thus making life harder for their bowmen and correspondingly easier for the Yorkists. According to Jean de Waurin, Edward's cavalry was driven from the field by the massed charge of a Lancastrian force under the command of the duke of Somerset, Lord Rivers and the ubiquitous Trollope. So successful was this manoeuvre that these Lancastrians believed that they had won the day; and probably they would have done if, on the other wing, the earl of Northumberland had acted with similar *élan*. As it happened, however, writes Waurin, Northumberland's slower advance gave Edward time to steady his troops. As usual, the climax of the battle was the mêlée of dismounted men-at-arms wielding swords, axes and maces. Edward himself fought on foot by his standard, determined not to flee, but to live or die that day amongst his soldiers. Many people were inclined to ascribe the final victory, after a day of fluctuating fortunes, to his personal prowess. This, of course, was a sensible way to write about a king, but it may also have had some basis in fact. A brave, heavily-armoured and powerfully built king (Edward, we know from his skeleton, was 6 foot $3\frac{1}{2}$ inches tall) was a force to be reckoned with on the field of battle, an inspirational asset all the more valuable in view of the complete absence of any equivalent figure on the Lancastrian side.

In the end the Lancastrian line broke. Most fled north, many of them hoping to find safety behind the walls of York. The battle itself had been fairly evenly matched; the pursuit turned into carnage. According to George Neville, the bridge at Tadcaster was down – broken, he said, by the Lancastrians themselves as part of their plan to check the Yorkist advance – and as a result many were drowned and others trapped in the town and slaughtered. The Yorkists escaped lightly. Apart from FitzWalter, only one name, that of the Kentish captain Robert Horne, appears on the casualty lists, but for the Lancastrians these two days were calamitous. Five peers were killed in action: Northumberland, Clifford, Neville, Dacre and Welles. The earl of Devon was captured next day and executed at York. There were heavy losses too amongst the gentry. According to Gregory's Chronicle no less than forty-two knights were taken and killed at the end of the battle. Whether or not he was still limping from the wound he received at St Albans, Sir Andrew Trollope was one of those who failed to escape to fight another day. The loss of this experienced soldier was a damaging blow to the Lancastrian cause. In all the heralds counted twenty-eight thousand slain at Towton, or so it was widely reported. Most other contemporary estimates were higher; one, by the Neville chronicler, much lower. He put the number of deaths at nine thousand. Whatever the real total, it is clear that Towton was generally regarded as a disaster, a cause for lamentation and for reflection upon the tragic misfortunes which could befall a poorly governed kingdom, a last, appalling commentary on the misrule of Henry VI.

Nine

THE WAR IN THE NORTH, 1461–4

QUEEN MARGARET heard the news at York and fled to Scotland, taking her husband and son with her. She was soon joined by the dukes of Somerset and Exeter, Lord Roos and others of her partisans such as the learned judge Sir John Fortescue. Edward IV, meanwhile, had entered York and taken down his father's head from the wall. He stayed there for three weeks, aware that much of the north was now at his disposal. The bloodshed at Towton had broken the strength of those families which had traditionally dominated northern society and which had hitherto been solidly Lancastrian: the Percies, the Cliffords, the Dacres. With them gone, the way was open for a thorough reorganization. Not that this would be easy. The old loyalties died hard. As John Harding, a fifteenth-century expert on Anglo-Scottish relations, pointed out, the Percies 'have the hearts of the people of the north and always have had'. In these circumstances it is hardly surprising that Edward preferred to seek a reconciliation with some of his old enemies. Laurence Booth, the courtier bishop of Durham, had been closely attached to Margaret, but Edward now made him his confessor. From Durham, where he spent the last week of April, Edward moved on to Newcastle. Here, on 1 May, he witnessed the execution of one of his father's chief enemies, the earl of Wiltshire. The earl's talent for getting away had failed him at last. Then, instead of pushing on into Northumberland, where the castles of Warkworth, Alnwick, Bamburgh and Dunstanburgh were still held against him, Edward turned south. There were pressing matters which required his attention: his coronation and a parliament to pass an act of attainder against the Lancastrians. Unfinished military business in the north would have to be left to the Nevilles, to the earl of Warwick and his brother, Lord Montagu, released from captivity when Edward's victorious army marched into York.

The key to the north now lay in Scotland. In the last few years the border between the two kingdoms had again been a troubled one. An energetic young king of Scotland, James II, had been making the most of the opportunities offered by the political disturbances in England. In 1456 he carried out a six-day raid into Northumberland and in 1457 launched an attack on Berwick. His diplomacy involved plotting with Lancaster against York and with York against Lancaster, while at the same time he was urging the French king, Charles VII, to make a (from the Scottish point of view) diversionary attack upon Calais. Other military preparations had included the purchase of iron and gunpowder abroad and the encouragement of archery practice at home. Distractions like football and golf were to be 'uttirly cryit doune and nocht usyt'. In the long term James II's programme may have had precious little influence on the Scottish character, but in the short run he achieved his aim of creating a well-equipped and effective army. At the end of 1460, as soon as he had heard the news of the Battle of Northampton, he led a great host across the border to lay siege to Roxburgh Castle. On 3 August his wife, Mary of Guelders, arrived to inspire the enthusiasm of the Scottish troops, and to celebrate her arrival, James ordered his bombards to fire a salute. Unluckily one of the guns exploded and the king's thigh was smashed by a flying fragment. His successor, James III, was only eight years old. The defeated Lancastrians had fled from Towton to take refuge at and look for aid from a court which was faced with all the problems of a royal minority.

It soon became clear that the Scottish regency council was divided into two factions: one group, known as 'the young lords', was headed by James II's widow; the other, 'the old lords', was headed by Bishop Kennedy of St Andrews. Inevitably this meant that Queen Margaret would be very fortunate indeed if she were to obtain much help from a court distracted by its own quarrels. Even so, she was prepared to pay a high price for hospitality and for the prospect of military assistance. On 25 April 1461, on her orders, Berwick was surrendered to the Scots. After more than a hundred years in English possession the vital stronghold of the east March had been freely handed over. Margaret of Anjou was prepared to go further and cede Carlisle, the key to the west March, as well. Since this was not hers to give, it had to be besieged by a combined Scottish–Lancastrian force. News of this attack led Edward to bring forward the date of his coronation to 28 June in order to 'speed him northward with all haste'. In the event, however, he stayed in the south. He had still not been anointed king when further news reached

London. Carlisle had been relieved by Lord Montagu. The bishop
of Durham, moreover, had proved loyal. In June a surprise raid
led by Lords Roos, Dacre and Richemont Gray had penetrated as
far as the earl of Westmorland's castle at Brancepeth, south of
Durham. There they had raised the Lancastrian standard, but
despite (or perhaps because of) the fact that they had brought
Henry vi along with them, they found very little enthusiasm for the
cause. Laurence Booth mustered the local levies and sent them pack-
ing. Reassured by these developments Edward decided to remain
south of the Trent.

This, however, did not mean that he was totally unaware of the
military problem. The north was not the only theatre of war. In
Normandy the seneschal, Margaret of Anjou's old friend Pierre de
Brézé, had assembled a fleet for the conquest of the Channel Islands.
When a French force landed on Jersey in May the first stage of this
project seemed to be well on the way to completion. The threat to the
south and west of England was one which Edward could not afford to
ignore. The death of Charles vii on 22 July 1461 from complications
following the removal of a diseased tooth, gave Edward a slight
breathing-space. The new king of France, Louis xi, had, as dauphin,
been moderately pro-Yorkist and his succession to the throne was at
once followed by de Brézé's disgrace and the cancellation of the expedition. But this turned out to be an expression of Louis's hostility to his
father's policies rather than of his friendship for Edward. By early 1462
beacons were being manned all along the south coast and preparations
made for a naval squadron to patrol the Channel.

As well as the threats of foreign invasion Edward had to deal with the
problem of local disorder, inevitably serious when civil war followed
upon a long period of weak government. The new king's authority was
insecure and easily flouted. Even in an area as apparently Yorkist as
East Anglia, Edward's agents had difficulty in carrying out royal
orders. The castle of New Buckenham in Norfolk, for example, had
been seized by two esquires, John and William Knyvet, and when, in
July 1461, Edward authorized a group of officials headed by Sir
William Chamberlain, Gilbert Debenham and John Twyer to take
possession of the castle, they were openly and successfully defied.
According to their own report, they managed to enter the outer ward,
but then found the drawbridge to the moat-encircled inner ward raised
against them and a garrison ready to defend the castle. John Knyvet's
wife, Alice, appeared at the drawbridge tower and addressed them.

'Maister Twyer, ye be a justice of the pees and I require you to kepe the peas for I woll nott leve the possession of this castell to dye therfore, and if ye begyn to breke the peas or make any warr to gete the place of me I shall defende me, for lever I had in suche wyse to dye than to be slayne when my husbond cometh home for he charget me to kepe it.' Edward had to call in bigger guns to deal with the problem, but even after the duke of Norfolk himself had received the king's commission, the dispute was resolved only by a compromise and a pardon for the Knyvets. By January 1462 Margaret Paston was writing to her husband: 'God in his holy mercy give grace that there may be set a good and a wise rule in this country [i.e., Norfolk] in haste, for I heard never say of so much robbery and manslaughter in this country as is now within a little time.' It was a conventional enough opinion, but such views, if widespread, could be very dangerous to a new regime which was still trying to prove itself.

A traditional means of reasserting royal authority was for the king to go on a progress through the shires. In July 1461 Edward hoped to kill two birds with one stone by combining this with the first moves in a campaign against Lancastrians still holding out in Wales. A progress, moreover, would serve to emphasize the contrast in styles between the old and the new king. Early in August he left London, accompanied by two of those who had appeared on his coronation honours list – the earl of Essex (formerly Viscount Bourchier), Lord Hastings (formerly Sir William Hastings) – and some of the judges. He visited Kent, Sussex, Hampshire, Wiltshire and Gloucestershire. At Bristol he himself presided over the trial of a west-country Lancastrian, Sir Baldwin Fulford. After the predictable outcome of the trial, Fulford's head was impaled in the market-place at Exeter and there it remained for eighteen months. Not until March 1463 was it removed, and then only on the grounds that 'it daily falleth down' among the feet of the citizens. From Bristol Edward progressed through the Marches of Wales and the west Midlands before returning to London for the first parliament of his reign. The original plan of a royal expedition to Wales had been abandoned. Nonetheless the problem still existed. Jasper Tudor, earl of Pembroke, Henry Holland, duke of Exeter, and other convinced Lancastrians were in possession of castles as important as Pembroke, Harlech, Carreg Cennen and Denbigh. For this reason, on 12 July, Edward had commanded Philip Harveys, his newly-appointed Master of the King's Ordnance, to mobilize his artillery. In the same month two new peers, Lord Herbert (formerly Sir William Herbert) and Lord

Ferrers (formerly Sir Walter Devereux) had been authorized to raise men in the border counties. Although Edward changed his mind about leading it himself, the muster of the army went on unchecked, and in the autumn Lord Herbert took command of a highly successful campaign. He captured Pembroke Castle on 30 September. Then, on 16 October, he defeated the earl of Pembroke and the duke of Exeter at Twt Hill just outside Caernarvon. After this defeat the Welsh Lancastrians were no longer capable of putting any army in the field. Their strongholds were isolated and picked off: Denbigh in January 1462, Carreg Cennen in May. Only Harlech continued to hold out. The capture of this great fortress, designed to be supplied from the sea, would have required a greater expenditure on ships and artillery than Edward was prepared to sanction. So for several years more this nest of rebels was allowed to survive under the captaincy of Sir Richard Tunstall, one of Henry VI's most loyal servants. Harlech was a potential bridgehead should the Lancastrians ever seek to land in force in Wales, but for the moment, from the king's point of view, no more than a distant pinprick.

The situation in the north remained much more precarious. The appointment of Warwick as warden of both east and west Marches in July 1461 suggested that the problem of Northumberland was being given high priority and, as in Wales, the autumn of that year witnessed some notable successes. In mid-September the chief Percy stronghold at Alnwick surrendered and a new garrison was installed. Soon afterwards Sir Ralph Percy surrendered the coastal fortress of Dunstanburgh. But instead of a Yorkist constable's being appointed to hold it, Sir Ralph was allowed to remain in command. Since his father had been killed at St Albans in 1455 and his elder brother at Towton this can only be described as a calculated risk on Edward's part and it was one which failed. On the other hand, the more obvious expedient adopted at Alnwick can hardly be accounted a success either. Within a few months Sir William Tailboys had retaken it for the Lancastrians. The establishment of Lord Dacre at Naworth Castle (east of Carlisle) was further proof – if proof were needed – that Edward's hold on the far north of his kingdom could never be secure as long as the Lancastrians had a base just across the border. Much therefore would depend on diplomacy and on the level of pressure which the English king could bring to bear on the Scottish court.

Ironically enough it was James II's greatest political triumph, the overthrow of the Black Douglases, which was making life difficult for his young successor. The disinherited earl of Douglas in exile in England since 1455 was keen to take his revenge on the house of Stewart. In February 1462, after several months of negotiation, James Douglas succeeded in persuading the powerful earl of Ross, Lord of the Outer Isles, and his kinsman Donald Balloch to join him in a confederacy subsidized by Edward iv. Its object was the restoration of the Black Douglases and the expulsion of the Stewarts. Scotland north of the Forth was to be partitioned equally between the three confederates as vassals of Edward iv. This was a far-reaching scheme, but also a far-fetched one, and Edward naturally did not pin much faith or spend much money on it. More promising was a direct approach to Mary of Guelders, especially if there was any truth in the rumour that the duke of Somerset had seduced her and now that he was in France was openly boasting of his conquest. Mary, moreover, was a niece of Duke Philip of Burgundy and her pro-Yorkist uncle could be relied on to lend his voice to those urging her to eject the Lancastrians. True, in March 1462, Mary paid for Margaret of Anjou's passage to France but this could have been just to get rid of her. Certainly when the earl of Warwick spoke to Mary in April and then again in June he came away from the meetings full of optimism, but always it seems it was only the 'young lords' who were sympathetic. Kennedy and the 'old lords' ensured that the regency council took no clear pro-Yorkist line. On the other hand, it is possible that Mary of Guelders too was only playing for time, waiting for news of Queen Margeret's mission to France, before she would show her hand. In the absence of private papers we cannot hope to unravel the devious diplomacy of the time with any certainty. What is clear, however, is that while Margaret was in France, her enemies were able to recover the initiative in Northumberland. A short Anglo–Scottish truce was made to last from June to the end of August and the Yorkist commanders took full advantage of this breathing-space. In July Lord Dacre surrendered Naworth to Montagu; Tailboys surrendered Alnwick to a force under Hastings, Sir John Howard and Sir Ralph Grey. Bamburgh was captured by Sir William Tunstall.

In the autumn of 1462, however, the pendulum swung back again when Queen Margaret returned from France. In June she and her cousin, Louis xi, had come to terms. In return for the cession of Calais Louis agreed to lend her money and release de Brézé to take command of a French expeditionary force. But in order to reach Calais Louis's troops had to cross Burgundian territory and this Duke Philip refused to allow. Denied access to Calais Louis became altogether less interested in Margaret's cause. Thus, when the queen set sail in October she and de Brézé had raised no more than eight hundred men and these had been paid for by de Brézé himself. Their voyage took them first to Scotland, where Henry VI came aboard, and then back to Bamburgh where they landed on 25 October. The castle soon opened its gates and was given into the keeping of the duke of Somerset. Sir Ralph Percy in Dunstanburgh reverted to the traditional allegiance of his family. Alnwick too, its garrison inadequately supplied with victuals, had to surrender after a short siege. The Lancastrians, however, were unable to capitalize on these early successes. When Henry VI's standard was raised, disappointingly few of the local gentry came to offer their support; most preferred to wait and see what would happen. What did happen was that Edward IV's government reacted with speed and vigour. Only five days after the landing at Bamburgh, the earl of Warwick left London on his way north, soon to be followed by a commission authorizing him to raise the levies of the northern shires. Supplies and the king's ordnance were sent by sea to Newcastle. By 4 November Edward himself was on the same road, having summoned to his side almost all the nobility still in Yorkist England. At the same time the earl of Douglas was given permission to harry the border. Faced by the imminent arrival of an army much bigger than her own, Margaret set sail for Scotland, leaving the garrisons of Alnwick, Bamburgh and Dunstanburgh to fend for themselves. Her fleet had hardly put to sea when it was struck by a storm. Four ships were wrecked, including her own. She, Henry and de Brézé managed to struggle into Berwick in an open boat, but the greater part of the soldiers and sailors found themselves stranded on Holy Island and at the mercy of the Yorkists.

Edward IV, meanwhile, had minor troubles of his own. He had reached Durham on 16 November only to be laid low by an attack of measles. This did not prevent his confiscating the estates of Bishop Booth and banishing him to Cambridge – a sensible political precaution as well as a profitable one – but it did mean that he was temporarily unable to undertake an active military role. In the king's absence Warwick acted as the Yorkist commander-in-chief. From a base at Warkworth he directed simultaneous operations against all three castles. In charge at Alnwick were the experienced Lord Fauconberg, recently created earl of Kent, and Anthony Woodville, Lord Scales, a former Lancastrian – he had fought at Towton – pardoned in July 1461. Dunstanburgh was besieged by the earl of Worcester and Sir Ralph Grey; Bamburgh by Montagu and Lord (formerly Sir Robert) Ogle.

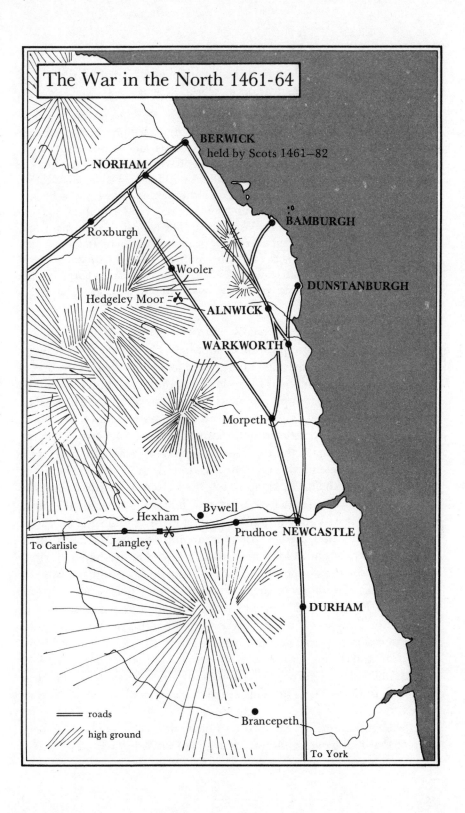

The War in the North 1461-64

BERWICK
held by Scots 1461—82

NORHAM

Roxburgh

BAMBURGH

Wooler

DUNSTANBURGH

Hedgeley Moor

ALNWICK

WARKWORTH

Morpeth

Bywell

Hexham

Prudhoe

NEWCASTLE

To Carlisle

Langley

DURHAM

Brancepeth

═══ roads

///// high ground

To York

One of John Paston's letters to his brother gives a useful picture of Edward IV's war administration at work.

My Lord of Warwick rideth daily to all these castles to oversee the sieges. If they need victuals or anything else, he is ready to supply them. The king commanded my Lord of Norfolk to send victuals and the ordnance from Newcastle to Warkworth Castle to my Lord of Warwick; and so my Lord of Norfolk commanded Sir John Howard, Sir William Peche, Sir Robert Chamberlain, Ralph Asheton and me, Calthorpe and Gorge and others to escort the victuals and ordnance; and so yesterday [10 December 1462] we were with my Lord of Warwick at Warkworth. The King lieth at Durham, and my Lord of Norfolk at Newcastle. We have people enough here. In case we stay longer I pray you see that more money is sent to me here by Christmas Eve at the latest, for I cannot obtain leave to send any of my waged men home. No one can depart – unless, of course, they steal away without permission, but if this were to be detected they would be sharply punished.

As John Paston's letter makes plain this winter campaign in the north was very largely a question of supplies. The three garrisons were to be starved into submission. There could, of course, be no question of a frontal assault against their formidable fortifications, but it is perhaps surprising that no attempt was made to use the king's artillery. The answer seems to be that Edward wanted the castles intact. Flattened walls would do very little to help maintain royal authority in Percy country. Undoubtedly the arrival of the king's great guns put extra pressure on the defenders, and if they could hasten the end of the sieges without actually being fired, so much the better. Whether or not the artillery should be used was a matter of fine judgment, all the more delicate since it was known that a relieving army would soon be on the way. The Scots had pledged their honour to rescue the garrison of Alnwick. One of the 'old lords', the earl of Angus, had a further inducement in the shape of the English dukedom promised him by Henry VI on 22 November 1462 in return for armed help. Shortly before Christmas Edward and Warwick learned that the relief army had in fact set out. They were able, however, to prevent this news reaching the beleaguered garrisons and on Christmas Eve the defenders of Dunstanburgh and Bamburgh (reduced to eating their horses) made a conditional offer of surrender. After some discussion their offer was accepted and two days after Christmas the two castles were in Yorkist hands.

The terms made by Edward at Christmas 1462 have often been criticized as being over-generous. He agreed to the full reinstatement of the duke of Somerset to all his lands and titles; within a matter of days the duke found himself at Alnwick helping Warwick against his former friends. More remarkable still was Edward's willingness to allow Sir Ralph Percy to take command of both Bamburgh and Dunstanburgh as soon as he had sworn an oath of allegiance. Percy indeed was authorized to receive repentant rebels into the king's grace at his own discretion. Probably, as has been suggested, Edward was over-confident, too much inclined to put faith in his own personal charm and in his ability to win over old enemies. On the other hand, he was not indiscriminately generous. Two of the lords defending Bamburgh and Dunstanburgh, the earl of Pembroke and Lord Roos, were unable to obtain such favourable terms. Furthermore, Edward's own bargaining position was not strong. Unless he made the terms of surrender sufficiently attractive, the garrisons would decide to fight on and he knew (as they did not) that the relieving army was on the way. In these circumstances Edward's generosity – even though, as it turned out, it failed to produce the desired result – was not necessarily foolish.

With two of the castles already in their hands, the Yorkists could now concentrate on the blockade of Alnwick. But then, on 5 January 1463, de Brézé and the earl of Angus appeared with the long-awaited relieving army. Warwick raised the siege and withdrew slightly, making no effort to bring the Scottish army to battle. Lord Hungerford, the hard-pressed commander of the Alnwick garrison, immediately took the chance to march out in full view of Warwick's men and join his friends, leaving only a token force behind to hold the castle. According to the rather later northern chronicler John Warkworth, Warwick was afraid of the Scots and the Scots, fearing a ruse, were afraid of him. Most contemporaries believed that the Scots were in the stronger position, whether by virtue of superior numbers or whether because Warwick's troops were in poort heart, having 'lain there so long in the field, grieved with cold and rain', and that, in consequence, the Scots should have attacked. 'Had the Scots been bold and sensible,' wrote the Neville chronicler, 'they might have destroyed all the nobility of England then and there.' This was de Brézé's opinion too – or so he claimed afterwards – but at the time more cautious counsels prevailed. Having rescued the bulk of the garrison, the Scots withdrew over the border. Next day, of course, Alnwick opened its gates to the earl of Warwick. It all seemed a bit of an anticlimax. Two substantial armies had been mobilized and had come within sight of each other, but there had been no battle. In the words of one unknown contemporary

observer, 'And in all this long time, when almost all the armed force of
England was assembled against our enemies, what, I ask, what action
memorable or deserving of praise was done, except the capture of the
aforesaid three castles?' Clearly the thought moved the writer to indignation, but his was the indignation of a southerner and it was almost
certainly misplaced. This war in the north was fought in the normal,
battle-avoiding pattern of war on the continent. It was fought, in other
words, according to methods which made good sense in lands accustomed to the regular occurrence of war – and unlike the rest of England,
Northumbria and the Scottish border were such a land. Here the
normal campaign strategy was not to seek battle, but to win control of
strongpoints. This, of course, though it seemed a trivial gain to our
southern writer, is precisely what the winter campaign of 1462–3
achieved. Summing up Edward's position at the beginning of 1463 it
seemed to John Warkworth that the king 'was possessed of all England
except a castle in north Wales called Harlech'.

It was still too early for Edward to relax: though much had been
achieved and key castles had been won, they still had to be retained. For
a while after Edward left the north, Warwick remained there, keeping a
watch on the Scottish border. Then he too came south, and with his
departure the Yorkist hold on Northumberland crumbled. In March
1463 Sir Ralph Percy allowed a force of French and Scots to reoccupy
Bamburgh and Dunstanburgh. Edward IV's gamble had clearly failed.
But in handing out these important commands it was not easy to find
the right political balance between local men and outsiders. At Alnwick, for example, the local man Sir Ralph Grey was appointed constable while the senior post of captain went to Sir John Astley, a knight
of the Garter and a former hero of the tiltyard, but a man whose
connexions were East Anglian. Grey, it seems, felt he had been treated
unfairly. In May he followed Sir Ralph Percy's example, tricking Astley
and welcoming Lord Hungerford back to Alnwick. For the third time
since the battle of Towton the three castles were in Lancastrian hands
and all the hard – and expensive – work of the winter campaign had
been undone. Edward had to find not just a military, but also a political
solution to the problem of the north. The appointment of Warwick as
warden of both Marches could be an answer only if Warwick was
prepared to stay in the north, but the fact was that the earl, like his royal
master, gave a higher priority to the problems and pleasures of the
south. Only during an emergency was he willing to stay in the north,
and this was a recipe for recurring emergencies. The first glimmerings

of a more permanent solution can be seen in the appointment of Lord Montagu as warden of the crucial east March on 26 May at an improved rate of pay. In the last two years John Neville had been the most energetic of all the northern Yorkists and he was very soon in action again, taking measures to guard against a threat to Newcastle. As it happened, the citizens of Newcastle turned out to be very capable of looking after themselves. Not only did they beat off the Lancastrian attack, they also succeeded in capturing four French supply ships heading for Bamburgh.

Meanwhile, since it was an emergency, Warwick had once again taken the road north. He left London on 3 June, accompanied by his brother-in-law Thomas, Lord Stanley. On their arrival they found the news so serious that they wrote at once to Edward, urging him to muster reinforcements and come with all possible speed. It was known that Queen Margaret had persuaded the Scottish regency council to try another invasion and rumoured that she had offered them seven English counties in return for their support. To Kennedy she was said to have held out the prospect of the archbishopric of Canterbury. Early in July 1463 the boy king of Scotland James III led a large army over the border to lay siege to Norham Castle. This was clearly a major effort. Henry VI, Queen Margaret and Mary of Guelders were all present; so too was the Scottish 'great ordnance'. The Lancastrian garrisons of Alnwick, Bamburgh and Dunstanburgh were in position to threaten the supply lines of any force which tried to march to the relief of Norham. Despite all this, the Scottish enterprise ended in a humiliating failure. Warwick and Montagu, aided by the archbishop of York and the northern levies, made their way to the siege without being intercepted. At their approach the invaders retreated in confusion, leaving southern Scotland defenceless. Warwick and Montagu seized the chance to launch a retaliatory raid, burning and pillaging over a wide area and only calling a halt when they ran out of victuals. Over on the west March the exiled earl of Douglas was also busy doing as much damage as he could to his countrymen. For the Scots the capture and execution of Douglas's brother was the only bright spot in a disastrous summer. After this fiasco it was evident that Queen Margaret could hope for no further active assistance from the Scottish court, so in August she set sail from Bamburgh, taking with her de Brézé and her son, leaving her husband in the care of Bishop Kennedy. Henry and Margaret never met again.

Edward IV, meanwhile, had obtained a parliamentary grant of

£37,000 (the first such grant of his reign) and a subsidy from the Canterbury convocation, both for 'the defence of the realm'. It was generally believed that this money was going to be spent on a follow-up campaign against Scotland. In a letter written on 7 August the king's intimate counsellor Lord Hastings told Jean de Lannoy that the Scots would be made to repent to the Day of Judgment the aid they had given to Henry and Margaret. On 9 August orders were given for the mobilization of the royal artillery and plans were made for a muster of troops at Newcastle in mid-September. Warwick provided at least six ships to form the core of a northern fleet under the command of the earl of Worcester. In June Edward had assured parliament that he would lead the army in person and so he was on schedule when he rode to York in September, but though he remained in the north until January 1464 no further military operations were undertaken. Naturally the taxpayers felt that they had been cheated. The southern churchman who had criticized last winter's campaign was now even more disillusioned. The king's grand army had failed to materialize. The fleet had skulked in port, the sailors doing nothing but eat and drink. 'Shame and confusion was the wretched outcome of it all.' William Gregory of London came to a similar conclusion: 'All was lost and in vain and came to no purpose, neither by water nor by land.' The resentment was sufficiently widespread to persuade Edward that he had better grant a remission of £6,000 from the aid voted in June. For the moment the young king was undoubtedly not as popular as he had been, but this apart, Edward had reason to be satisfied with the course of events in the second half of the year. The proceeds of the tax had been usefully employed in paying off some of the arrears of his standing military expenditure, the wages of the Calais garrison and of the wardens of the Marches towards Scotland. Diplomacy, moreover, promised to achieve just as much as a northern campaign and at far less expense.

The vital development here was the changing attitude of the French king. Louis XI's immediate ambition was the recovery of the Somme towns ceded to Burgundy in 1435. To carry out this plan he needed above all the friendship of the duke of Burgundy and this was hardly possible while one supported Lancaster and the other York. Louis therefore began to prepare the ground for a political volte-face. He refused to receive the earl of Pembroke and John Fortescue, envoys sent to him by Henry VI to seek further aid. He indicated his willingness to meet Edward's envoys at a tripartite conference between France, Burgundy and England to be held at Saint Omer. On 21 August 1463, shortly before he left for the north Edward had in fact been at Dover, giving last-minute instructions to Bishop George Neville, the leader of the English delegation. The prospect of a peace treaty between York and France was so devastating to Lancastrian hopes that Queen Margaret, on leaving Scotland, found herself driven to the desperate remedy of seeking an interview with her old adversary, the duke of Burgundy. Duke Philip listened politely but silently and Margaret had to go her way with a little money to ease her financial straits but not a single word to lighten her heart. What she feared took place. The tripartite conference at first made little progress, was then adjourned to Hesdin and there, on 8 October, an Anglo-French convention was signed. This provided for a year's truce on land, in ports and on rivers (though not at sea). Each king promised not to support the enemies of the other during the period of the truce. Not only did Louis specifically renounce all aid to the Lancastrians, but in buoyant mood – for Burgundy had agreed to return the Somme towns – he even told Edward's envoys that he was ready to abandon the traditional French protection for Scotland. Thus isolated the Scottish government felt it had no choice but to open negotiations with England. Bishop Kennedy's envoys met Edward at York and on 9 December a truce was agreed. It was to last until 31 October 1464 and in the meantime negotiations for a more permanent settlement were to begin in March. In return for his own undertaking to give no more aid to the earl of Douglas, Edward obtained the crucial promise: the Scots would no longer help the Lancastrians. Henry vi was moved from St Andrews to Bamburgh. Cut off from French and Scottish assistance the old king and his English adherents were now on their own. Unquestionably this was a triumph for Edward's national diplomacy.

Curiously enough it was precisely at this moment that Edward's personal diplomacy suffered one of its greatest setbacks. Ever since Christmas 1462 he had gone out of his way to bring about a genuine reconciliation between himself and Henry Beaufort, duke of Somerset. According to Gregory's Chronicle, 'the king made full much of him; in so much that he lodged with the king in his own bed many nights, and sometimes rode a-hunting behind the king, when the king had no more than six men in his party, of whom three were the duke of Somerset's men. And for his great love the king made great jousts at Westminster, that he should see some manner sport of chivalry after his great labour and heaviness.' In view of what had happened between their fathers, this remarkable attempt at peace-making highlights one of Edward's most attractive qualities. In July 1463, again according to Gregory, the king was at Northampton escorted by two hundred of Somerset's men, 'a lamb among wolves'. Not everyone, however, was as forgiving or as trusting as Edward. 'And the commons of the town of Northampton and of the shire about arose upon that false traitor the duke of Somerset and would have slain him within the king's palace. And then the king with fair speech and great difficulty saved his life for that time, and that was pity, for the saving of his life at that time caused many a man's death soon after, as ye shall hear.' In order to get him out of harm's way Edward sent Somerset to north Wales, but while he was there the duke began to forge links with diehard Lancastrians and apparently sent secret reports to Henry VI in Bamburgh Castle. Then, to continue Gregory's story, at about Christmas 1463 the duke showed his hand. Without first obtaining the king's leave, he left Wales and, accompanied only by a small household, attempted to reach Newcastle incognito. The two hundred men who had 'guarded' Edward at Northampton were now part of the Newcastle garrison and Somerset planned to use them to seize the town and hand it over to Henry VI. At Durham he was recognized and nearly captured while in bed. Two of his men were taken, but he escaped 'in his shirt and barefoot'. Edward then came to his senses and sent some more reliable men from his own household under the command of Lord Scrope of Bolton to Newcastle to replace Somerset's followers, some of whom were caught and executed. Whether or not we choose to believe this tale in all its romantic details, whether or not Edward was quite as naïve as Gregory depicts him, the essential fact remains that Somerset reverted to his old allegiance and made his way, somehow or other, to Bamburgh.

The timing of Somerset's move is interesting. On the international stage Henry VI's cause was now at its lowest point. On the other hand, the government's new unpopularity with the taxpayer had created more fertile ground for internal rebellion. Riots and disturbances might be exploited in the interests of the house of Lancaster. Early in 1464 there was unrest in Gloucestershire and in Cambridgeshire. Edward took these troubles sufficiently seriously to postpone the parliament which he had summoned to York and visit both places. He appointed commissioners to crack the whip in no less than fifteen southern counties. But it was only in Wales, Lancashire and Cheshire that the disturbances took on a clearly treasonable and dynastic aspect. These were regions which traditionally housed Lancastrian loyalists and doubtless the duke of Somerset had had a hand in bringing them to the boil once more. It was characteristic of Edward IV that he returned to London to discuss foreign policy with the Franco-Burgundian agent, Jean de Lannoy, and left others to deal with the disaffection in Wales. The duke of Norfolk, posted at Holt in Denbighshire, was made responsible for north Wales. On 25 February some men were executed at Chester and the troubles were reported to be over; Edward's agents in south Wales, John Donne and Roger Vaughan, had rather more to do. There the rebels had to be beaten in the field, at Dryslwyn near Carmarthen on 4 March, before they were prepared to submit.

Once again, however, the main confrontation was to take place in the north. On 27 March 1464 Edward publicly announced his intention of leading an expedition against the Lancastrians in the early summer. Unquestionably it was high time some action was taken. In recent weeks the Lancastrians had been doing ominously well. The Cliffords had managed to recover possession of their castle at Skipton-in-Craven in the Yorkshire dales and had declared for Henry VI. As yet this was a relatively isolated outpost, and whether or not it survived would depend on events in Northumberland where the remaining Lancastrians, having been driven out of Scotland, were now concentrated. At Bamburgh Somerset had been joined by two other former Lancastrians whom Edward had pardoned and restored to favour, Sir Henry Bellingham and Sir Humphrey Neville. Together with Sir Ralph Percy they had gone over to the offensive, capturing Norham, Langley, Hexham, Bywell and Prudhoe. They now controlled most of the countryside of the border and were in a position to threaten the vital Yorkist supply base at Newcastle. The immediate effect of this had been to put at risk the Anglo–Scottish talks due to be resumed at Newcastle on 6 March. They were postponed to 20 April and it was planned to hold them, for safety's sake, at York.

In mid-April Lord Montagu, as warden of the east March, was despatched to the border to meet the Scottish envoys and escort them back to York. It was to be a journey fraught with peril. On his way to Newcastle he was nearly ambushed by Sir Humphrey Neville with a force of archers and eighty men-at-arms. Fortunately Montagu's scouts warned him of the danger ahead and he was able to take another road. At Newcastle he picked up more troops and pushed on north past Alnwick. On 25 April at Hedgeley Moor, between Morpeth and Wooler, he was attacked by the main Lancastrian army under the command of Somerset, Hungerford, Roos, Percy and Grey, a force including, according to Gregory (who was probably following a Yorkist news-letter) no less than 5,000 men-at-arms. All we know about the engagement is that the rebels were disheartened by the death of Sir Ralph Percy and fled, allowing Montagu to continue his journey without being further molested.

Edward IV meanwhile was slowly and methodically pushing on with preparations for a major campaign. On 16 April he gave instructions for the mobilization of his artillery. The sheriffs of over thirty counties (though not Cheshire, Lancashire, Durham, Northumberland, Cumberland and Westmorland) were ordered to array all able-bodied men and have them ready to depart at twenty-four hours' notice. The Lancastrians were in desperate straits. Now that the Scottish envoys were at York they could safely assume that Scotland would soon be permanently barred to them. A massive royal army was mustering at Leicester. After the setback at Hedgeley Moor the only thing that might save them now was a morale-boosting quick victory. Their only hope lay in swift and aggressive action before they were crushed by the sheer weight of Edward's men, carts and guns. With this in mind they advanced south into the Tyne valley. Presumably hoping that their king's presence would bring in further support, they even removed Henry VI from his retreat on the Northumbrian coast and brought him to Bywell Castle, barely a dozen miles from Montagu's base at Newcastle. This time, however, Montagu did not wait to be attacked. As soon as he heard that Somerset's army was encamped at Hexham, he set out with all available men, including contingents led by two former Lancastrians, Lords Greystoke and Willoughby. Possibly Henry VI saw them as they went past Bywell on the other side of the river, but if he did, he was unable to send a warning to his followers upstream at Hexham. On 15 May Montagu came upon them suddenly and put them quickly to flight. Somerset himself was captured during the pursuit, brought before Montagu and beheaded that same day. Next day Hungerford and Roos were caught hiding in a wood near Hexham, taken to Newcastle and likewise executed. In all, over thirty Lancastrians were eliminated in this summary fashion, among them Sir William Tailboys, caught hiding in a coal-pit with £2,000 of Henry VI's war funds in his pockets. The money was shared out between Montagu's soldiers, men who in the last month had worked hard and suffered many casualties. According to Gregory, however, the money worked wonders for their war-weariness. The defeat at Hexham and the round of executions which followed it marked the virtual extinction of the Lancastrian cause. Their fortresses in the Tyne valley fell at once, though by the time Montagu's troops burst into Bywell Castle they found Henry VI already gone, leaving behind his coroneted helmet (his 'bycoket') and other regalia in the anxious haste of his departure. For another year the former king wandered forlornly from one hiding-place to another, but it was only a matter of time before he was delivered into the hands of his enemies.

Unquestionably the man who had been most vigorous on Edward IV's behalf was John Neville, Lord Montagu, and he now received the reward which was due to him. On 27 May he was invested at York with the lands and titles which had once belonged to Henry Percy, earl of Northumberland. All that remained now was for the new earl to take possession of his earldom. His brother, the earl of Warwick, went with him, and so did the royal army and siege-train, including the great bombards, the *Newcastle*, the *London* and the *Dijon*. Faced by this overwhelming power, Alnwick and Dunstanburgh capitulated at once, without a fight, on 23 and 24 June. Now the great natural fortress of Bamburgh stood alone, the last Lancastrian stronghold in England, its walls sheltering Sir Ralph Grey and Sir Humphrey Neville, the only two leaders to survive the devastating aftermath of Hexham. On 25 June Northumberland and Warwick advanced to demand its surrender. Heralds were sent to make an offer of pardon to the garrison, but this tactic, which had worked at Alnwick and Dunstanburgh, failed here, undoubtedly because the offer of pardon had pointedly excluded Grey and Neville. Grey replied that he was determined to stay in Bamburgh and live or die there, and he took no notice of the heralds' argument that he would, in that case, be responsible for the shedding of much blood. Another of the heralds' threats, though equally ineffective, is interesting for the light which it sheds on the government's military thinking. 'The king, our most dread sovereign lord, specially desires to have this jewel [Bamburgh] whole and unbroken by artillery, particularly because it stands so close to his ancient enemies the Scots, and if you are the cause that great guns have to be fired against its walls, then it will cost you your head, and for every shot that has to be fired another head, down to the humblest person within the place.' Whether or not Grey passed this grim message on to his subordinates, he certainly remained defiant. As a result, for the only time in these four years of fighting between Lancaster and York, there took place a full set-piece siege. The bombards were brought into action. Soon Bamburgh's battered walls began to crumble into the sea. Grey himself was badly injured by falling masonry; it was said that the brass gun *Dijon* 'smote through his chamber oftentimes'. Then, as the Yorkist men-at-arms and archers closed in for the assault, Sir Humphrey Neville indicated his willingness to give up the unequal struggle. He may have believed that Grey was already dead; at any rate he managed to win a pardon for himself. Sir Ralph Grey, though wounded, was brought before the king at Doncaster, put on trial in the court of the constable of England, condemned and beheaded. Not only had his defiance resulted in serious damage to one of the king's castles as 'appeareth by the strokes of the great guns in the walls', but at Alnwick in 1463 he had betrayed both the king and, in tricking Sir John Astley, a brother knight.

With the fall of Bamburgh the war in the north was over. Edward himself had taken almost no part in the fighting since Towton and for this he has been much criticized. He has sometimes been portrayed as a lazy or pleasure-loving king who let others do all the real work. On the whole this criticism is misconceived. There was certainly no point in the king's risking his own life except in those rare circumstances, as at Towton, when his presence was vital. The victory at Towton had given the Yorkists the upper hand and though it took three more years to stamp out the embers of Lancastrian resistance, there was no need for the king to play a front-line role. But this does not mean that his part had been a negligible one. Setting aside minor episodes, such as the surrender of Skipton-in-Craven, in which he may have been involved, his task had been to create the political, financial, administrative and diplomatic circumstances which virtually guaranteed victory in the field. Thus in late May and June 1464 Edward stayed at York, taking charge of the negotiations with the Scots. These were brought to a successful conclusion on 11 June when he ratified the fifteen years' truce agreed ten days earlier. Even more important was the fact that it had been Edward's ponderous preparations for war which had forced the duke of Somerset to take risks, to snatch at every opportunity of a quick success that happened to come his way. If the morale of the Lancastrian troops had been high, this strategy might have given them a fighting chance, but their performances at Hedgeley Moor and at Hexham suggest that, on the contrary, their confidence was low and they were being pushed into situations which were beyond their resources. Given Henry vi's precarious financial position, it seems likely that his troops were poorly paid and this might well go some way towards explaining their poor record against Lord Montagu – this, at least, is what William Gregory believed. None of this can detract from the skill and energy which Montagu displayed; the ablest of Edward's war captains he richly deserved his earldom. But the fact remains that Somerset, even though he must have known that just one heavy defeat would be fatal, had nonetheless been compelled to commit his men to the risks of battle. If Montagu had been worsted at Hexham, Edward IV would still have been in a strong position. Somerset, in other words, was reduced to fighting battles against the odds. If he won, he won little, but if he lost he might lose everything. Yet he had no other choice. Strategically he had been outmanoeuvred. Given Edward IV's vastly superior material resources, the king deserves no special credit for this, but to go so far as to criticize him for it does seem a little bit perverse.

Ten

RICHARD OF WARWICK: THE DISCONTENTED EARL, 1465–70

FOR FIVE YEARS Edward ruled England in peace. For the king they were prosperous years. The last remnants of Lancastrian opposition were gradually weeded out. Henry VI, after a year spent in hiding, was eventually captured in July 1465 and taken to the Tower. Even the castle of Harlech fell at last, on 14 August 1468. By this date Edward was sufficiently confident of his mastery of his realm to be planning an invasion of France. In May 1468 his chancellor informed parliament that the king had concluded, or was just about to conclude, treaties with Castile, Aragon, Denmark, Scotland, the Empire, Naples and, above all, with Brittany and Burgundy. These alliances would enable him to remind the French people that he was their rightful king. This aggressive stance was very different from the foreign policy of the early years of his reign, a policy which had been defensive in outlook, dominated by the need to deprive his internal enemies of outside support. In going over to the attack against 'his old and ancient adversary' Edward was doing exactly what his subjects expected of an energetic and successful ruler and they responded accordingly. The commons in parliament made a substantial grant of war taxation, and so did the convocation of Canterbury. On 3 August Edward signed an agreement to send 3,000 archers to help the duke of Brittany. By September the expedition was being actively prepared under the command of Lord Mountjoy; Breton transport ships were at Portsmouth, ready to ferry the army across; in addition, an English fleet was being assembled, intended, presumably, for an attack on the French coast. With one exception the political nation appeared to be united behind a king who was taking up the mantle of Henry V, but that exception was a notable one: the earl of Warwick.

By now Warwick was a very discontented man. Whether or not he had in fact been the kingmaker who put Edward on the throne in 1461, it is clear that this is how he saw himself and that, in consequence, he believed that English policy should be Warwick's policy. A man who saw the world in these unrealistic terms was only too susceptible to flattery, and this made him easy game for a diplomat as wily as King Louis XI. Thus Warwick became an advocate of a French alliance and chose to remain so even when Edward IV began to show unmistakable signs of a preference for Burgundy. But the earl's unyielding attitude to foreign policy was little more than an expression of the extent to which he was out of sympathy with prevailing trends at court. For it must be admitted that Warwick had reason to feel aggrieved. At the heart of the problem was the king's extraordinary marriage.

Very early in the morning of 1 May 1464 Edward had slipped away from his entourage and married Elizabeth Woodville, a widow whose former husband, Sir John Grey, had died fighting for the Lancastrian cause at St Albans three years earlier. Although Elizabeth's mother, Jacquetta of Luxembourg, belonged to the upper ranks of the European aristocracy, claiming indeed descent from Charlemagne, her father, Richard Woodville, was no more than a member of a minor gentry family. His marriage to Jacquetta, the widowed duchess of Bedford, had done wonders for his career, but whereas it was a fact of life, and accepted as such, that a dowager duchess might occasionally stoop to marry an attractive man, regardless of his social rank, it was quite out of the question for a ruling prince to indulge his fancy in this way. Politically speaking, Edward's marriage was a mistake – and he knew it. He kept it a secret even from his friends for more than four months and confessed what he had done only when it was impossible to stay silent any longer. It was not just that the wedding ruined Warwick's plans for a marriage between Edward and a French princess; nor just that Elizabeth Woodville's station in life was unsuitable; there was also the problem that she came as part of a Woodville package – no less than five brothers and seven unmarried sisters, not to mention her own two sons by her first husband, all of them clamouring to be provided for. For Edward's action on that May morning there can only be one explanation – and contemporaries were not slow to draw the obvious conclusion. 'Now take heed', wrote William Gregory, 'what love may do.'

Providing for the Woodvilles was no easy task. In 1461 Edward had had at his disposal the lands forfeited by a third of the nobility and many of the gentry. These 'Lancastrian' estates – worth perhaps £30,000 in all – had been used to reward the men who had brought him to the throne, the Nevilles, Sir William Hastings, Sir William Herbert, Humphrey Stafford and others, but by 1464 these vast reserves of patronage had gone. This meant that the only effective way to endow the queen's family was by arranging marriages for them – and this Edward did. The most notorious case was the marriage between Warwick's aunt, Katherine Neville, duchess of Norfolk, and one of the queen's brothers, John Woodville. According to the Neville chronicler this was a 'diabolical marriage' since the husband was twenty and the wife, as he put it, 'a slip of a girl almost four score years old'. More serious still from Warwick's point of view was the fact that between September 1464 – when the king's own marriage was announced – and 1470 every English earl who had an heir available to marry chose for him a Woodville wife. Warwick himself had no male heir, just two daughters, and the matrimonial triumphs of the Woodvilles made it very difficult for him to find suitable husbands for them. His great hope was that they might marry the king's younger brothers, George of Clarence and Richard of Gloucester, but this Edward would not allow. On these vitally important matters of domestic policy on which the future of the Warwick inheritance depended, the king had in effect blocked every reasonable avenue of approach. It is hardly surprising that, as the Neville chronicler makes crystal clear, Edward's pro-Woodville marriage policy was a very sore point.

It seemed to Warwick that he was being ousted from his rightful place at the head of the king's councillors by a set of *parvenus*. The worst of them were the Woodvilles, but there were others. Sir William Herbert, whose dominating position in south Wales ran counter to Warwick's own ambitions in this area, was one. He was created earl of Pembroke in 1468. Humphrey Stafford, created earl of Devon in 1469, was another. Undoubtedly Warwick's analysis of what was happening was an accurate one; undoubtedly also, Edward had made some mistakes in his handling of royal patronage, but this was not enough to justify rebellion. Edward continued to treat the earl as a friend, continued to grant him gifts and favours: some Percy manors in Cumberland as late as February 1469, for example. If Edward had other friends and more frequently preferred their advice to Warwick's, this was cause for disappointment, certainly, but not for revolt. The political system required that the king should rule, and Edward was ruling. Increasingly, however, Warwick's truculent attitude was based on the assumption that he, not the king, should be the real ruler of the country.

In these circumstances it was inevitable that men should begin to talk of a *rapprochement* between Warwick and his old Lancastrian enemies. Margaret of Anjou was in exile in France and Warwick's connexions with the French court were well known. Rumours of this were current on the continent as early as the spring of 1467. In the autumn of that year William Herbert captured a messenger from Margaret of Anjou to the garrison of Harlech who was prepared to make the same accusation. The fact that at court there were men who were ready either to manufacture or to believe such stories could have served only to increase Warwick's resentment. In reality he was looking elsewhere for allies, not to Margaret of Anjou, but to Clarence and to English public opinion. Apart from Edward's opposition to the proposal that he should marry Isabel Neville, George, duke of Clarence, had no obvious reason to be dissatisfied with his brother. He had been given lands and titles in plenty and the disagreement over the marriage, though aggravating, was, once again, not enough to justify rebellion. But while Edward and Elizabeth had no sons Clarence was heir presumptive to the throne and this opened up a glittering prospect which he may have found it hard to put out of his mind. Whether Warwick planned to put Clarence on the throne or whether he planned to capture Edward and then rule in his name, we do not know. Perhaps Warwick himself did not know. Once armies were on the march so many chance factors were involved that it was probably easiest to play it by ear, to wait and see who was killed or captured or ran away. But whatever it was that Warwick and Clarence hoped to gain from each other, it is clear that by the autumn of 1467 they had arrived at a secret understanding.

The second vital ingredient in Warwick's plan for a *coup d'état* was popular support. Throughout his political career he had shown himself to be both well aware of the importance of public opinion and extremely adroit at manipulating it. He was always careful to live in a style which befitted the richest nobleman in England. Wherever he went he dispensed hospitality on a lavish scale; to tradespeople and artisans everywhere the arrival of the earl of Warwick was known to be 'good for business', and late in 1468 he sensed that there was an opportunity to contrast his own popularity with the king's unpopularity. Edward's planned invasion of France had come to nothing. In September and October 1468 Louis xi made peace first with Brittany, then with Burgundy. Yet Edward had obtained a generous grant of taxation, and simply to disband the expeditionary force which he had assembled would have been too humiliating, so instead, on the pretext that Margaret of Anjou was at Harfleur preparing to invade England, he ordered his fleet to patrol the Channel. Late in November they returned ingloriously to port, having encountered only autumn gales, and with nothing to show for the money expended. According to the well-informed Neville chronicler £18,000 had been spent entirely frivolously since there had never in fact been a genuine threat. It is clear from other writers that views such as these were widely held: the taxpayers' hard-earned money was being wasted, law and order were breaking down, unworthy men were enriching themselves at the expense of church and people. What, however, cannot be shown is that such conventional opinions as these were more widespread in 1468–9 than, say, 1463–4. It is the time-honoured lot of taxpayers to be disillusioned with governments and as early as 1462 there were people proclaiming that 'We commons have brought King Edward to his prosperity in the realm of England and just as we have made him king so also we can depose him and put him down.' The difference was that in 1462–4 Warwick was with the king; in 1468–9 he was against him, secretly at first, but then coming out into the open.

The crisis began in a minor key with some local risings in Yorkshire during the spring of 1469. The leaders of the rebels were two rather mysterious figures known as Robin of Redesdale (or Robin Mend-All) and Robin of Holderness. What lay behind these movements it is impossible to say with any certainty. To some extent they seem to have been revolts of the taxpayers, protesting – as is usual in these cases – against too much government money going to line the pockets of the king's favourites. The insurrection in the East Riding (where Robin of Holderness was the rebel captain) also seems to have been a demonstration in favour of the traditional leaders of local society, the Percy family, and a demand that young Henry Percy should be restored to his 'rightful' earldom. To all appearances Edward IV's earl of Northumberland, John Neville, had little difficulty in suppressing these revolts, but appearances were deceptive. Though he succeeded in capturing and beheading Robin of Holderness, Robin of Redesdale slipped through his fingers and turned up again in June in Lancashire. This time Edward decided that he would deal with the trouble himself, but, for the moment, while he set in motion the business of mustering an army, he carried on with a leisurely tour of East Anglia. From Norwich on 18 June he sent instructions to the royal wardrobe to supply coat-armour, jackets for 1,000 men, banners and standards. Two days later he ordered the mobilization of his artillery. Letters were sent commanding the earls of Pembroke and Devon to muster troops in Wales and the west country and bring them to a rendezvous with the forces which Edward was assembling in the east Midlands. Then he went on a pilgrimage to the shrine at Walsingham before joining the queen for a week at Fotheringhay Castle. On 5 July, now at Stamford, he wrote to the city of Coventry asking them to provide a hundred archers. Thence, by easy stages, he moved on to reach Newark by 10 July. Evidently he still felt no great sense of urgency.

But on that day everything changed. He wrote again to Coventry, in a very different tone, asking for more troops, without fail, as quickly as possible, and sparing no expense. Instead of continuing his measured advance northwards Edward hurriedly retraced his steps and returned to Nottingham, there to await the arrival of more troops. What had caused this sudden about-turn? By 9 July at the latest he had heard some disquieting rumours. Warwick, Clarence and the archbishop of York were said to be involved in a plot against him, but Edward had heard such rumours before and, though he wrote to all three, asking them to come and see him, this did not check his northerly progress. What he learned next day at Newark was that Robin of Redesdale was marching rapidly south in command of a force which was, it was suggested, three times as big as the king's own. The nervous prior of Crowland, anxious for the safety of the abbey's treasures, put the rebel army at no less than 60,000 men. This is unquestionably a wild exaggeration; nonetheless Edward's actions make it plain that Robin of Redesdale represented a serious threat.

Who was Robin of Redesdale? It is probable that masquerading under this fictitious name was Sir William Conyers of Marske in Swaledale. He belonged to a family of prominent Richmondshire gentry closely attached to the Nevilles. His brother, Sir John Conyers, held the key position of steward of the lordship of Middleham, the engine-room of Warwick's power in Yorkshire. Other members of the Conyers clan followed Robin of Redesdale, as did several of the earl's own kindred, among them his nephew Sir Henry FitzHugh, and a cousin, Sir Henry Neville, son of Lord Latimer. A manifesto drawn up by the rebels reflects Warwick's complaints accurately enough. It accused the king of excluding the lords of his blood from the council chamber and of relying only on the advice of greedy favourites, William Herbert, earl of Pembroke, Humphrey Stafford, earl of Devon, Lord Audley and, above all, the Woodvilles, Earl Rivers and his brood. In a sinister phrase the manifesto compared Edward's favourites with Edward II's, Richard II's and Henry VI's. All of these kings had been deposed. Was this to be Edward's fate? Clearly if the Neville connexion was able to command such widespread support in the north, there must have been a degree of disenchantment with Edward's government which could well make him vulnerable to a *coup d'état*.

What, in the meanwhile, was Warwick himself up to? He, Clarence and George Neville had indeed been conspiring. On 12 June Warwick's flagship, the *Trinity*, after refitting at Sandwich, had been blessed there by the archbishop and, using this ceremony as a cover, the three of them discussed their plans. The rest of the month they spent in London and Kent and by 28 June their schemes were sufficiently well-advanced for Warwick to write to Coventry, announcing the forthcoming marriage between his daughter, Isabel, and Clarence, and asking the town to have a band of armed men ready to accompany him to the king – a request which was couched in ominously vague language. Then, accompanied by the earl of Oxford, the three plotters returned to Sandwich and crossed the sea to Calais. There, on 11 July, the archbishop of York officiated at the wedding of Clarence and Isabel. It was, wrote Waurin, a hasty affair, only two days of festivities. Busy with the final preparations for rebellion, Warwick had no time to spare for Waurin, though he had promised the historian that when he next came to Calais he would supply him with full details of recent events. On 12 July the conspirators came out into the open. They circulated copies of Robin of Redesdale's manifesto together with an open letter of their own, explaining that the king's true subjects 'with piteous lamentation' had called upon them to seek a remedy for the nation's ills. In response to this plea they were now summoning all who would help them in this 'reasonable and profitable' enterprise to come fully armed to meet them at Canterbury on Sunday 16 July. Warwick had prepared the ground well beforehand and he found a warm welcome in Kent. By 20 July he had left Canterbury at the head of a substantial force and was on his way to London. Edward, by this time, must have heard of Warwick's invasion, but he remained motionless at Nottingham waiting to be joined by Pembroke's and Devon's army which was marching north-west towards Northampton. Robin of Redesdale's army, meanwhile, was on its way south to a rendezvous with Warwick, by-passing the king in the hope of cutting him off from London. The two marching armies appeared to be on a collision course.

As Warwick approached the capital he continued to play the role of 'true subject' demanding the reformation of the realm. On these terms he was allowed to enter the city and even given a loan of £1,000. Before leaving London he took the precaution of sending a squadron of cavalry in advance of his army in order to make contact with the northerners. The earl of Pembroke, meanwhile, had become separated from the earl of Devon. This was serious because Pembroke's force was largely cavalry, while most of the archers were under Devon's command. The separation of the two ruled out that tactical combination of the two arms which was widely accepted – and with reason – as good military practice. Why this had occurred we do not know. It may have been, as Waurin says, simply carelessness, the consequence of Pembroke's ignorance of the proximity of the northern army. Or it may have been, as John Warkworth wrote later, the result of a quarrel over billeting arrangements in Banbury. But whatever the reason, it seems that it was this separation of the two arms which proved fatal to the army on which Edward was pinning all his hopes.

The only contemporary chronicler to give any details of the affray at Edgecote on 26 July 1469 was Waurin. Historians in general have not been inclined to trust him, but war was his subject and he had good sources of information both within the Calais garrison and at the Burgundian court. Though he made nonsense of the name Banbury (writing Thersbury) his brief narrative is perfectly coherent. Pembroke and Robin of Redesdale first made contact on 25 July and the two armies spent that night separated by a small river. Next morning Pembroke's Welsh men-at-arms, though outnumbered and hampered by the absence of archers, managed to hold their own in a fierce skirmish for control of the river crossing. Both sides then withdrew to attend to their casualties. After dinner the arrival of Warwick's advance guard under the command of Sir William Parr and Sir Geoffrey Gate encouraged the northerners to attack again. By this time Pembroke's hard-pressed troops ought to have been reinforced by the infantry under the earl of Devon, but they, apparently believing that the whole of Warwick's army had come to Robin of Redesdale's aid, decided that discretion was the better part of valour. So, for the second time that day, the northerners had the advantage in numbers and this time it proved decisive. The Welshmen were defeated and suffered heavy casualties. To judge from the lamentations of their bards, Edgecote was a national calamity. The earl of Pembroke and his brother, Sir Richard Herbert, were captured, taken to Northampton and beheaded next day on

Warwick's orders. For this there could be no legal justification. They
had been leading an army to help the king whom Warwick himself still
recognized. Like the executions of Earl Rivers and Sir John Woodville
soon afterwards these were purely acts of revenge perpetrated by
Warwick in pursuance of his private political ends.

Throughout this campaign King Edward seemed curiously out of
touch with events, and when he left Nottingham on 29 July he still did
not know of the disaster which had befallen Pembroke and Devon.
Expecting to meet them at Northampton he had got as far as Olney
when he heard the news. The immediate reaction of his troops was to
desert. Apparently stunned by his lack of success in the last month,
Edward allowed himself to be taken prisoner by George Neville.
Though treated with an outward show of deference, he was sent first to
Warwick Castle and later to the great Yorkshire stronghold of the
Nevilles at Middleham. But the game was not yet over. Warwick had
been remarkably successful in manipulating popular discontent, but he
had won the Edgecote campaign with almost no aid from his fellow
peers. Nor indeed, as it soon transpired, did he enjoy their support. It is
difficult to see what his aims were. There were rumours abroad that he
intended to have Edward declared a bastard and give the crown to
Clarence, but no evidence that he actually made any move in this
direction. If what he wanted was a chastened king who would accept
the friendship and advice of the man who had lifted him to the throne,
then he needed a king who was temperamentally prepared to be kept on
leading reins – and Edward IV was patently not such a king.

Within a matter of weeks Warwick found himself in a very awkward
situation. In many parts of the country the apparent absence of any
legitimate authority was taken as a licence for violence. There was
rioting and pillaging in London. Many nobles seized what seemed to be
a chance to pursue their private quarrels without official interference.
Worse was to come when that irrepressible Lancastrian, Sir Humphrey
Neville of Brancepeth, taking advantage of the general uncertainty,
raised the standard of revolt along the northern border. But Warwick
certainly had no intention of putting Henry VI back on the throne. He
decided to take personal command of operations in the north, only to
discover that there was hardly anyone who would follow him. The
proclamations calling for men to put down Humphrey Neville's insurrection went unheeded and it rapidly became clear that they would
remain so for as long as Edward IV was held prisoner. Evidently the
northerners who had followed Robin of Redesdale had been protesting

against unpopular ministers, not against the king; now that these people were either dead or out of office there was no justification for further action against Edward. Only the moral authority of the king in person could command their obedience and, however reluctantly, Warwick had to face that fact.

By mid-September Edward had been released from confinement and had made public appearances at York and Pontefract. After that there was no further difficulty about raising troops to put down the Lancastrian revolt. Humphrey Neville was captured, brought to York and executed on 29 September, in Edward's presence. This degree of freedom was all that the king needed in order to reassert his full authority. He summoned his brother, Gloucester, his brother-in-law, Suffolk, together with Arundel, Essex, Northumberland, Hastings, Mountjoy and other members of his council to come and join him in the north. Then, escorted as a king should be, he made a ceremonial return to his capital. Warwick's attempt to repeat the experiments of 1455 and 1460 and rule through a captive king had failed.

The last few months had witnessed some extraordinary twists and turns of fortune, but what was in some ways the most extraordinary aspect of the whole business was yet to come. Edward behaved as though nothing had happened. 'The King himself', wrote John Paston, 'hath good language of the lords of Clarence, of Warwick, and of my lords of York and Oxford, saying they be his best friends.' He invited them to attend a series of great council meetings which went on from November until mid-February 1470, culminating in an agreement by all parties that there should be 'peace and entire oblivion of all grievances'. The transfer to Richard of Gloucester of the Welsh offices which Warwick had accumulated in the previous summer was only to be expected. In these months Edward made only one major change and this too could be seen as part of a policy of general reconciliation: the restoration of the earldom of Northumberland to the Percy family. Ever since 1464 the 'rightful heir', Henry Percy, had been kept in prison in London, either in the Fleet or in the Tower. No sooner had he been released from his own confinement than Edward freed Percy and began the series of manoeuvres designed to restore him to his traditional place in society. The problem here was to find adequate compensation for the present earl, John Neville, a man conspicuous for his loyalty and effective service on Edward's behalf. The lands of the earls of Devon were available for this purpose since Humphrey Stafford's discretion at Edgecote had done him little good. On 17 August he had been captured and executed by the people of Bridgwater in Somerset. Not only did John Neville obtain the bulk of these lands, he also had the pleasure of seeing his son, George, betrothed to the king's eldest daughter, Elizabeth, and created duke of Bedford. In return, on 1 March 1470, John Neville surrendered the Percy estates which he had held for the last five years.

On the face of it the earl of Warwick had not emerged too badly from the ups and downs of 1469. His own estates were still securely held. He had removed from Edward's councils those men whom he hated most. By the marriage of his daughter to Clarence and by the betrothal of his nephew and heir to the eldest daughter of a king who had no son, he had all but put the Neville family on the throne. Nonetheless, he had good reason to feel very ill at ease. He could hardly forget the savage treatment he had meted out to the king's friends and the queen's kinsmen – even if the king himself might seem to. In public Edward was his usual good-humoured self, but what was he like in private? In public the king might use fair words, as John Paston noted, but, he continued, 'his household men have other language'. Did this 'other language' reflect Edward's own thoughts? It seemed only too likely. It was, after all, his household men who knew him best. One day surely the king would smile and strike. To an active and aggressive politician like Warwick, there was only one sensible course. He too must smile – and he must strike first, at the earliest opportunity. This time there could be no half-measures. Edward could not be manipulated like a puppet. Therefore he must be driven off the throne. The obvious replacement was Clarence: a man who, like Warwick, had every reason to feel insecure under the present dispensation.

Men who are determined to seize the first opportunity rarely have to wait very long. A feud blew up in Lincolnshire, involving one of King Edward's household men, Sir Thomas Burgh of Gainsborough, his master of horse. Burgh's quarrel was with the leading landowner in south-east Lincolnshire, Richard, Lord Welles and Willoughby. According to Waurin, Willoughby had been involved in Robin of Redesdale's rising so it is possible that the divisions of national politics had given a sharper edge to a local rivalry. At some date during the winter of 1469–70 Welles, assisted by his son, Sir Robert Welles, and by his brothers-in-law, Sir Thomas de la Lande and Sir Thomas Dymmock, attacked and destroyed Burgh's manor house, carrying off his goods and chattels. Violent episodes of this kind, though by no means normal, were certainly just as common in the fifteenth as in the fourteenth or sixteenth centuries. The duke of Norfolk's quarrel with the Pastons had recently come to a head with his siege of Caister Castle. On 20 March 1470, on the other side of the country, the Talbots and the Berkeleys met in a bloody confrontation at Nibley Green. What made the Lincolnshire feud particularly significant was Edward IV's decision to come to Sir Thomas Burgh's aid in an armed demonstration of household solidarity.

This decision had two consequences. In the first place, it drove Welles and his friends to seek equally powerful allies of their own, in other words it drove them into the arms of Warwick and Clarence. In the second place, Edward's announcement, made on 9 February, that he intended to muster an army at Grantham on 12 March, recalled his visit to Lincolnshire in the previous July and the humiliation he had suffered on that previous journey. It was easy enough to spread a rumour that the king was coming to exact retribution for Lincolnshire's part in Robin of Redesdale's rebellion; the general pardon granted earlier for all offences committed before Christmas was not going to be honoured; his judges had been instructed to 'hang and draw a great number of the commons'. This combination of circumstances gave Warwick and Clarence grounds for hoping that they would be able to use popular discontent to outmanoeuvre Edward, just as they had done last July. By February at the latest they were in touch with Lord Welles and his Lincolnshire supporters. In Warwickshire Warwick began to muster troops on pretence of bringing them to aid the king.

Edward meanwhile had summoned Welles and Dymmock to Westminster. They came and were granted pardons but, despite their submission, the king continued to press on with the arrangements for his journey north. On 3 March he ordered the mobilization of his artillery train. He had already sent out commissions of array to twelve eastern and south-eastern counties. He had planned to leave London on 4 March, but on hearing that Clarence was just about to arrive in the city, he decided to wait a little. According to the official accounts published a few weeks later, Clarence's plan was to delay Edward's departure for as long as possible. On Tuesday 6 March the two brothers met at Baynard's Castle, their mother's London residence, and if the king had any suspicions about Clarence's intentions, they were apparently dispelled when his brother told him that he was on his way to the west country to see his wife. Late that afternoon Edward left London, accompanied by the earl of Arundel, Lord Hastings and Sir Henry Percy. No sooner had they gone, however, than Clarence went to the

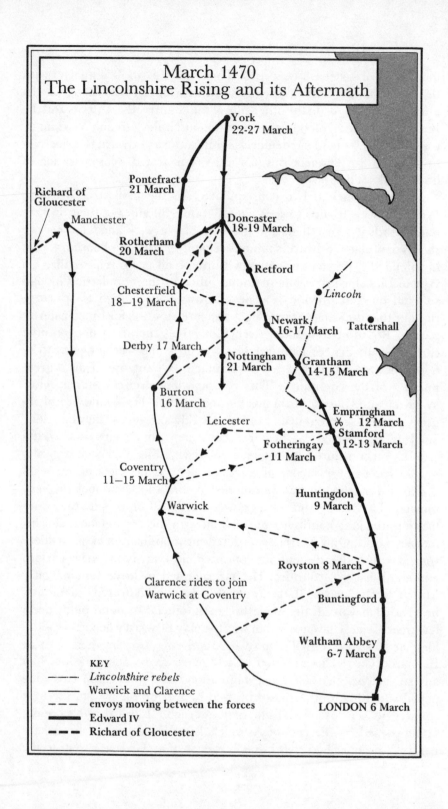

March 1470
The Lincolnshire Rising and its Aftermath

York
22-27 March

Pontefract
21 March

Richard of
Gloucester

Manchester

Doncaster
18-19 March

Rotherham
20 March

Retford

Chesterfield
18—19 March

Lincoln

Newark
16-17 March

Tattershall

Derby 17 March

Nottingham
21 March

Grantham
14-15 March

Burton
16 March

Empringham
12 March

Leicester

Stamford
12-13 March

Fotheringay
11 March

Coventry
11—15 March

Huntingdon
9 March

Warwick

Royston 8 March

Clarence rides to join
Warwick at Coventry

Buntingford

Waltham Abbey
6-7 March

KEY
·—·—·— Lincolnshire rebels
———— Warwick and Clarence
– – – envoys moving between the forces
▬▬▬ Edward IV
▬ ▬ ▬ Richard of Gloucester

LONDON 6 March

hospital of St John's at Clerkenwell for a conference with Lord Welles, with the prior of St John's (whom Warwick had appointed treasurer in August 1469 and who lost that office two months later when Edward returned to power) and with other friends. Then, instead of going to visit his wife, Clarence rode off to join Warwick.

While Edward was delaying in London, events were moving rapidly in Lincolnshire. Sir Robert Welles, calling himself 'great captain of the commons of Lincolnshire', summoned the men of the shire to his banner. He circulated a proclamation to be read on Sunday 4 March in every church in the shire, asserting that Edward was coming to 'destroy the commons' and calling for a muster of those who would oppose the king at Ranby Hawe near Lincoln in two days' time. Edward was at Waltham Abbey on the morning of Wednesday 7 March when he heard the news of Sir Robert's call to arms. His actions during the next twenty days are recounted in some considerable detail in a narrative known as the *Chronicle of the Rebellion in Lincolnshire*. This was clearly written by someone who travelled in the king's company, probably a privy seal clerk since he was particularly well informed on the letters sent out under the privy seal. Apart from possessing all the obvious advantages and disadvantages of an official account, the *Chronicle* has one special merit; it was composed very soon after 26 March, probably before the end of the month and certainly before its author knew the end of the story.

Edward's immediate response to this report was to send a messenger back to London, bearing orders that Lord Welles and Sir Thomas Dymmock were to be brought to him for questioning. Next day, as he was approaching Royston, a page dispatched from Tattershall Castle by Lord Cromwell's steward there, brought further news. So enthusiastic, apparently, was the response to Sir Robert's proclamation that, together with reinforcements from Yorkshire and other neighbouring counties, the rebels expected to have 100,000 men under arms in time to prevent Edward's reaching his muster point at Grantham. Fortunately this alarmist message was countered later that day when Edward received a promise of help from an unexpected quarter. A letter came from Clarence, explaining that he had not, after all, gone to visit his wife, but was now on his way to meet Warwick and he would join the king when the earl did. Not only did Edward reply to this with a letter of thanks in his own hand, but he forwarded to Clarence and Warwick authorization to array troops in Warwickshire and Worcestershire.

On Friday 9 March Edward reached Huntingdom and it was here

that Welles and Dymmock, together with their escort, caught up with him. They were interrogated separately and both made apparently full confessions, admitting their own parts in instigating the revolt, but saying nothing about either Warwick or Clarence. Edward, of course, had other uses for Lord Welles, quite apart from his questionable worth as a source of information. He was made to send a message to his son: submit or see his father and Sir Thomas Dymmock executed for treason. Sir Robert Welles had passed Grantham and was on his way to a rendezvous with Warwick and Clarence fixed for Monday when he received his father's message. Warwick's plan had been for the Lincoln- shire rebels to avoid a confrontation with the king. Instead, they were supposed to join him at Leicester while allowing Edward to proceed unhindered to his muster at Grantham. Since Warwick had also organ- ized a rising in Yorkshire, this should mean that Edward was both cut off from London and threatened from two sides at once. As a plan of campaign this had much to recommend it, but the whole scheme was ruined by the king's ruthless exploitation of the best card in his hand. Sir Robert Welles could not stand by and see his father die without putting up a fight to save him. Abruptly the Lincolnshire rebels changed direction. Sir Robert had no intention of submitting. He now reverted to what was thought to be the rebels' original plan: to attack the king at Stamford.

Edward arrived at Stamford on Monday 12 March. While he took up quarters in the town, his vanguard was sent ahead to give advance warning of the rebels' approach. Further letters were received from Warwick and Clarence, written at Coventry, and letting Edward know that on Monday night they expected to be at Leicester *en route* to join him. Possibly this was news which gave Edward further food for thought, since over the weekend his spies had informed him that the Lincolnshire rebels were also heading in the direction of Leicester. But whatever qualms he may have had, he still gave every public appear- ance of confidence in his brother's and Warwick's loyalty, sending them a letter of thanks in his own hand. By the time he wrote this he may already have known of the effect of Lord Welles's message to his son. Sir Robert Welles's army now lay at Empingham – only five miles from Stamford, and was clearly ready for a fight. Edward at once marched out to meet it. According to the *Chronicle of the Rebellion* the king was not prepared to put his own life in jeopardy on the field of battle while the traitors lived who had brought him to this pass. So, although it was widely believed that they should have been protected by the pardons granted them a week earlier, Lord Welles and Sir Thomas Dymmock were taken out and executed in the sight of the royal army, drawn up with its battle banners displayed.

Edward's rapid advance took the rebels by surprise. It seems that they had expected to attack him while he was still lodged in the town. We know almost nothing of the numbers involved at Empingham, though we can perhaps deduce from the figure of 30,000 rebels mentioned by the author of the *Chronicle* that the king's force was outnumbered. However, the rebels consisted almost entirely of infantry, under the command of the 'captain of the footmen' Richard Warren. In the retinues of the lords who were with him Edward doubtless had better equipped and more experienced soldiers than were available to Sir Robert Welles, as well as more cavalry. In artillery moreover he enjoyed total superiority. According to John Warkworth the contest opened with a barrage from the royal guns. The effect of this would have been to give the rebels no option but to attack at once; defensive tactics would merely have exposed them to a fire which they were unable to return. As the two lines advanced towards each other, Edward heard the rebels' battle-cry: 'A Clarence! A Clarence! A War-wick!' and several people were observed wearing Clarence's livery, including Sir Robert Welles himself. The mêlée was brief. By seizing the initiative Edward had been able to dictate the terms of the fight and it very quickly turned into a rout. The haste with which the fleeing rebels discarded the defensive clothing which they no longer needed gave to the engagement its name of 'Lose-cote Field'. One of Sir Robert's lieutenants, Sir Thomas de la Lande, a knight with a fine reputation in the lists, was captured in the pursuit, but the most important prize was a casket taken from the body of a man wearing Clarence's livery. He turned out to have been the duke's envoy to Sir Robert Welles and the casket contained letters which confirmed the state of affairs first revealed by the battle-cry of the Lincolnshire rebels. Late that evening Edward returned to Stamford, his soldiers happy after a long, successful and presumably profitable pursuit, and the king himself doubtless conscious of having had a narrow escape. As the author of the *Chronicle* pointed out, if the Lincolnshire men had joined forces with Warwick and Clarence there might have been a very different story to tell.

From Stamford Edward wrote next day to Warwick and Clarence, reporting his victory and commanding them to disband the shire levies which they had raised. They were to come to him escorted only as was appropriate to their status. Perhaps he was still prepared to continue his policy of turning a blind eye to their treasonable designs and hoped that by telling them of the defeat of their allies he could bring them to a discreet and timely submission. But to Warwick and Clarence, Edward's letters must have read like invitations to walk into a trap. In the last fortnight not everything had gone as well as they had hoped. In the west country Clarence had managed to stir some of the Courtenay family into revolt. With John Neville's being put in possession of estates which were traditionally theirs and which they might have hoped to recover after Humphrey Stafford's death, this was presumably not difficult and it is more significant that no one else of note was prepared to join in. Nor had Warwick succeeded in arousing much support in the west Midlands. Even Coventry had dutifully sent a contingent to Grantham in answer to the king's summons, though there is possibly a hint of the local problem of conflicting loyalties in the oath of allegiance which each of the city soldiers was required to take. With troops coming in more slowly than they had hoped, and perhaps also disturbed by news of Sir Robert Welles's change of direction, Clarence and Warwick had decided to spend Monday at Coventry instead of moving on to Leicester. They were still there when Edward's envoy, John Down, found them and delivered the king's letters, probably on Wednesday 14 March. In reply Clarence and Warwick told Down that they would do as Edward asked. They would disband their infantry levies and ride at once to see him accompanied by only a thousand, or at most fifteen hundred men. On leaving Coventry, however, Down was surprised to see them take the road to Burton upon Trent. When he pointed out that this was hardly the direction to travel in if they were intending to see the king, they explained that there were some footsoldiers who had gone on ahead by that route and they ought to speak with them. A lame enough excuse but it sufficed to send him on his way back to the king while they continued on theirs.

Edward meanwhile had allowed his troops a day's rest at Stamford before pressing on to Grantham where he spent the evening of Wednesday 14 March and the whole of Thursday. While he was there Sir Robert Welles and some of his friends were brought in and questioned. Upon examination they freely confessed 'not for fear of death nor under any other duress' (says the author of the *Chronicle*) that Clarence and Warwick were the chief instigators of the revolt and that its purpose was to put Clarence on the throne. At the same time Edward heard some details of the rising in Yorkshire. It was centred on Wensleydale and

Richmond where Lord Scrope of Bolton and Sir John Conyers were active on Warwick's behalf. To meet this challenge Edward developed a two-pronged strategy. Levies were to be raised in Northumberland and Westmorland in order to threaten the rebels in their rear, while John Neville was commissioned to tackle them head on. From now on Edward's position grew stronger each day. More lords came in to join him, bringing their retinues: the dukes of Norfolk and Suffolk, the earl of Worcester, Lord Mountjoy. At Grantham itself he should have seen the mustering of the shire and town levies.

From Grantham Edward continued his northward advance. On Friday 16 March he reached Newark; from there he ordered the mobilization of forces in the south-west to suppress the rebellion of the Courtenays. Next day he received letters from Warwick and Clarence. Still keeping up the pretence that they were obeying his summons, they announced that they would meet him at Retford. It later transpired that they had arranged a rendezvous with their Yorkshire allies at Rotherham. Over the next few days, as both parties moved north, there was a non-stop to-and-fro of envoys and heralds between them. Edward said that even if the accusations against them were true, he was prepared to treat them 'with favour and pity, remembering their ties of blood and the old love and affection which had been between them'. This offer was not enough for Warwick and Clarence. They wanted something less vague: safe conducts and pardons for themselves and for their followers, but this Edward would not grant. After formal consultation with his lords he refused to set so dangerous a precedent, a precedent which might have given too much encouragement to potential rebels. Instead of granting pardons, Edward issued a grim reminder that the penalty for taking up arms against the king was death. At Doncaster on Monday 19 March Sir Robert Welles and Richard Warren were beheaded in view of the whole army. At the same time, however, Edward made it plain that he would pardon those who deserted Warwick and Clarence and returned at once to his allegiance. It looks, indeed, as though one of the rebels' envoys, Warwick's retainer Sir William Parr, took advantage of this offer. Sir William became an influential figure in the royal household in the second half of the reign; his granddaughter, Catherine Parr, became queen of England.

With their supporters coming under this kind of pressure and, according to Waurin, succumbing to it, Warwick's and Clarence's position continued to deteriorate. Nonetheless, from Chesterfield they sent their harbingers on to Rotherham, apparently planning to continue their march to meet Edward. With negotiations in deadlock this advance threatened battle and Edward reacted accordingly. At nine o'clock on the morning of Tuesday 20 March he mustered his troops and marched out in the direction of Rotherham and Chesterfield. 'Never', wrote an anonymous correspondent of the Pastons, 'were so many goodly men seen in England, and so well arrayed in a field.' But whether Warwick and Clarence changed their minds, possibly on being warned that Lord Scrope had given up the struggle, or whether the move to take up quarters in Rotherham had all along been a feint, when Edward arrived there that evening, he found that they had in fact made off in the opposite direction. They had decamped during the night and were now riding through the Peak District on their way to Manchester in the hope – a desperate, last hope – of persuading Lord Stanley to help them.

To follow in their tracks would not have been easy. After the rebel troops had passed through that mountainous countryside there would have been precious little food and drink left to supply an army the size of Edward's. To cross the Pennines his army would need to start out with a wagon train that was full. So, in order to load up with provisions and then enter Lancashire by a different route, Edward gave the order to turn back north again and make for York, a city whose shops and market promised an abundant supply of victuals. Moreover, since at this stage Edward did not know that the Scrope–Conyers insurrection was on the point of collapse, the move to York seemed to offer the additional advantage of stationing his army where it was well placed to hinder an eventual junction between Warwick and Clarence and the rebels of the North Riding. Travelling via Pontefract, he reached York on Thursday 22 March and stayed there until the following Monday. On 24 March the king issued a proclamation against Warwick and Clarence. If they appeared before him by 28 March they might have his grace and favour. If not, they were to be treated as rebels and traitors. A reward of £1,000 cash or £100 a year in land was offered to their fortunate captor. But despite this appearance of patience, Edward was taking no chances. Remembering the events of 1460 he was determined to prevent Warwick and Clarence from using either Ireland or Calais as a base from which to return in strength. Thus, on 23 March, he had written to the deputy lieutenant of Ireland, informing him that Clarence had been replaced as lieutenant by the earl of Worcester and that he was to refuse all obedience and aid to him. Similar orders were sent to Warwick's deputy at Calais, Lord Wenlock.

Right Tattershall Castle, Lincolnshire, built by Lord Cromwell. Despite its name it was a house designed for peace not for war. With its side windows, this fifteenth-century brick residence has something of the air of a Victorian mansion.

Below Bodiam Castle, Sussex. Built in the late fourteenth century, Bodiam presents a much more warlike appearance than the 'castles' built a century later. Note the gun ports covering the causeway approach to the main gate.

Above The start of a pitched battle between two similarly-equipped armies. This scene illustrates the problems facing commanders in the Wars of the Roses.

Jean de Waurin's *Chronique d'Angleterre* is one of the most valuable and underrated sources of information on the period. Here we see the author presenting his chronicle to Edward IV.

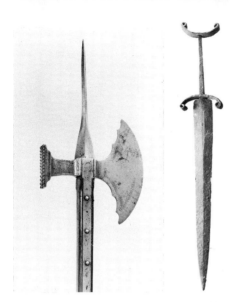

Far left A fifteenth-century pole-axe.

Left A fifteenth-century iron dagger found in Queen Victoria Street, London.

Below An English victory in the Hundred Years War as seen by a late fifteenth-century English artist. Richard Beauchamp, earl of Warwick and English bowmen put the French to flight.

Above Though none of the battles of the Wars of the Roses was a sea battle (in 1460, for example, Exeter avoided committing his fleet to the hazards of a sea battle against the earl of Warwick) control of the channel was often vital and here the Yorkists generally held the upper hand.

Right A scene which illustrates the importance of bowmen in warfare; though this is anything but a head-on clash between two armies, the archers on both sides are engaged.

Left Monumental brass of
Sir Walter Mauntell and his
wife dating from 1487 in
Heyford, Northamptonshire.
Sir William is shown in
the type of armour worn
by knights in the late
fifteenth century.

Below An Edward IV groat,
1483.

Bottom A silver groat of
Henry VI, king of England
and France.

This first chappitre of the first tractate sheweth vn=
der what kyng the playe of the Chesse was founden and
maade .   Capitulo primo

Monge alle the euyl condicions & signes that may
be in a man the first and the grettest is . Whan he fe
rith not ne dredeth to displese & make wroth god by synne
& the peple by kyuyng disordonatly / Whan he retcheth not .
nor taketh hede vnto them that reproue hym and his vy=
ces . But sleeth them . In suche wyse as did the emperour
nero . Whiche did do slee his maister seneque . for as moche
as he myght not suffre to be reproued & taught of hym . in
like wise was sotyme a kyng in babilon that was named

a iiij

Above and right The Princes in the Tower by Delaroche and Richard III as portrayed in the 1955 film show again how the Shakespearian myth has permeated the interpretation of the period, right up to the present day.

Opposite The first page of *The Game and Playe of the Chesse* printed by Caxton. Printing, reading and playing chess were three of the peaceful arts which flourished in the late fifteenth century.

Henry VII by Torrigiano.

Edward, meanwhile, devoted his chief energies to replenishing his army's supplies and to making new arrangements for a political settlement in the north. Lord Scrope and Sir John Conyers came to his presence, submitted and were received back in favour. Of greater long-term significance was the culmination, on 25 March, of Edward's policy of reinstating the Percies: the restoration of their earldom to Sir Henry Percy. John Neville, of course, had to be compensated; all the more so in view of his loyalty to Edward in the last few weeks. He was created marquis of Montagu – a more elevated title certainly, but whether it carried with it the traditional prestige of the earldom of Northumberland was more questionable. Always the same problem in the management of royal patronage. In making new friends, the king ran the risk of losing old ones, especially, in this case, when, in June, John Neville had to hand over the wardenship of the east March to the new earl of Northumberland.

In Lancashire, meanwhile, Warwick and Clarence had failed to find the support they were looking for. Lord Stanley had troubles enough of his own, having clashed with Richard of Gloucester, who was presumably advancing north-east from Wales in response to his brother's summons. With Stanley unable to spare any troops to help them, they now had little choice but to flee the realm. By 26 March Edward knew that they were heading south again, hoping that the Courtenays and others of Clarence's connexion in the west country would shelter them while they found ships to take them to Calais. He sent commissions of array, ordering the muster of forces against Warwick and Clarence, to Cornwall, Devon, Dorset, Somerset, Wiltshire and Gloucestershire as well as, further north, to Shropshire and Staffordshire. But the beaten rebels were in a hurry, and these commissions arrived too late to be effective. Next day Edward himself set off in pursuit, calling upon other mounted contingents to join him on the way, at Nottingham, Coventry and Salisbury, where – according to a letter he wrote to the city magistrates – he expected to find provisions for an army of 40,000 men. If ever the Salisbury magistrates had taken the king's demand at face value they must have been much relieved when Edward's army passed them by, reaching Exeter via Wells on 14 April.

By then it was too late. Taking with them the countess of Warwick and her daughters, including Duchess Isabel of Clarence, who was well advanced in pregnancy, the rebels had already sailed. Not entirely sure of their destination Edward sent a commission of array to Kent in case they should attempt a landing there. Then he mustered fresh troops in

Cornwall and Devon and set off eastwards. By the time he reached Salisbury on 25 April, he had compiled a list of fifty-three men who could still be considered as rebels, and ordered the seizure of their lands and property. It is not a very impressive list. Including the leaders of the Lincolnshire rising, all now dead, it names fewer than twenty knights and twenty esquires. Many of them had close professional associations with either Warwick or Clarence, men like Sir Geoffrey Gate, Sir Walter Wrottesley and Sir Edward Gray. In general it is clear that the rebels had failed to attract a wide section of the country gentry, and that after the submission of their Yorkshire allies – themselves a small group – they had found themselves disastrously isolated. Apart from Lord Scrope of Bolton the only lords who had risked involvement in any way were Warwick's brother-in-law Lord Stanley, who had presumably at one stage made some encouraging noises; John Talbot, earl of Shrewsbury, who seems to have been one of those who at Chesterfield decided that the game was up; another of Warwick's brothers-in-law, John de Vere, earl of Oxford, who made no overt move, but fled to France; and finally Warwick's brother, the archbishop of York, whose arrest Edward IV had ordered on 3 April. Taken as a whole, the English baronage had not rallied to Warwick's and Clarence's cause. The prospect of having Clarence as king was hardly an appealing one.

Warwick and Clarence, meanwhile, had set sail for Calais. As they passed the Isle of Wight, Warwick tried to strengthen his fleet by raiding Southampton and making off with some of the ships berthed there, including his old flagship, the *Trinity*. But Anthony Woodville, the new Earl Rivers, was not caught napping this time, as he had been ten years ago at Sandwich, when he and his father were seized and carried off to Calais. Warwick's attack was beaten off with the loss of some of his men and a ship or two. It may have been during this incident that Sir Geoffrey Gate was captured. Gate received a pardon, but others who were taken prisoner were less fortunate. When Edward arrived at Southampton they were tried and sentenced by the newly appointed constable of England, John Tiptoft, earl of Worcester. Their punishment, according to John Warkworth, was to be hanged, drawn, quartered and beheaded; then their bodies were hung up by the legs, 'and a stake made sharp at both ends, whereof one end was put in at the buttocks, while their head was impaled on the other'. As a result, continues Warkworth, the earl became 'greatly behated among the people'.

Warwick's failure at Southampton was followed by an even bigger disappointment at Calais itself. In command at Calais was his deputy, Lord Wenlock, and the earl had counted on his loyalty. It came, therefore, as a nasty surprise when, on 16 April, the guns of Calais opened fire on the refugees' fleet. Whatever Lord Wenlock's private feelings, the fact was that the bulk of the garrison, under the command of the marshal of Calais, the Gascon exile, Gaillard, Lord Duras, had decided to stick by Edward IV, and there was little that Wenlock could do about it.

Warwick's initial reaction was to try to fight his way in, but this was clearly hopeless, so he drew back out of range in order to negotiate. The garrison, however, sent envoys to the duke of Burgundy (who was at Saint Omer), asking for assistance, and refused to give ground. The best that Warwick could obtain was some wine to comfort the duchess of Clarence, now in labour, but though the mother survived, the child did not and was buried near Calais. Eventually Warwick decided to move on. Edward was delighted by Lord Wenlock's unexpected loyalty and rewarded him by promoting him to be lieutenant of the town and Marches of Calais in May. The duke of Burgundy too was pleased. He sent a messenger to Wenlock, congratulating him and granting him a pension of a thousand crowns. The messenger was none other than Philippe de Commynes, and in his *Memoirs* he reports that the loyal Wenlock was all along playing a double game. Apparently he had not so much opposed Warwick's entry into Calais as advised against it. To enter Calais at this moment when the garrison, the duke of Burgundy and the king of England were all ranged against him was to put his neck into a noose. Better to go to France; when the time was right he would see to it that Calais was delivered to his lord. 'No man', writes Commynes, 'ever served the earl of Warwick so loyally.'

As he left Calais on 20 April Warwick fell in with a large Flemish convoy. It was the kind of temptation which he never could resist, and even though an English fleet, under Lord Howard, had already put out in search of him, he decided to make the most of it. At the Burgundian court it was reported that he captured no less than sixty ships belonging to Duke Charles's subjects and had their crews thrown into the sea. Charles rushed to Sluys in order to supervise in person the mobilization of an avenging fleet, while Warwick sailed westwards snapping up more prizes. The pirate earl did not escape entirely unscathed. Lord Howard caught up with him and in a fierce sea-battle forced Warwick to give up some of his captures. However,

Warwick was still in possession of a great deal of plunder when his ships dropped anchor at Honfleur and asked for the protection of King Louis of France. This marked the beginning of a new stage in the Wars of the Roses. From now on they became deeply enmeshed in the wider network of European politics.

Eleven

THE RETURN OF THE OLD KING, 1470–1

ON 22 JULY 1470, at Angers, the earl of Warwick went down on his knees before Margaret of Anjou and he stayed there for a good quarter of an hour before she could bring herself to forgive him for all the wrongs he had done to her and her family. Even then he had to promise to repeat this ceremony of contrition in public at Westminster as soon as they had recovered England. Three days later, in Angers cathedral, Edward, Prince of Wales, was betrothed to Anne Neville. Plans were laid for an invasion of England, but so deep was their distrust of each other that Margaret would neither cross the Channel with Warwick nor allow her sixteen-year-old son to accompany him. They would join the earl only when his mission had been successfully accomplished. In the meantime, Lancastrian interests in England were to be represented by Jasper Tudor while Anne Neville remained behind in France, a hostage to ensure Warwick's good faith. In the long run, this decision was to prove fatal to their cause, but it was much more than just an unfortunate accident. It reflected a deep-seated split in the new alliance which, one way or another, was always likely to bring it down.

The man who had brought these two arch-enemies together at Angers was, of course, Louis XI of France. But although this little piece of political theatre had required a certain amount of tactful stage-management – Clarence had to be kept out of the way, for example – it had certainly not stretched his diplomatic talent to the limit. Much as they disliked each other, they neither of them had anywhere else they could go. So, as soon as he heard that Warwick and Clarence had landed at Honfleur, Louis realized that his moment had come. Now was the time to revive an old dream: the restoration of Henry VI followed by an Anglo-French military alliance against Burgundy. What Louis was after was the return of the Somme towns, chief among

them Amiens and Saint Quentin, to the crown of France, and organizing an invasion of England was just a means to this end. It was
undeniably a gamble. If he sheltered Warwick, then Duke Charles, who
looked upon the earl as a pirate, would at once draw closer to Edward
IV, but Louis very quickly decided to take the plunge. He sent messengers inviting Margaret of Anjou to come to court, persuaded her to meet
Warwick and promised to supply men, money and ships.

Louis XI's gamble ushered in the next stage of the War of the Roses, a
naval war in the Channel. Since Edward IV's fleet, under the command
of John Howard, had been at sea since the spring, he had already taken
an important initiative, but it was doubtful whether the English fleet on
its own could have prevented the invasion force from crossing the
Channel. Fortunately for Edward IV, Warwick's depredations had
ensured that he could call upon the assistance of the large Burgundian
navy. It is hard to believe that Warwick had been unaware of the likely
consequences of his piratical actions. Presumably his main priority had
been to keep his fleet together. Without this he had no bargaining
counter left. He had counted on having the resources of Calais at his
disposal but, deprived of these, what else could he do but offer his
sailors the opportunity to earn their pay in the shape of plunder?
Indeed, to Duke Charles's intense chagrin, Warwick's raids on Dutch
shipping continued throughout May and he even attempted to carry off
or destroy some ships of the Burgundian fleet being fitted out against
him at Sluys. Charles had in fact given orders for the immediate
mobilization of his fleet as long ago as 24 April, but it took time, and not
until 11 June was the Burgundian admiral, Henrik van Borselen, ready
to join Howard. United, however, the Anglo-Burgundian navy dominated the Channel. Borselen and Howard launched raids against the
towns of the Norman coast, then settled down to a blockade of the Seine
estuary.

But no fleet could stay at sea for long, especially not a war fleet
carrying extra complements of soldiers. Ships were small, provisions
limited, weather uncertain. At the end of June Henrik van Borselen
returned to refit. The English also drew off, alarmed by news of a hostile
Hansa flotilla off the east coast. Warwick and the French admiral took
the opportunity to move their ships out of the Seine estuary and down
the coast to Barfleur and La Hogue. Warwick and Clarence then took
up their headquarters at nearby Valognes and waited until Louis told
them that Margaret of Anjou was ready to sign a treaty of alliance.
Their plan was to land somewhere in the west country; this should

enable them to capitalize on Jasper Tudor's Welsh connexions. Moreover, Warwick had promises of support from the earl of Shrewsbury and Lord Stanley. He also planned to repeat the strategic formula which had been so successful in 1469. His own invasion would be preceded by risings in the north designed to draw Edward away from London and leave the coast clear in the south.

What, in the meantime, had Edward IV been doing? At the Burgundian court, the general opinion seems to have been that he was overconfident and negligent. According to Commynes, at this date still in the service of Duke Charles, Edward 'was not afraid. It seems to me that it was a great piece of folly not to fear his enemy and not to want to believe the duke's warnings, considering the great preparations which were being made. But Edward paid no attention and just carried on with his hunting.' He had, in fact, taken several precautions and indeed Commynes goes on to mention one of them. He sent 'a lady on a secret mission to Clarence, to persuade him not to be the agent of the ruin of his family, to ask him to consider very carefully what room there was for him now that Warwick had married his daughter to the Lancastrian prince of Wales'. He appointed the earl of Worcester as lieutenant of Ireland and even Wenlock, who had turned Warwick away from Calais, was replaced by John Howard. By such steps the two invasion springboards of ten years earlier were denied to the rebels of 1470.

This apart, he clearly relied chiefly on sea power. He did not know where an invasion force might land, but he did know where it intended to embark. In these circumstances a blockade was the most economical effective method of defence. Early in July the Anglo-Burgundian fleets returned to the Norman coast and re-imposed their blockade.

The first stage of Warwick's plan went ahead on schedule. Late in July his brother-in-law, Lord FitzHugh of Ravensworth, led a rebellion in the North Riding and there was another rising in Cumberland. Both movements involved gentry with close Neville associations. The Cumberland rising was led by Richard Salkeld, formerly Warwick's constable of Carlisle Castle. Lord FitzHugh's rebellion was on a more substantial scale. Its leader was able to call upon the resources of the Lovell and Latimer estates since the heads of these two families were both minors in FitzHugh's care. He was followed by at least twenty members of the Richmondshire and Cleveland gentry, very much the same group that had marched with Robin of Redesdale in 1469. It included, for example, John Conyers, son of the John Conyers who had died at Edgecote, grandson of the steward of Middleham. No less than three of the rebels were brothers-in-law of Warwick's steward and in the case of many others, yeomen as well as gentry, the Neville connexion was strong. Most sinister of all was the fact that one of the rebels, William Burgh, was a member of the council of Warwick's brother, the marquis of Montagu. Some of the other insurgents may well have been men who stood to lose, or had already lost, office as a result of the restoration of old Percy estates to the new earl of Northumberland. However that may be, it is clear that this was a Neville rebellion, not just the revolt of one baron and his following. By 5 August Sir John Paston, in London, was writing to his brother that 'there be many folks up in the north, so that Percy is not able to resist them'. So swift a challenge to Edward's reorganization of the north was a serious matter. He responded at once by calling up his retainers and marching to deal with it.

The decision to go north at this juncture has been criticized. It was, presumably, what Warwick hoped he would do and so, on the face of it, must have been an error of judgment. But, in fact, Edward's prompt action meant that he was able to disperse the rebels very quickly – in contrast to the disastrous consequences of his leisurely response in 1469. Moreover, his blockade was still in operation and his spies had presumably informed him that Warwick, Louis and Margaret were only just completing their own arrangements. By 14 August he was at York. Two days later he reached Ripon, on the edge of the North Riding. The rebels melted away at his approach and Lord FitzHugh fled across the border into Scotland. If Edward should be criticized, it is not for going north, but for staying there after the rebellion had been put down. He was still in Yorkshire in mid-September when news came of Warwick's landing – and this despite the fact that on 7 September he had written a letter announcing that he expected his enemies to land in Kent or somewhere near there. What was he doing in the north at the end of August and in early September? Commynes's portrait of a careless and pleasure-loving king, 'accustomed to more luxuries than any prince of his day, thinking of nothing but women, hunting and self-indulgence', is beside the point. If Edward wanted his pleasures, he could have found them in the south. If he went hunting in the north, it is not likely to have been the ladies' tents which held his attention, but the company of Henry Percy and John Neville. What line would the marquis of Montagu take if and when his brother invaded? So far this able soldier had always been loyal to Edward – even during the two crises of July 1469 and March 1470 – but since then he had lost both the earldom of Northumberland and the wardenship of the east March. Had he been adequately compensated? These were political problems which it was well worth spending some time over. Edward presumably felt that they had been satisfactorily dealt with because when the news of the invasion came he entrusted Montagu with the job of raising the levies of the north.

Warwick meanwhile had been facing considerable difficulties. Everything was ready, but the ominous presence of the blockading fleet meant that he could not move. English and Burgundian raiding parties attacked the Norman coast, killing, burning and pillaging. The local population can hardly have looked with favour upon the uninvited guests who had drawn these attentions upon them. Perhaps while Warwick's men had money they were made welcome, but as the weeks of enforced idleness went by so their money ran out. Inevitably relations became more and more strained, between the outsiders and the people of Normandy, between the outsiders and their own commanders who feared mutiny, between Warwick and Louis's officials, harassed by the earl's constant demands for money. On 21 August Warwick ordered his men to leave Valognes and go to Barfleur, to be ready to board ship. His orders were disobeyed. The men would do nothing until they had been paid. Warwick pawned what he had and asked Louis for more. Another awkward week went by, and another – and still the Anglo-Burgundian fleet kept station. Then, at last, Warwick's luck changed. A storm blew up and smashed the blockade, scattering ships, or so it was said, from Scotland to Holland. On 9 September, with not a hostile sail in sight, the allies put to sea.

They landed near Exeter and at once issued proclamations in the king's name, summoning all able-bodied men to support them. Jasper Tudor rode off to raise Wales, while Warwick, Clarence and the earl of Oxford headed north-east. Shrewsbury and Stanley kept their promises and came in to join them. By the time they reached Coventry they had gathered a large army estimated in the official Coventry records at 30,000. Does this mean, as had been argued, that popular sympathy had swung decisively against Edward IV? If it had, what could have caused such a drastic turn-around? Public opinion polls taken during the preceding fifteen months would have made interesting reading. Was the country really pro-Warwick one moment, pro-Edward the next, pro-Henry immediately afterwards? Unquestionably men did change sides, but in almost every case that we know about it happened after the event, not before it. They were adjusting to a new political dispensation, not struggling to bring it about. This is how writers like Sir John Fortescue, John Harding and John Rous behaved. Were writers in search of patronage more cynical than their fellows? Municipal records suggest that they were not. Towns tended to support whichever side happened to control the administrative machinery of the realm, the *de facto* government. This realistic attitude meant that only at moments when the government itself was in doubt did they have to think very hard about their political commitment – and the signs are that they did not enjoy having to do so. One such awkward moment occurred in September 1470. On 21 September Salisbury city council found themselves faced by two conflicting demands. Warwick's envoy appeared and asked them to send a contingent of forty men; at the same time a member of Edward IV's household, Thomas St Leger, arrived to insist that they should oppose the invaders. The council's reaction suggests embarrassment rather than a desire to support one side rather than the other. Their attempted compromise was rejected by Warwick's envoy and eventually Salisbury's contingent marched out to join the rebels under the command of a citizen who shortly before had volunteered to serve the king. Why, in the end, did they decide to join the invaders? Were they persuaded by the words of Warwick's Lancastrian manifestos? Or by the fact that Warwick's army was a great deal closer than Edward's? Just at this crucial moment the king in the north was a remote figure. His decision to concentrate on the problems of the north was a sensible one since all his recent troubles had had their origin in the north, but, like every alternative course of action, it had its drawbacks and in the south Edward was now paying the penalty. Farther north, in the Midlands, the Coventry records suggest that towns found it easier to send their contingents to Edward's appointed muster at Nottingham. The mayor of Coventry received a privy seal writ, dated 18 September, at three o'clock on the afternoon of 20 September and that same day forty men were in harness. Whether or not Edward's strategy was a mistaken one would depend on the extent to which he succeeded in achieving the political settlement in the north to which he had devoted so much time at a critical moment.

As Edward moved south to meet the army which was gathering at Nottingham he was, it seems, in a confident mood. He had a low opinion of Warwick's abilities on the field of battle and he counted on outnumbering him anyway. He halted at Doncaster to give the marquis of Montagu and the northern levies time to catch up with him. Since there was no immediate danger, his army was quartered in the surrounding villages. He and his entourage sat down to dinner knowing that Montagu would soon be with them. But the king's peace of mind was shattered by the news that John Neville had declared for Henry VI and was about to attack.

Evidently Edward's reorganization of the north had failed. John Neville looked upon the estates and titles which he had been granted as a mere 'magpie's nest' – in John Warkworth's graphic phrase – in comparison with the earldom he had lost. He had delayed showing his hand for as long as possible in the hope of taking Edward by surprise. Fortunately for the king, from the moment the marquis told his followers of his plans – as he was bound to – there was no way the secret could be kept. Edward just had time to send out messengers to check tidings which he could scarcely bring himself to credit and to hold a hurried consultation with his advisers. Although several lords were with him, Gloucester, Rivers, Hastings, Worcester, Howard and Saye, the fact that their troops were dispersed meant that there was no chance of opposing Montagu's compact force, nor of regrouping in order to carry out an orderly retreat. The king's only chance lay in headlong flight. With two Neville armies in the field against him, nowhere in England where he would be safe, particularly since the soldiers at Nottingham would disperse as soon as they heard that their commander had turned and run away, he would have to flee the realm. Montagu's defection, concealed until the last moment, had been decisive.

Edward and all those who could escape from Doncaster rode southeast, towards the Lincolnshire coast and away from the two Neville armies, Montagu's to the north and Warwick's to the south-west. Then, after a hazardous crossing of the Wash in small boats in the dark, they arrived at King's Lynn, late on the night of Sunday 30 September. Here Earl Rivers had some influence owing to the proximity of his seat at Middleton Castle. They were able to procure three ships and set sail two days later for the Low Countries. Still Edward's troubles were not over. His flotilla was sighted by a squadron of Hanseatic ships and pursued right up to the Dutch coast. Only the fortunate presence of Duke Charles's governor of Holland, Louis of Gruthuyse, prevented Edward's ships from being boarded as they lay at anchor waiting for the tide which would allow them to enter the harbour at Alkmaar. Gruthuyse, who on several occasions had served as a Burgundian ambassador to England, knew and liked Edward. By 11 October the exiled king was safely installed in Gruthuyse's house at the Hague.

The news of Edward's flight from Doncaster brought about the instant collapse of his regime. The queen fled from the Tower and took sanctuary at Westminster where, on 2 November, she was to give birth to Edward IV's first son. At the same time a mob of sanctuarymen, Warwick's followers and old Lancastrians as well as debtors and criminals, swarmed out of their various refuges and went on the rampage. With the prisons broken open and a crowd of Kentishmen, claiming to be Warwick supporters, looting and pillaging in Southwark, the city was in tumultuous confusion. In an attempt to restore law and order, custody of the Tower was granted to one of the men who had just broken out of sanctuary, Warwick's retainer, Sir Geoffrey Gate. Three days later, on 6 October, Warwick himself entered London, accompanied by Clarence, Shrewsbury and Lord Stanley. They went to the Tower, collected the old king, and swore allegiance to him. Henry VI was on the throne again.

In many ways the new government was bound to be an unstable one, composed as it was of groups which might be able to sink their differences for a short-term military alliance, but which were unlikely to form a permanent regime. Clarence's position was highly ambiguous. What would Warwick's own role be once Queen Margaret had returned? And there were other Lancastrians still abroad, notably the most bitter of Warwick's old enemies, Edward Beaufort, duke of Somerset, and Henry Holland, duke of Exeter. What would happen when they returned? In the meantime, the earl might try to build up a party of his own adherents, but this was by no means easy. The events of September–October 1470 gave very little scope for seizing the estates of defeated political opponents, and, with no forfeitures, there was equally no opportunity for a judicious exercise of generosity. Few men had cause to be grateful to Warwick; even men like Shrewsbury and Stanley went unrewarded. On the other hand if Warwick's long-term future looked bleak, so also did Edward IV's. The strength of his position as king had lain in the contrast between him and Henry VI. But when Margaret of Anjou returned to England she would bring back her son Edward, now seventeen years old. The not too distant – and peaceful – succession of this young prince to his father's throne might seem a more attractive prospect than the violent restoration of Edward IV. Edward, in other words, was under pressure to act quickly. The longer his return was delayed, the smaller his chance of success. Unfortunately for Edward his immediate prospects looked bleak too. The problem was the attitude of the man to whom he had gone for help, his brother-in-law, Charles of Burgundy. Charles refused to see him and indeed, according to Commynes, wished that he was dead – on the face of it a strange attitude for a prince whose fleet had recently been the mainstay of Edward's defence measures. But the duke's policy was both rational and consistent. He had wanted the king of England as an ally against Louis xi – whether that king was Edward or someone else was a matter of some indifference though, if pressed, Charles might have had a slight preference for a Lancastrian. Now that Edward was off the throne, the duke's over-riding aim was to renew the Anglo-Burgundian alliance by coming to terms with Warwick as soon as possible. In these circumstances the exiled king was hardly a welcome guest.

Luckily for Edward the earl of Warwick wasted no time in rejecting the duke's overtures. Warwick had long since been committed to a French alliance and was now bound still more tightly to Louis xi by treaty as well as by ties of gratitude and expediency: his daughter was at the French court; at the unlikely best, if the Anglo-French war against Burgundy were to go well, his share of the spoils would be the rich provinces of Holland and Zealand; at the worst, if Margaret turned against him, Louis's court might provide an honourable refuge. The harder Louis pressed for the opening of their joint campaign against Burgundy, the more likely Charles was to change his mind about Edward. On 3 December 1470 Louis published what was, in effect, a declaration of war against Burgundy and three weeks later the duke finally decided to grant his brother-in-law an interview. Until this moment the only continental prince to show any sympathy for Edward had been Francis of Brittany, but from now on his prospects were transformed. Edward's recovery, like his overthrow, was very largely conditioned by Louis xi's hostility to Burgundy. In public Duke Charles continued to forbid his subjects to help Edward, but in private he gave him £20,000, some ships and the facilities for fitting out a fleet at Veere on the island of Walcheren. In the weeks that followed, as France and Burgundy slipped further down the slope into war, Edward was able to acquire more ships (including no less than fourteen from the Hanseatic League) and borrow more money. Inevitably these prep-arations were observed with interest, and Louis xi and Warwick were kept well informed of their progress. Warwick in turn made his own preparations. He issued commissions of array, to Montagu for the north, to Clarence, Oxford, Scrope of Bolton and himself for the rest of England, and to Jasper Tudor with Clarence and himself again, for

Wales and the Marches. If these were the only men whom Warwick believed that he could trust to raise troops, then the Neville-Lancastrian regime of 1470–1 was as narrowly based as Richard III's Neville-Yorkist regime fourteen years later. But if Warwick was still a keen exponent of sea power then his main line of defence should have been the English and French fleets. An English fleet under the command of the Bastard of Fauconberg was indeed sent out to patrol the Channel. Unfortunately for Warwick, he was short of money – he had not dared risk unpopularity by demanding a grant from parliament – and so he could not afford committing his fleet to the unprofitable as well as tedious business of a blockade. Fauconberg kept his fleet in being by the traditional Neville method of allowing it to prey on merchant shipping. But attacks on, among others, Breton ships were followed by Breton reprisals and, at the crucial time, Fauconberg's fleet was lured away by the activities of a Breton squadron. As for Louis XI's fleet, that had important work to do; its task was to escort Margaret of Anjou to England. It lay at anchor in the Seine estuary waiting for her to embark, but she was anxious, worried about Warwick and his real intentions. While she still hesitated, Edward IV put to sea.

Twelve

COMING IN BY THE WINDOWS, 1471–83

THE HISTORIAN of Edward's recovery of his throne is fortunate in possessing a detailed contemporary narrative of these dramatic events: the *Historie of the Arrivall of Edward IV*. We do not know the name of the author of the *Arrivall*, but he was probably a member of the household. Certainly he travelled with the king and was an eyewitness of many of the scenes which he describes. His account was set down on paper at Edward's behest very soon after the last event it records (26 May) and copies (not all of them with exactly the same text) were sent abroad, to the Burgundian court and elsewhere. Unquestionably then we are dealing with an official version produced for purposes of propaganda. This, however, by no means renders it useless. It was, after all, in Edward's interests that both foreign princes and domestic readers should learn that they could count on his news-letters for accurate information. Moreover it is clear that the author of the *Arrivall* was not only exceptionally well-informed, but that he was also an intelligent observer of the political scene. The task of the historian of the Wars of the Roses would be much simpler if this writer had composed more such accounts, or if more had survived. For these reasons, while making due allowance for its propaganda element, the following narrative is very largely based on the *Historie of the Arrivall of Edward IV*.

On 2 March 1471 Edward embarked at Flushing. He had a fleet of thirty-six ships and a force of 1,200 combatants, including some Flemish hand-gunners, perhaps 2,000 men in all. It was not much of an army to conquer a kingdom and contemporaries put Edward's chance of success correspondingly low. 'It is a difficult matter to go out by the door and then try to come in by the windows,' wrote a Milanese ambassador. 'Men think he will leave his skin there.' The ambassador's information came from circles around Warwick, but he was undoubtedly correct in implying that this time Edward intended to stand and fight. On 2 March the wind was against him, but, in a public demonstration of his determination, he refused to disembark, forcing himself and his following to spend nine weary days aboard, before they could at last weigh anchor on the eleventh. By the evening of the next day they were off the coast of Norfolk near Cromer. Prudently Edward sent a small group ashore to assess the mood of the local population and they returned with warnings that it was unsafe to land. Warwick had been vigilant and had done his work well. Suspected supporters of Edward, like the duke of Norfolk, had been rounded up and held in custody. Led by the earl of Oxford those of the East Anglian establishment who were loyal to Warwick were alert and ready to repel any invasion. Edward decided to sail on northwards. But once again the weather turned against him. His fleet was hit by storms and scattered. Eventually on Thursday 14 March Edward made a safe landing at Ravenspur on the Humber – the very spot where, in 1399, Bolingbroke had landed at the start of his bid to become Henry IV.

If this was a good omen, other signs were less favourable. Edward's ship, the *Anthony*, was on its own. With Edward were his chamberlain, Lord Hastings, and 500 men, no more. His first night in England was spent in poor lodgings in a small village, two miles from Ravenspur. Next day brought both good news and bad. The other shiploads succeeding in making their way from their different landing places to join him, but, as the author of the *Arrivall* admits, almost no one else joined him. Many indeed preferred to join the force several thousand strong which was being mustered by Martin de la See and which threatened to corner him in Holderness. At this critical moment when his bid for the throne seemed on the point of being snuffed out almost before it had started, Edward held a hurried conference with his advisers and decided to adopt the ruse which had been used by Bolingbroke seventy-two years earlier. He announced that he had come to claim, not the crown, but only the duchy which had been his father's. He also let it be known that in this venture he had the support of the earl of Northumberland; in Yorkshire – again as Bolingbroke had known – the voice of the Percies counted for much. Reassured by these tidings, persuaded perhaps by the gifts of money which Edward sent their way and doubtless glad of an excuse for avoiding battle, Martin de la See's army melted away.

Rather than head directly for London, which would have meant returning to their ships for the crossing of the Humber estuary – and laid them open to the suspicion that they were sailing away for good – Edward decided to make for York. Hull, 'a good walled town' refused to open its gates. If more towns were to follow this example of loyalty to Henry VI, Edward's attempted *coup* would soon lose all credibility. On 18 March while still three miles away from York, the city recorder, Thomas Conyers, met him and advised him against approaching any nearer. He would either, he said, suffer the humiliation of being refused entry or, if he were admitted, he would be trapped and his cause lost. Edward, however, felt that he had to take the risk. If he withdrew now he would be lost anyway. No matter how poor the odds the only hope lay in boldness. A little further on he was slightly encouraged by two other citizens who said that, since he came only for the duchy of York, he probably would be allowed to enter. Further on still Conyers warned him off again and it was in this uncertain manner, with his fortune hanging in the balance, that his small force came to the gates of York.

There he was told that he could enter – but only with an escort of sixteen or seventeen men. The rest of his troops would have to stay outside. Perhaps Conyers had been right. It looked like a trap. But Edward still felt that he had no choice but to go on or give up. He went in and, according to one chronicler, he did it in style. Writing about ten years later John Warkworth describes how he entered wearing an ostrich feather (the emblem of the prince of Wales) and shouting 'A King Harry! A King and Prince Edward' to demonstrate his loyalty to the Lancastrian regime. Once inside, his personal charm worked its old magic on the mayor and aldermen. By the evening his whole army had been allowed in to spend the night in relative comfort and find refreshment – but only on condition that it left by noon next day. It had been a close-run thing. A few weeks later, after Edward had revealed his true colours, York became one of the centres of a northern rebellion against him.

From York, Edward turned south. His strategy was a twofold one. It was in the Midlands, where Lord Hastings had wielded great influence, that he had the best hope of reinforcements; and it was there too that he would have to challenge Warwick for control of the kingdom. On 20 March he came to the family castle of Sandal, near Wakefield, the scene of his father's death. Only seven miles away, at Pontefract Castle, the marquis of Montagu made no attempt to obstruct his progress. At this point the author of the *Arrivall* pauses in his narrative to give a realistic assessment of the possibilities open to Montagu, which shows clearly that the kind of shrewd political analysis which we associate with the name Commynes was by no means unique to him. Montagu, he says, allowed Edward to pass because the Yorkist army, though small, was well-armed and determined. It could be met only by a greater force, and the pretence that Edward came for the duchy of York only, made it difficult to muster men against him. Most important was the fact that the earl of Northumberland had remained immobile, for in that part of the world no action could succeed unless it had Percy backing. In other words, by remaining inactive, Northumberland had done Edward a great service – as great a service indeed as if he had summoned his retainers and called out his tenants to march in the Yorkist cause. This was because the Yorkshire gentry and yeomen had still not forgotten Towton where so many of their fathers and brothers had died fighting against Edward. If the earl were to summon them now, they would not flock enthusiastically to his banner and, in the present finely-balanced circumstances, half-hearted service might do more harm than good. 'And so it may reasonably be judged that the earl had given a notable good service, and politiquely done.' The earl's immobility had persuaded York to open its gates and persuaded many others to sit still, even those who in their hearts opposed Edward's coming. Moreover, by the time Edward reached Sandal those who lived nearby were less disposed to resist him than they might have been; since up to this point no one had opposed him, to do so now seemed to be flying in the face of the opinion of one's neighbours. All these considerations must have been in Montagu's mind and prevented him from standing in Edward's way.

This clear-sighted analysis by one of his followers only serves to highlight the fact that Edward had still failed to gain any wholehearted adherents in the week since his landing at Ravenspur. In 1399 Bolingbroke had done much better than this. From the region around the family stronghold of Sandal 'came some folk unto him, but not so many as he supposed would have come' confesses the writer of the *Arrivall*. Some came in at Doncaster, but not until he reached Nottingham did he receive any substantial reinforcements: six hundred well-armed men under two knights, Sir William Parr and Sir James Harrington. At the same time one of Edward's patrols reported the presence of a large Lancastrian force, some 4,000 men, at Newark. These were troops raised in the eastern counties by the duke of Exeter, the earl of Oxford and Lord Beaumont. Edward at once wheeled about and made for Newark, only to learn, when he had come to within three miles of the town, that Exeter and Oxford had observed the patrols and, guessing that Edward himself would follow hard on their heels, had decamped during the night leaving most of their army in disarray behind them. Once again Edward's reputation for boldness had paid dividends. On 25 March he crossed the Trent and finally at Leicester the long looked-for accession of strength materialized: 3,000 men led by Lord Hastings's retainers arrived at the agreed rendezvous. In the opinion of the *Arrivall*'s author they were not only well-equipped; they were also entirely trustworthy: 'They would abide with him for better and for worse, serving him truly with all their strength.'

Warwick, meanwhile, had also been raising men in the Midlands. Of the dozens of letters he must have written one still survives. It was sent to Henry Vernon of Derbyshire on 25 March, summoning him to come in haste to Coventry and ending with a postscript: 'Henry I pray you fail not now as ever I may do for you. R. Warrewyk.' But Henry Vernon was also in touch with Clarence and it seems likely that he did fail Warwick now. At this critical juncture Clarence held the balance of power and it was later reported that he had deceived Warwick by means of messengers advising him not to risk battle with Edward until he and the earl had joined forces. Certainly, for whatever reason, Warwick chose not to fight. On 27 March he took up his quarters in Coventry, 'a strong walled town', in the words of the *Arrivall*, and was not to be lured forth by the challenges to a pitched battle which followed Edward's arrival there two days later. If the author of the *Arrivall* was correct when he asserted that Warwick's army of six to seven thousand men was larger than Edward's, then it is most probable that the earl was reasonably confident and was simply waiting for the reinforcements led by Montagu, Oxford, Exeter and Clarence which he knew to be on the way. Edward, who had billeted his own army in Warwick, would then be hopelessly outnumbered. It was a sensible enough policy – if relying on Clarence could ever be said to be sensible – and it nearly succeeded. Although a Yorkist rearguard defeated Exeter and Beaumont at Leicester on 3 April, it failed to stop their getting through to Coventry. Montagu and the earl of Oxford also succeeded in joining Warwick there, but by that same day Clarence had made up his mind to switch sides – and with him he brought no less than 4,000 men, including Henry Vernon. The *Arrivall* contains a vivid description of the meeting of the brothers and their armies, three miles out of Warwick on the Banbury road. When they had approached to within half a mile of each other, they drew their forces up in battle array, and then, each taking only a handful of friends with him, they left the safety of their armies and went to meet each other. Clarence threw himself down on his knees, but Edward at once raised him up and kissed him many times. Then there was 'right kind and loving language betwixt them two, with perfect accord knit together for ever hereafter'. Next, Clarence and Richard of Gloucester embraced and there followed a general reconciliation of all the nobles in both parties. To the sound of trumpets and minstrels Edward led Clarence to visit his army. Then, still accompanied only by the select few, he went over to Clarence's host and welcomed them, assuring them of his grace and love. These demonstrations of mutual trust and affection over, the two armies marched into Warwick.

So the two sides had mustered their forces. After a fortnight of confusion and uncertainty the lines were now clearly drawn, all the more so since on his arrival at Warwick Edward had at last thrown off the mask which had served him so well and had openly proclaimed himself king. But, in the Midlands at least, this mustering of the armies led only to stalemate. Warwick would not budge from Coventry and Edward had no hope of being able to take so well-defended a city by assault. Nor could he afford to settle down to a siege. He had neither the cash resources which would be needed to reconcile a large army to the tedious business of a blockade, nor the time – any day now Queen Margaret and her followers might land on the south coast. Moreover, foraging was already becoming difficult as the Coventry–Warwick region felt the strain of feeding so large an influx of men and horses. Somehow Edward had to find a way of breaking the stalemate.

On 5 April his army broke camp and began to march east. After consulting his brothers Edward had decided to strike for London. There were obvious risks in leaving Warwick's army intact in his rear – but when had he not taken risks? And it was equally obvious that control of the capital would bring great advantages, not only in terms of the number of men and amount of war material which London could provide, but also because Westminster, as the seat of royal authority, offered an appearance of legitimacy and the resources of the central administration to the person who held it. So, taking care to appoint 'a good band of spears and archers, his behind-riders, to counter, if it had been needed, such of the earl's party as, peradventure, he should have sent to have troubled him on the backhalf', Edward marched on London via Daventry, Northampton, Dunstable and St Albans. In fact since he was taking his artillery with him, Warwick had little hope of catching up with Edward before the latter reached London. The news of Edward's approach threw the common council of London into a state of uncertainty bordering on panic. Edward wrote to them commanding them to seize Henry VI and keep him in custody until his arrival. Warwick wrote to them commanding them to hold the city at all costs until his arrival. To add to the complications, they had just had news of Queen Margaret and Prince Edward; they had embarked on 24 March and, though delayed by contrary winds, were expected at any moment. Hearing this the two most energetic Lancastrians then in London, Edmund Beaufort, duke of Somerset, and John Courtenay, heir to the earl of Devon, had left the city on 8 April. In their eyes going to meet the true leaders of the Lancastrian cause was more urgent than helping Warwick to hold London. After their departure the mantle of responsibility fell upon the shoulders of Warwick's brother, George Neville, the archbishop of York. The earl had written to him, begging him to keep Edward at bay for two or three days, just long enough for his army to catch up with Edward's as it lay before the city. George Neville did his best. He tried to rally support by organizing a parade of loyal Lancastrians on 9 April. The unfortunate Henry was himself dragged into the procession, but he had to be held by the hand all the way by the archbishop, and his unregal appearance sitting limply on his horse and dressed in 'a long blue gown of velvet as though he had no more to change with' may have excited pity but certainly did not inspire confidence. Persuaded by this demonstration of Lancastrian armed might, the common council resolved that: 'as Edward, late King of England, was hastening towards the city with a powerful army, and as the inhabitants were not sufficiently versed in the use of arms to withstand so large a force, no attempt should be made to oppose him'. Realizing that his position was hopeless, George Neville, on the evening of 10 April, secretly offered to submit to Edward, who by now had reached St Albans. So also did other Lancastrians, for during that night a party of Yorkists was able to seize the Tower. Next day Edward entered London in triumph, his army led – a Londoner reported – by five hundred of a 'black and smoky sort of Flemish gunners'. Edward's first concern was to go to St Paul's and there offer thanks for his safe return. Then he went to find Henry VI in the bishop's palace. The two kings shook hands and the older, feebler man is reported to have offered an embrace with the words: 'My cousin of York, you are very welcome. I know that in your hands my life will not be in danger.' Edward reassured Henry and sent him for safe keeping to the Tower, along with George Neville and various other Lancastrians. Edward next called in at Westminster Abbey for just long enough to enable the archbishop of Canterbury to set the crown on his head, and then he made his way to the sanctuary where his wife and daughters had spent the entire period of his exile and where his new-born son had spent the whole of his life. But there was little enough time for family reunions; already Warwick was approaching St Albans and a reception committee had to be got ready to meet him.

Friday 12 April, Good Friday, and the following Saturday morning were spent in hectic preparation for the coming struggle. It was clearly still in Edward's interest to bring Warwick to battle as quickly as possible in order to avert the danger of his joining forces with Queen Margaret. Warwick, understanding this, ought to have realized that there was no chance of his taking Edward by surprise by an attack during the Easter celebrations. Possibly he calculated that his political future in Lancastrian England would be bleak unless he could present himself before Queen Margaret in the guise of a victor. In this sense he too needed a quick success, but by this same logic his defensive posture in the Midlands had been a strategic mistake caused, presumably, by the political blunder of relying on Clarence. As he pressed southwards looking for the one decisive battle by which to retrieve his position, he could at least console himself with the reflection that it was now Edward who was relying on Clarence. Moreover, though Edward undoubtedly found more soldiers and cannon in London, it seems that in both respects Warwick still held the numerical advantage.

At midday on Saturday Edward held a muster of his army in St John's field. At four o'clock the march began, heading up the Great North Road in the direction of St Albans. With him were Gloucester and Clarence, Hastings, Rivers and half a dozen other lords. The size of their followings would suggest that Edward had an army of about 10,000 combatants. In addition there was at least one non-combatant: Henry vi. In a dynastic quarrel, to have the rival king in your hand was to hold a trump card and Edward was clearly determined to keep him. Even if he lost the battle, if only he could retain possession of Henry it might prove a useful bargaining counter. At Barnet Edward's clashed with Warwick's patrols, drove them out of the town and then, in pursuing them, came across the main body of their army drawn up along a ridge of high ground about half a mile to the north. With Warwick were Montagu, Exeter, Oxford and Beaumont. According to the author of the *Arrivall*, they numbered themselves at 30,000 men, but this is clearly a dubious figure. Before the battle they had good reason to exaggerate their numbers and, after the battle, Edward's partisans had good reason to accept an estimate which lent so much additional splendour to their victory. Other sources are, if anything, less reliable; nonetheless they all agree that Warwick had the larger army. On receiving his patrols' reports, Edward pushed on. Despite the gathering darkness he rode straight through Barnet and refused to allow any of his soldiers to find a more comfortable bed in the town. As quietly as he could, he drew up his army on an east–west line north of Barnet and close to Warwick's. This night manoeuvre, however, did not go exactly as he had planned. Because his troops could not see their enemy's positions at all clearly, they ended up even closer than they had supposed. In addition the two armies were not quite opposite each other, each army's right extending beyond its opponent's left. But once again it shows that Edward was deliberately taking risks in order to retain the initiative. Warwick tried to extract the maximum advantage from his superiority in artillery by bombarding Edward's position throughout the hours of darkness. Precisely because, however, the two armies were so close, his gunners constantly overshot their target. Edward very sensibly did nothing to disabuse them of this error. His own artillerymen made little attempt to return the fire and the whole army was under strict orders to maintain silence. As the night passed, a mist rolled up, thickening with the approach of Easter Sunday's dawn.

Edward was still conscious of Warwick's guns, determined that the weight of fire power would play no part in the coming battle. He planned to launch his attack in the half-light before sunrise thus ensuring that there was no time for an accurate cannonade before the struggle was joined hand-to-hand. So, very early in the morning, between four and five o'clock, to the ear-shattering accompaniment of a blast of trumpets, his soldiers advanced into the mist. Firing almost blind, his hand-gunners and archers had time only for a few shots before they were in among the enemy. Curiously enough the mist which made it so hard for the combatants to see one another makes it easier for the historian, following the account in the *Arrivall*, to see the unfolding pattern of the battle. On Edward's left, his troops were outflanked and outnumbered by Warwick's right commanded by the earl of Oxford. It was not long before the Yorkist left broke and fled, first to Barnet and some then on to London, the fugitives bringing with them the news that Edward had been defeated. So poor was the visibility, however, that Edward did not realize this. Those fighting in other parts of the field had no idea what had happened and as a result they

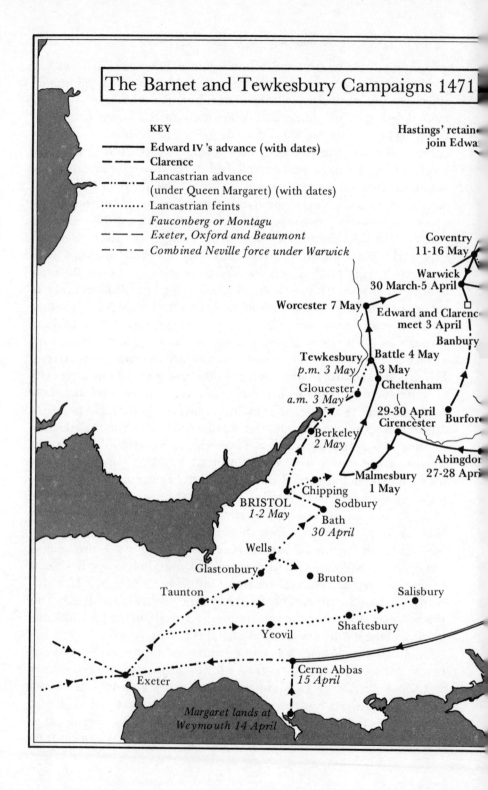

The Barnet and Tewkesbury Campaigns 1471

KEY

—————— Edward IV's advance (with dates)
— — — Clarence
—··—··— Lancastrian advance
(under Queen Margaret) (with dates)
··········· Lancastrian feints
—————— *Fauconberg or Montagu*
— — — *Exeter, Oxford and Beaumont*
—·—·—· *Combined Neville force under Warwick*

Hastings' retain[...]
join Edwa[...]

Coventry
11-16 May

Warwick
30 March-5 April

Worcester 7 May

Edward and Clarenc[...]
meet 3 April

Banbury

Tewkesbury
p.m. 3 May

Battle 4 May
3 May
Cheltenham

Gloucester
a.m. 3 May

29-30 April
Cirencester

Burfor[...]

Berkeley
2 May

Abingdo[...]
27-28 Apri[...]

Malmesbury
1 May

Chipping
Sodbury

BRISTOL
1-2 May

Bath
30 April

Wells

Glastonbury

Bruton

Salisbury

Taunton

Shaftesbury

Yeovil

Cerne Abbas
15 April

Exeter

*Margaret lands at
Weymouth 14 April*

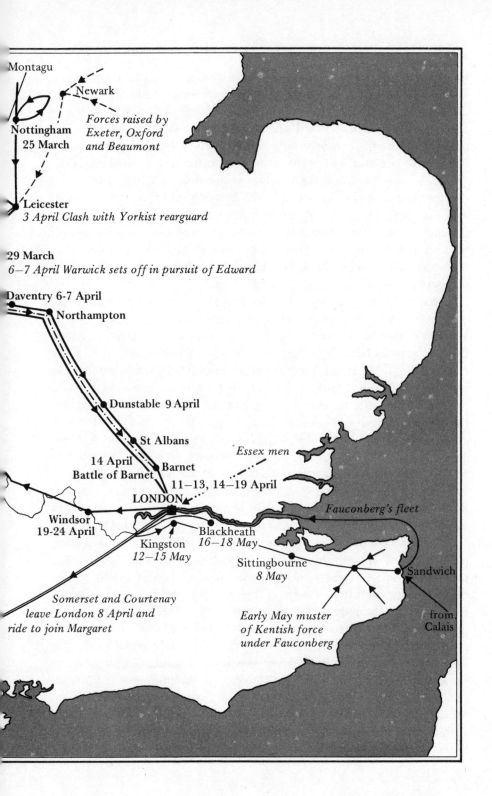

Montagu

Newark

*Forces raised by
Exeter, Oxford
and Beaumont*

Nottingham
25 March

Leicester
3 April Clash with Yorkist rearguard

29 March
6–7 April Warwick sets off in pursuit of Edward

Daventry 6-7 April
Northampton

Dunstable 9 April

St Albans

14 April
Battle of Barnet
Barnet

Essex men
11–13, 14–19 April

LONDON

Fauconberg's fleet

Windsor
19-24 April

Kingston
12–15 May

Blackheath
16–18 May

Sittingbourne
8 May

Sandwich

*Somerset and Courtenay
leave London 8 April and
ride to join Margaret*

*Early May muster
of Kentish force
under Fauconberg*

from
Calais

hammered away neither encouraged nor dismayed by this turn of events. On the other wing, the roles were reversed but with a crucial difference. Warwick's left, though it was rolled back, did not collapse and, in consequence, Edward's right was not drawn away from the field in pursuit. Instead, by swinging round to the left, it gave additional impetus to the king's own thrust in the centre and, according to the *Arrivall*, it was here that the battle was decided. In a slogging match between men-at-arms on foot, Edward's physique and courage – as well as the quality of his armour – made him a dominant figure. 'With great violence he beat and bore down before him all that stood in his way, and turning first one way and then another he so beat and bore down that nothing might stand in the sight of him.' Some three hours after it began the battle was over and Edward had won.

Accounts of the battle of Barnet which were composed later frequently contain personal touches and vivid anecdotes. One such is Warkworth's story of the confusion caused by the similarity between Edward's and Oxford's badges (see p. 38). Another is Commynes's statement that Montagu, 'a very courageous knight', had persuaded his brother to dismount and send away his horses, contrary to his usual practice. Normally, says Commynes, once he had brought his men into the battle, Warwick was in the habit of mounting. 'If the battle was going well for him he would throw himself into the fray, but if it was going badly he would make an early escape.' This time, in order to strengthen the fighting spirit of his troops, Warwick agreed to demonstrate his willingness to live or die at their side. These stories may or may not be true. They can certainly be fitted into the pattern of established fact. Thus it is true that both Warwick and Montagu were killed that day – though according to Warkworth, Warwick was trapped in a wood while fleeing on horseback. On the other hand, they are told by writers whose facts are sometimes wildly wrong. Commynes, for example, says that it was only on the morning of the Battle of Barnet that Clarence changed sides and went over to Edward. Clearly it is not possible to use the details provided by a source of this kind to reconstruct the events of the battle, though they do have a certain value for military historians in illustrating the kind of thing which contemporaries believed to be possible. By contrast, the author of the *Arrivall* was writing very soon after the events – before the stories had time to grow – and though he was writing propaganda he was also concerned with accuracy. For this reason the foregoing account of the battle was based on the *Arrivall* alone.

Casualties had been high. Sir John Paston, who had fought in the earl of Oxford's company and whose brother, also confusingly called John, had received an arrow wound in the arm, put them at more than a thousand on both sides. The battle, all men agreed, had been fiercely contested but it was not so much on this account that so many had fallen; rather it was because, owing to the mist, the fighting had been one-sided on both wings and, as was well known, it was when a line broke that casualties were at their heaviest. On Edward's side Lords Saye and Cromwell, Sir Humphrey Bourchier and Sir William Blunt were killed. The bodies of their two chief opponents, Warwick and Montagu, were brought to St Paul's and put on display – not in a gloating mood, but to forestall any attempt to pretend that they had escaped and were still alive, for, as the *Arrivall* puts it, 'such false, feigned fables and slanders were wont to be seditiously sown and blown about all the land by such persons as could use – and long had used – that accursed custom'.

Just two days later other news, long expected, arrived in London. On the evening of Easter Sunday, a matter of hours after the conclusion of the Battle of Barnet, Queen Margaret, bringing her son, Prince Edward, with her, landed at Weymouth. The war was far from being over. On 18 April Sir John Paston wrote home, advising his cousin to tread warily and avoid any open commitment to Edward's cause: 'For the world, I assure you, is right queasy, as ye shall know within the month; the people here [i.e., the Yorkists in London] feareth it sore. God hath showed himself marvellously like him that made all, and can undo again when him list; and I can think that by all likelihood shall show himself as marvellous again, and that in short time.' Three days earlier, at Cerne Abbey, Margaret had conferred with the duke of Somerset and John Courtenay and they encouraged her to hope that the Lancastrian cause was not altogether lost. It could indeed be argued that they were well rid of Warwick, for so uneasy and unnatural an alliance could only complicate matters and confuse their true supporters. This optimistic diagnosis seemed to be confirmed by the queen's success in raising an army in the west country. Moreover, in the person of Somerset, she had a military adviser with experience of war on the continent; he had accompanied Charles of Burgundy on the Montlhéry campaign. Margaret's movements, of course, were closely observed and reports sent back to Edward and to London. By 30 April the wounded John Paston, though short of ready money owing to the size of the doctors' bills which he was having to meet, was nonetheless in an optimistic frame of mind: 'With God's grace it shall not be long ere my wrongs and other men's be redressed.'

Edward too had been busy, hard at work raising and supplying fresh troops to replace those whose services, through death, injury or exhaustion, he had lost at Barnet. Between 18 and 26 April requests for men were sent to various towns, and commissions of array sent to fifteen counties in the west country, west Midlands and Welsh Marches. On 19 April he left London and rode to Windsor. Five days he waited there, watching the gradual completion of the muster. If it seemed a slow process he at least had the satisfaction of knowing that this new army was well-equipped – possession of the Tower armoury and the capture of Warwick's artillery train had seen to that. Margaret, meanwhile, having summoned Somerset, Dorset and Wiltshire to her banner, had gone to Exeter. There she met Sir John Arundel and Sir Hugh Courtenay and with their assistance mustered the levies of Cornwall and Devon.

What would she and Somerset do next? Somehow Edward had to anticipate her movements and in the *Arrivall*'s assessment of the various strategies open to her there is surely a reflection of the thinking in the king's council. Since at Exeter she was 'in an angle of the land' she had two basic alternatives. In the first place she might head for London, which she could do either by taking the inland route via Salisbury or by marching along the coast into Hampshire, Sussex and Kent. If this strategy of direct confrontation was to work she would have to be able to raise the levies of the counties through which she passed, though once she reached Kent she should be able to count on the strong support which Warwick had built up during his period of office as warden of the Cinque Ports. Alternatively she could adopt a more cautious strategy and head north towards the traditionally Lancastrian counties of Lancashire and Cheshire. This would have the advantage of facilitating a junction between her army and the Welsh troops which Jasper Tudor was said to be raising on her behalf. If she took the first course, then Edward would need to move fast in a south-westerly direction in order to bring her to battle before she could draw on that additional strength on which she would necessarily be counting. If she took the second course, then his priority must be to prevent her crossing the Severn, which she could do either at Gloucester or Tewkesbury or Worcester; in this case he would have to march west by north. Which would she do? It was essential that he guess correctly. Naturally he had his scouts out gathering information. Equally obviously Margaret knew what he wanted and was laying false trails and spreading false news in an attempt to mislead him. In the end he would have to use his judgment, relying on his assessment of the mind of the enemy on the other side of the hill. And whether he marched west by south or west by north he would, in either event, be leaving Kent and Calais unsubdued in his rear.

From Exeter Margaret sent an advance party, a flying squad, on to Shaftesbury and Salisbury, but it was a feint. In fact, she had decided to head north, and her main army took another road, to Taunton. From there she detached another squadron in the direction of Yeovil, another feint. Again the same trick when she reached Wells, a patrol sent to Bruton in order to put into circulation the report that they were aiming at Reading. At first Edward moved cautiously. On 24 April he left Windsor and travelled slowly up the Thames valley. By 27 April he had only reached Abingdon, heading west by north it is true, but still within easy reach of Reading and the western approaches to London. Next day he dallied at Abingdon and then he made up his mind. On 29 April his army marched to Cirencester. For four days he had averaged less than ten miles a day, then in one he covered thirty. He was now on the edge of the Cotswolds, less than a day's march from the Severn at Gloucester. At Cirencester Edward received further information. The Lancastrians were on their way to Bath and were apparently planning to bring him to battle somewhere beyond Bath on Wednesday 1 May. Again Edward waited, but the news that they had reached Bath on the Tuesday seemed to confirm the accuracy of the information. Edward acted at once. He arrayed his army and advanced three miles out of Cirencester to spend the night in a field. On the Wednesday morning, however, his scouts reported no sign of the enemy anywhere in front of him. So Edward decided that he would move forward to Malmesbury, towards the Lancastrians, as he hoped – but further away from the vital passages across the Severn. In luring him forward Margaret and Somerset had achieved their first tactical success. They themselves had in fact swung left down the Avon to Bristol, 'a good and strong walled town'. There they were well received and obtained a plentiful supply of provisions, men, money and artillery. They also sent an advance patrol on to Chipping Sodbury and beyond. It seemed that the Lancastrians, encouraged by the reinforcements received in Bristol, were looking for a suitable battleground and believed that they had found it at Sodbury Hill, one mile along the road between Chipping Sodbury and Malmesbury. Once again this was a challenge which Edward felt he could not

afford to ignore. On Thursday 2 May, he left Malmesbury on the
Bristol road. Simultaneously Margaret and Somerset marched out of
Bristol. Edward's reading of the situation seemed to be confirmed by
the arrival of news that some of his harbingers had been chased out of
Chipping Sodbury by a party sent out on a similar errand by the
Lancastrians. It looked as though the two armies were set on a collision
course. Shortly after noon Edward came within sight of Sodbury Hill,
but of his enemies there was no sign at all. Fearing a trap Edward halted
and sent out more reconnaissance patrols. When it was clear that the
Lancastrians were nowhere about, he pushed on as far as Sodbury Hill
where he camped for the night while his scouts ranged further and
further afield in search of their foe. At three o'clock on Friday morning
he heard the news which he must have feared. For the second time in
two days Somerset and Margaret had given him the slip, and had lured
him a little further away from Gloucester. They had moved out of
Bristol in the direction of Sodbury Hill, but had suddenly swung left
and were now heading for Gloucester by way of Berkeley. Moreover,
since they had not stopped when evening came, it looked very much as
though they intended to march all night. The time for shadow-boxing
was over. It was now a race for the Severn.

But having been outmanoeuvred Edward had no chance of reaching
Gloucester in time to disrupt the passage of the Lancastrians. His only
hope now was that Margaret would be refused entry to Gloucester and
thus barred from access to the Severn bridge. Governor of Gloucester
and constable of the castle was Sir Richard Beauchamp, a man whom
Edward had appointed. To him Edward sent some members of his
household with an urgent message. He must hold Gloucester at all
costs. He need have no fear, Edward was on the way. Any attempt by
the Lancastrians to launch an assault would be observed by Edward's
scouts and the king would come at once to their rescue. Luckily for
Edward, Sir Richard Beauchamp was prepared to remain loyal. When
Somerset and Margaret arrived at Gloucester at ten o'clock on Friday
morning, they found the gates closed against them. Since they had
taken the trouble to ascertain that many of the townspeople were
favourably disposed towards them, this was a bitter disappointment.
Frustrated and angry, they threatened to storm the town unless it was
opened to them, but they knew as well as Sir Richard Beauchamp that
these were idle words. Edward was too close at hand and would take
them in the rear if they tried any such thing. Though they were tired
and the day was hot, there was nothing for it but to push on to the next

crossing, the ford at Tewkesbury. They arrived there at four o'clock on the afternoon of Friday 3 May. In thirty-six hours they had marched almost fifty miles through awkward terrain, 'in a foul country, all in lanes and stony ways, betwixt woods, without any good refreshing'. The greater part of the army consisted of footmen and they were now totally exhausted. With Edward hard on their heels, there was no prospect of the whole army getting across in safety. Just conceivably the cavalry might have made it, but this would have meant the deliberate abandonment of their infantry. Besides which, their horses too were very weary. So, though it meant the failure of their strategy, Somerset and Margaret decided to stand and fight.

Edward, meanwhile, had left Sodbury Hill early that same morning. His army was arrayed in three battles, ready for action. Ahead of him and on every side rode his scouts and patrols. He took the old road running high along the western edge of the Cotswolds. Here, in good, open, sheep-grazing country he had better marching conditions than the Lancastrians as they struggled through the orchards and wood-lands of the Severn Vale below. As the day passed, he began to catch up with them and by late afternoon was only seven or eight miles behind. By this time, of course, his own soldiers were in trouble, particularly the three thousand infantrymen. Up on the ridge of the Cotswolds there was neither food nor drink to be had, just the sun beating down. The horses too were in difficulties, suffering from a lack of both forage and water. They had come across one small brook, but as the carts churned their way through it, the water became muddied and undrinkable. Not until they had reached Cheltenham and Edward learned that the Lancastrians had come to a halt at Tewkesbury, did the king allow his hard-driven troops a brief rest and the chance to help themselves to meat and drink from the wagon train. They had already covered more than thirty miles that day. Then they were off again before finally settling down to spend the night within three miles of the enemy, knowing for certain that many of them would be dead before twenty-four hours were out.

Though their strategy had gone awry and Margaret, together with the other ladies, had taken shelter in a nearby religious house, the Lancastrians were still in a strong position. Encamped just to the south of Tewkesbury, they had chosen a site well-suited to a defensive battle in the classic English mode. In front of them, and to every side, there were 'foul lanes and deep dykes, and many hedges with hills and valleys' so that it was 'as evil a place to approach as could possibly have been devised'. Edward, nonetheless, was determined to attack. On the morning of Saturday 4 May he armed himself, and arrayed his troops in the customary three battles. He remained with the main battle, and placed the van under the command of Richard of Gloucester. Observing a large wood (Tewkesbury Park) to the left of the Lancastrian position (as he looked at it), Edward ordered a squadron of two hundred men-at-arms to stay wide on his flank and keep an eye on the wood. If there were any Lancastrians lying in ambush for him in the park they were to deal with them as soon as they made a move; otherwise they were to act at their own discretion. When everything was ready, Edward ordered the trumpeters to sound the advance.

As soon as they were in range his gunners opened fire. A little later the archers of his vanguard followed suit. The Lancastrians returned fire, but in this department they were outgunned and the rain of arrows and shot that poured down on them they found hard to bear. Realizing that his solid defensive line was in danger of being broken by the weight of Yorkist fire power, Somerset decided to go over to the attack. Before the battle started he had seen that it might well be possible to use the broken and wooded terrain to swing some of his troops round to his right without the Yorkists being able to see them. Taking advantage of a sunken lane and hedges, he very skilfully succeeded in bringing his troops to a sloping field from which they were able to launch a downhill attack on the flank of Edward's main battle. The king's men turned and fought back manfully. The drawback to Somerset's manoeuvre was the fact that it took the pressure off the front of the Yorkist van, freeing Gloucester to go to his brother's aid. The combined power of the two Yorkist battles was sufficient to turn the tide. In a fierce hand-to-hand struggle Edward and Gloucester drove Somerset's men from the hedge and ditch at the field bottom and began to push them back up the slope. At this point Somerset's hard-pressed force was hit by a surprise flanking attack launched by Edward's mobile force of two hundred men-at-arms. This unforeseen blow came so magically on cue that, as the author of the *Arrivall* pointed out, it was almost as though the whole thing had been arranged in advance. Somerset's men broke and scattered. Some fled along the lanes, some into the park, and others down to the meadow by the river, but many of them were cut down and killed as they ran. To this day the meadow retains the name it acquired that Saturday morning in May: Bloody Meadow.

Edward was too good a commander to allow his company the luxury of a pursuit while there were still enemy forces in the field. He brought them round again and advanced against the second Lancastrian battle under the command of Prince Edward. This time the hand-to-hand struggle was brief and the issue never in doubt. Edward's soldiers had the confidence of a winning side, while the Lancastrians were demoralized by the fate of their vanguard. Once it was all over Edward gave his soldiers the freedom to pursue their enemies, capture, kill and despoil them. Most of the fugitives looked for shelter in Tewkesbury and many hoped for sanctuary by taking refuge in the abbey church. Others fled towards the Avon and some were drowned in a mill-race in their desperate efforts to escape the Yorkists' swords. Many more did not escape, among them John Courtenay, the earl of Devon, Somerset's brother, John Beaufort, and John, Lord Wenlock. Most important of all, the prince of Wales was himself killed as he fled the field. In political terms this meant the extinction of the house of Lancaster.

When the battle was over, Edward visited Tewkesbury Abbey to give thanks to God for his victory. In the elation of the moment he granted a free pardon to all who had fled to the abbey church, but soon afterwards he regretted his generosity. His soldiers entered the church and dragged the fugitives out; the king's apologist pointed out that Tewkesbury Abbey had never been granted the legal status of a sanctuary and that in arresting rebels Edward was well within his rights. On Monday 6 May Somerset and a dozen other leading Lancastrians were brought to trial before the dukes of Gloucester and Norfolk as constable and marshal of England. They were sentenced to death and immediately beheaded. Nearly all of them were, in Edward's eyes, traitors twice over. They had defected after receiving his pardon for previous offences. By contrast, other captives, men like the former Chief Justice John Fortescue, who had remained steadfastly loyal to the Lancastrian cause and who therefore had never received Edward's pardon, now did so. Next day Edward learned that Margaret of Anjou had been captured.

But despite the disaster which had befallen the Lancastrian dynasty at Tewkesbury, Edward's trials were not over yet. There were reports of insurrections in Kent. This and other business seemed to call for the king's presence in London, but then the news of further risings in the north, at York and elsewhere, must have made him wish he could be in two places at once. He had to choose and choose quickly. Making up his mind to head north he gave orders for a fresh muster at Coventry. He arrived there on 11 May together with a contingent of the men who had served him so well in the last few weeks. For three days these soldiers, some of them now veterans of two pitched battles in less than a month, rested and took on supplies in preparation for a third campaign. By now, however, the northern rebellion had fizzled out. The rebels had risen in response to the news that Queen Margaret had landed and was gathering troops; they dispersed in response to the news that her army had been overwhelmed at Tewkesbury. Since the leaders of northern society, the Nevilles and the Percies, had either been crushed or were loyal to Edward IV, there was no way that a northern rising could succeed without the active co-operation of a Lancastrian royal army. Once that had been destroyed the rebels had no real option but to submit. They applied to the earl of Northumberland and sought his help in obtaining the king's pardon. On 14 May, Northumberland's messengers, followed soon afterwards by the earl himself, arrived at Coventry to report the pacification of the north. This turn of events left Edward's hands free to deal with the trouble in the south-east. The news from that quarter had grown daily more alarming. Many of his prime political assets were in London – not just Henry VI but also Edward's queen and the heir to his throne – and it seemed that they were now at risk. Kent, led by one of Warwick's cousins, the Bastard of Fauconberg, was up in arms.

Thomas Fauconberg was one of the illegitimate sons of William Neville, Lord Fauconberg. We know nothing of his life or career until 1470, but when Warwick fled the country in April of that year, Thomas sailed to join him. In the autumn he returned to England to share in his cousin's triumph and seems to have been chiefly employed on naval duties. His most famous exploit was the capture of a dozen Portuguese merchant ships. Although the plunder gained in this way would undoubtedly have made him popular with seamen and those inhabitants of the Cinque Ports who catered to seamen's needs, if it meant that acts of piracy had diverted him from carrying out patrols against Edward's return, then clearly he had failed to perform what was strategically the most vital task. Originally, as self-proclaimed 'captain and leader of our liege lord King Henry's people in Kent' as well as 'captain of the navy of England', he began to raise men to help Warwick, but by the time he had gone across to Calais and brought back some troops from Sir Geoffrey Gate's garrison there, his cousin was already dead. Even so, Fauconberg's was not a hopeless enterprise. The news of Margaret's landing meant there was still hope that the outcome of Barnet might be reversed.

By early May the Bastard – as most contemporary writers call him –

had a considerable force at his disposal. Besides his seamen and the Calais soldiers he had succeeded in attracting a good deal of support in Kent. A document preserved at Canterbury lists the names of over two hundred citizens who, in one way or another, were involved in the rising. Ninety-two of them were said to have given financial or material aid only under duress, but this still leaves more than a hundred who joined the Bastard's march on London. At their head was the mayor of Canterbury, Nicholas Faunt. Most of them were working men from the clothing, food and building trades, together with a sprinkling of inn-keepers, yeomen, parish clerks and the like. Finally, there was John Thornton, town sergeant, who had taken Edward IV's wages to go with him to the west country but in fact went with Fauconberg. Dover, Sandwich, New Romney, Hythe, Lydd and other towns, including Rye in Sussex, presumably sent similar, if perhaps smaller, contingents. In addition, gentry and yeomen mustered followers from the manor-houses and villages of every part of Kent. All in all, according to the author of the *Arrivall*, Fauconberg's men claimed to have raised an army of sixteen or seventeen thousand. Their motives for joining the revolt will for ever remain unknown, whether it was out of loyalty to the Nevilles or loyalty to the Lancastrian dynasty, or out of a desire for 'good government', or for excitement or plunder. Perhaps some of them shared the anti-London feelings attributed to the Essex men who joined the assault on the capital. A London chronicler who lived through these events as a young man, thirty or forty years later still retained a vivid memory of the march of the dairy farmers of Essex, armed with clubs, staves and pitchforks, and wearing their wives' smocks and cheese-cloths in protest against the low prices which they were getting for their produce in the London market.

The counsellors whom Edward left in charge of affairs at London and Westminster when he moved west, did their best to stem the tide of revolt in Kent. On 3 May a commission, including some of the most influential local landowners, was appointed to arrest and imprison the rebels. But by Wednesday 8 May Fauconberg had advanced as far as Sittingbourne, apparently without meeting any opposition. From there he sent letters to the city authorities asking for permission to pass through London on his way to seek out Edward. He promised that there would be no pillaging (despite the rumours which his enemies were circulating); no victuals or supplies of any kind would be taken without payment. He wrote in haste and gave them until nine o'clock on Friday morning for a reply to be sent to him at Blackheath. But the leading citizens of London were not at all anxious to re-live the experiences of the previous autumn, not to mention 1381 and 1450, when Kentishmen joined with the London poor to go on a rampage through the city, and they were sceptical of Fauconberg's claim that he could discipline his host. Moreover, it seemed likely that he would try to rescue Henry VI from the Tower, and this could certainly not be done without creating a major disturbance. There were, in any event, very few people who wanted to see the return of Henry VI's queen and now that Warwick was dead this was what the defeat of Edward IV would unavoidably mean. So, in a firmly worded reply, drafted on 9 May, they told the Bastard that they intended to hold London on behalf of their sovereign lord Edward IV. No one who was making unlawful assemblies of his people would be allowed to enter. During the Wars of the Roses few towns, including London itself, ever resisted the entry of an army. In taking this unusually tough line the city was undoubtedly encouraged by news which they had only just received – the news of their sovereign lord's victory at Tewkesbury. In a thoughtful gesture they passed a copy of Edward's letter on to the rebels.

Undeterred Fauconberg pressed on. Evidently his men were made of sterner stuff than the northern rebels – or possibly they were simply carried away by the enthralling prospect of the sack of a great city, the chance of winning the loot of a lifetime. By 12 May they had reached Southwark. They had brought their fleet up the Thames estuary and it was now moored near the Tower. The city authorities meanwhile had been busy preparing to stand siege. Along the river bank from Castle Baynard to the Tower they stationed men-at-arms, bombards and other instruments of war. At every gate they built bulwarks and stocked them with guns, but their main worry concerned the attitude of the Londoners themselves. Could they be relied upon? How many were partisans of Warwick or of the Lancastrians? And how about the poor and less respectable? Were there not many servants and apprentices who would 'be right glad of a common robbery so that they might get their hands deep into rich men's coffers'? They wrote to Edward asking him to come as quickly as possible. His queen, his son and daughters were all like London itself, in the greatest jeopardy. Long before Edward received this letter, the assault on the city had already begun.

He had no sooner arrived at Southwark than Fauconberg launched his first attack, hoping to force a passage over London Bridge. The new gate at the southern end was burned down, but the bridge itself was vigorously and successfully defended. Over on the other bank some beer-houses near the hospital of St Katherine by the Tower were set ablaze. These rather derisory achievements led to a change of plan. Next morning, instead of renewing the assault the Bastard marched west. He let it be known that he intended to cross the Thames at Kingston, then sweep back and take Westminster and the suburbs by storm before forcing his way into the city to take revenge on those who had denied him entrance. Earl Rivers, who was in charge of the defence of the Tower, reacted to this by sending some of his garrison up-river in barges in order to hold Kingston Bridge against them. Whether or not these soldiers were ever put to the test we do not know, but once again Fauconberg changed his mind. That same evening his army returned to Southwark and, in a gesture doubtless meant to intimidate the Londoners, was drawn up in battle array in St George's Fields. The author of the *Arrivall* believed that Fauconberg had been put off by receiving further information about the strength of the Yorkist position. The idea of seeking Edward iv out and challenging him to battle seemed more and more impractical. If they crossed the river the bridges might be broken down behind them or held to prevent their return; they ran the risk of being trapped between London and Edward iv's advancing army. Better to stay on their own side of the river; better, after all, to get what plunder they could from London and clear off home than cross swords with the victor of Barnet and Tewkesbury. Undoubtedly this was a realistic assessment of the situation, but the fruitless marching of Monday 13 May must have shaken the Kentishmen's confidence in Fauconberg's leadership.

Next morning he launched a determined and apparently well-organized attack on the city. The only way to retrieve his waning reputation was to capture London before Edward came up to its relief. The day began with a cannonade. Fauconberg had had the guns removed from his ships and lined up along the south bank, pointing at the city waterfront across the river. But London's own artillery returned the fire and they possessed the greater weight of shot. Under a fierce barrage the rebels were forced to abandon their gun positions. Then, at about eleven o'clock in the morning, came the assault itself. Armed with handguns as well as bows and other weapons they attacked the city simultaneously at three points: the bridge, Aldgate and Bishopsgate. Fauconberg had used his ships to ferry more than 3,000 Kentishmen across the Thames to join forces with the men from Essex. According to the city journal no less than 5,000 men were involved in the attacks on Aldgate and Bishopsgate. The outer defences of London

Bridge had been demolished during the first assault on 12 May and this time the rebels advanced as far as the tower guarding the drawbridge. As they pushed forward they set fire to the houses on the bridge, intending to clear a path into the city. But in fact they were held at the tower and, in the opinion of the author of the *Arrivall*, even if they had managed to burn a gaping hole in London's fortifications they would not have been able to fight their way through it, so heavy and so well-aligned was the artillery which the mayor and aldermen had brought to bear on that spot.

At Bishopsgate the attackers set fire to the gate as well as to some of the neighbouring houses, but their greatest success came at Aldgate. Here not only did they fire the gate but for a moment they managed to get their hands on the bulwark. It required a major, and co-ordinated, effort on the part of the defenders to dislodge them. Earl Rivers in the Tower opened the postern and launched a sortie against the rear of the Kentishmen with four or five hundred troops. At the same time the Londoners sallied out in a counter-attack of their own. According to the *Arrivall* the mayor and citizens had been well instructed in this kind of thing by the earl of Essex and various gentlemen who had come with their retinues to add a seasoning of military experience to the city's defence measures. The weight and timing of this combined attack decided the day. Fauconberg's men were driven back from Aldgate. Then the retreat became a rout. As they fled towards their boats and ships at Blackwall, several hundred were killed and more captured, to be 'ransomed like Frenchmen'. Those who escaped joined up with their fellows south of the river, where the attacks on the bridge had also been called off.

Even after this reverse, Fauconberg seemed to be reluctant to give up. He stayed another day in St George's Field and then withdrew only as far as Blackheath where he remained until 18 May. Eventually the whole gathering broke up. The appearance in London of an advance guard of 1,500 men whom Edward had dispatched from Coventry on 14 May was probably the final straw, heralding as they did the arrival of the king himself. The Bastard's fleet put to sea and sailed round to Sandwich. The Calais contingent returned to their garrison and Fauconberg rode with them as far as Sandwich. The Kentish men dispersed and found their own way home. By the time Edward made his triumphal entry into London on Tuesday 21 May it was all over, save for the rewarding of loyalty and the punishing of rebellion. The mayor, recorder and some of the aldermen of London received knighthoods.

The mayor of Canterbury was hanged, drawn and quartered. The heads of two of Fauconberg's lieutenants were displayed on Aldgate. As for the Bastard himself, the fact that he still commanded a fleet of more than forty ships meant that he still presented a threat of sorts. The easiest way to deal with him was to offer him a pardon in return for his submission. On these terms Fauconberg surrendered his fleet to Richard of Gloucester on 27 May. For a while the pardon protected him, but in September, possibly partly on account of new offences, he was beheaded and his head placed on London Bridge 'looking towards Kent'. During the summer and autumn of 1471 commissioners of inquiry, arrest and punishment moved through Kent and Essex, identifying rebels and bringing them to trial. 'Such as were rich were hanged by the purse, and the others that were needy were hanged by the neck,' was one writer's sardonic comment on their visitation. Only the soldiers of the Calais garrison escaped entirely unscathed – a further indication, if one were needed, of their vital military importance.

Edward had stayed in London only for a day or so before leading his army of retribution into Kent, but though his visit to the capital was brief, there was time enough for some important business. In the carefully chosen words of the *Arrivall*, when Henry VI realized that the Lancastrian cause was now finally and completely finished, 'He took it to so great despite, ire and indignation that, of pure displeasure and melancholy, he died.' All other sources take it for granted that Henry met a violent end and there can be no doubt that, if he did, then the well-informed author of the *Arrivall* had very good reason to conceal the truth. Assuming that Henry was murdered, there can equally be no doubt that, no matter who carried it out, the responsibility for the deed was Edward's. While Henry's heir was alive and free there had not been much to gain from killing the old king, but once Prince Edward was dead, his father became the last representative of the Lancastrian dynasty, the likely focus of future revolts. It looks very much as though, as the Milanese ambassador in France put it, Edward had 'chosen to crush the seed'. If such was Edward's calculation, it cannot be denied that he had calculated accurately. The next twelve years were years of domestic peace. Apart from the earl of Oxford's abortive occupation of St Michael's Mount for four months in 1473 there was no further fighting on English soil for the rest of Edward's reign.

'Coming in again by the windows' was not easy, yet Edward had done it. As the author of the *Arrivall* very properly observed, he had enjoyed 'the help of Almighty God, the most glorious Virgin Mary his

mother, Saint George and of all the saints of heaven'. If his enemies had
managed to take concerted action in 1471, then Edward would surely
have failed. If Warwick had been more decisive, if Fauconberg had
moved earlier, if the northern rebels had pressed harder, if Margaret
had not been delayed in France for three weeks by contrary winds, if. . .
As things turned out Edward was undeniably very lucky – or had very
great cause to be grateful for God's help, but at least Edward had taken
full advantage of every piece of good fortune which came his way. His
energy and determination had been phenomenal. He had shown
generalship of the highest order. At Barnet he had not allowed Warwick
to exploit his superior artillery. At Tewkesbury his tactic of placing a
squadron of two hundred men-at-arms by the park on his left flank had
worked like a dream. But looking at his battles in isolation is not the
best way to measure a commander's skill. Once both sides were
committed to battle there was relatively little a general could do to
influence the course of events. Luck and the courage of his soldiers
mattered much more. A battle was part of a campaign, and it is his
conduct of the whole which has to be studied, not just the most
dramatic part. When Edward landed at Ravenspur on 14 March the
odds were stacked heavily against him, but in the following breathless
weeks he hardly put a foot wrong. Throughout the Barnet campaign
he demonstrated the strategic importance of capturing and retaining
the initiative. In the Tewkesbury campaign he correctly evaluated
Margaret's strategic options and though once or twice tactically outmanoeuvred, his tremendous driving force swept his army to an overwhelming victory. As the author of the *Arrivall* put it, his opponents had
every reason to fear not only his 'great fortunes' but also his 'good
speed'.

There were still a few military problems left to solve. In Wales, for
example, Jasper Tudor and his nephew, Henry Tudor, earl of Richmond, remained in control of Pembroke Castle. Indeed they registered
one or two striking successes, capturing and beheading Roger Vaughan
(who was said to have led Owen Tudor to the block in 1461) and
beating off a Yorkist siege of Pembroke. But as the weeks went by they
became increasingly isolated and in September Jasper Tudor decided
to return to France. If his nephew was now the Lancastrian candidate
for the throne, then he was safer at the court of Louis XI than cooped up
in a castle in Wales. But bad weather intervened and brought their ship
to Brittany and the court of Edward IV's ally, Duke Francis. Both Louis
and Edward made diplomatic and financial offers to acquire possession

of the Tudors but the duke of Brittany knew when he had been dealt a useful card and had no intention of relinquishing it, not yet at any rate. The most he would promise Edward IV was that uncle and nephew would be kept under strict surveillance.

Only two Lancastrian peers were still at large, John de Vere, earl of Oxford, and Viscount Beaumont. After the battle of Barnet de Vere had managed to escape first to Scotland, then to France. With Louis XI's help he set about harassing Edward IV, raiding the Marches of Calais and attempting a landing in England. On 28 May 1473 he came ashore at St Osyth's in Essex, not far from the de Vere family estates, but despite rumours that there were a hundred gentlemen in Norfolk and Suffolk ready to join him, prompt action by the earl of Essex and Lords Dinham and Duras compelled him to put to sea again. After a profitable summer's piracy in the Channel, he was joined by Beaumont and together they took the small garrison of St Michael's Mount by surprise and seized the fortress on 30 September. Described, accurately enough, by John Warkworth as 'a strong place and a mighty. If it be well victualled twenty men may keep it against the world', Oxford and Beaumont held this off-shore island for several months. But the military threat they posed was negligible. Initially Edward was content with measures intended to prevent provisions getting through to the rebels. Unfortunately, the man put in charge of this operation, Sir Henry Bodrugan, the political boss of Cornwall, was notoriously corrupt and unscrupulous. He was soon plausibly suspected of coming to a very satisfactory arrangement with Oxford and allowing food in. Not until December 1473, when John Fortescue and several other members of the king's household arrived on the scene, did the real siege of St Michael's Mount begin. Guns were sent down under the command of John Wode, master of ordnance; ships and naval stores were supplied by two of the royal household's experts in this field, John Sturgeon and Edward Brampton. As the pressure on the besieged tightened, they were also offered the prospect of escape: free pardons and even rewards for those who would give themselves up. According to Warkworth, so many defected that out of the original force of 397 men only eight or nine were left when Oxford decided to capitulate early in February 1474 – even though, as was widely reported, there was food and drink enough to hold out till midsummer. By the terms of the surrender their lives were spared, the earl himself being taken to Calais and then to a cell in Hammes Castle.

Apart from this isolated episode, Edward IV ruled England in peace from 1471 until his early death in 1483. There was still the threat of political intrigue, but after the deaths of George Neville in 1476 and Clarence in 1478, even this danger lost whatever sting it might once have possessed. The near permanent political problem of the north seemed at last to have been settled by allowing the king's brother, Richard of Gloucester, to step into Warwick's shoes, and by the establishment of a successful working arrangement between him and the earl of Northumberland. As the single most successful family at court, the Woodvilles continued to arouse jealousies, but rivalries such as these were standard features of court life everywhere; for many kings the manipulation of court factions was an essential part of the political management of their realm. There were a few wars against external enemies (France in 1475 and Scotland in 1482–3), but none to disturb the peace of England. In 1472 indeed Edward's spokesman in parliament argued that external war acted as a safeguard against internal commotion. There was always that obscure exile in Brittany, Henry Tudor, but while there was a stable regime in England he had no prospective allies and therefore no hope of being a serious contender for the crown. An heir to the throne, Edward, had been born on 2 November 1470 in the sanctuary at Westminster. A second son, Richard, was born in August 1473. The future of the Yorkist dynasty seemed doubly secure. Then, in the spring of 1483, Edward IV went on a fishing trip and caught a cold.

Thirteen

THE USURPATION OF RICHARD III: 1483

THE DEATH OF EDWARD IV was followed, almost immediately, by a struggle for power. When the heir to the throne was a child this was inevitable. What was not inevitable was the savage intensity with which it was fought, nor the way it ended. The deaths of Edward III and Henry V had been followed by struggles for power within the royal family and inner ring of councillors, struggles which some men lost and others won. They had not ended, as this one ended, with usurpation and murder. It has been suggested that political behaviour had become brutalized as a result of events since 1455. Between 1455 and 1471 twenty-six peers had been killed and thirteen executed; in addition six of Edward III's descendants in the male line had met violent ends. In these circumstances it is perhaps arguable that the 'good manners' of 1377 and 1422 could no longer be expected to prevail. Against this it should be remembered that the record of the last twelve years – after Warwick's death – had been much better. We should not be too severe on Edward IV's 'lack of political foresight'. Quarrels he could and did anticipate, but not his brother's actions. The dying king was not alone in this. More than two months later Richard of Gloucester was still able to take men by surprise – even men as shrewd as Bishop Morton and Lord Hastings. However brutalized society might have been in 1483, Richard's behaviour was extraordinary and unforeseeable: that is why, in the short run, he succeeded.

For the historian of war Richard's *coup d'état* is important because it ushered in the third stage of the Wars of the Roses. Although the *coup* involved no actual fighting, force and the threat of force were crucial to its success. The first struggle was for possession of the boy king Edward V. Richard was in the north when the expected news of his brother's death reached him, presumably by 13 or 14 April. At the same time he must have learned that Edward had appointed him protector. As the boy king's only surviving paternal uncle he was the obvious choice, all the more so since his long residence in the north meant that he stood somewhat aloof from the factional rivalries which had been the stuff of court politics. As protector he would act as chairman of the minority council. The question was, as chairman how much power would he have? Not much certainly, if the young Edward remained in the care of his mother and her numerous relatives. The wishes of a twelve-year-old king could not be simply disregarded, particularly once he was an anointed king, and if he remained in the hands of the Woodvilles, there could be little doubt that he would wish to do what they wanted. Whatever thoughts may or may not have flitted through Richard's mind as he heard the news that his brother was dying, we can at least be sure that he did not want to see a Woodville-dominated court. And there were others who shared Richard's view. The author of the Croyland chronicle, who was there, describes the council meeting which followed Edward iv's funeral. 'All wanted to see the prince succeed his father, but there was a great divergence of opinion because the wiser wished to withdraw him from the guardianship of his maternal uncles and half-brothers; in particular Lord Hastings feared that if power slipped into the grasp of the queen's relatives they would avenge the injuries they claimed that he had done them – for between him and them there was a feud of long standing.' Between Hastings and Richard of Gloucester therefore there was a natural alliance of interests; both wished to 'rescue' the young king from the baleful influence of the Woodvilles.

At this first council meeting of the new reign the main item of business concerned the arrangements for Edward v's coronation. Edward, as prince of Wales, had been at Ludlow when his father died, in the care of his maternal uncle, Earl Rivers. The council agreed that he should be brought to Westminster and that the coronation should take place on 4 May. All this was very much in the Woodville interest and makes it clear that the group whom the Croyland chronicler calls 'the wiser' were in a minority. While the protector stayed in the north, the Woodvilles kept a grip on London and the machinery of government. The Tower, together with its treasure and its armament, was held by the queen's eldest son and Lord Hastings's greatest rival, Thomas, marquis of Dorset. If Edward v was brought to London by a strong force of Woodville troops, their continuing ascendance would be ensured. Thus, as Hastings realized, much depended on the size of the royal escort. Somehow he had to persuade the Woodvilles to accept a limit on the number of men accompanying the king. In the circumstances anything but an easy task – yet he did it. He held one strong card and he played it. If the king did not come to London with a moderate number, he would flee to Calais. On the face of it not much of a threat, but the Calais garrison – recently strengthened by an extra contingent of 500 archers – was still the only English standing army. Hastings had been captain of Calais ever since 1471 and he had exploited this position to maintain good contacts with both the French and Burgundian courts. A hostile Hastings, entrenched in Calais, represented a military threat which the Woodvilles could not afford to ignore. They agreed to limit Edward's escort to 2,000 men at most.

All this time Richard had remained in the north. In public he insisted on his loyalty to his nephew and adopted a conciliatory attitude towards the queen. He was evidently, however, in touch with Hastings and with at least one other magnate who resented Woodville ambitions. This was Henry Stafford, second duke of Buckingham. As an eleven-year-old boy he had been married to one of the queen's sisters but he gained little or nothing from this court connexion and by 1483 he clearly disliked in-laws whom he regarded as *parvenus*. Now was his chance of escaping from the political limbo to which he had been relegated for the last ten years. On 29 April Richard and Buckingham met at Northampton. Edward v and his escort had already passed through and were now at Stony Stratford, fourteen miles nearer London, but they obviously had no idea that they had anything to fear, since Earl Rivers and his nephew Sir Richard Grey rode back to Northampton in order to welcome the king's protector. It seems that they enjoyed a convivial evening and were completely taken by surprise when, next morning, they were placed under arrest. Immediately afterwards Richard and Buckingham rode into Stony Stratford, took charge of Edward v, and arrested Sir Thomas Vaughan and some other members of his household. Doubtless Richard's position as the king's uncle and protector designate played some part in persuading Rivers and Edward's escort to submit, but it is hard to believe that the presence of a sufficient number of armed men did not lend extra authority to his words.

Late that evening, 30 April, the queen heard the terrifying news. Her first thought was to try to recapture her brother and her children, but it very quickly became clear that she had no hope of raising the necessary armed force. For most people the fact that the king was now in his uncle's care was no great cause for alarm and they saw no reason to risk their lives in an over-hasty defence of the Woodvilles. Once she had realized this, the queen decided she had no option but to seek sanctuary. So she and her children, including Edward v's younger brother Richard, duke of York, fled that same night to Westminster Abbey, taking with them at least some of the royal treasure from the Tower. On 4 May Gloucester and Buckingham, accompanied by a token force of 500 armed men, entered London, announcing that they had rescued the king from evil counsellors who would have led him astray. Cartloads of weapons were paraded, meant to prove that the Woodvilles had been planning to use force of arms to stay in power. Soon afterwards Richard was formally appointed protector and a new date was set for Edward v's coronation: 22 June. Richard's enemies now had only one asset left – a fleet under the command of another of the queen's brothers, Sir Edward Woodville. As soon as Gloucester learned that it lay at anchor in the Downs, he sent troops to defend Sandwich and Dover against attack and then set to work to win control of the fleet for himself. His best weapon was the offer of a free pardon to all who would desert Sir Edward. This approach was particularly appealing to the captains of two Genoese carracks. Their great ships had been hired by the Woodvilles, but their main concern was to remain on good terms with whichever government happened to be in power. Realizing the problem, Sir Edward stationed armed guards in each ship, but the Genoese plied them with drink, overcame them and then, to a great blast of trumpets, set sail for London. The fleet scattered in confusion, all but two of the ships eventually following the Genoese example. The recovery of the fleet completed Richard's triumph and the discomfiture of the Woodvilles. To his chief ally, Buckingham, Richard gave wide powers of government and military control in Wales and some western counties. The constables of several royal castles were dismissed and replaced by his own nominees. The protector's exact legal position, particularly after the coronation, still had to be worked out, but in this, as in everything else in the foreseeable future, it is clear that Richard's voice would be the dominant one. And so it might have remained – had Richard been content to play the kind of role which John of Gaunt had played in the early years of Richard II's reign. But he was not content.

The steps by which Richard mounted the throne included some which were set in the same mould as those by which he had 'captured' his nephew: acts of violence backed up and made possible by the threat of armed force. For several weeks all was peaceful enough and preparations went ahead for Edward v's coronation as planned. But by 10 June Richard was calculating that, for some reason or another, he would soon be in need of soldiers. In a letter to the city authorities of York he asked them to supply as quickly as possible 'as many as ye can defensibly arrayed, to aid and assist us against the queen, her blood adherents and affinity, which hath intended and daily doth intend, to murder and utterly destroy us and our cousin the duke of Buckingham and the old royal blood of this realm ... fail not, but haste you to us hither.' A letter dated 11 June, but carried north by the same bearer, Sir Richard Ratcliffe, omits the anti-Woodville propaganda and speaks more privately and more obscurely.

> My Lord Neville,
> I recommend me to you as heartily as I can; and as ever ye love me and your own weal and security, and this realm, that ye come to me with that ye may make, defensibly arrayed, in all the haste that is possible, and that ye give credence to Richard Ratcliffe, this bearer, whom I now do send to you, instructed with all my mind and intent.
> And, my Lord, do me now good service, as ye have always done before, and I trust now so to remember you as shall be the making of you and yours.
> And God send you good fortunes. ·

Similar letters were sent to the earl of Northumberland and, presumably, also to other men to whom Richard looked for support. The plan was for them to muster at Pontefract on 18 June and then march south under Northumberland's command.

What were the soldiers for? As it happens they were never sent into action, indeed their departure from Pontefract was delayed, possibly deliberately, for about a week. We cannot know what was in Richard's mind on 10 and 11 June. Could the queen in sanctuary have posed the kind of threat which needed armed force to counter it? The phrase in the letter to Lord Neville, this 'shall be the making of you and yours' seems to hint at great prospects opening up. Very few men knew what Richard intended, but that men knew his army had been sent for and was on the way is clear from another contemporary letter, this one written on 21 June by Simon Stallworth, a member of the chancellor's staff: 'It is thought there shall be 20,000 of my lord protector's and my lord of Buckingham's men in London this week: to what intent I know not but to keep the peace.' In other words they were coming to keep the peace – perhaps.

By the time Simon Stallworth wrote his letter two further acts of violence had already taken place and had possibly caused Richard to send instructions delaying the departure of his northern troops. The first of these events was the elimination of those members of the minority council who were opposed, or whom he believed to be opposed, to his plans – whatever they were. On 13 June[1] Lord Hastings, Thomas Rotherham, archbishop of York, John Morton, bishop of Ely, and Oliver King, the king's secretary, were arrested while sitting in council at the Tower. Hastings was taken out and beheaded on the spot; the others were put in prison. According to Dominic Mancini, the Italian cleric who was in London throughout these crucial events and who composed his account of them before the end of the year, the arrest was carried out by armed men acting under orders from Richard and Buckingham. Sir Thomas More, whose dramatic account of the scene was doubtless based on Morton's reminiscences – for he was brought up in Morton's household – describes how Richard accused Hastings of treason, banging his fist on the table as though in anger. 'At which token given, one cried "Treason" without the chamber. Therewith a door clapped and in came there rushing men in harness, as many as the chamber might hold.' However biased More's version of history might be, it could hardly have been done otherwise. The speed with which Hastings was executed suggests either that he knew something and Richard wanted him silenced, or that, alive, even in prison, he might retain the loyalty of his retainers and deputies (particularly the Calais garrison) and was therefore better dead. As the astonishing news of Hastings's death spread round London, Richard sent out a herald with

1. *It has recently been ingeniously argued that Hastings was arrested and executed on 20 June, that is to say after the young duke of York had been taken from sanctuary, and much closer to Richard's first overt move to seize the throne. Although this sequence of events would make Hastings's execution more readily comprehensible and is, indeed, the sequence given by Mancini as well as by Tudor historians, there are, unfortunately, serious objections to it. In the first place, there are so many early references to 13 June as the date of Hastings's death that it is necessary to assume a massive official falsification of records if he, in fact, was killed a week later. Governments, obviously, do falsify, especially governments as precariously placed as Richard's, but there has to be some purpose behind the fraud – and if the purpose here was to portray Hastings as a villainous plotter, this seems to be a curiously unemphatic way of going about it. If the date actually had been deliberately altered to this end (in other words if the date had really mattered), I would have expected the 'true' date to have been restored in the autumn of 1485. Although the precise date matters to modern historians, I doubt if Richard's agents cared so much about it in 1484 that they were prepared to spend time and effort changing it. In the second place, although Simon Stallworth's letter (written on Saturday 21 June) may be ambiguous when it refers to Hastings being 'headed' 'on Friday last' (does this mean 'Friday last week' or 'this last Friday'?), it does contain a postscript with the news that all Hastings's men are now transferring their allegiance to Buckingham. Is it credible that Hastings was executed 'yesterday' and 'today' it is reported that all his men have immediately gone over to a lord involved in their old lord's death? There is much evidence to suggest that Hastings was well-liked, a 'good lord', and in these circumstances even a week seems a short period for such a drastic switch as this – though the build-up of pressure in the last few tense days must have been immense and the flow of the political tide clearly visible.*

the official explanation of what had happened. A plot had been discovered and the chief plotter punished. This apart, there is no contemporary evidence for the widely-held modern theory that Hastings was
conspiring with the queen – a combination so unlikely that it surely
could only have been brought into being if Hastings actually had
learned of a plan to seize the crown, in which case it would indeed be for
his opposition to this course of action that Richard had him eliminated.
On the other hand, if Hastings *had* known of such a plan it seems
improbable that he would have walked so unwarily into Richard's trap.
The balance of probabilities – it can be no more than this – suggests that
Hastings and the others had opposed the use of force to remove Edward
v's brother from sanctuary. To a suspicious mind this could readily be
interpreted as evidence that they were in alliance with the queen and if
Richard had already determined to 'capture' the duke of York (as we
know he had) as a necessary preliminary to seizing the throne (which
we do not know), then opposition on this point would be desperately
important to Richard but would not be seen as such by Hastings and his
associates. Only by some such hypothesis as this can we explain *both*
why Richard was determined to kill Hastings and why Hastings failed
to see what was coming. But once Hastings was out of the way, then the
likelihood of effective armed opposition to a *coup* would have been
substantially diminished and the urgency which – undoubtedly – had
filled Richard's mind on 10 and 11 June would have been much
reduced.

The second act of violence took place on 16 June. On that day a band
of soldiers surrounded the sanctuary at Westminster Abbey and the
queen was persuaded to hand over her second son, Richard of York, to
the care of the archbishop of Canterbury. It was argued that it would be
improper if Edward v were to be crowned while his young brother
cowered in sanctuary. It was doubtless an argument which the queen
had heard before – for weeks there had been negotiations between her
and the council – but this time she was persuaded. According to
Mancini, cardinal Bourchier, the eighty-year-old archbishop, had
agreed to put the case to the queen 'in order to prevent a violation of the
sanctuary'. In other words, the decision to use force if necessary had
been taken. The upshot, of course, was the removal of the second prince
to the comfort of the state apartments in the Tower.

According to the Croyland chronicler, from that day onwards
Richard and Buckingham made no secret of their plans. If this is so,
then Simon Stallworth was being remarkably discreet when he wrote to

Sir William Stonor on 21 June, but it is undoubtedly the letter of a
worried man, full of veiled allusions. What it does not conceal is the
disturbed atmosphere in London. 'Worshipful Sir, I hold you happy
that you are out of the press, for with us is much trouble and every man
doubts everyone else.' The fear of armed men casts a shadow over
almost every line. Not just the 20,000 whom Stallworth believed to be
on the way from Wales and the north or the 'great plenty of harnessed
men' at Westminster Abbey; there were also the men occupying the
town houses of the protector's prisoners and the men due to be sent to
occupy their country houses. Mancini remembered how, when the
marquis of Dorset escaped from sanctuary, he was hunted, though in
vain, by soldiers and dogs. The mounting tension in the city was
reflected in the mayor's instructions, issued on 20 June, for a careful
keeping of the watch. By this date it must have been obvious that
Edward v's coronation was not, after all, going to take place on 22 June.
What in fact happened that day was that Richard, at last, publicly
showed his hand. That Sunday the sermon in St Paul's was preached by
the mayor's brother, Dr Ralph Shaw, and he turned it into an invitation
to Richard to ascend the throne on the grounds that Edward iv
and Elizabeth Woodville had not been validly married and that
their children were in consequence illegitimate. Four days later
Richard accepted the invitation, taking his seat on that same chair in
Westminster Hall to which his father had once stretched out his
hand in vain.

   Richard of Gloucester's *coup* had been better and more ruthlessly
prepared than his father's had been. It had not, of course, simply been a
question of the weapons carried by Gloucester's and Buckingham's
retainers; there had also been the political bargaining typified by the
recognition of Lords Howard and Berkeley as co-heirs of the Mowbray
estates – as a result of which, on 28 June, Howard became duke of
Norfolk, his son earl of Surrey, and Berkeley became earl of Nottingham. But the political bargaining had taken place in an atmosphere
dominated by the haunting thought of Hastings's fate – a fate shared by
Earl Rivers, Richard Grey and Thomas Vaughan, executed at Pontefract on 25 June. Sometimes the armed men were visible, as they were
when they surrounded the sanctuary at Westminster, but even when
they could not be seen, there was always the possibility that they were
in the next room, waiting for the signal to burst in. The possibility, it
may be, was more fearsome than the fact. When, eventually, the earl of
Northumberland marched into London at the head of Richard's army,

the citizens liked to think that the northerners were not, after all, quite so terrible as they had expected, just four or five thousand men 'evil apparelled and worse harnessed, in rusty harness neither defensible nor scoured'. It was, nonetheless, entirely appropriate that they should stand guard over London while Richard, on 6 July, went to Westminster Abbey to be crowned and anointed, for it was they who had taken him to the throne.

Naturally, the new king had brought his old northern friends and servants with him. Viscount Lovell was appointed chief butler of England in succession to Earl Rivers, and lord chamberlain in succession to Hastings; he was put in charge of the strategically placed Thames valley castle and honour of Wallingford. Sir Robert Brackenbury became master of the King's Moneys (a lucrative office also formerly held by Hastings) and constable of the Tower. They were both appointed to the king's council. Other new councillors were Lord Scrope of Bolton, his brother-in-law Sir Richard Ratcliffe, Sir James Tyrell and Sir Richard FitzHugh. Not everyone who found a place in the new scheme of things was a northerner. Lord Dinham, for example, formerly Hastings's deputy at Calais, was granted the stewardship of the duchy of Cornwall and stayed on as captain of Calais. Other influential northerners were men like the earl of Northumberland and Lord Stanley who had already been councillors during Edward IV's reign. Even so, there can be no doubt that 1483 marked, to some extent, a take-over of the south by the north – and was perceived as such. The Croyland chronicler records the displeasure felt by southerners as they saw northerners rise higher and higher in the king's favour. By the same token it also meant that some old-established servants of the Yorkist dynasty were displaced by a new and fairly close-knit group, many of them belonging to families which were traditionally thought of as being loyal to the house of Neville rather than the house of York. Some degree of displacement was inevitable whenever a new, adult king ascended the throne, but the contrast between the Neville–northern affiliation on the one hand and the York–southern on the other made it particularly acute in 1483. All of which, added to the moral stigma attaching to the manner in which Richard III ascended the throne, meant that in this case the ending of a minority government did not so much resolve a crisis as create one.

As protector, Richard might well have maintained the precarious balance of the Yorkist political system; instead, he threw it into disarray and, by so doing, put at risk the whole future of the dynasty. One

immediate effect of the disinheriting of Elizabeth Woodville's children was to make the Woodvilles respectable again. Instead of being
parvenus they could now pose as the champions of legitimacy against the
usurper. They could be confident of winning widespread sympathy for
their plan of rescuing Edward IV's sons from the Tower, as well as for
the contingency plan of smuggling his daughters out of sanctuary 'in
case any mishap should befall his sons'. Inevitably it was rumoured
that the princes were already dead and Richard's failure to put them on
parade in order to scotch a story so damaging to his shaky reputation is
a clear indication of the truth of the rumour.

During the summer of 1483 while Richard travelled north, the south
buzzed with tales of meetings and conspiracies. According to the Croyland chronicler, Westminster Abbey took on the appearance of a fortress as Richard found himself forced to order the doubling and
redoubling of the guard placed there to prevent messengers visiting the
queen. Elsewhere, however, messengers came and went freely enough.
Two of the queen's brothers, the marquis of Dorset and the bishop of
Salisbury, came out of hiding to take over the organization of a
counter-coup. Three interlocked groups of plotters emerged, a Kentish
group, a Wiltshire–Berkshire group and a Devonshire group. Some of
the conspirators were gentry with well-established Woodville connexions, men like Sir Richard Haute and John Guildford. More important
was the large group whose Woodville affiliations were less noteworthy
than the fact that they had all been prominent members of Edward IV's
household: his brother-in-law Sir Thomas St Leger, the former treasurer of the household, Sir John Fogge, chamber knights like John
Cheyne, George Brown, William Norris, William Stonor, William
Berkeley, Giles Daubeney, and Peter Courtenay, now bishop of Exeter,
previously Edward's secretary, men who stood for the continuation of
an old and stable regime now overturned by the intrusion of a northern
faction. Among the Devonshire rebels was Peter Courtenay's distant
kinsman, Edward, head of the – traditionally Lancastrian – main line of
the family, and doubtless hoping to recover the Courtenay earldom.
Edward Courtenay's participation gave the first hint of a Yorkist–
Lancastrian alliance against the new usurper.

Up to this point the marquis of Dorset had been the only peer in the
conspiracy and although to some extent this was no more than a
reflection of the fact that Edward IV had created few new peers after
1471, it also meant that any addition to the number was especially
welcome. But the one who did join them, they must have thought of as

the peer least likely to: the duke of Buckingham. What on earth his motives were has been a theme for endless speculation from that day to this, but it does at least seem clear that his prisoner, Bishop Morton, played a part in persuading him. Perhaps he also listened to the advice of those of Lord Hastings's retainers who entered his service after their master's death. It also seems clear that, after Buckingham had joined it, the plot took on a new purpose. Instead of aiming at the restoration of Edward v, it became directed towards the replacement of Richard III by Henry Tudor. In other words the conspirators now accepted that Edward IV's sons were dead.

Later writers like Polydore Vergil and Sir Thomas More may well have exaggerated the importance of the conspiratorial role played by men who afterwards became great figures at Henry VII's court, men like John Morton and Reginald Bray, but it is certain that there were links of some kind between the duke of Buckingham and Henry Tudor's mother, Margaret Beaufort. Since for the last ten years she had been married to Lord Stanley, now steward of the household, she was in a position which was both ambiguous and influential. Although for twenty years she can have seen very little of her only child, she was quick to realize that his prospects had suddenly been transformed. While her husband travelled around the country at the king's side, she stayed in London. She raised money, talked to Elizabeth Woodville – apparently the two ladies shared the same doctor and the sanctuary guard allowed him to pass – and sent advice and messages of encouragement to her son in Brittany. Presumably it was at this stage that the possibility of a marriage between Henry Tudor and Elizabeth of York was first discussed.

As early as the end of August 1483 Richard knew that something was afoot. He appointed commissioners to deal with disturbances and murmurings of revolt in the south, but since he placed Buckingham at the head of the commissioners, he was presumably unaware of the duke's remarkable change of heart. We do not, indeed, know when this change of heart occurred, only that, according to the act of attainder brought against Buckingham, he was in touch with Henry Tudor before the end of September. Just what was contained in the messages which went to and fro between London, Brittany and Buckingham's castle at Brecon, we do not know, though some modern historians believe that they have detected a grand design, a concerted series of simultaneous revolts. The men of the south-east were to muster at Maidstone and march on London. Other rebels were to assemble at

Newbury, Salisbury and Exeter. Henry Tudor, with a force supplied by the duke of Brittany, was to land somewhere on the south coast. The duke of Buckingham, having mustered his following at Brecon, would cross the Severn and advance east. Richard III would be unable to deal with insurrections at so many places at once and the net would soon close in around him. The date on which each of these actions should begin was set for Saturday 18 October.

Unfortunately there is no real evidence that this is what the rebels intended. 18 October is clearly the date which Richard III's legal advisers took to mark the beginning of treasonable activity. It was, for example, the date from which the bishops of Ely, Salisbury and Exeter were said to have forfeited all their temporal possessions. The act of attainder passed in parliament only three months later distinguished five groups of rebels and stated that in each case they had committed their treason on 18 October. But there is other, non-legal evidence which shows that in Kent, at least, the revolt had started earlier than this. On 10 October the duke of Norfolk wrote to John Paston: 'The Kentishmen be up in the Weald and say that they will come to rob the city.' By 11 October Richard III, then at Lincoln, was able to refer to the duke of Buckingham as 'the most untrue creature living'. By combining these pieces of evidence, historians have deduced that the revolt was meant to start on 18 October, and that the Kentish rebels not only showed their hand too early but also gave the game away by proclaiming that Buckingham was the chief of their design. If, however, the date 18 October has purely legal, formal value for the Kentish revolt, it follows that this may also be true of the other risings. We do not know when they actually began, nor when they were planned to begin. The notion of 18 October as a kind of D-day depends upon assumptions about military co-ordination and timetable which are more appropriate to the late nineteenth and twentieth centuries than to the fifteenth. It seems likely that the rebellion was due to get under way in October, but to argue that in Kent it erupted prematurely and that, as a result, the whole thing went off at half cock and therefore failed, is to go further than the evidence will allow. It failed because the men who betrayed Richard in 1485 did not do so in 1483.

Buckingham, for example, clearly hoped for help from the Stanleys. Lord Strange, Stanley's son by his first wife, was in Lancashire in October 1483 and his secretary, in a letter to a kinsman, reported that 'messengers cometh daily both from the king's grace and the duke into this country'. These conflicting pleas and sets of instructions had placed the local gentry in an awkward position: 'People in this country be so troubled that they know not what to do.' Although the writer was himself evidently hostile to Buckingham, his employer's attitude may not have been so straightforward. 'My Lord Strange goeth forth from Latham upon Monday next [20 October] with 10,000 men, whither we cannot say.' But despite the obscurity and possible ambiguity of this phrase, the Stanleys, in fact, decided to support Richard – and were well rewarded for doing so. Margaret Beaufort's forfeited estates were granted to her husband in return for his 'good and faithful services and for the good love and trust that the king has in him'. At all events, whether people joined the army which Richard was mustering or whether they sat at home, wondering what to do, it is clear that Buckingham's call to arms against the usurper failed to win him the expected adherents. To judge from the numbers of those attainted, the rebels won a substantial following among the gentry and yeomanry of the south, but hardly any in Wales and the Marches. Who could trust the duke after so spectacular a change of allegiance?

Richard, meanwhile, had learned of the revolt on 11 October and had immediately begun to take countermeasures. An army was summoned to assemble at Leicester on 21 October and it was from there, on 23 October, that he issued a proclamation offering a free pardon to all yeomen and commoners who had the good sense to lay down their arms at once. For their leaders, men whom he termed 'traitors, adulterers and bawds', Richard had other treatment in mind and a price was put on their heads: £1,000 or lands worth £100 a year for the capture of Buckingham, 1,000 marks or lands worth 100 marks a year for the marquis of Dorset and the bishops of Salisbury and Exeter; for the knights 500 marks or lands worth £40 a year. To judge from the Croyland chronicler's account of the campaign against Buckingham, a policy of this kind had already achieved the desired result. The king, he wrote, 'arranged for armed men to be posted in the vicinity [of Brecon] so that, as soon as the duke left his home, they would be able to pounce upon his property. To encourage them to undertake this, he held out to them the prospect of the duke's wealth for themselves. The result was that Thomas, son of Sir Roger Vaughan, with his brethren and kinsmen, kept careful watch on all the routes leading west from Brecon, while to the east Humphrey Stafford broke down some of the bridges and stationed troops to guard others.' Even the elements seemed to be against Buckingham. A violent storm struck the west country in mid-October. Rivers burst their banks and flooded the countryside.

Harassed by Welshmen and hindered by the weather, the duke's advance down the Wye valley was miserably discouraging. None of the looked-for reinforcements came in and by the time he had got as far as Weobley, north-west of Hereford, he was ready to believe that he had marched into a trap. In a panic he disguised himself and made off, leaving his soldiers to their fate. What happened to them we do not know. Presumably they dispersed and went back home to dry their clothes. Their noble commander was less fortunate. He took refuge in the house of one of his followers, Ralph Bannister of Lacon Hall near Wem, and was promptly handed over to the sheriff of Shropshire. As a reward Bannister was given one of the duke's manors in Kent.

From Leicester Richard III moved to Coventry on 24 October. This move south-westwards suggests that he was confident of John Howard's ability to hold London and that, accompanied by the vital northern contingents led by the Stanleys and the Percies, he was ready to deal with Buckingham and the south-western rebels. It seems, however, that it was not long before he heard the news of the duke's discomfiture. Whatever his plans may have been on 23 and 24 October, this meant that he was now free to concentrate on the risings at Newbury, Salisbury and Exeter. But the remaining rebels were inevitably demoralized by Buckingham's collapse and Richard encountered virtually no opposition. At the end of the month he entered Salisbury in triumph, the rebels having fled at his approach. It was here, in the city market-place on 2 November, that the duke of Buckingham paid the penalty for treason. Next day Richard marched west. He reached Exeter on 8 November, again without encountering any resistance. Most of his enemies had either gone into hiding or taken ship to Brittany, but a few were captured, among them his brother-in-law Thomas St Leger. He too was executed. By this time Henry Tudor had landed somewhere on the south coast, probably at Plymouth, had heard the news and had put to sea again.

Twenty years later Polydore Vergil heard a rather more dramatic version of these events, presumably from informants in Henry's entourage. According to this account, Henry set sail on 10 October 1484 [*sic*] with 5,000 men and fifteen ships. That same evening a sudden storm blew the greater part of his fleet back to France, but early next morning Henry and just two ships found themselves in calm waters off Poole. Seeing plenty of soldiers on the shore, Henry ordered that no one was to disembark until the rest of his ships had arrived and, in the meantime, sent a boat to within hailing distance of the beach. Richard's soldiers – for that is who they were – tried to persuade the boat's crew that they were followers of Buckingham, that the duke's camp was nearby and that King Richard had fled, but Henry was too astute to be taken in. After waiting a while for his fleet, he set sail and landed in Normandy. If there is any truth at all in this tale of adventure and wisdom, it is at any rate clear that the date is quite wrong. Even in 1483 11 October is too early for Richard to have troops stationed on the shore. Henry would unquestionably have turned back only after he had received bad news from a reliable source and this can hardly have been before the end of the month. The chances are, therefore, that the loan of 10,000 crowns which he received from Duke Francis on 31 October at Paimpol on the Channel coast, was a loan intended to speed him on his way to England; and that, even if there was a near landfall at Poole, it was at Plymouth (as the Croyland chronicler states) early in November that he heard what had happened.

From Exeter Richard made his way back through the southern counties where there were a few last embers of resistance – at Bodiam Castle, for example – to be extinguished. By 25 November he was in London. The rebellion of 1483 had turned out to be a fiasco. In the months since his coronation the king had worked hard to make himself popular. In this he had doubtless been assisted by having much of Edward IV's accumulated treasure at his disposal. Presumably this had also helped him to raise an army and keep it in being. Given the depleted state of the peerage in 1483 Richard was unbeatable for as long as he retained the loyalty of the Howards, the Percies and the Stanleys. That the Woodvilles and a number of Edward IV's displaced servants should run the risks of an early rebellion is understandable, but to succeed they needed support from at least some of the men who, just three months earlier, had acquiesced in Richard's *coup*. Unfortunately only Buckingham was ready to change sides so soon and, as a rebel captain, he was the last man in the world to inspire confidence.

After the revolt there were few executions; most of the leaders escaped. But though they managed to save their lives, their property was forfeit. In the only parliament of Richard's reign no fewer than a hundred people were attainted (whereas during the reigns of Edward IV and Henry VII the totals were 140 and 138 respectively). The fact that Richard attainted so many at once suggests that he was in a state of insecurity bordering on panic. Naturally this meant that still greater responsibilities and greater rewards were placed in the hands of the few he did trust. As a result the grip of the northerners on the country as a whole was tightened further. In January 1484 Sir Marmaduke Constable was put in charge of Buckingham's forfeited Kentish lordship of Tonbridge and Penshurst. Sir Robert Brackenbury was made sheriff of Kent for life; Sir Robert Percy sheriff of Essex and Hertfordshire; Lord Scrope of Bolton was appointed head of a commission for Cornwall and Devon. Along with these men came their officials and their officials' servants. A great many northerners at all sorts of social levels enjoyed power and profit thanks to Richard III's nervous generosity; it is hardly surprising that his stock continued to remain high in the north. Equally it would hardly be surprising if, in the aftermath of the revolt of 1483, southern resentment of outsiders continued to grow. More momentous still, the failure of Buckingham's rebellion pushed to the centre of the political stage a man who had hitherto been condemned to wait in the wings. *Faute de mieux* all those who were opposed to Richard III now had to turn their eyes to the impoverished court of Henry Tudor.

Fourteen

HENRY TUDOR: THE ENDING OF THE WARS 1483-7

FOR TWELVE YEARS Henry Tudor had lived in almost total obscurity. Obviously he had some companions in exile, but until 1483 his uncle, Jasper Tudor, is the only one to whom we can give a name. Then in the early summer of 1483, he was joined by Sir Edward Woodville with the *Trinity* and the *Falcon* – all that remained of the fleet of which Woodville had been the commander. His main accession of strength came later that year. For the rebels who scattered in the face of Richard III's army Brittany was the obvious haven and, apart from John Morton who stayed in Flanders, nearly all seem to have made their way there: the marquis of Dorset, Bishop Peter Courtenay and Edward Courtenay, Sir John Cheyne, Sir William Berkeley and Sir Giles Daubeney among them. The presence of a group of Edward IV's courtiers in Brittany could only strengthen Henry's resolve to marry Edward IV's daughter. In the cathedral at Rennes on Christmas Day 1483 he swore to marry Elizabeth of York as soon as he became king; then the assembled company swore homage to him as though he were king already.

If Henry had ever been a useful diplomatic pawn in the hands of the Breton duke, then he was doubly so now. Naturally Richard's reaction was to increase the pressure by which he hoped to persuade Duke Francis to surrender his pawn. His first step was to try to drive home the point that the duke could ill afford to incur the English king's anger. In the last few years of his reign Edward IV had built up a formidable navy and Richard now sent this to sea to fight a winter war in the Channel against Breton shipping and, if it could be pinned down, the Breton fleet. More worrying for Duke Francis, however, were politics on land. His only child was a daughter, Anne of Brittany, and it was taken for granted that when he died, the king of France would go all out to acquire the duchy. At the Breton court, therefore, England was looked upon as an ally whose military aid might be crucial in the forthcoming struggle for the duchy's independence. The death of Louis XI on 30 August 1483 and the succession of a thirteen-year-old, Charles VIII, had brought temporary relief from French pressure and had enabled the duke to lend his support to Henry's first attempted invasion two months later. But once the French regency council settled down, it was clear that it would resume the traditional policy of the crown and that Brittany would need help from the king of England, even from a king who was widely suspected of having murdered his nephews. In June 1484 the war at sea came to an end and Richard promised to supply 1,000 archers for use in the defence of the duchy.

This was an agreement which was bound to strike fear into Henry's heart. Polydore Vergil has a complicated and exciting story of how John Morton in Flanders got wind of a plot by which Pierre Landois, the treasurer of Brittany and acting head of the government while Duke Francis was ill, promised to hand Henry over to Richard, and how, by a series of deceptions, disguises and frantic rides, Henry managed to escape across the Breton border into Anjou, barely an hour ahead of the troops Landois had sent to arrest him. It is stirring stuff and a fine demonstration of the way in which providence looked after Henry Tudor and 'the fortune of the English commonwealth', but that circumspect man would have needed no warning from Morton to know that the agreement of June 1484 spelt danger. Even so, Henry may well have been reluctant to leave the Breton court, the only political world he knew at all well. Not until October 1484 is there documentary evidence of his presence in France and it remains possible that the timing of his departure from Vannes was precipitated by a message from Morton.

Henry and his party had not been long at the court of Charles VIII* when they were able to welcome an unexpected addition to their strength: John de Vere, earl of Oxford. After ten years' imprisonment in Hammes Castle, de Vere suddenly 'escaped' and made his way to the French court at Montargis. Not only was the earl an experienced soldier but he was also a genuine Lancastrian – and such men were like gold dust in the Tudor camp, composed as it was chiefly of Yorkists driven out by Richard III. Indeed, so far as numbers went, the earl's arrival hardly made any difference to the Yorkist–Lancastrian balance, since with him came two more Yorkists: James Blount and John Fortescue. From Richard's point of view their defection was probably more serious than Oxford's escape. The earl, after all, always had been

an enemy, but Blount and Fortescue were men who had held positions
of trust, Blount as captain of Hammes Castle – de Vere, in other words,
had not really escaped – and Fortescue as gentleman porter of Calais,
an office once held by Andrew Trollope. Clearly the military implications of their defection were serious. Hammes itself was now held in
Henry's name by Blount's wife. And how secure was Richard's grip on
the rest of the Calais complex of fortresses, still the only permanent
military base in the crown's possession? How loyal was the garrison?
Blount's brother, Lord Mountjoy, was captain of Guînes. What would
his attitude be? Richard did not wait to find out. He sent in a fresh
garrison under a new captain, the reliable Sir James Tyrell. In
December 1484 Lord Dinham was ordered to recapture Hammes and
this he eventually did, but only on terms which allowed the garrison to
depart and guaranteed them a free pardon. In March 1485 Richard
went a step further. The old Yorkist, Lord Dinham, was removed and a
new captain appointed: John of Gloucester, Richard's own bastard son.
Since John was still a minor this was, in effect, the king taking Calais
into his own hands and may well be a further indication of the difficulty
he was facing in finding people he could trust. It also meant that Calais
would have to be governed from a distance and through deputies and
this can hardly be said to have solved the problem. In the same way, by
moving Tyrell to Guînes, Richard found himself insisting on Glamorgan's being governed from a distance, instructing people there to take
their orders from Tyrell even though he was no longer on the spot. The
king was becoming increasingly dependent on a dangerously small
group of men. Plugging one gap in his defences meant the creation of a
new gap somewhere else. Calais, of course, was vitally important, but
so, as it turned out, was south Wales.

Very little seemed to go right for Richard. In the parliament of 1484
he assembled the lords spiritual and temporal and had them promise to
recognize his son Edward as his successor, only for Edward to die soon
afterwards. He came to terms with Elizabeth Woodville so that she and
her daughters were able to leave sanctuary, only for Richard, after his
own wife's death in March 1485, to fall foul of the damaging rumour
that he was planning to marry his niece and that he had, indeed, to this
end hastened his wife's death either by poison or by refusing to share
her bed. Since his wife had been a Neville and the Neville connexion
was the focus of many northern loyalties, this was an accusation which
Richard had to take seriously and go to great lengths to deny. Throughout 1484 and 1485 he remained on the defensive. During the greater

part of the summer of 1484 he made his headquarters at Nottingham, presumably believing that its central location meant that he was strategically placed to deal with a threat at any quarter of his kingdom. But no invasion came. The troubled state of French and Breton politics meant that Henry failed to obtain the necessary financial, naval and military support. Perhaps it was just as well. According to the Croyland chronicler, in 1484 Richard's defence capacity was at its height, chiefly because he was able to give generously, and still keep something in hand. But once the lands confiscated from the rebels of 1483 had been redistributed and Edward IV's treasure spent, then, for the first time, Richard – even though he had managed to economize by eliminating the rest of the royal family – would have to face the financial problems posed by the costs of war.

In these circumstances it is not surprising that as the year drew to a close so Richard's nervousness increased. Henry Tudor's arrival at the French court meant that he was now effectively out of reach. The events at Calais triggered off a series of responses which, in view of the fact that it was midwinter, throw an interesting light on Richard's state of mind and even give a kind of substance to the famous Tudor portrait of a twitching king, incessantly biting his lip and fiddling with his dagger. On 7 December 1484, for the first time, he issued a proclamation against Henry Tudor, accusing him of abandoning the rights of the English crown in France and of intending 'to do the most cruel murders, slaughters and robberies and disinheritances that ever were seen in any Christian realm'. Next day he issued commissions of array to most of the English counties; finally on 18 December he ordered a military census of the lords and gentry, demanding to know how many men each could call up at half a day's notice. None of this can have helped his subjects to enjoy a relaxed Christmas, but it does tend to confirm the Croyland chronicler's account of the following Twelfth Night. In the midst of the festivities, as the king wore his crown in splendour, his spies entered and told him that, beyond all doubt, his enemies would invade next summer. 'Nothing', wrote the chronicler, 'could have been more pleasing to him than this news.' The strain of waiting had been beginning to tell.

In the spring of 1485 Henry Tudor moved to Rouen. The French government had at last been persuaded to grant him some financial aid, presumably in order to prevent Richard III from sending troops to Brittany. With money in his pocket Henry was able to assemble a fleet in the Seine estuary and begin the work of fitting it out. In April

Richard countered by ordering his own Channel fleet to sea under the command of Sir George Neville, and by sending Viscount Lovell to Southampton to take charge of the defence of the south coast. In June he reissued the proclamation against Henry Tudor, this time laying special emphasis on his rival's bastard descent; he ordered the commissioners of array to review the shire levies and the sheriffs to remain at their posts to be ready for action the instant they heard that Henry had landed. In the same month Richard returned to Nottingham Castle and waited. Since he did not know where the blow would fall, there was little else he could do.

Henry, on the other hand, was in a position to make more definite arrangements. His first priority had been to ascertain how much support he could look forward to receiving in the crucial days which followed a landing. Once he had some indication of this, he could begin to plan the details of his invasion, its time and place. Inevitably these inquiries were conducted in secrecy, but we know that he had been in touch with the Stanleys and it is probable that he had also made contact with the earl of Northumberland; with two, in other words, of the three most powerful families in England. Since the only clearly encouraging messages he received came from the Stanleys it was natural that his agents should then concentrate on the west and, in particular, on Wales, where Sir William Stanley (Lord Stanley's brother) held high office and where Henry's uncle, the Lancastrian earl of Pembroke, might still have friends. Eventually he received promises of aid from Gilbert Talbot, uncle of the fourth earl of Shrewsbury, from Sir John Savage, a Cheshire landowner who was Lord Stanley's nephew and had been a member of Edward iv's household, from Rhys ap Thomas, a prominent figure in south Wales, and from a few others. These promises at least gave Henry a chance, if not much more than that. It was, moreover, doubtful whether he could afford another year of apparent inactivity if he wanted to keep his band of exiles together – already the marquis of Dorset had tried to break away and had had to be 'recaptured'. The risks of delay were certainly as great as the risks of action. In July a Welsh cleric called John Morgan sent word that the time had come. On 1 August 1485 Henry's fleet commanded by the French admiral Guillaume de Casenove, left Harfleur and sailed out into the Channel, heading for Wales.

Shortly before sunset on 7 August, after a slow but apparently uneventful voyage, Henry landed at Milford Haven. His army consisted of his companions in exile, several hundred in all, and of a

Norman contingent supplied by Charles VIII. According to Commynes
the Normans were 'three thousand of the most unruly men that could
be found', whereas Polydore Vergil puts the entire force at no more
than two thousand. But whatever the number and quality of the French
soldiers, Henry was clearly grateful to their commander, Philibert de
Chandée, whom he created earl of Bath early in 1486. He spent that
first night at Dale and then advanced next day to Haverfordwest. Here
he was joined by a small troop supplied by Pembroke but received the
disquieting news that John Savage and Rhys ap Thomas were actually
preparing to resist him. Despite this, Henry pressed on for a further five
miles in the direction of Cardigan before pitching camp. By now his
troops were well aware that Richard's officials knew that they had
arrived and their nerves were on edge at the thought of the impending
reception committee. That evening a rumour that Walter Herbert was
about to attack them 'with a huge army' sent a wave of panic through
the camp; it subsided only after their scouts rode back with the reassuring news that there was no sign of the enemy – a minor incident but one
which highlights the problems which Henry faced. Unless his followers
were encouraged by a fairly rapid inflow of reinforcements, their morale
would sink, and his army, already a small one, would become even
smaller as more and more men took the decision to leave an expedition
which seemed to be heading for disaster. Thus every new arrival was
fêted, but in the first three or four days there were distressingly few of
them. As the history of Buckingham's rebellion had made clear there
was no automatic Welsh enthusiasm for a Tudor.

Immediately after his landing Henry had dispatched messengers to
Talbot and the Stanleys, informing them of his intention of crossing the
Severn at Shrewsbury and arranging a rendezvous, but unless some
substantial aid came in quickly it must have been doubtful whether he
would even get as far as Shropshire. Crucial to the expedition's survival,
therefore, was the attitude of Rhys ap Thomas. Further envoys were
dispatched with authority to offer him the 'lieutenancy' in Wales
should Henry succeed. If, while they waited for the envoys' return,
Henry's line of march took him northwards by the coast road to
Aberystwyth, it may be that his followers found comfort in the sight of
their fleet, particularly the Norman troops who still made up the
greater part of the army. Fortunately the inducement worked. Rhys ap
Thomas agreed to keep his earlier promise, and Henry, who had been
preparing to bring him to battle, found himself, after all, able to
welcome him as an ally on the road to Shrewsbury.

At Shrewsbury he received further encouragement. His envoys rode in bearing messages and money. At the appropriate moment, he was told, his friends would keep their word. For some that moment came quickly. The very next day, at Newport, Gilbert Talbot arrived and five hundred men with him. For others it was not so easy. The following day, at Stafford, Sir William Stanley rode in, but he was accompanied only by a small retinue and he stayed only for a short talk. We are not told what they talked about, but it is not difficult to guess. The Stanleys were caught in a tangled web. Shortly before Henry landed at Milford Haven Lord Stanley had asked and been granted permission to leave King Richard's court, but only on condition that his son, Lord Strange, came to court in his place. As soon as he knew of Henry's landing (i.e., on 10 or 11 August), Richard summoned Stanley back to Nottingham, but the latter pleaded the sweating sickness and said that he could not come. His son then tried to escape but was arrested and questioned. He made a partial confession, admitting that his uncle Sir William Stanley and Sir John Savage had indeed conspired to join Henry Tudor, but insisting that his father still intended to remain loyal. He was then allowed, or perhaps forced, to write to his father, telling him of his plight and begging him to come at once with all his forces. Although Sir William Stanley had, as a result of his nephew's confession, been publicly denounced as a traitor, it was by no means clear what his best course of action was – and even less clear, of course, what his brother should do. In the circumstances they had little choice but to wait and see. Sir William presumably told Henry that they would, in the end, give him their support, but that it would indeed have to be at the very last moment, for if they committed themselves too early, Richard would have time to make Lord Strange pay with his life. For this reason Lord Stanley, who had been at Lichfield, had just fallen back to the east, moving away from Henry, and looking as though he might be heading for Leicester, the place of muster for Richard's army. All this Sir William could have explained to Henry, and undeniably it made sense – but it still left open the possibility that, at the last minute, the Stanleys would calculate that the best way to save George Stanley's life was to throw in their lot with Richard III. They had, after all, disappointed the rebels of 1483, and they might do so again. In that case Henry would be overwhelmingly defeated. But the die was cast. He had no option but to listen to what Sir William told him, hope that it was true, and press on regardless.

From Stafford Henry moved to Lichfield and then Tamworth. He had been heading straight for Nottingham; this slight change of direction meant he was now heading towards Leicester. Clearly he was intent upon bringing Richard to battle as soon as possible. At Tamworth he was joined by Walter Hungerford and Thomas Bourchier, two former members of Edward IV's household who had been involved in Buckingham's rebellion and who, though pardoned, had not yet recovered the entirety of their estates. Next day Henry went to a secret meeting with both Stanleys at Atherstone. A battle was now imminent and it was vital to know what they planned to do. But probably more reassuring than their words was the arrival late in the afternoon of Sir John Savage; one of the Stanley group had at last committed himself. That evening Henry pitched camp knowing that he was very close to Richard's army and that the next twenty-four hours would be the make-or-break crisis in his life.

According to the Croyland chronicler Richard rejoiced, or at least appeared to rejoice, when he heard that the invasion had come. He must have realized that until Henry had been defeated he had no hope at all of reigning in peace; on the other hand, he cannot have been entirely confident that he had won the loyalty of his subjects. The statement of the Croyland chronicler that he sent out 'threatening writs' ordering men to fight on pain of losing their goods, estates and lives, is confirmed by the terms of the summons sent to the Vernons. That he was having to call upon men whom he did not trust is suggested not only by his summons to Lord Stanley but also by Polydore Vergil's account of how he instructed Sir Robert Brackenbury to keep a close watch on various unreliable gentry as they made their way from London to the rendezvous at Leicester. Just past Stony Stratford, however, Thomas Bourchier and Walter Hungerford gave Brackenbury the slip and stole away by night. Other reluctant soldiers stayed away altogether. The duke of Norfolk sent a polite note to his 'well-beloved friend John Paston':

Wherefore I pray you that you meet with me at Bury [St Edmunds], for, by the grace of God, I purpose to lie at Bury as upon Tuesday night [16 August], and that you bring with you such company of tall men as you may goodly make at my cost and charge, besides that which you have promised the king; and, I pray you, ordain them jackets of my livery, and I shall content you at your meeting with me,

Your lover,
J. Norfolk

But two months after Bosworth, John Paston was appointed sheriff of Norfolk. He clearly had done nothing that day to earn either Henry's or the earl of Oxford's disfavour.

There were, of course, some men whom Richard could count upon. The duke of Norfolk was one; the citizens of York too were anxious to demonstrate their loyalty. By 16 August they had heard of Henry's landing, yet they had received no word, from the king or anybody else, about mustering the city's contingent. They decided to take the initiative themselves and sent two messengers to Nottingham to ascertain the king's instructions. Pleased as he may have been by York's enthusiasm for the fray, this was probably disquieting news. If the citizens had received no instructions what was the earl of Northumberland doing? He had made a major contribution to Richard's success in the summer and autumn of 1483. He had been duly rewarded with massive grants of land, in value second only to those given to Norfolk, but the implications of this news from York were, in the event, borne out by Henry Percy's conduct at Bosworth. Most contemporaries felt that his behaviour that day was a betrayal. Despite the benefits he had received, Percy was obviously, as it turned out, less than happy with Richard's rule. The problem may have been that, unlike most kings, Richard did in fact know the north. He intervened directly there and, as king, he had an overriding claim on the service of men whom the earl of Northumberland doubtless thought of as his own clients. Sir Marmaduke Constable, for example, whom Richard had brought down to Tonbridge, was an old Percy retainer. While Richard was duke of Gloucester he and Northumberland had got on well together; thus the earl's behaviour in 1483, but in 1484 and 1485 it seems that Henry Percy gradually came to realize that a northern king, in effect a Neville king, was not in his own best interests. In August 1485 he came reluctantly to Richard's call.

By 17 August, then, it must have been apparent to the king that he was facing a crumbling of loyalty: Henry had been allowed to advance undisturbed to Shrewsbury; George Stanley's confession; the news from York – all pointed in this direction. Knowing that both Northumberland and Norfolk were on the way and knowing how small Henry's army was, he must still have felt reasonably confident, but if the crumbling were not to continue an early battle was desirable. Thus, for their different reasons, both commanders were determined to fight it out as soon as possible. On learning that Henry had reached Lichfield, Richard set out from Nottingham (probably early in the morning of 20

August) to join the troops who were mustering at Leicester. Next day he marched east and selected a likely field of battle somewhere near Bosworth. He pitched camp early, giving his soldiers plenty of time to rest and prepare themselves for the coming ordeal. Apart from Norfolk, Northumberland and Lord Strange (as a hostage) the only peers in his army were Norfolk's son, the earl of Surrey, Viscount Lovell and Lords Ferrers and Zouch. This means that twenty-eight peers who might have come to the rendezvous at Leicester preferred to stay away. To judge, moreover, from the list of commoners attainted in Henry's first parliament, twenty-three in all, a significantly high proportion of the gentry had, like John Paston, also decided to ignore the king's summons. Even so, both the Croyland chronicler and Polydore Vergil believed that Richard's army was a large one, considerably bigger than Henry's. Since Henry was accompanied by only two peers, Oxford and Pembroke, and both of them were exiles, this assessment may well be accurate. In addition, there is some evidence to suggest that Richard's army, like Henry's, included a contingent of foreign mercenaries, in this case probably Flemings, dispatched by Archduke Maximilian in furtherance of his quarrel with Charles VIII of France.

Despite its enormous mythical importance, Bosworth is as poorly documented as most of the other battles of the Wars of the Roses. Local tradition has its uses but in matters such as this it is totally unreliable. There are only two accounts worth mentioning. One, by the Croyland chronicler, is very brief. It tells us only that Henry fought against Richard, that Oxford attacked Norfolk and that where Northumberland stood, there was no fighting at all. The other, by Polydore Vergil, is almost certainly based upon eyewitness reports, and – despite the fact that the author did not arrive in England until eighteen years later – it undeniably provides a very plausible version of a battle which seems to have been less confused than most. This, of course, may only be a tribute to Polydore's artistic skill, but it may also be a reflection of the fact that several contingents seem to have remained stationary throughout the battle. What these two accounts do not allow us to do is to make a map of the battlefield. Many such maps have been drawn but, apart from the fun of making them, they are all quite worthless. From the York city records we know that the battle was fought on Redmoor Plain – between Market Bosworth to the north, Sutton Cheney to the east, Stoke Golding to the south and Upton to the west – but we cannot locate it any more precisely than this. Only one geographical feature is mentioned, a marsh, and we do not know where this was. According to the proclamation which Henry issued after the battle, Richard was killed at 'Sandeford in the county of Leicester', but we do not know where Sandeford was, nor do the occasional finds of cannon-balls help. No narrative source mentions the presence of guns, and although either or both sides may well have possessed some field artillery, we do not know when these particular cannon-balls were fired, nor from which direction. We do not know where Richard's camp was, nor Henry's, nor Lord Stanley's. Not knowing their starting-point we certainly cannot plot their movements on a map.

What then are we left with? Enough, at least, to be able to discern both a chronological sequence of events and a decisive moment. Richard drew up his army with what Polydore Vergil called a terrifyingly large vanguard, containing both cavalry and infantry, with archers placed to the front, under the command of the duke of Norfolk; behind came the king 'with a choice force'. Early that morning as Henry began his preparations he sent a message to Lord Stanley who was now nearby, 'betwixt the two battles', asking him to bring his contingents in to join the array. Stanley's reply was that Henry should put his own forces in order and he would then come in with his army well appointed. Clearly Lord Stanley's policy was still one of 'wait and see'. His son was still Richard's hostage and might even yet be executed on the brink of battle – as Lord Welles had been executed in March 1470. He was determined to be on the winning side, whichever that might be. After their conference of the previous day Henry was taken aback, 'vexed and somewhat appalled'. He had no choice, however, but to do as Lord Stanley said. His vanguard, also with archers to the front under the earl of Oxford, was much smaller than Richard's. Its wings were commanded by Gilbert Talbot to the right and John Savage to the left. Behind came Henry, knowing that he must put his trust in Lord Stanley, with just one troop of horse and a few footmen. In all Henry now had about 5,000 men (Polydore Vergil's estimate).

Between Henry's and Richard's armies there lay a marsh which Henry used 'as a fortress' as he marched with the sun on his back – all of which implies that, at one – presumably dangerous – stage, he was marching roughly north and across the enemy's front. Indeed as soon as Henry had passed the marsh Richard gave the order to attack, first the archers and then hand-to-hand. After a while, the earl of Oxford ordered his men to stay close to the standards – not further than ten feet away – so as to present a short and solid line. Although contracting the

line was a standard textbook response to the problem of being outnumbered, it involved a momentary withdrawal which seems to have dis-
concerted the enemy. As a result, there was a lull in the fighting, either
because they suspected a trick or because – as Vergil suspected – they
had not been very keen to fight in the first place. However, Oxford soon
renewed the struggle, his men advancing to attack in traditional wedge
formation. A fierce conflict ensued. We do not know how long it
continued – according to Polydore Vergil the whole battle lasted two
hours – but at some stage Richard believed he saw an opportunity to
win the day by a single decisive stroke. From afar he identified Henry's
small squadron by its banners and led his own troops around the edge
of the fighting to launch a charge against it. If a battle was itself a form
of trial by which the 'Lord of hosts' decided who had the right, this was
to be trial by single combat: king against anti-king. Polydore Vergil
records the names of those who stood between Henry and death at
Richard's hands: William Brandon, his standard-bearer, was killed;
John Cheyne, a man of great strength, was knocked down; Henry had
to fight for his life and 'he bore the brunt longer than even his own men
could have expected'. Doubtless Polydore Vergil exaggerated the
extent to which it was a man-to-man encounter between Richard and
Henry; presumably it was a clash of two households, but the effect was
the same. Richard was now cut off from the main part of his army.
Moreover, he was close enough to Sir William Stanley's force – no less
than 3,000 men according to Polydore Vergil – to make it possible for
Stanley to intervene with decisive effect. For Sir William it was just a
question of which of the two contending households he would support;
to whichever he chose he could bring victory. It is unlikely that Richard
would have gambled in the way he did if he had known what Sir
William Stanley's choice would be; presumably he, like Henry, hoped
that, in the end, the Stanleys would throw their weight in on his side.
And since, in 1485, Henry Tudor was an unknown quantity, the fact
that Sir William decided to support him means, in effect, that he was
deciding against Richard. Given a free choice – and that, for one
astonishing moment, is what Sir William Stanley did have – he would
prefer not to have this man as king any longer. If ever there was a battle
which was a continuation of politics by other means it was Bosworth.

   Most of Richard's 'choice force' fled before the overwhelming weight
of Sir William Stanley's charge. 'King Richard alone was killed fighting
manfully in the thickest press of his enemies ... his courage was high
and fierce and failed him not even at the death which, when his men

forsook him, he preferred to take by the sword rather than, by foul flight, to prolong his life.' The words are Polydore Vergil's. Even Henry VII's court historian could not withold his Froissart-like admiration for the heroic and chivalrous way in which the usurper met his end, head on and unflinching. But desperately brave knight though he may have been, as a king Richard was a disaster and the fact that he felt he had to risk that final throw is a measure of the extent to which he had already failed. Once Richard was killed there was no point in fighting on. Most men threw away their weapons and surrendered.

Only in the vanguard where, by a sensible soldier's convention, the best men were normally placed in the front rank and where the battle had indeed been keenly contested, were the casualties heavy, chief among them the duke of Norfolk. Also killed were Lord Ferrers, Sir Robert Brackenbury and Sir Richard Ratcliffe. Others managed to escape, notably Viscount Lovell and two Stafford brothers, Thomas and Humphrey, who fled to the sanctuary of St John's at Colchester. Most significant of all, however, was the number who came to the battlefield and then did nothing except stand and wait. At their head were two of the greatest magnates of the realm: Lord Stanley and the earl of Northumberland. Stanley's preference in 1485, though muted, is clear enough. He it was who was credited with 'crowning' Henry VII on the field of victory. In return for his services he was created earl of Derby. Northumberland's attitude seems to have been more ambiguous and is certainly much harder to penetrate. Conflicting loyalties among his own retainers may have made it difficult for him to take a positive step in either direction but, unlike Lord Stanley, he had attended Richard's rendezvous. Thus, when the battle was over he was imprisoned but – and here Henry's response is equally ambiguous – he was not attainted. The crucial fact remains, however, that the two lords who, apart from the duke of Norfolk, had benefited most from Richard's regime had most signally not remained loyal to him. As Sir Thomas More wrote, 'With large gifts he got him unsteadfast friendships.' Was there ever a king who lost the allegiance of his chief supporters – Buckingham, Stanley, Northumberland – in so short a time? In these facts lies the vindication of the underlying truth, for all its rhetorical extravagances, of the Tudor portrait of Richard III.

Richard's performance as commander of the English invasion of Scotland in 1482 suggests that he was a competent general. But on that occasion a demoralized and outnumbered Scottish army had disbanded before the coming of the English; in consequence, when

Richard came to Bosworth it was the first time that he had been in overall command of an army at a pitched battle. So far as military organization went, he had done enough to win. Even if Lord Stanley stayed away, the force which Northumberland led should have been sufficient. We can only guess at its size but it should have been a large one. The earl had led 6,700 men against the Scots in 1482; in 1475 only the royal dukes, Gloucester and Clarence, had made larger contributions to Edward iv's invasion of France. But, in the last resort, Richard lacked the ability to make men fight for him. If, as some historians suggest, the charge at Bosworth was 'a brilliant tactical manoeuvre', this must imply that he was already on the brink of losing the battle; otherwise it was reckless and foolish. Either way he was defeated. A successful soldier-king needed other qualities; military competence alone was not enough.

That evening Henry, having been acclaimed king on the battlefield, marched into Leicester. There his army was rested and Richard iii's naked body put on display. The new king's first act of government was to send Robert Willoughby to Sheriff Hutton in Yorkshire to secure the person of his most obvious rival for the throne and take him to the Tower of London. This was Edward, earl of Warwick, the fifteen-year-old son of Clarence and Isabella Neville. With the heir to the house of York in his hands – together with most of the York and Neville estates – Henry's position was a strong one. Since he himself claimed to be the heir of Lancaster this meant that both the dynastic avenues to the throne were blocked. As the curious history of the later imposters makes clear, in these circumstances there could be no real contenders. Moreover, although Henry dynastically speaking was a Lancastrian, in practical terms he was a Yorkist. Most of the lords and gentlemen who supported him were men who had been associated, both at court and in the country, with the government of Edward iv. Politically speaking, Henry vii represented the continuity of York after the calamitous but brief interlude of Richard iii's reign, but because the political base of Richard's regime had been a notably narrow one, its collapse was not attended by a flood of forfeitures. Henry, in other words, was not confronted by a substantial number of families who needed to bring about a reversal of the verdict of 1485 in order to secure the restoration of their estates. Only one great magnate family, the newest one, the Howards, had stood by Richard to the end. The surviving representative, Thomas Howard, had been captured at Bosworth and he too was a prisoner in the Tower. Only in the north had Richard enjoyed much gentry support and it was only there that Henry was to face a genuine military threat. The last act of the Wars of the Roses was to be the violent death-throes of Richard's northern partisans.

The position in the north was further complicated, as always, by the Scottish border. Although the king of Scotland, James III, was well-disposed towards Henry, and had indeed allowed him to recruit Scottish mercenaries for his invasion of England, he had very little control over his own border barons. Their taste for a life of raiding had, if anything, been increased by the English capture of Berwick in 1482, and to Henry the possibility of co-operation between them and his domestic enemies seemed a very real one. Within a very few months he had come to recognize that his first choice as warden of the Marches, Lord Strange, carried insufficient local weight and in December 1485 he set free the earl of Northumberland. Once again a Percy was made warden of the east and middle Marches. Then Henry planned to visit the north himself, and it was rumoured that he was coming 'to do execution quickly on such as have offended against him'.

Despite this early concern for the unsettled state of affairs in the north, the king seems to have been taken aback, early in April 1486, by the news that a conspiracy against him was already in train. The chief plotters were Lord Lovell and Humphrey Stafford. While they were in sanctuary at Colchester, sentences of attainder were passed against them, their estates confiscated and granted to others, but now they had broken out and were said to be raising the standard of revolt: Lovell in Yorkshire and Stafford in Worcestershire. It seems that Henry was right to be surprised. Despite the rumours that Lovell had gathered a large army to the north of Richard's old stamping-ground of Middleham, it is clear that he had, in fact, miscalculated badly. Some of the most influential Richmondshire families, Conyers and Metcalfe, for example, had already decided to throw in their lot with the new regime, and very few indeed were prepared to run the risk of rebellion. Even without summoning an army, the king was able to deal with Lovell; the royal household in arms disposed of sufficient force. Henry had been at Lincoln, on his way north, when he received the first reports of the conspiracy. Undeterred he continued on his leisurely progress, accompanied by a large entourage. Not until he reached York, on 23 April, did he take any military action. While he remained behind in the city, he sent the greater part of his entourage on ahead, under the command of his uncle Jasper, now duke of Bedford. On approaching the rebel camp,

Bedford offered a pardon to all who would lay down their arms. This alone was enough to give Lovell cause to doubt the loyalty of his followers. Some time during the night he slipped away, leaving the rest with no option but to surrender. Lovell managed to escape to the house of Sir Thomas Broughton in north Lancashire and for a little while longer a small group of rebels, led by Broughton and Sir John Huddleston, two Cumbrian knights whose horizons had widened during Richard's reign, held out in the far north-west. Eventually, however, most of these men accepted the pardons they were offered and, deprived of their protection, Lovell fled abroad, to Flanders.

Henry VII, meanwhile, had left York and had visited Worcester, Gloucester and Bristol. By the time he got to the west country the rebellion raised by Humphrey Stafford and his brother Thomas had already collapsed. In their bid to win support they had relied heavily on the manufacture of false news such as the story that Lovell had captured the king. As soon as the truth was known, their adherents melted away. On 11 May Humphrey Stafford again took refuge in sanctuary, at Culham near Abingdon but this time in vain. Two days later he was forcibly dragged out. In July 1486 the judges of the King's Bench, interpreting the law as Henry required, decided that sanctuary could not be pleaded in cases of treason. Humphrey Stafford was executed, but his brother and everyone else who was brought to court for his part in the rising was pardoned.

The Lovell–Stafford revolt had failed miserably. But it has some significance as a first indication that the name of the earl of Warwick might yet serve as a focus for discontent. One of the wilder rumours to circulate during the revolt had been to the effect that he had been set free on Guernsey and then taken to meet Lovell at York. The indictments laid against Stafford's followers were to charge them with shouting, 'A Warwick! A Warwick!' There had been some disturbances around London early in May which were probably linked with the revolt – and one of the banners which the rioters were said to have brandished was the standard of the ragged staff. Given the prominent position accorded Warwick in the rumours which swirled about the Lovell rebellion, it is hardly surprising that its suppression was followed by a rumour that he had been murdered. It was presumably this story which gave an Oxford priest named Richard Simons the idea of taking Lambert Simnel to Ireland and passing him off as the young earl. By late January 1487 Henry knew that something was afoot and on

17 February he countered the imposture by parading the real earl of Warwick through the streets of London. Though it is unlikely that anyone of any consequence actually believed in Simnel, it was easy enough for the pretender's supporters to claim that the young man whom Henry had put on parade was the 'real imposter'.

No matter which of the two was Warwick, what made Lambert Simnel a real threat to Henry was the fact that, for reasons of their own, three very influential people were prepared to support him. The first was Gerald Fitzgerald, eighth earl of Kildare; the second, Margaret of Burgundy, and the third, John de la Pole, earl of Lincoln. For the last thirty years, no matter who was lieutenant of Ireland, it had been the earls of Kildare, as deputy lieutenants, who had ruled the country. When Henry VII came to the throne, Gerald Fitzgerald, the eighth earl, petitioned for a renewal of his office, but instead of this being automatically granted he found himself invited to come to England. Seven or eight years went by before the earl could be persuaded to accept that invitation; in the meantime he decided to take a friendly interest in the career of Lambert Simnel. Margaret, sister of Edward IV and widow of Duke Charles of Burgundy, still wielded great authority in Flanders and was prepared to use it against a Tudor usurper. She gave shelter first to Viscount Lovell and then to her nephew, the earl of Lincoln, eldest son of John de la Pole, duke of Suffolk, and Elizabeth, another of Edward IV's sisters. Lincoln, then, was another potential Yorkist heir; indeed, after the death of Richard III's son in 1484, he may have been encouraged to look upon himself as the designated heir to Richard's throne. Despite this, the young man – he was about twenty-four years old in 1485 – had submitted to Henry VII and, to all appearances, he had remained loyal. He may have been encouraged in this attitude by his father, always a dutiful servant of the crown, no matter who was wearing it. Lincoln had not been implicated in the Lovell–Stafford revolt and he was present at a council meeting on 2 February 1487 when Lambert Simnel was on the agenda. Only when he fled to the Low Countries did his real attitude become suddenly and startlingly clear. Whether he had been involved in the early stages of the Simons–Simnel plot and what he hoped to do on reaching Flanders are questions on which no certainty is possible. All we know is that by early April Henry VII was expecting an invasion of the East Anglian and Essex coast, the obvious landing stage for an expedition led by a de la Pole and launched from the Low Countries. In fact, however, Henry's enemies decided to join forces and, on 5 May, Lincoln and Lovell landed at Dublin. Most important of all, they brought with them a company of mercenaries supplied by Margaret: 2,000 German troops under the command of a well-known soldier, Martin Schwartz.

From now on events moved swiftly. On 24 May Lambert Simnel was proclaimed King Edward VI and crowned in Christ Church with a circlet of gold taken, or so it was said, from a statue of the Blessed Virgin Mary. Then, reinforced by a contingent of Irish troops under Thomas Fitzgerald, the allies set sail from Dublin and landed at Furness on the coast of Lancashire on 4 June. Odd assortment though their army was, in military terms it was probably rather more formidable than the force with which Henry had landed at Milford Haven two years earlier. In one crucial respect, however, the 1487 invaders were less well prepared than Henry Tudor had been. While in France he had been in communication with men in England and he had been able to offer himself as an alternative king. What alternative could the invaders of 1487 hold out to potential supporters? Would they be fighting for Edward VI? Or for an imposter? Or was the earl of Lincoln intending to make himself John II? There was a degree of uncertainty here which made it difficult for anyone to commit himself wholeheartedly to their cause.

But Henry, of course, could not be sure. He was bound to wonder how many nobles had already given their word to Lincoln. In April while he believed that the blow would fall on the east coast, he visited East Anglia, not just to pray at the most important local shrine, the church of the Blessed Virgin Mary at Walsingham, but also to make sure that the region's nobility and gentry were aware of his watchful presence. Of the earl of Oxford's loyalty there could be little doubt. But what line would the duke of Suffolk adopt if his son invaded? Long suspicious of the marquis of Dorset, when he heard that the latter was coming to meet him at Bury St Edmunds he had him arrested and imprisoned in the Tower, saying that if he were a true friend he would put up with a little indignity in a good cause. At the end of April Henry moved to the west Midlands, to Coventry and Kenilworth. Either he was now more confident of East Anglia's loyalty or his agents had informed him that Lincoln's and Lovell's thoughts were moving in quite another direction. At any rate, not unlike Richard III in 1484 and 1485, he now took up his residence in the centre of the country and waited.

From his landing-point at Furness, Lincoln was ideally placed to make contact with the disaffected in both Cumberland and Richmond-shire, men whom he knew from the days when he had presided over

Richard III's council in the north. While Sir Thomas Broughton brought in his north-western friends, Lincoln advanced across the Pennines through Wensleydale. By 8 June he was at Masham and in touch with Lords Scrope of Bolton and Scrope of Masham, both of them active supporters of Richard III's regime in the North Riding. Five days later the Scropes moved on York where Lincoln was known to have 'many good friends'. Other former retainers of Richard's joined in and it may well have been the threat they posed that caused the earl of Northumberland to stay in Yorkshire rather than join the army which Henry VII was mustering. Lincoln himself moved south fairly rapidly, covering a hundred miles in a week. By 15 June he was approaching Newark.

— Henry, meanwhile, had begun to move north as soon as he was informed of the landing at Furness. By the evening of 11 June he had reached Loughborough, but at this point the pace of his advance slowed, and three days later his army was still quartered around Nottingham, barely fifteen miles north of Loughborough. There were at least two good reasons for the delay. In the first place, he needed accurate information about Lincoln's movements before committing his force either to the east or to the west of the Pennines. In the second place, he was waiting to be joined by the Stanleys at a rendezvous south of Nottingham. Undoubtedly this was worth waiting for. On 14 June Lord Strange rode in, in command of both his own and his father's troops, 'all fair embattled'. In the opinion of the writer, probably a herald, who described Henry's manoeuvres before the battle of Stoke, the Stanleys' army was large enough to have defeated all the king's enemies on its own. Nonetheless, the apparent lack of decisiveness between 11 and 14 June had caused some problems as the army 'wandered here and there for a long time' without always being able to find good billets. Fortunately the weather was fine, but even so the troops began to wonder what was going on and at one stage it was plausibly rumoured that Henry had fled. Finally, on 15 June, the king's scouts brought the information he wanted. Lincoln had marched down the east side of the Pennines and was now advancing on Newark. Henry immediately turned east and camped that night at Radcliffe, fourteen miles from Newark.

By now Henry was in command of a very large army including contingents contributed by several bishops, notably by Morton, now archbishop of Canterbury, and by Courtenay, now bishop of Winchester (the richest see in England). Nobles present were Lord Strange, the earl of Devon, the earl of Shrewsbury and the earl of Oxford, in command of the van. Some indication of the number of gentry present can be gathered from the fact that Henry made thirteen bannerets and fifty-two knights that day, while Sir John Cheyne was later promoted to the rank of baron. On the other side, the 1487 act of attainder names one knight, Thomas Broughton, eight esquires and twelve gentlemen among a total of 8,000 men said to have levied war against the king on 16 June (a later act of attainder puts the total at 5,000). What these details suggest is that Lincoln brought relatively few Englishmen with him to Stoke and that his largely foreign army was heavily outnumbered. Next morning the king's army made an early start. Some villagers from Radcliffe had been persuaded to act as guides; they pointed out marshy ground and likely spots for ambush on the road to Newark. It was still not yet nine o'clock when the vanguard made contact with Lincoln's army drawn up near Stoke.

About the events of 16 June the herald with Henry's army tells us little; only that Lambert Simnel was captured by Robert Bellingham, an esquire of the king's horse, that Lincoln and several gentlemen were slain, that Lovell fled, that there were 4,000 casualties in all, and that 'by the help of Almighty God he [the king] had the victory'. For further details we are again, as at Bosworth, thrown back upon Polydore Vergil's later account. The one thing which this makes clear is that the battle was won by the king's vanguard alone, and this has led some historians to speculate whether Stoke was not indeed another Bosworth, a battle in which the number of participants was matched by the number of those who stood aside and awaited the outcome. On several grounds this is an implausible theory. Firstly, there is no direct evidence for it. Secondly, there would seem to be something wrong with a theory which puts the main body of royalist troops, under Henry's command, into the category of those who preferred to wait and see what happened. Thirdly, Henry VII was not Richard III and not all the reasons which made men unwilling to fight for the one can be said to have applied to the other. On the other hand, there is equally no evidence that Stoke was a keenly contested battle which could have gone either way. According to Polydore Vergil while it lasted it was hard fought, but if it was only the royalist van which did the fighting the outcome can hardly be said to have hung in the balance. What probably happened is that Lincoln, realizing that he was outnumbered, launched a quick attack, hoping to win a decisive advantage before the rest of Henry's forces came up. According to Polydore – who seems to have thought they were Swiss – the German troops fought well but were in the end demoralized by having to witness the heavy losses suffered by the poorly armed Irish. From Henry's point of view what really mattered was the elimination of the leaders. Lincoln, Schwartz, Fitzgerald and Broughton were killed; Lovell may have escaped but, whether dead or alive, at this point he disappears from the pages of history. Lambert Simnel was spared and put to work in the royal kitchen. By the time Polydore wrote his account he had been promoted to king's falconer.

From Stoke Henry returned to Kenilworth, but as reports of the way Lincoln had been received in Yorkshire filtered south, it became clear that another royal visit to the north was called for. After a week in York he moved on to Durham and Newcastle (by 14 August) and then returned via Richmond, Ripon and Pontefract (by 25 August). The entire progress was marked by a stream of men coming in to submit and seek pardon for their political offences. Most of them were indeed pardoned – doubtless at a price – but not all escaped so lightly. Scrope of Bolton and Scrope of Masham were taken south and detained in Windsor and Wallingford Castles; even after their release from prison they were prevented from travelling north of the Trent. Henry's journey through Yorkshire and Durham in August 1487 completed the political destruction of the remnants of Richard III's following. This mopping-up operation in the north marked the real end of the Wars of the Roses, not with a battle but a progress.

There were still, of course, a few people, notably Margaret of Burgundy, who refused to give up the dynastic struggle, but from now on the 'war' was fought by diplomatic rather than military means. A second imposter, Perkin Warbeck, became an instrument of foreign policy in the hands of neighbouring princes, but in England he had no prospect of winning a following. In consequence there were no more wars. Right from the start of his reign the position of Henry VII, the Lancastrian king who had pieced together the shattered Yorkist political establishment, had been a strong one. After Stoke it was even stronger. This does not mean that there was an end to court intrigue or to violent objections to unjustified taxation. Nor does it mean that Henry VII stopped looking over his shoulder. But it did mean a return to an essentially stable political system – and in a sense a rather belated return since only Richard III's ruthless ambition had reopened a struggle settled in 1471.

CONCLUSION

WHAT THEN were the Wars of the Roses? First, it is important to be clear what they were not. They were not a single series of wars caused by a single problem, a malignant disease of the body politic known as 'bastard feudalism'. 'Bastard feudalism' is an unfortunate term, but stripped of its negative overtones, it simply refers to a system of relationships linking lords, gentry and yeomen. As a system it was as characteristic of fourteenth-century or sixteenth-century society as of fifteenth. Effective kings governed through 'bastard feudalism'; ineffective or dangerous kings were overthrown by means of it; it posed no threat to the crown as such. Powerful and ambitious magnates, men like Simon de Montfort, Thomas of Lancaster, Richard Neville, earl of Warwick, John Dudley, duke of Northumberland, were bred no more frequently in the fifteenth century than in any other.

In reality there were three separate wars. The first was caused by Henry VI's manifold shortcomings, his inability either to hold France or govern England. It began in the 1450s, came to a crisis in 1459–61, and then continued to simmer in the north until 1464. The second, caused by Warwick's violent discontent, lasted from 1469 to 1471. The third, precipitated by Richard III's murderous ambition, began in 1483 and ended in 1487. The dynastic issue, the struggle between Lancaster and York, emerged into the light of day only in 1460 and was effectively settled by 1464, if not already by 1461. It would not have been resurrected had it not been for Warwick's and then Richard III's extraordinary behaviour. In European history up to the eighteenth century there always was a dynastic element in politics, but in this case it was secondary rather than primary. Its function here was not to create the conflicts but to channel them and permit them to be resolved.

The Wars of the Roses, then, were three separate wars and, politically speaking, they should be kept distinct. Nonetheless, they all occurred within a single society and within the space of a single generation. For this reason it is possible to look upon them as a set of wars having certain characteristics in common and susceptible of analysis as a group. When Philippe de Commynes looked at them in this light, his conclusion was one which bears repeating: 'If a conflict breaks out in England one or other of the rivals is master in ten days or less.' In the fifteenth century, it is true, men's arithmetic was no better than ours; it was intended to be rhetorically effective rather than merely accurate. In essence, however, Commynes was right. The wars were short. Indeed they were fought in a peculiarly English style that was designed to bring them to a rapid conclusion. Anything less like the First World War it would be hard to imagine. By contrast, wars abroad, including wars fought by Englishmen abroad, were fought in the normal 'medieval' manner – that is to say in the manner that was to remain characteristic of European warfare until the eighteenth century. These wars were long-drawn-out struggles based on devastation, attrition, fortification and siege. If English wars were different this was because Englishmen did not expect war and, in consequence, had made no preparations for it. Perhaps this meant that when war did come, it was felt to be both shocking and memorable. But the fact remains that however well-remembered the Wars of the Roses came to be, what was remembered was the myth not the reality.

All that now remains is to set the reality in a wider perspective, wider both in time and space. First, in time. The wars were not the last dying convulsion of the middle ages. The old argument that they marked an important watershed in English history, the divide between 'medieval' and 'modern' is one which cannot be sustained. By and large, economic, social and religious life went on unhindered. The temporary havoc which the wars caused in the political establishment was real enough and for many individuals it was deeply tragic, but it made little difference to the structure of politics. It is true, as many historians have pointed out, that Tudor noblemen were unwilling to rebel – but so too were the lords of Lancastrian England. It is not true that the Tudor monarchs pursued an avowedly anti-aristocratic policy or waged a royal war against private armies. In order to govern their realm, they depended on lords just as much as their predecessors had done. It is true that Henry VII did not create many new peers, but nor did Edward IV after 1471, the Lancastrian kings before 1437, nor, to go further back still, did Edward I. There was no significant break with the past here; this was just an area, albeit an important one, in which each king had his own individual style. This is not to say that during the period of the Wars of the Roses nothing changed. Important educational, linguistic, technological, economic and social developments have already been mentioned (in Chapter One) and they flowed on, unchecked, independent of the political and military struggle. In time these underlying developments were to have a profound effect on the political super-structure – but that time was not yet.

Second, in space. Fifteenth-century England was a small, compact, unfortified and relatively unified society. Compared with France, Spain, Italy, Germany and the kingdoms of eastern Europe, provincial loyalties here, though not negligible, were weak. Here there was only one city, London, which could begin to match the multitude of urban centres in northern Italy, the Rhineland and the Low Countries. During the Wars of the Roses Englishmen were divided neither by economic conflicts nor by religious differences. The wars were caused, not by structural tensions, but by the shortcomings of individuals: by Henry vi, by Warwick, by Richard iii. That these three human beings should follow one another in swift succession was unfortunate, but that is all. In these circumstances, violent political disputes were unlikely to last long, since there was very little for them to feed on, neither separatist loyalties nor ideological commitments.

Commynes was surely right to argue that out of all the countries which he had known 'England is the one where public affairs are best conducted and regulated with least violence to the people.' It could also be argued that there was a price which had to be paid. As a compact, unified and relatively centralized society, a society increasingly dominated by its one and only centre, London, Westminster, the court, England was also a very uniform society. As we have seen in the history of the printing press, government regulation could act as an intellectual strait-jacket. Moreover, the number of presses to be found in England compared with the number found in many parts of the continent, tends to suggest that in the fifteenth and sixteenth centuries England was a cultural backwater. The extraordinary genius of one man, Shakespeare, should not deceive us into thinking that Tudor society, as a whole, was a great European centre of high culture. In the arts of painting, architecture and music England lagged behind. In the fields of scholarship, scientific inquiry, religious vitality, reform and debate, Englishmen followed where others led. In the fields of exploration and exploitation – for good or ill – of distant parts of the globe, Englishmen, as in so much else, were piratical parasites, living off the achievements of others. Not until the mid-seventeenth century did what happened in England – Shakespeare apart – matter much to anyone else in the world. In part, of course, this was because England was a small country, but in part it may also be because it was a rather cosy one. There were no rival courts here, no competing towns, nothing to match the creative tensions which existed in more fragmented societies, notably the Low Countries, Germany, Spain and Italy. By comparison with the continent, there were few causes of tension in sixteenth-century England and fewer still in the fifteenth century. Those that there were were short-lived ones. Even during the period of the Wars of the Roses most Englishmen contrived to live in characteristically comfortable but unadventurous fashion.

BIBLIOGRAPHICAL GUIDE

This book is based chiefly on chronicles, letters, manifestos and reports written by heralds or by envoys, in other words on literary rather than administrative evidence. With rare exceptions I have used record evidence only where it has already been cited by twentieth-century historians. But since, in contrast to wars fought against foreign enemies, civil wars left relatively little trace in the records of government, to attempt to use them systematically would have meant a great deal of effort and many years' work for, comparatively speaking, a small return.

Abbreviations
EHR   English Historical Review
BIHR   Bulletin of the Institute of Historical Research
C.S.   Camden Society

The major study of the narrative sources remains C. L. Kingsford, *English Historical Literature in the Fifteenth Century* (1913). There is also an excellent brief guide in Charles Ross, *Edward IV*, Appendix I (1974). For some general comments see D. Hay, 'History and Historians in France and England during the 15th Century', BIHR, 35 (1962).

Narrative and literary sources
'Annales rerum Anglicarum' (anonymously written by an author whom I have called the Neville Annalist) in ed. J. Stevenson, *Letters and Papers Illustrative of the Wars of the English in France during the reign of Henry VI*, vol. 2, pt. ii, pp. 756–92, R[olls] S[series] (1864). There is a useful, though not entirely accurate description of this work in K. B. McFarlane, 'William Worcester: A Preliminary Survey' in ed. J. Conway Davies, *Studies presented to Sir Hilary Jenkinson* (1957).
'Bales Chronicle' in ed. R. Flenley, *Six Town Chronicles of England* (1911).
'Brief Latin Chronicle' (probably written by a churchman from the south of England) in ed. J. Gairdner, *Three Fifteenth Century Chronicles*, C.S. (1880).
Calendar of State Papers and Manuscripts existing in the Archives and Collections of Milan, I, ed. A. B. Hinds (1913).

Chronicle of the Rebellion in Lincolnshire 1470, ed. J. G. Nichols, C.S. (1847).
Philippe de Commynes, *Memoirs. The Reign of Louis XI, 1461–1483*. Translated with an introduction by Michael Jones (1972).
'The Croyland Chronicle': Historiae Croylandensis Continuatio in ed. W. Fulman, *Rerum Anglicarum Scriptores Veterum*, pp. 449–592 (1684). See J. G. Edwards, 'The second continuation of the Crowland Chronicle; was it written in ten days?' *BIHR* 39 (1966).
An English Chronicle of the reigns of Richard II, Henry IV, Henry V and Henry VI written before the year 1471, ed. J. S. Davies, C.S. (1856).
The Great Chronicle of London, ed. A. H. Thomas and I. D. Thornley (1938).
'Gregory's Chronicle' in ed. J. Gairdner, *The Historical Collections of a London Citizen*, C.S. (1876). See J. A. F. Thomson, 'The Continuation of "Gregory's Chronicle" – a possible author?' *The British Museum Quarterly*, 36 (1971–2).
Historie of the Arrivall of King Edward IV, ed. J. Bruce, C.S. (1838). See J. A. F. Thomson, ' "The Arrivall of Edward IV" – the Development of the Text', *Speculum*, 46 (1971).
Dominic Mancini, *The Usurpation of Richard III*, ed. and translated by C. A. J. Armstrong (1969).
Sir Thomas More, 'Richard III' in ed. R. S. Sylvester, *Complete Works of Sir Thomas More*, vol. II (1963).
Paston Letters and Papers of the Fifteenth Century, ed. N. Davis.
Paston Letters 1422–1509, ed. J. Gairdner, 6 vols. (1904).
Plumpton Correspondence, ed. T. Stapledon, C.S. (1839). See J. Taylor, 'The Plumpton Letters 1416–1522', *Northern History* 10 (1975).
Six Town Chronicles of England, ed. R. Flenley (1911).
Three Fifteenth Century Chronicles, ed. J. Gairdner, C.S. (1880).
Polydore Vergil, *Three Books of Polydore Vergil's English History*, ed. H. Ellis, C.S. (1844).
The Anglica Historia 1485–1537, ed. D. Hay, C.S. (1950). See D. Hay, *Polydore Vergil: Renaissance Historian and Man of Letters* (1952) and H. A. Kelly, 'English Kings and the Fear of Sorcery', *Medieval Studies*, 39 (1977).
John Warkworth, *A Chronicle of the First Thirteen Years of the Reign of King Edward IV*, ed. J. O. Halliwell, C.S. (1839). See J. R. Lander, *Crown and Nobility*, pp. 259–61.
Jean de Waurin, *Recueil des croniques*, ed. W. and E. Hardy, Vol. 5, R.S., (1891).
John Whethamstede, *Registrum Abbatis Johannis Whethamstede*, ed. H. T. Riley, R.S. (1872–3).

Secondary works

There are two excellent modern studies of the Wars of the Roses:
J. R. Lander, *The Wars of the Roses* (1965). With extensive quotations from original sources.

C. Ross, *The Wars of the Roses. A Concise History* (1976). With fine illustrations.
For a brief interpretation of the subject, now almost a classic, see K. B.
McFarlane, 'The Wars of the Roses', *Proceedings of the British Academy*, 50
(1964).

Chapter One

On Shakespeare's view of fifteenth-century politics see C. L. Kingsford,
Prejudice and Promise in Fifteenth Century England (1925); E. M. W. Tillyard,
Shakespeare's History Plays (1944); G. B. Churchill, *Richard III up to Shakespeare*
(1900).

On the rate of extinction of noble families see K. B. McFarlane, *The Nobility
of Later Medieval England*, pp. 172–6 (1973). For a cautionary note, T. B. Pugh,
'The magnates, knights and gentry' in ed. S. B. Chrimes, C. D. Ross and R. A.
Griffiths, *Fifteenth-Century England* (1972); also M. Hicks, 'Descent, Partition
and Extinction: the Warwick Inheritance', *BIHR* 52 (1979). On the other
hand there is some related evidence which suggests that the landowning class
was doing rather better in the second half of the fifteenth century than in the
previous hundred years (since the Black Death), T. H. Hollingsworth, *Historical Demography*, pp. 378–9 (1969). For a recent case-study of one member of
this class, see C. Richmond, *John Hopton* (1981).

On language and literacy in fifteenth-century England see B. Cottle, *The
Triumph of English 1350–1400*; V. J. Scattergood, *Politics and Poetry in the Fifteenth
Century*; H. Suggett, 'The Use of French in England in the Later Middle Ages',
Transactions of the Royal Historical Society 28 (1946); J. H. Fisher, 'Chancery and
the emergence of standard written English in the fifteenth century', *Speculum* 52
(1977); N. Orme, *English Schools in the Middle Ages* (1973); S. L. Thrupp, *The
Merchant Class of Medieval London* (1948); and, in general, F. R. H. Du Boulay,
An Age of Ambition, English Society in the Late Middle Ages (1970).

On printing and the printed book: D. M. Stuart 'William Caxton' in ed.
C. M. D. Crowder, *English Society and Government in the Fifteenth Century* (1967);
H. S. Bennett, *English Books and Readers 1475–1557* (1952); R. Hirsch, *Printing,
Selling and Reading 1450–1550* (1967).

For a 'positive' view of the fifteenth-century economy see A. R. Bridbury,
Economic Growth: England in the Late Middle Ages (1962); note also the well-
balanced conclusion to J. L. Bolton, *The Medieval English Economy 1150–1500*
(1980). See J. R. Lander, *The Wars of the Roses*, pp. 20–1, reprinted in J. R.
Lander, *Crown and Nobility*, p. 62, for the statement that 'active campaigning'
lasted only twelve or thirteen weeks, and W. H. Dunham, *Lord Hastings'
Indentured Retainers 1461–1483*, pp. 24–5 (1955) for the calculation about 'actual
fighting'.

Chapter Two

For a wide-ranging comparative approach see J. P. Cooper, 'Differences
between English and continental governments in the early seventeenth cen-

tury' in ed. J. S. Bromley and E. H. Kossman, *Britain and the Netherlands* (1960).

On town fortifications see H. Turner, *Town Defences in England and Wales 900–1500* (1970) and, for the contrast with France, P. Contamine, 'Les fortifications urbaines en France à la fin du Moyen Age: aspects financiers et économiques', *Revue Historique*, 260 (1978).

On guns: R. Coltman Clepham, 'The ordnance of the 14th and 15th centuries', *The Archaeological Journal*, 68 (1911); T. F. Tout, 'Firearms in England in the 14th century', EHR 26 (1911); O. F. C. Hogg, *The Royal Arsenal*, 2 vols, 1963.

M. G. A. Vale, 'New Techniques and Old Ideals: the Impact of Artillery on War and Chivalry at the end of the Hundred Years War' in ed. C. T. Allmand, *War, Literature and Politics in the Late Middle Ages* (1976). For the impact of guns on architecture see J. R. Hale, 'The Early Development of the Bastion: an Italian Chronology *c.* 1450 – *c.* 1534' in ed. J. R. Hale, R. Highfield and B. Smalley, *Europe in the Late Middle Ages* (1965); B. H. O'Neil, *Castles and Cannon* (1960).

On continental warfare in the fifteenth century see the important study by P. Contamine, *Guerre, État et Société à la fin du Moyen Age. Études sur les armées des rois de France* (1972) as well as his general survey, *La Guerre au Moyen Age* (1980). There is much that is useful in R. Vaughan's biographies of the fifteenth-century Burgundian dukes, *John the Fearless* (1966), *Philip the Good* (1970) and, in particular, *Charles the Bold* (1973). Also helpful is R. Vaughan, *Valois Burgundy* (1975). For another comparison see M. Mallett, *Mercenaries and their Masters. Warfare in Renaissance Italy* (1974).

For the impact of war on society, C. T. Allmand, 'The War and the Non-combatant' in ed. K. Fowler, *The Hundred Years War* (1971).

On the north see R. L. Storey, 'The North of England' in Chrimes, Ross and Griffiths, *Fifteenth-Century England*; R. L. Storey, 'The Wardens of the Marches of England towards Scotland 1377–1489', *EHR* 72 (1957); *Memoirs of a Renaissance Pope. The Commentaries of Pius II. An Abridgement*, ed. L. C. Gabel, translated by F. A. Gragg (1959).

Chapter Three

On the recruitment and composition of armies: J. R. Lander, 'The Hundred Years' War and Edward IV's 1475 Campaign in France' in *Crown and Nobility*; C. Rawcliffe, *The Staffords, Earls of Stafford and Dukes of Buckingham 1394–1521* (1978); W. H. Dunham, *Lord Hastings' Indentured Retainers 1461–1483* (1955); W. I. Haward, 'Economic Aspects of the Wars of the Roses in East Anglia', *EHR*, 41 (1926). The material on Coventry's contribution is taken from ed. M. D. Harris, *The Coventry Leet Book* (1907–13).

On the fifteenth-century literature of war: ed. A. T. Byles, *The Book of Fayttes of Armes and of Chyvalrye* translated and printed by William Caxton from the French original by Christine de Pisan (1937); D. Bornstein, 'Military Manuals in 15th century England', *Medieval Studies* 37 (1975); ed. R. Dybosky and Z. Arend, *Knyghthode and Bataile. A XVth Century Verse Paraphrase of Flavius Vegetius Renatus' Treatise 'De Re Militari'* (1935). There is a partial translation of Vegetius into modern English in ed. T. R. Phillips, *Roots of Strategy* (1943).

On numbers see A. E. Prince, 'The Strength of English Armies in the Reign of Edward III', *EHR* 46 (1931); J. H. Ramsay, 'The Strength of English Armies in the Middle Ages', *EHR* 29 (1914); G. Perjés, 'Army Provisioning, Logistics and Strategy in the second half of the 17th century', *Acta Historica* 16 (1970).

On Edward IV's planned Scottish campaign of 1481 I have had the benefit of reading an unprinted study by D. Cook, *The Capture of Berwick on Tweed and its consolidation under English Rule 1480–1483*.

Chapter Four

On Henry VI there is now the recent biography B. Wolffe, *Henry VI* (1981). Unfortunately this appeared too late for me to use and I relied instead on B. P. Wolffe, 'The Personal Rule of Henry VI' in ed. S. B. Chrimes, C. D. Ross and R. A. Griffiths, *Fifteenth-Century England* (1972). The muddle of his foreign policy is well illustrated by M. H. Keen and M. J. Daniel, 'English Diplomacy and the Sack of Fougères in 1449', *History* 59 (1974). For the king's religious reputation see ed. M. R. James, *Henry the Sixth: A reprint of John Blacman's Memoir* (1919) and Cardinal Gasquet, *The Religious Life of King Henry VI*. J. J. Bagley, *Margaret of Anjou* remains the only reasonable biography of this formidable lady.

A full-scale study of Cade's rebellion is badly needed. In the meantime there is a useful Historical Association pamphlet, H. M. Lyle, *The Rebellion of Jack Cade 1450* (1950).

On the breakdown of the Lancastrian regime in the 1450s R. L. Storey, *The End of the House of Lancaster* (1966) is invaluable.

Chapter Five

On Richard of York's political and financial problems see chapters 4 and 6 of R. L. Storey, *The End of the House of Lancaster* (1966) and chapter 3 of K. B. McFarlane, *The Nobility of Later Medieval England* (1973). An important assessment of his plans is to be found in R. A. Griffiths, 'Duke Richard of York's intentions in 1450 and the origins of the Wars of the Roses', *Journal of Medieval History*, 1 (1975).

Chapter Six

The Neville–Percy feud is best studied in R. A. Griffiths, 'Local Rivalries and National Politics: the Percies, the Nevilles and the Duke of Exeter 1452–1455', *Speculum* 42 (1968). See also J. R. Lander, 'Marriage and Politics in the fifteenth century: the Nevilles and the Wydevilles' in Lander, *Crown and Nobility*. By far the best study of any of the battles is C. A. J. Armstrong, 'Politics and the Battle of St Albans', *BIHR* 33 (1960).

Chapter Seven

On the Courtenay–Bonville dispute see R. L. Storey, *The End of the House of Lancaster*, chapters 5 and 13. I have taken the account of Sir Nicholas Radford's murder from J. R. Lander, *The Wars of the Roses*, pp. 82–5. See also J. R. Lander, 'Henry VI and the duke of York's second protectorate 1455–6' in Lander, *Crown and Nobility*.

The vital importance of Calais was first emphasized by G. L. Harriss, 'The Struggle for Calais: an Aspect of the Rivalry between Lancaster and York', *EHR*, 75 (1960). A similar study of Calais's role in the next thirty years is much needed.

Chapter Eight

The aristocracy's involvement in these tumultuous events has been thoughtfully analysed in C. Richmond, 'The Nobility and the Wars of the Roses 1459–61', *Nottingham Medieval Studies*, 21 (1977). Of the battles, only Northampton has been seriously studied, R. I. Jack, 'A quincentenary: the battle of Northampton, July 10th 1460', *Northamptonshire Past and Present*, 2 (1960).

The significance of the Yorkist dynastic claim has been freshly evaluated by R. A. Griffiths, 'The Sense of Dynasty in the Reign of Henry VI' in ed. C. Ross, *Patronage, Pedigree and Power in Later Medieval England* (1979).

Chapter Nine

The war in the north was narrated by D. Charlesworth in two articles, 'The Battle of Hexham 1464', *Archaeologia Aeliana*, 4th series, 30 (1952) and 'Northumberland in the early years of Edward IV', *ibid.*, 31 (1953). For the events at New Buckenham in 1461 see *Calendar of Patent Rolls 1461–7*, p. 67.

On all Scottish affairs in this period the best general guide is R. Nicholson, *Scotland. The Later Middle Ages* (1974).

Chapter Ten

P. M. Kendall, *Warwick the Kingmaker* (1957) is an admirably vivid and imaginative biography of the earl. But, like all Kendall's work, it contains too many anachronistic judgments and must be used with caution. Very different, and very much better, is C. Ross, *Edward IV* (1974).

On Edward's political personality see also J. R. Lander, 'Edward IV: the modern legend and a revision' in *Crown and Nobility*; and the important, all too brief study by D. A. L. Morgan, 'The King's Affinity in the Polity of Yorkist England', *Transactions of the Royal Historical Society*, 23 (1973).

On the Woodvilles see J. R. Lander, 'Marriage and Politics in the fifteenth century' in *Crown and Nobility*, and M. Hicks, 'The Changing Role of the Wydevilles in Yorkist Politics to 1483' in ed. C. Ross, *Patronage, Pedigree and Power*. In the same volume on Robin of Redesdale see A. J. Pollard, 'The

Richmondshire Community of Gentry during the Wars of the Roses'. R. L. Storey has looked at the background to the Lincolnshire rising in 'Lincolnshire and the Wars of the Roses', *Nottingham Medieval Studies*, 14 (1970).

Chapter Eleven
Kendall on Warwick can be complemented by P. M. Kendall, *Louis XI* (1971), a book in similar vein.

For the Burgundian dimension, R. Vaughan, *Charles the Bold* (1973) and A. R. Myers, 'The Outbreak of War between England and Burgundy in February 1471', *BIHR*, 33 (1960).

On naval blockades and the whole problem of warfare at sea, C. F. Richmond, 'English Naval Power in the fifteenth century', *History*, 52 (1967). For the Neville revolt in the north see A. J. Pollard, 'Lord FitzHugh's Rising in 1470', *BIHR*, 52 (1979).

Chapter Twelve
Useful for the topography of Tewkesbury is J. D. Blyth, 'The Battle of Tewkesbury', *Transactions of the Bristol and Gloucestershire Archaeological Society*, 80 (1961), but the only good study of any of the campaigns of 1471 is C. F. Richmond, 'Fauconberg's Kentish Rising of May 1471', *EHR*, 85 (1970).

Chapter Thirteen
P. M. Kendall, *Richard the Third* (1955) takes an over-indulgent view of its hero. There is much to be said for the older view of J. Gairdner, *The Life and Reign of Richard III* (1878). See also A. Hanham, *Richard III and his early Historians 1483–1585* (1975). The north–south problem in Richard's reign is emphasized by A. J. Pollard, 'The Tyranny of Richard III', *Journal of Medieval History*, 3 (1977).

For the debate about the date of Hasting's death see A. Hanham, 'Richard III, Lord Hastings and the historians', *EHR*, 87 (1972); B. P. Wolffe, 'When and why did Hastings lose his head?', *EHR*, 89 (1974); A. Hanham, 'Hastings Redivivus', *EHR*, 90 (1975) and, though it appeared too late for me to use, C. H. D. Coleman, 'The execution of Hastings: a neglected source', *BIHR*, 53 (1980).

On the revolt of 1483 see A. E. Conway, 'The Maidstone Sector of Buckingham's Rebellion', *Archaeologia Cantiana*, 37 (1925).

Chapter Fourteen
The standard biography is now S. B. Chrimes, *Henry VII* (1972), though it is very brief on the early years, as is also R. L. Storey, *The Reign of Henry VII* (1968).

For the crucial attitude of the earl of Northumberland see M. A. Hicks, 'Dynastic Change and Northern Society: the career of the fourth earl of

Northumberland', *Northern History*, 14 (1978). See A. Goodman and A. Mackay, 'A Castilian Report on English Affairs 1486', *EHR*, 88 (1973) for rumours of Bosworth abroad. The most realistic assessment of the sources for Bosworth is still J. Gairdner, 'The Battle of Bosworth', *Archaeologia*, 55 (1897).

For the Lovell–Stafford revolt see C. H. Williams, 'The Rebellion of Humphrey Stafford in 1486', *EHR*, 43 (1928). The account of Henry vii's movements up to Stoke is based on the proclamation and herald's report printed in R. Brooke, *Visits to Fields of Battle in England*, Appendix iv (1857).

INDEX

Abergavenny, Lord, 112
Accord, Act of (1460),
  117–18
Alberti, Leon Battista, 25
Alkmaar, 185
Alnwick castle, 136, 140–2,
  144–7, 153–4
Angus, earl of, 144–5
Anjou, 56–8
Anjou, Margaret of, see
  Margaret of Anjou, queen
  of England
Annals of England (Stow,
  1580), 7
archers: king's bodyguard of,
  29; Dominic Mancini
  describes, 35–6, 41;
  proportion of, to
  men-at-arms, 36; cavalry
  vulnerable to, 37; high
  cost-effectiveness of, 40–1;
  with men-at-arms,
  interdependent, 41;
  unsupported, slaughtered
  at Brouwershaven (1426),
  42; for protection of
  victuallers, 47; at 1st St
  Albans, 88–9; at Barnet,
  197
armies: no standing armies in
  England, 15; high cost of,
  to Burgundy & France,
  28–9; recruitment of, 32–5;
  composition of, 36; size of,
  in Wars of Roses, 42–4
armour: noted by Dominic
  Mancini (archers), 35–6; of
  men-at-arms, 37–8; special
  weapons to crush, 37–8
Arnolfini, Michele, 130
artillery: well established by
  Wars of Roses, 18;
  manufacture of iron &
  bronze, 19; projectiles,
  powder charges, rate of
  fire, ranges, 19–20; effect
  of, on fortifications, 24;
  expenditure on, 25–7;
  minor role in Wars of
  Roses, 27; Lancastrian,
  silenced by rain at

Northampton, 113; at
  Barnet, 197; and
  Fauconberg revolt, 210–12;
  types bombards, 18–19,
  153, 210; crapaudeaux, 18;
  culverins, 18–19; orgues,
  ribaudequins, 18;
  serpentines, 18, 26–7
Arundel, earl of (1461), 124,
  126, 165, 167
Arundel, Sir John (1471), 202
Astley, Sir John, 146, 154
Audley, Lord (i), 103–4, 107;
  (ii), 107, 110, 161
Ayscough, William, bishop of
  Salisbury, 59, 64

baggage trains, 45–7
Bale, Robert, 26
Balloch, Donald, 141
Bamburgh Castle, 136,
  141–2, 144–7, 149–50, 151,
  153
Bannister, Ralph, 230
Barnet, b. of (April 1471), 19,
  38, 196–7
Baynard's Castle, 167, 210
Beauchamp, Anne, 78
Beauchamp, Sir Richard, 204
Beaufort family, 68, 71
Beaufort, Edmund, see
  Somerset, dukes of
Beaufort, John, 207
Beaufort, Henry, see
  Somerset, dukes of
Beaufort, Joan, 77
Beaufort, Lady Margaret,
  227, 229
Beaumont, Lord, 113–14,
  192, 196, 215
Bedford, George Neville,
  duke of, 166, 216
Bedford, John, duke of, 71
Bellingham, Sir Henry, 151
Berkeley, Thomas, Lord, 20
Berkeley, Sir William, 226,
  233
Berkhamsted Castle, 74
Berners, Lord, 126
Berwick, 20, 22, 30, 137
billmen, 40

Blackman, John, 53–6, 59
Blore Heath, b. of (Sept.
  1459), 46, 103–4
Blount, James, 234–5
Blunt, Sir William, 201
Bodiam Castle, 231
Bodrugan, Sir Henry, 215
Bonville, William, Lord, 46;
  71–2, 94–7, 126, 129
*Book of Fayttes of Armis and of
  Chyvalrye*, 39
Bordeaux, 23, 72, 74
Borselen, Henrik van, 180
Bosworth, b. of (Aug. 1485),
  35, 242–6
boulevards, 22–3
Bourchier, Sir Henry, 201
Bourchier, Henry, Viscount
  see Essex, earl of
Bourchier, Thomas,
  Archbishop see Canterbury,
  Thomas Bourchier,
  archbishop of
Brackenbury, Sir Robert,
  225, 232
Brampton, Edward, 26
Brancepeth Castle, 138, 164
Brecon Castle, 227
Brézé, Pierre de, 18, 138,
  141–2, 145
Brittany, 61, 156, 159,
  214–15, 227, 230
Brittany, Francis, duke of,
  215, 231, 233
Brown, Sir George, 226
Brouwershaven, b. of (1426),
  42
Brustem, b. of (1467), 46
Buckingham, Humphrey
  Stafford, duke of, 32–3,
  85–6, 86, 88–90, 100, 102,
  113, 114
Buckingham, Henry Stafford,
  2nd duke of, 219–25,
  227–32
bulwarks, 22–3
Burgh, Sir Thomas, 166–7
Burgh, William, 182
Burgundy: standing army of,
  15, 28; ruin of, caused by
  duke's death in battle, 40;

English archers in army of, 40–1; strategy of (1430), 48; Warwick negotiates assistance from, 101, 107; French/English negotiations with, isolate Scotland, 148–9, 156; peace with France, 159; navy of, aids Edward IV, 179–81, 183; no official aid for exiled Edward IV (1470), 187
Burley, William, 13–14
Bywell Castle, 152–3

Cabot, John, 11
Cade, Jack, revolt of (1450), 32, 64, 67–9, 73
Caen, 16–17
Caister Castle, 167
Calais: fortifications of, 23; garrison of, 29; (1445), 56; Somerset captain of, 71; French besiege, 72; Warwick captain of, 92; importance, cost of, to York, 97–9; and Warwick's pirate raids (1458), 101; (1459–60), 102, 107–8, 115–16; Queen Margaret agrees to cede, 141; and Warwick's revolt (1469), 162–3; Warwick repelled from (1470), 177; and Fauconberg revolt (1471), 208–9, 212–13; (1473), 215; (1484), 234–5
caltrap, use of, 125
Cambridge, Richard, earl of, 65
Canterbury; West gate defences of, 17; gunports at, 21; Yorkists take (1460), 110–11; (1471), 209
Canterbury, Thomas Bourchier, archbishop of, 223
Carlisle, 22, 30, 137
Carlisle, William Barrow, bishop of, 5, 84, 90
Carreg Cennan Castle, 139–40
Casenove, Guillaume de, 237
Castillon, 74–5
castles, 1, 23–4, 36, 37 *and see* individual castles
Caxton, William, 9, 39
Chamberlain, William, 138
Charles the Impetuous, duke of Burgundy: and Strasbourg (1475–6), 17; artillery tactics of (1465), 20, 25; untrained cavalry of, at Montlhéry (1465),

36, 42; killed at Nancy (1477), 40; tactical use of archers (Brustem 1467), 41; Swiss defeat at Murtin (1476), 45; Somerset accompanies on campaign, 201
Charles VI, king of France, 51, 75
Charles VII, king of France, 29, 51–2, 56–61, 68, 98, 137, 138
Charles VIII, king of France, 234–5
Chaucer, Geoffrey, 8
Chester, Queen Margaret in, 100, 102, 116, 151
Cheyne, Sir John, 226, 233
Chronicle of the Rebellion in Lincolnshire, 169–71
Cirencester, 119, 203
Clarence, George, duke of: troops raised by (1475), 32, 158; heir presumptive, conspires with Warwick, 159, 161–2, 165–6; (1470), 167, 169–77, 183, 186–7; holds balance of power (1471), 193; *rapprochement* with Edward IV, 193–4; at Barnet, 196–7, 200; dies, 216
Clarence, Isabel Neville, duchess of, 159, 162, 175
Clarence, Lionel, duke of, 65
Clere, Edmund, 83
Clifford, John, Lord, 3–4, 118, 120, 126, 134
Clifford, Thomas, Lord, 73–4, 79, 84–5, 88–90, 111, 112
Columbus, Christopher, 11
Commynes, Philippe de: on light casualties in Wars of Roses, 1; on peaceful condition of England, 15–16, 24; on armies of Louis XI, 25; on English inadequacy in siege warfare, 27; on English readiness to give battle, 28; on burden of taxation in France, 29; on untrained cavalry (Montlhéry, 1465), 36; on archers, 40–2; Paris region able to maintain two large armies, 47; on successes of Louis XI, 49; on origins of Wars of Roses, 50; on Calais, 97; quoted, 181; on Edward IV, 182; on Barnet, 200
Complaint of the Commons of Kent (1450), 64

Constable, Sir Marmaduke, 232
Constitutional History of England (Stubbs), 11–12
Conyers, Sir John, 102, 161, 173, 175
Conyers, John, 181
Conyers, Thomas, 191
Conyers, Sir William, 161
Corfe Castle (1460), 118
Courtenay family, 71–2, 94–7, 172–3, 175
Courtenay, Edward, 226, 233
Courtenay, Sir Hugh (1471), 202
Cromwell, Ralph, Lord, 76–7, 82, 169, 201
crossbowmen, 40, 47
Crowmer, William, 63–4
Croy, Philippe de, 41
Croyland Abbey (1460–61), 122–3
Cumberland, 76–7, 152, 181

Dacre, Lord, 134, 138, 140–1
Dartford, 73, 81, 86, 88, 93
Daubeney, Sir Giles, 226, 233
De Re Militari (Vegetius), 20, 49
Debenham, Gilbert, 138
Denbigh Castle, 139–40
Devon, John Courtenay, earl of (1471), 195, 201, 207
Devon, Thomas Courtenay, earl of, 70–1, 71–2, 81, 85, 94–6, 97, 118, 126, 134
Devon, Humphrey Stafford, earl of, 158, 161, 162–3, 165–6, 172
Dictes and Sayings of the Philosophres, 9
Dinham, John, 105, 108, 110, 215, 225, 235
Doncaster, 154, 184, 186, 192
Donne, John, 151
Dorset, Thomas Woodville, marquis of, 218, 224, 226, 229, 233
Douglas, James, earl of, 141–2, 147, 149
Down, John, 172
Dryslwyn, b. of (March 1464), 151
Dudley, Lord, 103
Dunham, W. H., 14
Dunstable, 127, 129–30, 194
Dunstanburgh Castle, 136, 140, 142, 144–6, 153
Duras, Gaillard, Lord, 109, 177, 215
Durham, 77, 150, 152
Durham, Laurence Booth, bishop of, 100, 136, 138, 142

Dymmock, Sir Thomas, 166–7, 169–71

East Anglia, 138–9
Edgecote, b. of (July 1469), 41, 44, 163–5, 181
Edward III, king of England, 16, 65, 68, 98
Edward IV, king of England: 1, 26–7, 35, 104–5, 144–5, 148, 189–90; updates Calais fortifications, 23; composition of expeditionary army of (1475), 32, 36, 43; at Barnet (1471), 38; size of Towton army of, 42–3; size of army of (1471), 44; 1470 campaign of, 48; and Northampton battle (1460), 113–14; in Wales (1460–1), 119; first victory of (1461), 124, 132–5; proclaimed king, 130–1; enters York, 136; in north (1462), 142, 144; wins alignment with France, 148–9, 154; foreign policy of (1465–70), 156–7; marries Elizabeth Woodville, 157; abandons invasion of France, 156, 159–60; and Robin of Redesdale, 160–3; captured in Warwick revolt (1469), 164; and Lincolnshire rising (1470), 167–77; flight of, to Holland (1470), 184–6; builds up invasion fleet, 187–8; enters York, 191; reconciled with Clarence, 193–4; returns to London, 195; and Barnet campaign, 196–202; and Tewkesbury campaign, 202–7; and Fauconberg revolt (1471), 210–13; achievement, reign, sudden death of, 213–17
Edward V, king of England (b. 1470), 186, 216, 217–19, 224
Edward, Prince of Wales, 80–1, 99, 129; disinherited (1460), 117–18; betrothed to Anne Neville, 179; prospects for (1470), 186; lands in England, 201; killed at Tewkesbury, 207
Egremont, Thomas Percy, Lord, 76, 79, 82, 83, 100, 113–14

Elizabeth, Queen of England, 11
Elizabeth Woodville, Queen of England, 157, 186, 219–20, 223, 226, 235
Elizabeth of York, 233
Ely, John Morton, bishop of, 222, 227–8, 233–4
Empingham, b. of (1470), 170–1
England, fifteenth century: crucial social changes in (English language, printing, literacy), 8–9; high wages in, 11; no govt. censorship in, 8–11; and technological breakthroughs (printing, shipbuilding), 11; false image of chaos in, 13–14; most peaceful country in Europe, 15; few walled cities in, 16–18; no standing army in, 15, 29; and Scottish border defences, 30–1
Essex, Henry Bourchier, earl of, viscount, 92, 102, 112, 115, 126, 139, 165
Exeter, 94–6, 139, 202, 230–1
Exeter, Peter Courtenay, bishop of, 226, 228–9, 233
Exeter, Henry Holland, duke of: backs Percies (1454), 82–3; released, 100; replaced as admiral by Warwick (1457), 100; shuns sea battle with Warwick (1460), 109–10; supporters of, hanged at Tyburn (1460), 115; at 2nd St Albans (1461), 126, 132, 139–40; (1470), 186; (1471), 192–3; at Barnet (1471), 196

Fastolf, Sir John, 24
Fauconberg, Joan, 77
Fauconberg, Lord William, *see* Kent, earl of
Fauconberg, Thomas, 208–13
Faunt, Nicholas, 209
Ferrers, Sir Walter Devereux, Lord, 140
Feuerwekbuch (Kauder), 19
Fitzhugh, Sir Henry, 161
Fitzhugh, Lord, 79, 126, 181
Fitzhugh, Sir Richard, 225
Fitzwalter, Lord, 133
Fogge, Sir John, 111, 226
foraging, 47
Fortescue, Sir John, 15, 136, 148, 184, 207, 215, 234–5

fortification, 16–18, 17–18, 17–25, 97–8
Fotheringay Castle, 161
Fougères, sack of (1449), 61–2
Foxe, John, 7–8
France: standing army of, 15; walled cities of, 16–17; English vulnerability to raids from, 18, 23; English 'scorched earth' strategy in, 24–5; Henry VI king of, 51–2; negotiates for Maine & Anjou, 56–61; conquers Normandy, 61–2; and Calais, 97–9; raids Kent coast (1457), 100; Somerset in, 116; Queen Margaret and (1462), 141–2; Edward IV and, 156–7; and peace with Burgundy and Brittany, 159
Freeman, Agnes, 55
Fulford, Sir Baldwin, 108–9, 139

Gascony, 56, 71, 72–3, 74–5
Gate, Sir Geoffrey, 119, 163, 175, 186
Gaunt, John of, *see* Lancaster, John of Gaunt, duke of
Gigli, Carlo, 130
Gloucester, Richard, duke of *see* Richard III, king
Gloucester, Humphrey, duke of, 59–60, 60, 66, 69, 93
Golden Fleece, Order of, 28, 41
Gomez, Gutierre Diáz de, 16
Grafton's *Chronicle* (1569), 7
Grantham, 123, 167, 170, 172–3
Gray, Sir Walter, 176
Gregory, William, 125, 129–31, 148, 151, 157
Gregory's *Chronicle*: on size of Yorkist army at Towton, 42–3, 132; on b. of Blore Heath (1459), 103–4; on execution of Owen Tudor (1461), 124–5; on 2nd b. of St Albans (1461), 125–7, 129–31; on Towton battle (1461), 134–5; on Somerset's breach with Edward IV (1462–3), 149–50
Grey of Codnor, Lord, 126
Grey of Ruthin, Lord, *see* Kent, earl of
Grey, Sir John, 157
Grey, Sir Ralph, 141–2, 146, 151, 153
Grey, Sir Richard, 219

Greystoke, Lord, 126, 152
Gruthyse, Louis of, 185
Guildford, John, 226
Guînes (Calais), 97, 107–8,
  115–16, 235

Hall, Edward, 6, 124
Hammines Castle, 97, 215,
  234–5
hand-gunners, 40, 124–5, 197
harbingers, 44–5, 173
Harding, John, 184
Harlech Castle, 118, 139–40,
  146, 156, 159
Harrington, Sir James, 192
Harrington, Sir Thomas, 102,
  104, 120
Harveys, Philip, 139
Hastings, William, Lord, 33,
  139, 141, 148, 158, 165,
  167, 185, 190, 193, 196–7,
  218–19, 222–3
Hatton, Randolph, 25
Haute, Sir Richard, 226
Haynin, Jehan de, 46
Hedgely Moor, b. of (April
  1464), 151–2, 154
Henry IV, king of England:
  first king to write English,
  8; and Percy rebellion, 15,
  77; takes Berwick (1405),
  20; and defence of Scottish
  border, 30; York denounces
  as usurper (1460), 117
Henry V, king of England:
  captures Caen 16–17; on
  use of fire in war, 24;
  composition of army of
  (1415), 36, 43; dies with
  work unfinished (1422),
  51–2, 71
Henry VI, king of England
  and France: Shakespeare
  on, 4; artillery purchases of
  (1456–9), 26; attempts to
  recruit troops from
  Coventry (1455), 34;
  inheritance, minority,
  character of, 51–6; cedes
  Anjou & Maine, 56–61;
  and loss of Normandy,
  61–2; advisers of, lynched,
  62–4; humiliated by Cade
  revolt, 64; alienates
  Richard of York, 66–7;
  rejects York's demands,
  70–1; and Courtenay/
  Bonville feud, 71–2;
  breakdown of (1453), 74–5,
  79, 81; recovery of,
  disastrous 83–4; defeated,
  captured at St Albans
  (1455), 86–9; joins
  Margaret at Kenilworth

(1456), 100; and Blore
  Heath campaign (1459),
  102–3; presence of,
  demoralizes Yorkists at
  Ludford Bridge (1459),
  105; and Northampton
  battle (1460), 112–14;
  Yorkists escort to London
  (1460), 114; compromises
  with York, over succession
  (1460), 117; and 2nd b. of
  St Albans (1461), 127, 129;
  in north (1462), 142; last
  parting from Queen
  Margaret, 147; isolated by
  Yorkist diplomacy (1463),
  149; joined by Somerset,
  150; escapes from Bigwell
  (1464), 152–3; troops of,
  poorly paid, 154; captured,
  in Tower, 156; restored to
  throne (1470), 186; returns
  to Tower (1471), 195; at
  Barnet (1471), 196; and
  Fauconberg revolt (1471),
  210; death of, in Tower,
  213
Henry VII, king of England:
  and innocent image of
  Henry VI, 55; in Brittany,
  214–15; Buckingham's
  revolt in favour of, 227–8,
  230–2; prepares to invade
  England, 233–6; lands at
  Milford Haven, 237; march
  to Bosworth, 238–42;
  victor at Bosworth, 243–6;
  restores stability,
  prosperity in England,
  246–53
Henry VIII, king of England;
  as censor, 9; reign of,
  extolled by Tudor
  propaganda as golden age,
  11; coastal fortifications of,
  22; conventional use of
  Calais, for French wars, 97
heralds, role of, 86, 88, 153
Herbert, Sir Richard, 163
Herbert, Lord William, *see*
  Pembroke, Lord William
  Herbert, earl of
Heworth Moor, 33, 76–9, 83
Hexham, 151–2, 154–5
*Historie of the Arivall of King
  Edward IV*, 46, 189–93,
  197, 200–1
History of King Richard III
  (More), 4
Holland, 185
Holt, Denbighshire, 151
Holy Island, 142
Honfleur, 178–9
Horne, Robert, 111, 134

Hotspur, Lord Harry, 77
Howard, Lord John *see*
  Norfolk, John
Howard, duke of
Hundred Years War, 18, 23,
  24–5
Hungerford, Lord, 111, 115,
  145–6, 151–2
Hyde, Richard, 32

Ireland, 65–6, 68, 105–6,
  108–9

Jacquetta of Luxembourg,
  duchess of Bedford, 157
James II, king of Scotland, 20,
  137, 140
James III, king of Scotland,
  147
John the Fearless, duke of
  Burgundy, 44
Joseph, William, 92
Judde, John, 26

Kauder, Konrad, 19
Katherine, Queen of
  England, 51, 124
Kemp, Cardinal, chancellor,
  81
Kendal, earl of, 111
Kenilworth, 26
Kent, 32–3, 62–3, 64, 73,
  100, 139, 162, 207–13,
  228–9
Kent, William Neville, Lord
  Fauconberg, earl of, 85;
  commands Calais garrison
  (1459), 102; takes
  Sandwich (1460), 110; and
  Northampton battle
  (1460), 113–14; at 2nd St
  Albans (1461), 126; at
  Alnwick (1462), 142, 208
Kent, Lord Grey of Ruthin,
  earl of, 113–14, 126
King, Oliver, 222
Knyvet, John, 138
Knyvet, William, 138
Kyriel, Sir Thomas, 129

Lancaster, house of: and
  usurpation of (1399), 2, 5;
  descent of, 68; close
  association of, with
  Nevilles, 77; avenges Blore
  Heath at Ludford Bridge
  (1459), 104–5; diplomatic
  nadir & recovery of
  (1463–4), 149–51;
  rapprochement with Warwick,
  159; restored (1470),
  179–88; extinction of, with
  d. of Prince of Wales at
  Tewkesbury, 207

Lancaster, John of Gaunt, duke of, 68, 77
Lande, Sir Thomas de la, 171
Langley, Prince Edmund, grandfather of Richard of York, 65
Lannoy, Jean de, 151
Latimer, Lord, 161
Le Mans, 60–1, 66
Leicester, 84–5, 170, 193, 229–30
Lincolnshire rising (1470), 166–7, *168*, 169
Livre des faiz darmes (Christine de Pisan), 39
logistics, 43–8
Lollards, 7–8
London: and Cade's revolt (1450), 32, 64; Margaret of Anjou crowned in, 58; Richard of York returns to (1450), 68–9; York & Nevilles leave (1455), 84; scant support for Somerset in, 85; tensions in (1455), 93; and (1458) Loveday, 101; Yorkists march on (1460), 111–12; Henry VI escorted to, 114; backs Yorkists, after 2nd St Albans battle, 129–30; riots in (1469), 164; Warwick supporters loot in (1470), 186; Edward IV re-enters (1471), 195–6; and Fauconberg rising (1471), 208–13; and usurpation of Richard III (1483), 218–19, 221–5
Louis XI, king of France: tactics of, 24–5; vast expenditure of, 29; Commynes on military success of, 49; accession of, 138; and Margaret of Anjou, 141–2; renounces Lancastrians (1463), 148–9; at peace with Burgundy and Brittany, 159; Warwick appeals to (1470), 178–9; ambitions of, against Burgundy, 179–80, 187; bids for control of Tudor exiles, 214
Lound, Peter, 83
Lovell, Lord, 111, 225
Lucy, Sir William, 114
Ludford Bridge, 40, 104–5
Ludlow, 74, 102–4, 105
Lufwyk, John, 26

Macfarlane, K. B., 5–6, 14
Maine, 56–8, 61

Mancini, Dominic, 35–7, 222–3
March, Edward, earl of *see* Edward IV, king
marches, 29–30, 78
Margaret of Anjou, Queen of England: Shakespeare on, 4; and strengthening of royal artillery (1456–9), 26; Henry VI seeks to please, by ceding Maine & Anjou, 57–61; dominates Henry VI, 59; pregnancy of (1453), 74–5; mother of Prince Edward, opposes York, 80–1; prepares to challenge Yorkists (1456), 99–100; new appointments of (1456–7), 100; seeks Warwick's resignation, 101–2; triumphs at Ludford Bridge, 103–5; support for, after Northampton battle, 118–19; after Wakefield battle, 122; beats Warwick at 2nd St Albans (1461), 125–7; fails to take London, 129; army of, beaten at Towton (1461), 132–5; fights on in north, 136–8; in France (1462), 141; invades Northumbria (1463), 147; abandoned by France, Burgundy, Scotland (1463), 149; *rapprochement* with Warwick, 179; sails for England, 195; lands, 201; and Tewkesbury campaign, 202–7; captured, 207
Mary of Guelders, queen of Scotland, 137, 141, 147
men-at-arms: strengths & weaknesses of, in training & combat, 36–8; interdependent with archers, 41; maintenance of, on campaign, 43–4; for protection of victuallers, 47
Merbury, Nicholas, 26
Middleham, 161, 164, 181
Midlands, 102–3, 116, 122, 161, 191–4
Moleyns, Adam, bishop, 62, 66
Mons Meg, 18
Montagu, Alice, 77
Montagu, John Neville, marquis of, 79, 83; (1459), 102; at 2nd St Albans (1461), 126; spared, 129; released, 136; relieves Carlisle, 138; at Bamburgh

(1462), 142; warden of east March, 147; beats Lancastrians at Hedgley Moor (1464), 151–2; earl of Northumberland, 153–5; (1469), 165–6; (1470), 175, 182; declares for Henry VI (1470), 185, 187; (1471), 191–3; at Barnet (1471), 196; killed, 200–1
Montlhéry, battle of (1465), 36, 38, 42, 201
More, Sir Thomas, 4–5, 8, 9–10, 222
Mortimer family, 65, 68
Mortimer, Anne, mother of Richard of York, 65
Mortimer's Cross, b. of (Feb. 1461), 124
Morton, John, *see* Ely, John Morton, bishop of
Mountfort, Sir Osbert, 110
Mountjoy, Lord, 156, 165, 173, 235
murage, *see* taxation
Murten, battle of (1476), 45

Naworth Castle, 140–1
Negra, Raffaelo de, 58
Neuss, siege of (1475), 41
Neville family: and defence of northern marches, 30; indicts Percy followers (1454), 33; denies Richard of York armed support (1452), 73; feud of, with Percies, and Heworth Moor 'battle' (1453), 76–9; close association of, with house of Lancaster, 77; Richard of York a natural ally for, 79; beats Percies at Stamford Bridge (1454), 83; threat to, from Queen Margaret, 99; northern estates of, devastated (1460), 118; alienated by Woodville ascendancy, 158; 1470 risings by, in Northumberland, 182
Neville, Anne, 179
Neville, Cecily, 79
Neville, George, *see* (i) Bedford, George Neville, duke of; (ii) Clarence, George, duke of; (iii) York, George Neville, archbishop of
Neville, Sir Henry, 161
Neville, Sir Humphrey, 151, 153–4, 164–5
Neville, Sir John, *see* Montagu, John Neville, marquis of

Neville, Katherine, *see*
Norfolk, Katherine,
duchess of
Neville, Ralph, *see*
Westmorland, earls of
Neville, Sir Thomas, 76, 79,
83, 102, 119
Newark, 161, 173, 192
New Buckenham Castle, 138
Newcastle, 45, 142, 147, 150,
151–2
Newgate, 83, 100
Norfolk, John Howard, duke
of, 34, 177, 180–1, 224,
228, 240–1
Norfolk, John Mowbray,
duke of, supports Richard
of York (1450), 70; joins
Yorkists (1460), 112;
(1461), 124; at 2nd St
Albans (1461), 126;
supports Edward IV
(1461), 131–2; in Wales
(1464), 151; (1470), 173
Norfolk, Katherine Neville,
duchess of, 158
Norham Castle, 147, 151
Normandy, 56, 61–2, 68,
183
Norris, Sir William, 226
Northampton, 150, 163–4,
194, 219
Northampton, b. of (July
1460), 112–15, 116, 118,
126
Northumberland: Yorkist
successes in (1461–2),
140–1, 144–5; Lancastrians
recover (1463), 146–7;
Lancastrians rally in
(1464), 151–2; (1470),
173
Northumberland, Henry
Percy, 2nd earl (1453), 76,
79, 84–5, 89–90
Northumberland, Henry
Percy, 3rd earl, 100, 118,
120, 126, 134
Northumberland, John
Neville, earl of, *see*
Montagu, John Neville,
marquis of
Northumberland, Henry
Percy, 4th earl: demands
for reinstatement of (1469),
160; Edward IV reinstates,
165–6, 167, 175, 182;
(1471), 191–2, 208; (1483),
221, 224–5, 241–3
Nottingham (1459), 102;
(1469), 162; (1471), 192;
(1484–5), 236, 238
Nottingham, Lord Berkely,
earl of, 224

Ogle, Lord Robert, 89, 142
Oldhall, Sir William, 68,
70–2
Oxford, John de Vere, earl of:
(1469), 162; (1470), 176;
183; (1471), 192–3; at
Barnet (1471), 38, 196;
(1473), 213, 215; (1484), 234

Paris, 24, 47–8
parliament: commons indict
earl of Suffolk (1450), 62;
supports Richard of York,
70–1; appoints York
protector (1454), 80–2;
grants Yorkists pardon
(1455), 92–3; Coventry
(1459), attaints Yorkists,
106; speaker Tresham
murdered, 113; summoned
by Yorkists, 115; first, of
Edward IV, 139; grants
defence funds to Edward
IV, 147–8; York, postponed
(1464), 150
Parr, Katherine, Queen of
England, 173
Parr, Sir Thomas, 102, 120
Parr, Sir William, 173, 192
Paston, John, 201
Paston, Sir John, 201
Paston letters: create
distorted image of
lawlessness, 13; quoted
(John P., 1450), 63, 69–70;
(1455), 83, 93; (1461), 34;
(1462), 144; (1469), 165–6;
(Margaret P., 1462), 139
pavise, use of, at 2nd St
Albans, 125
Pembroke Castle, 139–40,
214
Pembroke, Jasper Tudor, earl
of, supports Queen
Margaret (1460), 118;
(1461), 124, 139–40, 145;
rejected by Louis XI, 148;
ally of Warwick &
Margaret, 179, 181; returns
to Wales (1471), 183, 187;
in Brittany (1471), 214–15,
233
Pembroke, William Herbert,
earl of, 41, 139–40, 158–9,
161–3
Percy family: revolt of (Henry
IV), 15, 77; and defence of
northern marches, 30;
indicted by Nevilles, 33;
retainers of, 33; and
Heworth Moor 'battle'
(1453), 76–9; Richard of
York ousts from Yorkshire,
82–3; compensation for,

promised by Yorkists, 101;
supports Queen Margaret
(1460), 118–19; broken
after Towton, 136; support
for, in Yorkshire (1469),
160
Percy, Sir Ralph (1462), 140,
142, 146; (1464), 151–2
Percy, Sir Richard, 83
Percy, Sir Robert, 232
Philip, count of Flanders, 24
Philip the Good, duke of
Burgundy, 41, 46, 48,
141–2, 148–9
Pisan, Christine de, 25,
39–40, 47
Pius II, Pope, 110
Poitiers, battle of (1356), 39
Pontefract, 119, 132–3, 165,
191, 221
Powderham Castle, 96
Poynings, Edward, 127
Poynings, Henry, Lord, 78–9
press, the, 8–9, 9–11
Prudhoe, 151

Radford, Nicholas, 94–6
Ratcliffe, Sir Richard, 221,
225
recruitment, 32–3, 34–5
René of Anjou, father of
Margaret of Anjou, 58
retainers, 101
Richard II, king of England,
2, 5
Richard III, king of England:
Shakespeare's caricature
of, 2–3; invades Scotland,
43, 45; duke of Gloucester,
158; and Warwick revolt
(1469), 165; (1470), 175,
185; (1471), 194; at Barnet
(1471), 196–7, 200; at
Tewkesbury (1471), 206–7;
under Edward IV, 216;
protector (1483), 217–19;
usurps throne (1483),
219–25; conspiracies
against, 226; and
Buckingham revolt,
227–32; prepares to
intercept Henry Tudor,
233–6; and Bosworth
campaign (1485), 238–42;
killed at Bosworth, 243–6
Richemont, Lord, 138
Richmond, Henry Tudor,
earl of, *see* Henry VII, king
Rivers, Lord (1460), 108;
(1469), 162, 164
Rivers, Anthony Woodville,
earl, 108, 176, 185, 196;
and Edward V (1483),
218–19, 225

Robin of Holderness, 160
Robin of Redesdale
  (Mend-All), 160–3, 166–7,
  181
Roos, Lord (1459–60), 107,
  118; at 2nd St Albans
  (1461), 126, 132, 138, 145;
  (1464), 151–2
Ross, earl of, lord of Outer
  Isles, 141
Rous, John, 184
Roxburgh Castle, 137
Rutland, Edmund, earl of
  (son of Richard of York),
  3–4, 104–5, 119–20

St Albans, 1st b. of (May
  1455); Shakespeare's
  version of, 3, 14, 32, 34;
  Lancastrians beaten in,
  85–90 (*map*, 87), 92–3, 120
St Albans, 2nd b. of (Feb.
  1461), 43, 123, 125–9 (*map*,
  128)
St Andrews, Bishop Kennedy
  of, 137, 141, 147, 149
St Leger, Sir Thomas, 226,
  230
St Michael's Mount, 213, 215
St Omer, 48–9
Salisbury, 184, 203
Salisbury, Richard
  Beauchamp, bishop of, 43,
  121
Salisbury, Richard Neville,
  earl of: at Blore Heath, 46;
  and Richard of York, 73–4;
  and Heworth Moor
  'battle', 76–8; warden of
  west March, 78; demands
  justice, 79; with Warwick
  against court & Percies,
  84–5; escorts Henry VI to
  London, 91; takes field
  against Lancastrians
  (1459), 102–3; and Yorkist
  march on London (1460),
  110, 112; takes Tower of
  London, 115; executed
  after Wakefield, 119–20,
  122
Salisbury, Lionel Woodville,
  bishop of, 226, 228–9
Salkeld, Richard, 181
Sandal Castle, 100, 119,
  191–2
Sandwich, 18, 23, 100, 108
Saye, John, 85
Saye, Lord, treasurer, 63–4,
  112, 185, 201
Scales, Anthony Woodville,
  Lord, 111, 114–15, 142
Scotland, 29–30; Edward IV
  plans invasion of, 45;

Queen Margaret seeks
  support in, 118; key to war
  in north (1461–4), 136–42;
  aids Lancastrians, 144–7;
  Edward IV's non-invasion
  of (1363), 148; isolated,
  settles truce with Edward
  IV (1463), 149; 154
Scott, John, 111
Scrope of Bolton, Lord, 79,
  112, 150, 173–6, 187, 225,
  232
See, Martin de la, 190
Shakespeare, William, 2–7,
  28, 52–3, 118
Shaw, Dr Ralph, 224
Shrewsbury, John Talbot,
  earl of, 39, 74
Shrewsbury, John Talbot,
  2nd earl, 100, 113–14, 126,
  176, 183, 186
siege warfare, 18–19, 20–3,
  27, 144, 153–4
Somerset, 202
Somerset, Edmund Beaufort,
  earl and duke of:
  Shakespeare on, 3; Richard
  of York's feud with, 66,
  68–73; and breakdown of
  Henry VI, 74–5; and
  Neville/Percy feud (1453),
  79–80; Nevilles aid York
  against, 80; in Tower, 80;
  released, 84; scant support
  for, in London, 86;
  defeated, killed at 1st St
  Albans, 86–9; blamed by
  1455 parliament, 92–3
Somerset, Henry Beaufort,
  earl of: seeks revenge for
  father's death, 100; takes
  field against Yorkists, 103;
  attacks Calais, 107–10,
  115; flees to France, 116;
  raises south-west for Queen
  Margaret, 118; at
  Wakefield, 119–20, 122; at
  2nd St Albans (1461), 126,
  136, 140; restored to lands
  & titles by Edward IV, 145;
  breaks with Edward IV,
  149–51, 154–5; (1470),
  186; (1471), 195, 201;
  executed after Tewkesbury,
  206–7
Southampton, 18, 21, 176–7
Stafford, John (1460), 114
Stallworth, Simon, 221, 223–4
Stamford Bridge, b. of (Nov.
  1454), 83
standing armies, *see* armies
Stanhope, Maud, 76
Stanley, Lord Thomas,
  103–4, 147, 174–5, 176,

183, 186, 225, 228, 233–6,
  238–42
Stanley, Sir William, 103,
  233–6, 238–42, 239
Staple, Company of the, 98–9
Stationers' Company, 10
Stoke, b. of (June 1487), 14
Stonor, Sir William, 224, 226
Stow, John, 7
Strange, Lord, 228–9, 239–42
Stubbs, Bishop William,
  11–12
Sturgeon, John, 27, 215
Suffolk, John de la Pole, duke
  of, 126
Suffolk, William de la Pole,
  earl of: influence of, on
  Henry VI, 56–8; opposes
  cession of Anjou & Maine,
  59; and arrest of Duke
  Humphrey, 60;
  banishment, murder of,
  62–3; hatred of, respect for
  York, 68–9
Surrey, troops recruited in
  (1455), 32–3
Swynford, Katherine, 68

tactics, 19–20, 41, 44, 46,
  202–3
Talbot, Gilbert, 239
Tailboys, Sir William, 140–1,
  152
Tattershall Castle, 23, 76–7,
  169
taxation, 15, 17, 29
Terni, Francesco Coppini,
  bishop of, 110
Tewkesbury, b. of (1471);
  campaign, dictated by
  logistics, 48, 202–5; battle,
  205–7
Thomas, Rhys ap, 237–8
Thornton, John, 209
Thorp, Thomas, 92
Tower of London: main
  armoury & arsenal, 25;
  Suffolk in, 62–3; Somerset
  in, 80; Lancastrians hold
  (1460), 111–15; Henry VI
  in (1471), 195; and
  Fauconbridge revolt
  (1471), 209–13; York
  princes in (1483), 223–7
Towton, b. of (March 1461),
  4, 6, 35, 42–3, 132–5
Tresham, William, 113
Trollope, Sir Andrew, 102;
  defects to Lancastrians at
  Ludford Bridge, 105, 107;
  and Wakefield campaign
  (1460), 119–20, 122; and
  2nd St Albans (1461), 129;
  131; killed at Towton, 135

Troyes, Treaty of (1420), 51
Tudor, Henry *see* Henry VII,
　king
Tudor, Jasper, *see* Pembroke,
　Jasper Tudor, earl of
Tudor, Owen, 124, 214
Tudor propaganda, 5–6,
　9–11, 55
Tunstall, Sir Richard, 32, 140
Tunstall, Sir William, 141
Turner, Hilary, 17–18
Twt Hill, b. of (Oct. 1461),
　140
Twyer, John, 138–9
Tyndale, William, 5, 7–8
Tyrell, Sir James, 225, 235

Ulster, 65

Vaughan, Roger, 151, 214,
　229
Vaughan, Sir Thomas, 219,
　229
Vegetius, 20, 24, 49
Vergil, Polydore, 230, 234
Vernon, Henry, 193
Vescy, Lord de, 111
victualling, 45–7

wages, 11, 32–3
Wakefield, b. of (Dec. 1460),
　3–4, 48, 119–22, 120, *121*,
　122
Wales: Yorkist estates in, 65;
　Queen Margaret in (1460),
　118; Edward IV moves
　against, 139–40; support
　for Lancastrians in
　(1463–4), 150–1; (1470),
　188; Tudors quit (1471),
　214; Buckingham in
　(1483), 220; and Henry VII
　235–8
Wallingford Castle, 74
Walsingham, 116, 161
War of the Public Weal
　(France 1465), 24
Ware, 86
Warkworth Castle, 136
Warkworth, John: on Pierre
　de Brézé 18; on confusion
　at Barnet (1471), 38–9; on
　Pembroke's defeat at
　Edgecote (1469), 44; on
　Alnwick siege (1463), 145;
　on apparent security of
　Edward IV (1463), 146; on
　Empingham battle (1470),
　171; on Montagu's
　defection (1470), 185; on St
　Michael's Mount (1473),
　215
Warr, Lord de la, 111
Warren, Richard, 171, 173

Warwick (1471), 193–4
Warwick, Richard Neville,
　earl of ('kingmaker');
　Shakespeare on, 6; raises
　troops from Coventry
　(1461), 35; at Barnet, 38;
　rich inheritance of, 78; and
　Percy feud, 79–80;
　supports York against
　Henry VI and Percies,
　84–5; at 1st St Albans
　88–9; escorts Henry VI to
　London, 91; captain of
　Calais (1455), 92, 99, 101;
　raids Spanish, Hanseatic
　fleets 101–2; rebellion of
　(1458), 102; takes field
　against Lancastrians
　(1459), 102–3; defends
　Calais, 107–10; invades
　England, takes London
　(1460), 110–12; and
　Northampton battle
　(1460), 113–14; summons
　parliament 115; recovers
　Gûines, 116; splits with
　York, 117; beaten at 2nd St
　Albans (1461), 125–7;
　supports Edward IV
　(1461), 131; wounded
　before Towton, 133;
　northern campaigns of
　(1461–4), 136–41 (*map*,
　143) 145; reluctant to stay
　in north, 146–7; conquers
　Lancastrian north (1464),
　153; breaks with Edward
　IV, 156–60; conspires with
　Clarence, 161–2; and
　Lincolnshire rising (1470),
　166–77; in France, 178;
　restores Henry VI (1470),
　179–88; (1471), 193–5;
　defeat and death of, at
　Barnet 196–7, 200–1
Warwick Castle, 164
Waurin, Jehan (Jean) de, 23,
　44, 50, 103, 109, 120, 122,
　133–4, 162–3
weapons, 35–8
Welles, Lord, 126, 134,
　166–7, 169–70
Welles, Sir Robert, 166–7,
　169–73
Wenlock, Lord John, 110,
　112, 174, 177, 181, 207
Westminster Abbey, 51, 83,
　220, 226
Westmorland, Ralph Neville,
　earl of, 77
Westmorland, Ralph Neville,
　2nd earl of, 78, 122,
　138
Whethamstede, John, Abbot

of St Albans, 114, 116, 123,
　125, 127, 134
William I, king of England,
　17
Willoughby, Lord, 126, 152,
　166
Wiltshire, 139, 200
Wiltshire, James Butler, earl
　of, 85, 89–90, 124, 136
Wode, John, 27, 215
Woodville family:
　place-finding for, alienates
　Warwick, 157–8; jealousy
　of, under Edward IV, 216;
　threat of domination of
　Edward V by, 218–220;
　champions of Yorkist
　legitimacy, 226; and
　Buckingham revolt (1483),
　228–32
Woodville, Sir Edward, 220
Woodville, Sir John, 158, 164
Woodville, Richard, 157
wool trade, 18–19
Worcester, John Tiptoft, earl
　of, 142, 173, 176, 185
Wrottesly, Sir Walter, 176
Worde, Wynkyn de, 9

York, 33, 45, 119, 120, 149,
　152, 154, 165, 174, 191
York, George Neville,
　archbishop of, 102, 115,
　131, 132–3, 149, 161–2,
　164, 176, 195
York, Thomas Rotherham,
　archbishop of, 222
York, Richard, Duke of:
　Shakespeare on, 3–4;
　recalled from France
　(1445), 56–7; lineage,
　wealth, grievances of,
　65–7; returns to England,
　68–9; parliament supports,
　70–1; settles
　Courtenay/Bonville feud,
　72; plans armed rebellion
　(1451–2), 72–3;
　humiliation, apparent
　failure of, 74–5; natural
　ally of Nevilles (1453),
　79–80; protector (1454),
　81–2; gaols Exeter &
　Egremont (1454), 82–3;
　and Henry VI's recovery,
　raises army against court
　& Percies, 84–5; wins 1st
　St Albans (1455), 86–90;
　escorts Henry VI to
　London, 91; constable, and
　1455 parliament, 92–4; and
　Courtenay/Bonville feud
　(1455), 96–7; and Calais
　(1455–6), 97–9; relieved of

York, Richard, Duke of: –
contd.
2nd protectorship (1456),
99; Queen Margaret takes
field against (1459), 102–3;
flees to Ireland (Oct.
1459), 105, 106; intentions
of (1460), 115; lands in
England, claims throne
(1460), 116–17; killed at
Wakefield (Dec. 1460),
119–22

York, Richard, duke of (son
of Edward IV), 216, 220,
223
Yorkshire, 65, 79, 160,
169–70, 172–3, 207
Young, Thomas, 71